Data-Driven Innovation, Curriculum Transformation, and Learner Success in Higher Education

Caroline M. Crawford
https://orcid.org/0009-0006-6507-1960
University of Houston-Clear Lake, USA

IGI Global
Scientific Publishing
Publishing Tomorrow's Research Today

Vice President of Editorial	Melissa Wagner
Director of Acquisitions	Mikaela Felty
Director of Book Development	Jocelynn Hessler
Production Manager	Mike Brehm
Cover Design	Jose Rosado

Published in the United States of America by
IGI Global Scientific Publishing
701 East Chocolate Avenue
Hershey, PA, 17033, USA
Tel: 717-533-8845 | Fax: 717-533-7115
Website: https://www.igi-global.com E-mail: cust@igi-global.com

Library of Congress Cataloging-in-Publication Data

LCCN: (CIP Data Pending)
ISBN13: 9798260026069
Isbn13Softcover: 9798260026076
EISBN13: 9798260026083
British Cataloguing in Publication Data
A Cataloguing in Publication record for this book is available from the British Library.

Table of Contents

Detailed Table of Contents

Transitioning to Industry 4.0 (I4.0) has not only transformed curriculum, instruction, and research but also has created a pressing need to reform processes and practices implemented to assure and maintain quality in higher education. One of the central constituents of Higher Education 4.0 (HE 4.0) is 21st century skills, which are regarded as crucial for success in the modern workplace shaped by the influences of I4.0. This book chapter will examine the current status and role of soft skills, particularly communication, collaboration, creativity, and critical thinking, also referred to as 4 Cs, in higher education teaching, learning, and accreditation practices, highlighting their function as a critical component of quality assurance in the contemporary academic landscape. Practical implications will be presented in line with the analysis and evaluation of the current situation for stakeholders in higher education teaching, learning, and administration.

When considering the integration of research into undergraduate programs, a pedagogical approach can help students go beyond mere technical competencies and towards a holistic learning experience. Coming from Kolb's Experiential Learning Cycle, learning is a construction process where knowledge is born out of real-life experiences. Concrete experiences come from the fieldwork, and thoughtful self-reflection enables them to critique what they have found and encountered. Bloom's Taxonomy is a hierarchical framework for sharpening critical thinking skills and mental abilities. By applying that, teachers can fine-tune research opportunities that progressively push their students. University professors can be role models, instructors and leaders of research projects, and show their students the ropes of the research process. Successful mentorship is all about being supportive, allowing the students to figure things out for themselves. With respect to engineering programs, the use of research-led curricula showcases a very effective blend of theoretical concepts and mentoring.

This chapter advances a future-focused framework for embedding social-emotional competency and well-being into curriculum planning. Drawing on social-emotional learning theory, positive psychology, and curriculum as lived experience, it conceptualizes human flourishing as both a moral imperative and a strategic indicator of institutional quality. Through narrative inquiry, the chapter presents composite cases from international, interdisciplinary, and blended-learning contexts to illustrate how SEC-informed practices emerge, evolve, and encounter resistance in real settings. Building on these accounts, it proposes a multi-level strategic framework encompassing guiding principles, a cyclical planning process, curriculum and assessment design, faculty, and staff development, and enabling institutional structures. Policy and practice implications are outlined for institutional leaders, program teams, educators, and external stakeholders, arguing that resilient, equitable higher education systems must treat SEC and well-being as central design criteria rather than peripheral concerns

The curriculum is the core of quality education, guiding what students learn to prepare them for societal and global challenges. A well-designed curriculum and its development are essential for building a strong educational foundation. It not only frames the knowledge and skills to be imparted but also highlights the socio-economic condition of the country. Thus, the curriculum designed plays a vital role in shaping the professional and ethical capacities of learners. Curriculum frameworks must adapt to address evolving global challenges and promote sustainable learning. This chapter explores the theoretical concept of curriculum design and evaluates the trend of digital pedagogy, competency-based education, and outcome-based education The study outlines a global and Indian strategy for higher education institutions, using

Section 2
Learning Theories and Knowledge Acquisition

This chapter addresses the above situation from a university context intending to promote the international entrepreneurial mindset of future entrepreneurs. First, the evolution of the entrepreneur concept and the types of entrepreneurial mindset are addressed through the entrepreneurial matrix diagram. Then, the scenarios that need to be considered in order to create policies that support the training of international entrepreneurs are described, emphasizing the VUCA and BANI frameworks. The barriers and facilitators in the university environment for promoting international entrepreneurship are then analyzed. Next, some interdisciplinary strategies that could be developed to improve the impact on the international entrepreneurship mindset in the university environment are mentioned. Finally, conclusions and limitations of the research are presented. In this way, this research can help universities establish a starting point for proposing short-, medium-, and long-term roadmaps to enhance their impact on the international entrepreneurial mindset of students.

Higher education institutions worldwide are working in an increasingly unstable environment shaped by fluctuating enrollments, constrained funding, evolving faculty expectations and ongoing limits on international mobility. This chapter examines how systematic educational research, together with responsible use of institutional and learning analytics, can inform strategic decisions related to curriculum design, student recruitment and retention, faculty workload planning and resource allocation across diverse higher education contexts. The chapter reviews key sources and there effects of educational data such as enrollment trends, student engagement indicators, learning outcomes and faculty performance metrics. It also addresses challenges related to data quality, interpretation, ethical use and contextual variation across institutions. The chapter concludes that integrating educational research into strategic planning is essential for building sustainable, inclusive and responsive higher education institutions capable of addressing both immediate pressures and long-term goals.

This conceptual review synthesizes the theoretical foundations of AI-powered Learning Analytics (LA) in higher education within the framework of Education 4.0. Drawing on an extensive literature base, it examines how major learning theories—behaviorism, cognitivism, constructivism, and connectivism—along with methodological approaches such as Educational Data Mining and LA process models, inform the design and application of AI-driven analytics systems. Adoption theories, including the Technology Acceptance Model, Theory of Planned Behaviour, and Diffusion of Innovations, are analyzed to explain factors shaping institutional uptake. Ethical and sociotechnical issues, such as algorithmic bias, surveillance, and data privacy, are integrated to emphasize responsible implementation. The review argues that these perspectives must converge to frame AI-powered LA as a socio-technical educational practice. The synthesis provides a structured conceptual map to guide theory-informed research, policy, and practice in the evolving landscape of AI in higher education.

Evidence-based strategies have become an essential component of current educational policies and practice creating the chance to enhance learning outcomes, organizational efficiency, and system-wide responsibilities through the use of data-driven decision making. This has been aided by the growing access to digital learning platforms, administrative data, and massive test scores in offering new vistas of reviewing student performance, instructor excellence, and patterns of resource distribution. Educational data, when properly used, can aid in specific interventions, well-informed policymaking, and the steady improvement of all education system levels. This chapter discusses how the use of data-driven methods can enhance educational

Preface

INTRODUCTION

This edited book is focused upon higher education within the realms of data-driven innovation, curriculum transformation, and learner success. This triumvirate of strengths are forward-leaning in nature and evolve the higher education institution into not merely a viable entity but a creatively engaged organization that is evolving with the needs of the local, regional, national, and international communities within which it is embedded. This topic is inclusive of university systems, universities, colleges, and community colleges, that may be private or public, as well as non-profit or for-profit organizations. Further, the topics that evolve within the bounds of this edited book touch upon the multi-faceted recognition of citizenry and scholarly colleagues who choose to engage within Historically Black Colleges and Universities (HBCUs), Hispanic Serving Institutions (HSIs), Minority Serving Institutions (MSIs), and Primarily White Institutions (PWIs). It is an inherent recognition that the higher education institution serves different bodies of people who are drawn to what the institution offers, academically and socially, with an overarching focus upon learner success in the hallways of higher education. The breadth and depth of engagement throughout the chapters of this edited book reflect a data-driven approach and understanding, emphasizing the transformation of curriculum that occurs through the inherent innovations of scholarly as well as workforce needs, while equally emphasizing the learner supports and engaged successes necessary to support the reformations and futurist revolutions in cognitive and humanist evolution. The chapters throughout this edited book evolve a recognition that the success of the learner is the primary mission of each institution, while the curricular transformation and equally inherent data-driven innovations that occur within the walls of each higher education institution drive the prosperity of the community. This is an inclusive, global scale of consideration and support that understands the discussion of higher education within a much larger and ever-evolving world that is eternal and synergistic in nature.

The primary objective of this edited volume is to capture the forward-leaning, shifting landscape of higher education during this time of significant evolution and evolving understandings. Data-driven innovation discussions are balanced with cognitive needs of the learner, with equal recognition of the humanist emotional and wisdom-compelled realities. This unstable time within higher education may be considered as a revisionary earthquake, yet the opportunities to evolve the higher education institutions as anthropomorphic thinking entities that includes desirably perceptive and connected acumen offers a binding associative relationship and interwoven institution that is the best of the citizenry while also meeting the needs of the community. The short-term and long-term approaches towards data-driven innovation, curriculum transformation, and learner success in higher education guides the important, impactful, and hot topics within this insightful publication that assembles an exciting array of authors and book chapters.

ORGANIZATION OF THE BOOK

The book is organized into twelve chapters, within three distinct sections. The sections are: curriculum design and Transformation; learning theories and knowledge acquisition; and, educational research, data analytics, and technology. A brief description of each of the chapters follows:

Chapter 1 is titled *Four Cs as Pillars of Educational Quality: A Catalyst for Systemic Change in Contemporary Higher Education* by Nilüfer Ülker. Transitioning to Industry 4.0 (I4.0) has not only transformed curriculum, instruction, and research but also has created a pressing need to reform processes and practices implemented to assure and maintain quality in higher education. One of the central constituents of Higher Education 4.0 (HE 4.0) is 21st century skills, which are regarded as crucial for success in the modern workplace shaped by the influences of I4.0. This book chapter will examine the current status and role of soft skills, particularly communication, collaboration, creativity, and critical thinking, also referred to as 4 Cs, in higher education teaching, learning, and accreditation practices, highlighting their function as a critical component of quality assurance in the contemporary academic landscape. Practical implications will be presented in line with the analysis and evaluation of the current situation for stakeholders in higher education teaching, learning, and administration.

Chapter 2 is titled *Integration of Research into Undergraduate Curriculum - A Pathway to Transformative Engineering Education: Integration of Research into Undergraduate* Curriculum by Muthamil Sudar K, Mepco and Nagaraj P. When considering the integration of research into undergraduate programs, a pedagogical approach can help students go beyond mere technical competencies and towards a holistic learning experience. Coming from Kolb's Experiential Learning Cycle, learning is a construction process where knowledge is born out of real-life experiences. Concrete experiences come from the fieldwork, and thoughtful self-reflection enables them to critique what they have found and encountered. Bloom's Taxonomy is a hierarchical framework for sharpening critical thinking skills and mental abilities. By applying that, teachers can fine-tune research opportunities that progressively push their students. University professors can be role models, instructors and leaders of research projects, and show their students the ropes of the research process. Successful mentorship is all about being supportive, allowing the students to figure things out for themselves. With respect to engineering programs, the use of research-led curricula showcases a very effective blend of theoretical concepts and mentoring.

Chapter 3 is titled *Embedding Social-Emotional Competency and Well-Being in Curriculum Planning: A Future-Focused Strategy for Resilient Higher Education* by Priyal Malhotra and Sneha Saha. This chapter advances a future-focused framework for embedding social-emotional competency and well-being into curriculum planning. Drawing on social-emotional learning theory, positive psychology, and curriculum as lived experience, it conceptualizes human flourishing as both a moral imperative and a strategic indicator of institutional quality. Through narrative inquiry, the chapter presents composite cases from international, interdisciplinary, and blended-learning contexts to illustrate how SEC-informed practices emerge, evolve, and encounter resistance in real settings. Building on these accounts, it proposes a multi-level strategic framework encompassing guiding principles, a cyclical planning process, curriculum and assessment design, faculty, and staff development, and enabling institutional structures. Policy and practice implications are outlined for institutional leaders, program teams, educators, and external stakeholders, arguing that resilient, equitable higher education systems must treat SEC and well-being as central design criteria rather than peripheral concerns

Chapter 4 is titled *Curriculum Design and Development in Higher Education: Frameworks, Innovations, and Future Directions for Quality Education (SDG 4)* by Tarana Afrin Chandel. The curriculum is the core of quality education, guiding what students learn to prepare them for societal and global challenges. A well-designed curriculum and its development are essential for building a strong educational foundation. It not only frames the knowledge and skills to be imparted but also highlights the socio-economic condition of the country. Thus, the curriculum designed plays a vital role in shaping the professional and ethical capacities of learners. Curriculum frameworks must adapt to address evolving global challenges and promote sustainable learning. This chapter explores the theoretical concept of curriculum design and evaluates the trend of digital pedagogy, competency-based education, and outcome-based education The study outlines a global and Indian strategy for higher education institutions, using the National Education Policy 2020 as a guide to help them become more relevant, adaptable, and excellent in their teaching and learning through integration of digital technologies and alignment with Sustainable Development Goal 4.

Chapter 5 is titled *Embedding Learning to Earn Pedagogies in Future-Focused Higher Education: A Conceptual Framework for Strengthening Employability and Work Transition* by Preet Kanwal and Anjali Sharma. The education systems of higher education globally experience the growing pressure to address the continuing mismatch between academic qualifications and the labour market demands. This chapter presents a conceptual framework of integration of learning-to-earn pedagogies, educational strategies that formally integrate academic learning with earning opportunities, into a future-oriented higher education. In the chapter, it determines five fundamental dimensions of such pedagogies including experiential and project-based learning, work-integrated learning, entrepreneurship and innovation, digital and platform-based earning, and community engagement. It follows their conceptual roots in the experiential learning theory, human capital theory, constructivism, and work-integrated learning scholarship. The proposed framework theorizes the curriculum design, institutional strategy, industry collaboration, and student agency as four symbiotic supports that jointly make a dynamic learning bionetwork.

Chapter 6 is titled *Investigations of AI-Driven Personalization and Learning Analytics for Enhanced Education: The Algorithmic Classroom* by G. Revathy, M. C. Savithri, S. Gokulraj, and J. Vijaya Barathy. The exploration of the disruptive possibilities and far-reaching implications of the "Algorithmic Classroom" is undertaken here. Such an innovative form, the Algorithmic Classroom, is inherently attended by widespread applications of Artificial Intelligence (AI)-enabled individualized learning within educational environments. Various learning technologies allow instructors to use AI to fit knowledge involvements into the requirements of individual students, provide pedagogical innovations, and supply data-driven insights to teachers and institutions. This research will comprehensively examine the plan, execution, and impact of AI-enabled systems within different educational settings and across levels. Learning pathways, adaptive assessments, and intelligent tutoring systems are facilitated by the algorithms and architectures that this project will explore. New research data will assess how these AI interventions can effectively boost student engagement, learning achievements, and critical skills for the 21st century.

Chapter 7 is titled *Empowering Minds A Learner-Centric Approach to Transforming Higher Education in India* by Yash Vardhan Gupta, Mihira Bembey, Kapish Bansal, Kshirja Khurana, Sathish Pachiyappan, and John Paul Raj V. The study examines the factors influencing student engagement and academic outcomes in Indian higher education, with a focus on the transition from traditional teacher-centered approaches to learner-centric education as emphasized in the National Education Policy (NEP) 2020. It considers key determinants such as teaching methods, faculty training, technology integration, assessment practices, and institutional support. Data were collected from 588 students across various universities using a structured questionnaire. Student engagement and academic outcomes. Descriptive statistics and correlation analysis were used to explore relationships, followed by structural equation modelling to assess the impact of each factor. The findings reveal that teaching methods, technology integration, and institutional support positively influence engagement and performance, while faculty training and assessment methods were found to be significant positive predictors of engagement and performance.

Chapter 8 is titled *Developing an International Entrepreneurship Mindset in University Students Through Strategies: Barriers, Facilitators & Interdisciplinary Scenarios* by Josue Aaron Lopez-Leyva, Sialia Karina Mellink-Méndez, Gloria Janeth Murillo-Aviña, and Diana Esther Woolfolk-Ruiz. This chapter addresses the above situation from a university context intending to promote the international entrepreneurial mindset of future entrepreneurs. First, the evolution of the entrepreneur concept and the types of entrepreneurial mindset are addressed through the entrepreneurial matrix diagram. Then, the scenarios that need to be considered in order to create policies that support the training of international entrepreneurs are described, emphasizing the VUCA and BANI frameworks. The barriers and facilitators in the university environment for promoting international entrepreneurship are then analyzed. Next, some interdisciplinary strategies that could be developed to improve the impact on the international entrepreneurship mindset in the university environment are mentioned. Finally, conclusions and limitations of the research are presented. In this way, this research can help universities establish a starting point for proposing short-, medium-, and long-term roadmaps to enhance their impact on the international entrepreneurial mindset of students.

Chapter 9 is titled *Educational Research and Data-Driven Decision Making for Future-Focused Higher Education Planning* by Vipin Tyagi. Higher education institutions worldwide are working in an increasingly unstable environment shaped by fluctuating enrollments, constrained funding, evolving faculty expectations and ongoing limits on international mobility. This chapter examines how systematic educational research, together with responsible use of institutional and learning analytics, can inform strategic decisions related to curriculum design, student recruitment and retention, faculty workload planning and resource allocation across diverse higher education contexts. The chapter reviews key sources and their effects of educational data such as enrollment trends, student engagement indicators, learning outcomes and faculty performance metrics. It also addresses challenges related to data quality, interpretation, ethical use and contextual variation across institutions. The chapter concludes that integrating educational research into strategic planning is essential for building sustainable, inclusive and responsive higher education institutions capable of addressing both immediate pressures and long-term goals.

Chapter 10 it titled *Conceptual Foundations of AI-Powered Learning Analytics in Education 4.0 A Theoretical Review* by Ivan Marcelo, Justin Pierce, and Alex Bolt. This conceptual review synthesizes the theoretical foundations of AI-powered Learning Analytics (LA) in higher education within the framework of Education 4.0. Drawing on an extensive literature base, it examines how major learning theories—behaviorism, cognitivism, constructivism, and connectivism—along with methodological approaches such as Educational Data Mining and LA process models, inform the design and application of AI-driven analytics systems. Adoption theories, including the Technology Acceptance Model, Theory of Planned Behaviour, and Diffusion of Innovations, are analyzed to explain factors shaping institutional uptake. Ethical and sociotechnical issues, such as algorithmic bias, surveillance, and data privacy, are integrated to emphasize responsible implementation. The review argues that these perspectives must converge to frame AI-powered LA as a socio-technical educational practice. The synthesis provides a structured conceptual map to guide theory-informed research, policy, and practice in the evolving landscape of AI in higher education.

Chapter 11 is titled *Data Driven Decision Making for Strengthening Educational Policy and Practice* by Ashutosh Bhardwaj. Evidence-based strategies have become an essential component of current educational policies and practice creating the chance to enhance learning outcomes, organizational efficiency, and system-wide responsibilities through the use of data-driven decision making. This has been aided by the growing access to digital learning platforms, administrative data, and massive test scores in offering new vistas of reviewing student performance, instructor excellence, and patterns of resource distribution. Educational data, when properly used, can aid in specific interventions, well-informed policymaking, and the steady improvement of all education system levels.This chapter discusses how the use of data-driven methods can enhance educational policy and practice by emphasizing the data source and methodologies of data analysis and system frameworks that can be utilized in supporting decision making that is evidence-based.

Chapter 12 is titled *Data-Informed Educational Research and Evidence-Based Decision Making in Modern Education Systems* by Shikha Sharma. The growing nature of educational data has altered the manner in which research, policy and practice are being conducted in present education systems. Data-based learning research This approach to learning research focuses on the application of quantitative and qualitative evidence to comprehend the learning processes, assess interventions, and direct learning instruction and institutional decision making. This chapter will look at the premises of data informed and evidence-based approaches to education by discussing how various sources of data, the ways data analysis is conducted and how research designs can be used inform decisions at the classroom, institutional and policy levels. It also explains the purpose of education technologies and learning analytics to produce actionable insights and how to address the ethical, privacy, and equity issues related to the use of data.

CONCLUSION

The intention of this edited book was to offer a spece in which data-driven innovation, curriculum transformation, and learner success in higher education institutions are recognized as at the precipice of strategic shifts due to the significant advancements that are occurring with data structures and the availability of large language models that equally are evolving at a record pace within the artificial intelligence realm. The investigation into "*how do we move forward*" in this current space within which higher education finds itself is a curious question, with the authored chapters throughout this text offering an initial foray into this discussion. The intention of this edited book is for use by higher education administration, higher education faculty, as well as master's and doctoral students who desire to evolve into higher education faculty. Equally, this publication may be viable for political and strategic persons who are looking at the current state of higher education and wanting to rethink and strategize the evolution of higher education with a forward-leaning outlook.

Section 1
Curriculum Design and Transformation

Chapter 1
4 Cs as Pillars of Educational Quality:
A Catalyst for Systemic Change in Contemporary Higher Education

Nilüfer Ülker
http://orcid.org/0000-0002-9866-0642
Istanbul Technical University, Turkey

ABSTRACT

Transitioning to Industry 4.0 (I4.0) has not only transformed curriculum, instruction, and research but also has created a pressing need to reform processes and practices implemented to assure and maintain quality in higher education. One of the central constituents of Higher Education 4.0 (HE 4.0) is 21st century skills, which are regarded as crucial for success in the modern workplace shaped by the influences of I4.0. This book chapter will examine the current status and role of soft skills, particularly communication, collaboration, creativity, and critical thinking, also referred to as 4 Cs, in higher education teaching, learning, and accreditation practices, highlighting their function as a critical component of quality assurance in the contemporary academic landscape. Practical implications will be presented in line with the analysis and evaluation of the current situation for stakeholders in higher education teaching, learning, and administration.

INTRODUCTION

There have been unprecedented changes in in line with transition to Industry 4.0, which is reported to have commenced in 2011 in Germany (Xu et al., 2021). The new industrial revolution, mainly characterized by digitalization of processes, has

DOI: 10.4018/979-8-2600-2606-9.ch001

revolutionized every sphere of life including but not limited to education. Throughout history, education has evolved in parallel with advancements brought by industrial revolutions so as to respond to the needs of the society and meet the demands of the prevailing context, which was also the case in the emergence of Higher Education 4.0 (HE 4.0). As the sector responsible for equipping individuals with necessary skills and competencies of the era, higher education institutions started to adopt policies and strategies to serve the necessities of the professional workplace as well as the society in the context of Industry 4.0. Within this scope, as Kumar asserts, HE 4.0 has emerged as the new mode of tertiary education primarily characterized by flexibility, mainly due to strong emphasis on digitalization and uncertainties brought by technology (2025), and its influence has accelerated by the circumstances encountered during the COVID-19 pandemic.

It is important to note that 4.0 does not solely indicate digitalization as perceived by the name; rather, it is an indication of a combination of multiple skills required to survive and excel in the knowledge society in the post-pandemic world. The new teaching and learning paradigm in higher education encompasses an array of modifications in academic practices ranging from collaborative learning and working on authentic real-life projects to formative assessment of student performance and life-long learning. 21st century skills and competencies have come to the spotlight promoting the concept of soft skills, also referred to as social skills, in our everyday conversations in educational settings. Soft skills can be described in numerous ways and categorized under different domains, which are primarily career and life skills, digital literacies skills, and learning and innovation skills. Regardless of the form or category they belong to, the majority feature communication, collaboration, creativity and innovation, and critical thinking and problem solving as the essentials, referred to as the 4 Cs by P21, which pertain to learning and innovation skills domain and which will be the focus of this chapter (2019). It is evident that too much emphasis is attached to technical skills in higher education engineering curricula and assessment systems whereas soft skills are not placed sufficient amount of importance. A large body of scientific and practical research has been conducted to investigate various aspects of the topic proposing strategic courses of action to instill the engineering students with relevant skills and competencies so that they become qualified for a competitive job market upon graduation (Beagon & Bowe, 2023; Chen et al., 2023; Miranda et al., 2021; Passow & Passow, 2017; Qadir et al., 2020; Shuman et al., 2005).

While universities are expected to incorporate the aforementioned skills into their engineering curricula and assessment systems regardless of the field of study, there should also be other mechanisms to assure that university graduates are provided with the right skills in line with the demands of the current era. In this scope, transitioning to Industry 4.0 has not only transformed curriculum and research but also procedures adopted to assure and maintain quality as part of higher education management practices. Alzahrani et al. argue that higher education quality 4.0 functions as a response to changing circumstances as a result of transition to Industry 4.0 (2021). Accreditation has been the most prevalent form of quality assurance where higher education institutions are expected to meet predefined standards as specified by accrediting agencies. In the scope of accreditation, such crucial constituents of a program as curriculum, assessment, student admission, learning outcomes, student services, and quality improvement are meticulously reviewed against specified standards and recommendations are offered to assure and maintain those aspects of program quality. As part of continuous improvement practices, accreditation standards are also regularly revised and improved by accrediting agencies through input from various stakeholders to respond to the requirements of such a fast-changing academic landscape. Thus, soft skills being this much central for the success of graduates in their professional lives as emphasized by Succi and Canovi (2020), it is expected that higher education places emphasis on the incorporation of 4 Cs into their educational practices, and the accreditation frameworks across the world, regardless of the field they serve, include statements referring to soft skills, specifically 4 Cs, so that they remain up-to-date with societal demands.

This book chapter will present the existing situation about the place and importance of soft skills, particularly 4 Cs, in higher education teaching, learning, and accreditation practices as a crucial component of quality assurance in the current academic context. Although there is still controversy about whether accreditation is the appropriate mechanism to assure quality and its influence on the improvement of educational practices is widely debated, it is an undeniable fact that in this more than ever globalized world, where the number of accredited programs is rapidly increasing and university rankings have come into this much prominence, accreditation serves as a benchmarking instrument and brings competitive advantage to higher education institutions in attracting quality students and maintaining and enhancing their status in the international arena.

The chapter will include the background of the study encompassing various perspectives and relevant previous studies conducted in HE 4.0 and the place and importance of soft skills with a specific emphasis on 4 Cs as implemented in engineering education, 4 Cs in quality assurance and accreditation for engineering education, 4 Cs in engineering education accreditation framework, evaluation of accreditation criteria with regard to inclusion of 4 Cs accompanied by samples of contexts from a number of accrediting agencies located in different parts of the world, specifically ABET EAC (2025), EUR-ACE (2021), Engineers Ireland (2021), and Engineers Australia (2019). This will contribute to explaining the current situation as well as addressing the role and significance of inclusion of soft skills in contemporary higher education as critical constituents of educational quality across different quality frameworks. Implications for practice are provided for a variety of stakeholders of higher education teaching, learning, and administration. It is believed that the combination of theory and analysis in this chapter will foster the enhancement of individuals' awareness about 4 Cs in the context of HE 4.0, which will in turn bring wider benefits in terms of advancement of graduate skills and competencies for the 21st century workplace as well as service to the society as a whole.

Higher Education 4.0 and the Place and Importance of Soft Skills

Industry 4.0 has brought many substantial reforms in every sphere of our lives including higher education. In line with their critical role in transforming the society and to help graduates to keep up with the speed and complexity of societal challenges, universities are now expected to adopt interdisciplinary approaches that are unified in nature giving rise to joint resolutions as well as integrating collaborative skills in students' learning experiences. These skills are essential to survive and succeed in current global context grounded in knowledge-based society, which is characterized as a very aggressive universe of trade, business, and life that requests a larger number of abilities than those required for the alumni of the Industrial Age (Rajest & Suresh, 2018). However, as advocated by Brown (2023), existing economic constraints can direct attention towards challenges requiring immediate attention, which leads to a reorientation from creating a knowledge-based society, limiting the scope of higher education to achieve its objectives.

In the 21st century professional life, young people are expected to overcome complex situations and adapt to changing circumstances to be able to respond appropriately to societal challenges. As is widely acknowledged, this has become more significant in parallel with the influences of the pandemic. However, there is a growing gap between the skills that the university graduates have and the ones that employers seek due to abundance of information and increasing complexity of societal problems (Seely, 2005). Thornhill-Miller et al. assert that higher education systems encounter challenges in equipping students with the required skills and competencies for rapidly evolving work environments (2023). To be able to accommodate the needs of their stakeholders, as Baumber underlies, it is important for higher education institutions to assure that the future workforce does not remain as only recipients but become active creators of knowledge and be provided opportunities to use their knowledge (2023). However, as also argued by Caruana (2011), using the same materials and methodologies for modern 21st century students, who are significantly different from previous generations in terms of their characteristics, backgrounds, experiences and expectations, will not address the needs of the contemporary society.

Under the circumstances, HE 4.0 gains prominence as the new version of university education which emerged in alignment with the changing conditions of the 21st century. Transformation in higher education processes and practices in line with the features of the evolving field necessitates restructuring as a strategic vision in the post-pandemic era (Holmes & Corbett, 2022). Therefore, higher education institutions implement new tools and methods primarily supported by evolving information and communication technologies to enhance knowledge creation and transfer mechanisms, and utilizing this during the education process to facilitate enhancement of skills as desired by the professional world (Miranda et al., 2021). In this framework, Ülker and Otrar define the essential components of HE 4.0 as knowledge management and communication, continuous improvement, global competitiveness, and digitalization, in order of priority (2025). In the new educational context, students are provided with various forms of learning opportunities, short-term certificate programs, career development support, and collaborative networking programs to develop and sustain relationships with the academics, researchers, and the industry (Dewar, 2017). Still, despite substantial improvements in individual campuses or programs, a systemic change in higher education has yet to occur.

The need for this systemic change in higher education has recently become a priority as international business context is now shaped by creative and critical thinkers who can perform competently as a team member communicating and collaborating effectively to find innovative solutions for humanity. This is particularly important for engineers, who have the potential to respond to the constantly changing context of the new era. Therefore, there is a pressing need for a paradigm shift in engineering education, one that incorporates soft skills into curriculum design. Integration of social skills into engineering education aligns with the evolving role of engineers, requiring not only technical expertise but also ethical considerations and social responsibility. This is highlighted by the UNESCO (2017) Education Sector's recommendations for sustainability competencies that encompass cognitive, socio-emotional, and behavioral objectives essential for fostering global citizenship among students.

While some researchers have emphasized the importance of incorporating affective outcomes, communication skills, and the need to align with changing societal expectations into engineering education, the technical focus of these programs has typically limited opportunities for consistently incorporating these essential but less tangible skills (Rouvrais & Gaultier-Le Bris, 2018; White & Hastings, 2018). Whereas engineering teaching objectives are expected to represent a mixture of scientific, social, and engineering dimensions (Chen, Yin & Feng, 2023), there seems to be a considerable amount of focus on teaching objectives addressing scientific and engineering aspects, and the social dimension seems to be usually neglected. However, as also suggested by Kjellgren and Richter (2021), soft skills such as team work, critical thinking, and communication should become integral constituents of the engineering curricula.

4 Cs as Implemented in Engineering Education

Partnership for 21st century learning (P21, 2019) was formed as a not-for-profit consortium that encompasses leading corporate entities such as Microsoft, Cisco, and Dell (Qadir et al., 2020). In line with the needs of the industry that have changed to an unprecedented extent, they developed a framework identifying the skills and competencies required from the future workforce. They determined three types of core skills sets: Life and career skills, information, media and technology skills, and learning and innovation skills which comprise communication, collaboration, critical thinking, and creativity, referred to as 4 Cs. As also advocated by Reid-Griffin et al. (2023), preparing students for a complex global world requires equipping them with 4 Cs.

There have been various definitions and explanations of 4 Cs as implemented in higher education settings (Ayoub et al., 2024; Miranda et al., 2021; P21, 2019; Qadir et al., 2020; Thornhill-Miller et al., 2023):

Communication

Communication is a key skill which involves active listening, expressing oneself clearly and interacting in meaningful discussions. It is characterized as conveying one's thoughts and opinions in an effective manner by means of written, verbal, and non-verbal skills across diverse forms and contexts. Although engineering students are excessively exposed to technical courses during their undergraduate education, once they are in professional life, they are expected to perform actions requiring them to communicate effectively for a substantial part of their workday. Therefore, it is expected that higher education institutions put special emphasis on improving students' oral and written communication skills.

Creativity

Creativity features generating novel conceptual and practical solutions. Creative individuals know that "creativity and innovation is a long-term, cyclical process of small successes and frequent mistakes" (P21, 2019, p. 4). Engineering is a forward-looking profession that concentrates on envisioning and developing entirely novel technologies and inventions for the benefit of humanity. Higher education institutions are expected to acknowledge the significance of creative thinking by offering such activities that help students approach issues from new perspectives and develop innovative pathways. This skill can be enhanced through activities that foster student involvement in developing and creating novel solutions to problems.

Critical Thinking

Critical thinking comprises analysis and evaluation of situations by using relevant and reliable information to be able to make sound decisions. While getting prepared for 21st century professional life, university students have the chance to learn how to analyze a problem considering different aspects and develop problem-solving strategies. Critical thinking skill helps to "work viably and imaginatively with PCs, with huge measures of data, with uncertain circumstances, and with other individuals from an assortment of foundations" (Rajest & Suresh, 2018, p. 892). Critical thinkers are defined as individuals that have the ability to analyze and critically assess evidence, lines of reasoning, assertions and beliefs. Engineering students complete many technical courses but this has a negative influence on identifying the underlying cause of a problem without critical thinking skills that are expected to be gained through extensive exposure to arts, humanities, and social sciences during undergraduate education.

Collaboration

Collaboration entails working with other people towards the same goal. People with desired collaboration skills undertake shared responsibility for the shared goal while appreciating the contributions of other members of the team. In higher education context, it is important that students improve their communication and interpersonal skills as well as developing problem-solving competencies by means of collaborative work. Collaboration skills can be enhanced through problem solving in groups, in which every student is responsible for resolving a certain aspect of a defined problem. This kind of an experience in a collaborative environment is a core skill for prospective engineers to succeed in their professional lives.

Teamwork is the most prevalent form of instructional methodology and learning approach that is included under the umbrella of collaborative learning. Based on the importance of gaining experience of working collaboratively with people from different disciplines, offering the students chances for involvement in teams is becoming more widespread as part of higher education practices. Kolmos et al. (2024) define teamwork as a mechanism where members work together and collaborate so as to accomplish a shared goal. The variety of backgrounds and experiences feature the significance of collaboration in interdisciplinary teams, where each member is expected to have sufficient awareness of other members' areas for co-construction of knowledge to reach the common goal. As Bulter and Zander (2008) assert, members of the teams experience team learning through having face-to-face discussions in small groups, managing conflict, and finding solutions to problems.

There are many ways to improve individual skills as part of 4 Cs through curricular and extra-curricular activities; however, a shift is required in the learning environment and teaching pedagogies for a holistic integration. In general, 4 Cs can be improved through offering learning environments where students are asked to address and solve real world problems and exposing them to collaborative problem-based learning experiences (Levin-Goldberg, 2012). Project-based learning model (PBL), which is grounded in active and student-centered pedagogical approaches where the students are expected to learn by doing, is one way of accomplishing this. In this model, students work in groups and carry out scientific projects that are of their own interest and develop skills that are in essence related with 4 Cs. The process and the outcomes are both meaningful to them as they deal with real world problems (Kumaro & Barliana, 2022). Therefore, as also emphasized by Vithanage (2024), with its focus on autonomous inquiry and active involvement of the students in their educational process, PBL has the potential to enable the accomplishment of 4 Cs in learning for STEM (Science, Technology, Engineering, and Mathematics) education.

PBL is only one of the instructional approaches that can be employed to enhance students' competencies in 4 Cs. A holistic integration is needed to make these practices permanent and to instill 4 Cs in students within the school culture. In this respect, the Whole School Approach offers a parallel foresight that prepares students for a future characterized by complexity and change. According to Whole School Approach, sustainability is integrated into all elements that constitute the university and transforms the university campus into a learning space where different learning experiences take place (Michelsen & Burandt, 2017). Engaging in sustainability initiatives improves students' problem-solving and critical thinking skills (McMillin & Dyball, 2009). Students, as autonomous learners, manage their learning processes according to their existing knowledge base and experiences, and educators assume a facilitating role in this process (student-centered approach); students actively create knowledge and apply what they have learned by reflecting on their experiences in this process (action-oriented learning); students revise and change their existing ways of thinking to better understand the world they live in (transformative learning) is a fundamental pedagogical approach suggested by UNESCO (2017) for a holistic transformation of student experiences. According to UNESCO (2020), the primary consideration is to create an environment where students experience learning and learn from these experiences; therefore, in line with Whole School Approach, all aspects of the learning environment in which students' learning experiences take place, and all different learning environments should be considered.

According to Gamage et al. (2022), research-based learning, inquiry-based learning, experiential learning, and case studies are the most suitable instructional approaches that can be employed in addition to PBL. A central consideration, as underscored by McKeown and Hopkins (2017), is to provide university students with opportunities to work in environments that resemble real life through concrete tasks where they will use their skills, competencies, and problem-solving abilities in the process of developing skills and competencies. When evaluated in terms of learning outcomes, equipping students with the necessary social skills to achieve the sustainable development goal in higher education is essential (Kohl & Hopkins, 2021), and the holistic integration of Education for Sustainable Development (ESD) into educational practices contributes to realization of this goal. In this context, as highlighted by Michelsen and Burandt (2017), subjects play an important role in equipping students with critical thinking, creativity, collaboration, and other fundamental skills through formal and informal curriculum practices and innovative pedagogical approaches, as well as meeting the demand for personal and social competencies that are important in daily and professional life.

While initiatives have been taken and efforts have been made in curriculum design, assessment practices, and other essential constituents of higher education systems, additional measures are needed to remain competitive in this increasingly dynamic context. It is a fact that, in line with accelerating globalization, the number of institutions seeking accreditation has reached a very high level and the society is more informed about educational quality both through and due to global university rankings. Therefore, accreditation could be utilized as a means to reach parity with global leading institutions and inclusion of 4 Cs in the quality standards of accreditation schemes could function as a benchmark in pursuit of educating future-ready graduates.

4 Cs in Quality Assurance and Accreditation for Engineering Education

The state of engineering education has been questioned in many policy documents, reports, and studies in the past two decades, leading to inclusion of soft skills in the form of learning outcomes as part of engineering curriculum (Shuman et al., 2005). These learning outcomes are translated into graduate competencies as identified by accrediting agencies. Accrediting agencies are expected to make alterations in their quality criteria to serve better to future societal needs by assuring necessary graduate competencies, and, as contended by Beagon and Bowe (2022), accreditation criteria could be adapted as a top-down approach before establishing standards to guide curriculum design integrating soft skills in engineering education.

The study conducted by Passow and Passow (2017) revealed that technical skills are closely interlinked with effective collaboration skills in regular engineering practices; engineers spend approximately 55%-60% of their workday communicating with others in social interactions and they need to manage a variety of competencies to achieve an objective. When the mean importance scores (standardized) for emergent skills of engineering disciplines are displayed alongside ABET skills, it is seen that thinking creatively presents an upper-intermediate level of importance. When ABET and Washington Accord graduate attributes and learning outcomes are examined, it is seen that they are different from important emerging competencies of engineering practices in the real-world context. Therefore, it is not possible to teach soft skills separate from the operational environment where these skills will be applied.

Incorporating soft skills into accreditation criteria may be adopted as an approach for engineering programs to attain equal standing with the professional requirements of the era in a more rapid and effective way, which also requires prescription of innovative pedagogies by accrediting bodies to support the students' learning process to acquire these competencies. In parallel with this approach, engineering programs are supposed to include soft-skills-related concepts and activities as integral constituents of their programs to be able to fulfill quality criteria. However, as highlighted by Skvarenina (2008), the soft skills as described in ABET documents are expected to be developed by the students in the Humanities and Social Sciences electives in several contexts. It should also be the responsibility of engineering faculty to examine and assess student attainments of these skills. Therefore, by making adaptations in the course materials, "the technical courses in the curriculum should contribute to the teaching and assessment of the soft-skills" (p. 3).

Although soft skills are incorporated into accreditation criteria, it might be difficult to evaluate these skills and meet the defined learning outcomes due to lack of rigorous assessment tools, as also accentuated by Shuman et al. (2005). Also, engineering faculty feel more confident assessing the technical skills. Assessing and evaluating soft skills require examination of learning both through in-class and out-of-class activities through a process-based approach. Alternative assessment tools need to be created to be able to effectively assess and evaluate the soft skills acquisition. In this regard, the study by Shuman et al. (2005) demonstrated that ABET professional skills can be taught through new pedagogies implemented in engineering education and can be assessed through alternative additional assessment tools such as peer evaluation and self-evaluation.

As explained by ABET (2025), in ABET EAC's accreditation criteria, student outcome criterion 3 encompasses a broad set of skills and competencies that engineering programs are expected to cultivate in their students. This includes the "ability to recognize ethical and professional responsibilities in engineering" and to consider "the global, economic, environmental, and societal" impacts of engineering decisions when making informed judgments. Another important competency is the ability to work effectively within a team, fostering collaboration, leadership, and an inclusive atmosphere while establishing goals and planning tasks to achieve objectives. These criteria are foundational for all accredited engineering programs and are aimed at promoting continuous improvement in engineering education. Institutions seeking accreditation must demonstrate that their programs fulfill these criteria, ensuring that they meet the evolving needs of their stakeholders in a competitive and dynamic environment.

To the knowledge of the researcher, the research on the inclusion of soft skills in the accreditation frameworks is scarce and has only been limited to ABET standards as ABET is regarded as the most established accreditation agency in engineering education. There is no single study focusing on the existence and the extent of inclusion of the core learning and innovation skills, 4 Cs, in accreditation frameworks of engineering education accrediting bodies in different parts of the world. While accrediting agencies may seem to include the above-mentioned concepts about soft skills and 4 Cs specifically as constituents of accreditation criteria, the extent to which this would influence engineering programs to realize the educational reform in their curriculum, assessment and operational practices remains unclear.

4 Cs in Engineering Education Accreditation Framework

As a well-established mechanism for quality assurance and enhancement, accreditation assures whether higher education institutions meet the quality criteria, which are consistently reviewed through feedback from relevant stakeholders in line with recent advancements in the field of higher education. Under the circumstances, accreditation frameworks are expected to include standards related to professional skills. To examine this, employing a qualitative approach, publicly available accreditation frameworks as specified by EUR-ACE (2021), Engineers Ireland (2021), ABET EAC (2025), and Engineers Australia (2019) were analyzed and certain extracts from data were presented to provide explanatory illustrations. While doing this, the 4 Cs were examined in different parts of speech throughout the whole document specifically with regard to their contribution to student learning. If it existed in a different context than targeted as part of the analysis (i.e. characteristics of the self-study review team rather than students working as a team member), it was excluded to provide consistency.

This approach is in line with the descriptive nature of qualitative studies where researchers focus on absolute messages in data instead of trying to decipher the hidden meaning as highlighted by Braun and Clarke (2012). For this type of studies, in place of conducting and presenting an analysis of the extracts, certain extracts from data are presented to provide explanatory illustrations. In this particular type of content analysis, examination and presentation of what is not mentioned is as important as what is mentioned in the text (Cardno, 2018). This form of an analysis "provides insight into complex models of human thought and language that may be difficult for other strategies to analyze" (Armstrong, 2021, p. 5). Table 1 below shows the analysis of 4 Cs as included in the current accreditation frameworks of EUR-ACE (2021), Engineers Ireland (2021), ABET EAC (2025), and Engineers Australia (2019).

Table 1. 4 Cs as Addressed in Different Accreditation Frameworks

	Communication	Collaboration	Creativity	Critical thinking
ABET EAC	Student outcomes; curriculum features for two different programs of study	Student outcomes; curriculum features for two different programs of study	Definition of Engineering Design	Not addressed
EUR-ACE	Learning Area; Glossary of Terminology	Collaboration not addressed; Teamwork in Program Outcomes Framework	Glossary of Terminology for two areas of study; Teaching and Learning Process Standard	Glossary of Terminology for four areas of study
Engineers Ireland	Program outcomes; engineering definitions; indicative graduate attributes; two different program areas	Collaboration not addressed; Teamwork in Foreword in the form of a new Program Outcome; Program Outcomes	Program area in Accreditation Criteria Overview; definitions of skills	Indicative graduate attribute; competencies for two program areas
Engineers Australia	Professional and personal attributes; indicator of attainment for Knowledge and Skill Base	Collaboration not addressed; Teamwork in role descriptions; professional and personal attributes; indicator of attainment for Engineering Application Ability; Knowledge and Skill Base and Personal and Professional Attributes	Role descriptions; professional and personal attributes; indicator of attainment for defined levels of engineering	Indicator of attainment for Knowledge and Skill Base; Engineering Application Ability and Personal and Professional Attributes

Communication

Communication is available in EUR-ACE (2021) accreditation framework in the form of Communication and Team-working as one of the eight learning areas that are indicated to provide a reference for the outcomes described for both Bachelor and Master Degree programs. It is also provided in the Glossary of Terminology for Making Judgments, Communication and Teamworking, presented with detailed examples.

Engineers Ireland (2021) defines different standards for different levels of engineering as Chartered Engineer (CE), Associate Engineer (EA), and Engineering Technician (ET). Communication is explicitly stated as one of the program outcomes and different levels of engineering are characterized using different variations. For example, a CE is defined as "a leader, a visionary and an excellent communicator". While an AE is expected to have "the ability to communicate effectively on broadly defined engineering activities to diverse audiences", these are specified as "well-defined engineering activities" for an ET. It is also elaborated on as part of the indicative graduate attributes mainly with a focus on the effective use of communication strategies for different aims and in different contexts, as illustrated in "the ability to communicate effectively on complex engineering activities to diverse audiences". As program areas, Software and Information Systems and Societal and Business Context address communication through statements such as "develop the student's ability to .... communicate technical information to a range of audiences".

In ABET EAC (2025), communication is provided under the general criteria for Baccalaureate Level (BL) and Integrated Baccalaureate-Master's Level student outcomes articulated through "an ability to communicate effectively with a range of audiences". It also appears as part of the features described for the curriculum of Architectural and Similarly named Engineering Programs and Construction and Similarly Named Engineering Programs to be incorporated as a skill relevant for area-specific contexts.

Engineers Australia (2019) refers to communication as one of the Professional and Personal Attributes for Professional Engineer (PE), Engineering Associate (EA), and Engineering Technician (ET) stated in the form of "effective oral and written communication in professional and lay domains". "Proficiency in listening, speaking, reading and writing in English" is described with reference to "appreciating the impact of body language, personal behavior and other non-verbal communication processes". It is also mentioned as an indicator of attainment for Knowledge and Skill Base for defined levels of engineering relevant to different domains. For example, an ET "fluently applies relevant investigation, analysis, modelling, decision making,....knowledge management and communication tools and techniques pertinent to the technology domain".

Collaboration

Although collaboration is not explicitly stated throughout the accreditation criteria documents except for ABET EAC (2025), teamwork is presented in a variety of contexts. EUR-ACE (2021), for example, refers to it as part of the Program Outcomes Framework and Learning Areas in the form of "communication and team-working".

In the foreword section of the Engineers Ireland (2021) document, a new program outcome is presented, which includes "the ethical usage of technology and data; coverage of equality, diversity and inclusion in professional practice, teamwork and communication". Teamwork is also addressed as a program outcome titled Teamwork and Lifelong Learning in all forms of engineering practice. It is mainly defined as "the ability to work effectively" as a member of a team.

Program outcomes for CE with further learning under the title of Investigation, it is presented as "the ability to design and conduct experiments ....under guidance in a peer or team relationship". In the Program Areas of Societal and Business Context, there are many references to teamwork such as "Engineering invariably involves a team approach". Teamwork is also included under the program area Sustainability as "promoting dialogue and negotiation, learning to work together, so as to strengthen ownership of and commitment to sustainable action through education and learning". Moreover, "adequate workspaces should be provided for students to engage in projects and teamwork outside tabled activities" according to Program Management Criteria.

Collaboration is explicitly stated as part of ABET EAC (2025) general criteria for Baccalaureate Level and Integrated Baccalaureate-Master's Level student outcomes in the form of "an ability to function effectively on a team whose members together provide leadership, create a collaborative environment, establish goals, plan tasks, and meet objectives". It also appears as one of the characteristics defined for curriculum of Architectural and Similarly Named Engineering Programs and Engineering Management and Similarly Named Engineering Programs, in which curriculum must include "management topics which may include project management, technology management, team building, and strategy".

In Engineers Australia (2019), it is included in the role description of the mature engineers for PEs and EAs; ETs "may lead teams responsible for the implementation, operation, quality assurance, safety, management, and maintenance .... within specialist practice area(s) of the technology domain". Teamwork is also addressed as one of the Personal and Professional and Attributes for PEs, EAs, and ETs described in the form of "effective team membership and team leadership".

Participating in a team is reflected as an indicator of attainment for Engineering Application Ability presenting different standards for different levels of engineering. For example, EAs and ETs are "aware of the accountabilities of the members of the engineering team in relation to the 'design authority' role and contributes to well-defined and technical project activity as a member of the engineering team". It is also an indicator of attainment for Knowledge and Skill Base and Personal and Professional Attributes presented through such statements as "functions as an effective member or leader of diverse engineering teams, including those with multi-level, multi-disciplinary and multi-cultural dimensions".

Creativity

Creativity is included in EUR-ACE (2021) Glossary of Terminology for Engineering Design (MA level) and Glossary of Terminology for Investigations (MA level) through domain-specific references. For example, Engineering Design explains "to select and apply the most appropriate and relevant design methodologies or to use creativity to develop new and original design methodologies". The Teaching and Learning Process in the Program Aims also refers to creativity through the following standard: "Does the curriculum embed a student-centered learning and teaching approach that enables flexible learning paths and encourages students to take an active role in co-creating the learning process?".

In Engineers Ireland (2021), creativity is provided under the title Creativity and Innovation as a program area in the accreditation criteria overview and presented in the form of "Research and design are central components of creativity and innovation.....For example, consideration should be given to including in the program, the art of problem solving, heuristics, theory of inventive problem solving (TRIZ), etc. By these means, a student's ability to contribute to the creative process should be developed". Also, it is mentioned in the Definitions section as "in the context of the European Qualifications Framework, skills are described as cognitive (involving the use of logical, intuitive and creative thinking) or practical (involving manual dexterity and the use of methods, materials, tools and instruments)".

In ABET EAC (2025) criteria, creativity appears in the Definitions Section while defining Engineering Design, which is explained as "an iterative, creative, decision-making process in which the basic sciences, mathematics, and engineering sciences are applied to convert resources into solutions". Also, engineering sciences are "based on mathematics and basic sciences but carry knowledge further toward creative application needed to solve engineering problems".

Engineers Australia (2019) refers to creativity in the role description of the PE as "primarily concerned with the advancement of technologies and with the development of new technologies and their applications through innovation, creativity and change". It is also included as part of Professional and Personal Attributes for PEs, EAs, and ETs as "creative, innovative and pro-active demeanor", whose indicator of attainment is presented through different variations in line with the requirements of the roles. For example, a PE "applies creative approaches to identify and develop alternative concepts, solutions and procedures, appropriately challenges engineering practices from technical and non-technical viewpoints".

Critical Thinking

Critical thinking is available in EUR-ACE (2021) Glossary of Terminology for Knowledge and Understanding (MA level), Glossary of Terminology for Engineering Analysis (MA level), Glossary of Terminology for investigations for both Bachelors and Master's Degree programs, and Glossary of Terminology for Engineering Practice (MA graduates) through such statements as "critical awareness of the wider, multidisciplinary context of engineering and of knowledge issues at the interface between different fields" and "to critically interpret the outcomes of analyses of new and complex engineering products".

Engineers Ireland (2021) refers to it as an indicative graduate attribute as part of the CE with further learning presented through such statements as "the ability to conduct searches of literature and consult and critically use databases and other sources of information pertinent to an unfamiliar problem that is within the current boundaries of the field and the ability to critically evaluate problems within the boundaries of knowledge in the particular branch of engineering". It is also included as a constituent of Program Areas under the title of Creativity and Innovation as "Since engineering is ultimately about practical activities, such innovation should include the practical testing of ideas in the laboratory and conducting research for information to develop these ideas further. These activities should be linked to technical analysis and the critical evaluation of results". Similarly, under the Program Area Sustainability, it is presented as one of the "core competencies for achieving the SDGs: Critical thinking and reflection [Problem Analysis] – learning to question our current belief systems and to recognize the assumptions underlying our knowledge, perspectives and opinions".

In Engineers Australia (2019), it is articulated as an indicator of attainment for PE Knowledge and Skill Base for different levels of engineering. For instance, an ET "identifies and critically appraises current developments and emerging issues professionally disseminated in specialist practice area(s) of the technology domain". It also appears as an indicator of attainment for Engineering Application Ability described for all engineering levels. For example, a PE "critically reviews and applies relevant standards and codes of practice underpinning the engineering discipline and nominated specializations". An indicator of attainment for Professional and Personal Attributes is to be "proficient in listening, speaking, reading and writing English, including: critically assesses the accuracy, reliability and authenticity of information and thinks critically and applies an appropriate balance of logic and intellectual criteria to analysis, judgement and decision making".

Taken together, the analysis of 4 Cs in the accreditation criteria documents of EUR-ACE (2021), Engineers Ireland (2021), ABET EAC (2025), and Engineers Australia (2019) indicates variations in the extent and depth of content and orientations. While some refer to these competencies in their Glossaries of Terminology and definitions and role descriptions of different engineering levels, others elaborate on 4 Cs in such different contexts as program or student outcomes, indicative graduate attributes, and quality standards specified for engineering curriculum. In certain cases, they are not used throughout the document or may not be accompanied by detailed contextual elaboration. While the extent is still questionable, this suggests an increasing attention for the incorporation of soft skills, specifically the core learning and innovation skills, 4 Cs, into accreditation frameworks across different countries particularly in terms of how required competencies are conveyed to relevant stakeholders.

CONCLUSION

Engineering students need to be equipped with 4 Cs throughout their undergraduate education by means of higher education teaching and learning activities and administrative practices. In this context, accreditation frameworks may provide a benchmark through direct or indirect references to these core competencies in their quality standards. However, despite the increase in the number of institutions pursuing accreditation in line with increasing globalization, these frameworks may fall short in responding to the requirements for the long-anticipated systemic change in engineering education. This change necessitates a holistic approach, where individual components of higher education teaching, learning, and administration are transformed, leading to a whole university transformation.

Turning the campus into a living lab where students are provided with ample opportunities to experience real-life, in parallel with Whole School Approach, will help the restructuring of learning experiences for students, thus facilitating the improvement of 4 Cs. Engagement of students with sustainability issues of the campus through multidisciplinary projects is considered one of the most effective methods. Using the campus as a test bed for conducting experiments and projects imitating real-life practices where the students are assigned concrete tasks, which will enhance their competencies for co-creating joint solutions for complex problems; providing extracurricular collaborative learning opportunities such as campus activities and student-led events; using diverse teaching models such as MOOCs, flipped classrooms, and blended teaching and learning environments; creating a pathway for students through online, shorter and more intense course elements are suggested. This will also support the transformative, action-oriented and learner-centered pedagogies as suggested by UNESCO (2017), where learners are able to think critically as well as being able to actively participate in solutions of societal issues. In this type of teaching and learning environments, learners are expected to be active participants of the learning process, where their previous learning experiences are considered in course design and delivery. Active engagement in campus issues as a stakeholder will also help enhance learners' sense of belonging to the institution along with creating the potential to transform students from consumers to creators of knowledge.

As 4 Cs are reported to be more difficult to assess compared to technical skills, there also need to be changes in the assessment and evaluation methods. In the living campus, the students should be provided with numerous opportunities that reflect real-life, where they are anticipated to communicate and collaborate with others to find solutions to previously defined open-ended problems using their creativity and critical thinking skills. Therefore, using a mixture of formative and summative assessment methods and complementing assessment with peer evaluation, self-reflection and self-evaluation, feedback based on evaluation as well as engaging students in collaborative projects and creation of policy reports will not only contribute to students taking the responsibility of their own learning but also ease the transfer of these skills into the professional life upon graduation. There needs to be a focus on the assessment of turning knowledge into action and the variety of assessment methods should be determined accordingly.

It is important to note that it is not possible to teach or asses the 4 Cs individually due to their interdependent nature. Therefore, incorporating a single course into curriculum or creating individual exercises or activities to improve these skills independent of each other will not suffice. Creating the systemic change to cater for the needs of a completely different generation of students in a rapidly transforming environment will require a reform in teaching pedagogies. As the role of the students changes into active creators and co-creators of knowledge, the pedagogies implemented need to reflect the facilitating role of the instructor. This will be possible through continuous professional development activities where the instructors are acquainted with emerging technologies, teaching and assessment methods to support the learning experiences of new generation of students such as AI and other educational technologies, flipped, challenge-based, problem-based, inquiry-based, and project-based teaching and learning methodologies and students' active involvement in their own instruction and assessment activities, creating multidisciplinary research based learning environments. Moreover, considering these skills solely as an integral part of Humanities and Social Sciences electives represents a limited perspective; they should also be taught within the engineering courses and assessed and evaluated by the engineering faculty to meet the requirements for a holistic adaptation.

In addition to incorporation of 4 Cs into higher education teaching, learning, and assessment practices, they could be addressed in a more detailed way through explicit or implicit references across different accreditation frameworks as part of definitions, glossaries as well as individual quality standards. Making references to contemporary pedagogies that will help improve the 4 Cs in accreditation frameworks and placing emphasis on continuous professional development activities for instructors to keep up with the changing student profiles and the emerging forces at play in the academic landscape will contribute to raising awareness of programs or institutions in pursuit of accreditation. Also, presentation of sample teaching and assessment activities that promote 4 Cs in the form of ideal practices will guide applicant programs or institutions in navigating their ways while conducting their accreditation self-study evaluations. Adopting a bottom-up approach to implement these practices holistically at the institutional level, complemented by accreditation frameworks to assure and improve educational quality, will significantly contribute to achieving the long-anticipated systemic change necessary for educating future-ready graduates.

REFERENCES

Accreditation Board for Engineering and Technology (ABET). (2025). Criteria for Accrediting Engineering Programs, 2025-2026. Available online: https://www.abet.org/accreditation/accreditation-criteria/criteria-for-accrediting-engineering-programs-2025-2026/ (Accessed March 2025)

Alzahrani, B., Bahitham, H., & Elshennawy, A. (2021). Exploring the applicability of Quality 4.0 in higher education institutions. *Proceedings of the 2021 IEMS Conference*, 27, 1-8. DOI: 10.62704/10057/24719

Armstrong, C. (2021). Key methods used in qualitative document analysis. *OSF Preprints*, 1-9. DOI: 10.2139/ssrn.3996213

Ayoub, M. T., Malik, A. H., Tariq, M. J., Ali, S., Abbas, N., & Ftima, M. (2024). 21st Century Skills 4 C's in Higher Education English Language Classroom: Teachers' Perspectives. [JALT]. *Journal of Applied Linguistics and TESOL, 7*(4), 872–883.

Baumber, J. (2023). Developing Ideas-Informed Young Citizens. In *The Ideas-Informed Society* (pp. 265–284). Emerald Publishing Limited. DOI: 10.1108/978-1-83753-010-620231021

Beagon, U., & Bowe, B. (2023). Understanding professional skills in engineering education: A phenomenographic study of faculty conceptions. *Journal of Engineering Education, 112*(4), 1109–1144. DOI: 10.1002/jee.20556

Braun, V., & Clarke, V. (2012). Thematic analysis. In H. Cooper, P. M. Camic, D. L. Long, A. T. Panter, D. Rindskopf, & K. J. Sher (Eds.), *APA Handbook of Research Methods in psychology, Vol. 2: Research Designs: Quantitative, Qualitative, Neuropsychological, and Biological* (pp. 57–71). American Psychological Association. DOI: 10.1037/13620-004

Brown, C., Luzmore, R., & Groß Ophoff, J. (2023). Facilitating the ideas-informed society: A systematic review. *Emerald Open Research, 1*(1). Advance online publication. DOI: 10.1108/EOR-01-2023-0008

Butler, C., & Zander, L. (2008). The business of teaching and learning through multicultural teams. *Journal of Teaching in International Business, 19*(2), 192–218. DOI: 10.1080/08975930802118903

Cardno, C. (2018). Policy document analysis: A practical educational leadership tool and a qualitative research method. *Educational Administration: Theory and Practice, 24*(4), 623–640. DOI: 10.14527/kuey.2018.016

Caruana, S. (2011). Accreditation of soft skills in higher education using ICT. *Soft Skill Accreditation*, available at https://www.academia.edu/1561384/Accreditation_of_Soft_Skills_in_Higher_Education_using_ICT (Accessed May 2024)

Chen, Q., Yin, H., & Feng, J. (2023). Construction of course content integrating ideas of engineering education accreditation for higher education in China: An example of geochemistry course. *Sustainability (Basel)*, *15*(17), 12709. DOI: 10.3390/su151712709

Dewar, J. (2017). Call for tertiary sector to gear toward University 4.0. https://www.ceda.com.au/news-and-resources/news/education/call-for-tertiary-sector-to-gear-toward-university. (Accessed October 2024)

Engineers Australia. (2019). *Stage 1 Competency Standard for Engineering Associates*. Available at: https://www.engineersaustralia.org.au/sites/default/files/2025-05/stage-1-competency-standard-engineering-associate-may-25.pdf (Accessed January 2025)

Engineers Australia. (2019). *Stage 1 Competency Standard for Engineering Technologists*. Available at: https://www.engineersaustralia.org.au/sites/default/files/2025-05/stage-1-competency-standard-engineering-technologist-may-25.pdf (Accessed January 2025)

Engineers Australia. (2019). *Stage 1 Competency Standard for Professional Engineer*. Available at: https://www.engineersaustralia.org.au/sites/default/files/2022-07/stage-1-competency-standard-professional-engineer.pdf (Accessed January 2025)

Engineers Ireland. (2021). *Accreditation Criteria* (January 2021). Available at: https://www.engineersireland.ie/LinkClick.aspx?fileticket=Mz3SCCk_uRg=&portalid=0&resourceView=1&utm (Accessed November 2023)

European Network for Accreditation of Engineering Education (EUR-ACE). (2021). *EUR-ACE® Framework Standards and Guidelines* (November 2021). Available at: https://www.enaee.eu/wp-content/uploads/2023/11/EAFSG-approved-4-Nov-2021.pdf (Accessed June 2024)

Gamage, K. A. A., Ekanayake, S. Y., & Dehideniya, S. C. P. (2022). Embedding sustainability in learning and teaching: Lessons Learned and Moving Forward—Approaches in STEM Higher Education Programmes. *Education Sciences*, *12*(3), 225. DOI: 10.3390/educsci12030225

Holmes, P., & Corbett, J. (Eds.). (2022). *Critical Intercultural Pedagogy for Difficult Times: Conflict, Crisis, and Creativity* (1st ed.). Routledge. DOI: 10.4324/9781003150756

Kjellgren, B., & Richter, T. (2021). Education for a sustainable future: Strategies for holistic global competence development at engineering institutions. *Sustainability (Basel), 13*(20), 11184. DOI: 10.3390/su132011184

Kohl, K., & Hopkins, C. (2021). Aligning higher education's promise of well-being with sustainability as a purpose of education. In van't Land et al. (Eds.), *The Promise of Higher Education: Essays in Honour of 70 Years of IAU* (pp. 355-361). Springer Publishing. DOI: 10.1007/978-3-030-67245-4_53

Kolmos, A., Egelund Holgaard, J., Worm Routhe, H., Winther, M., & Bertel, L. (2024). Interdisciplinary project types in engineering education. *European Journal of Engineering Education, 49*(2), 257–282. DOI: 10.1080/03043797.2023.2267476

Kumar, S. (2025). Education 4.0: Transforming learning for the Fourth Industrial Revolution. *Higher Education for the Future, 12*(2), 144–162. DOI: 10.1177/23476311251326140

Kumaro, M., & Barliana, M. S. (2022, March). Integration of 4 Cs skills into learning by using the Project Based Learning (PBL) model to face the challenges of the 21st century. In *4th International Conference on Innovation in Engineering and Vocational Education* (ICIEVE 2021) (pp. 88–93). Atlantis Press.

Levin-Goldberg, J. (2012). Teaching Generation TechX with the 4 Cs: Using technology to integrate 21st century skills. *Journal of Institutional Research, 1*, 59–66. Available at: https://files.eric.ed.gov/fulltext/EJ1127608.pdf

McKeown, R., & Hopkins, C. (2017). Quality education and education for sustainable development. In Michelsen, G., & Wells, P. (Eds.), *A Decade of Progress on Education for Sustainable Development: Reflections from the UNESCO Chairs Programme* (pp. 28–38). UNESCO.

Mcmillin, J., & Dyball, R. (2009). Developing a whole-of-university approach to educating for sustainability: Linking curriculum, research and sustainable campus operations. *Journal of Education for Sustainable Development, 3*(1), 55–64. DOI: 10.1177/097340820900300113

Michelsen, G., & Burandt, S. (2017). Sustainable development as a guideline for higher education: An innovative concept for teaching and learning. In G. Michelsen and P. Wells, *A Decade of Progress on Education for Sustainable Development: Reflections from the UNESCO Chairs Programme* (pp. 38-48). UNESCO.

Miranda, J., Navarrete, C., Noguez, J., Molina-Espinosa, J. M., Ramírez-Montoya, M. S., Navarro-Tuch, S. A., Bustamante-Bello, M.-R., Rosas-Fernández, J.-B., & Molina, A. (2021). The core components of education 4.0 in higher education: Three case studies in engineering education. *Computers & Electrical Engineering, 93*, 107278. DOI: 10.1016/j.compeleceng.2021.107278

Partnership for 21st Century Learning (P21). (2019). Framework for 21st century learning definitions. Available at: https://static.battelleforkids.org/documents/p21/p21_framework_definitionsbfk.pdf. (Accessed April, 2025).

Passow, H. J., & Passow, C. H. (2017). What competencies should undergraduate engineering programs emphasize? A systematic review. *Journal of Engineering Education, 106*(3), 475–526. DOI: 10.1002/jee.20171

Qadir, J., Yau, K. L. A., Imran, M. A., & Al-Fuqaha, A. (2020, October). Engineering education, moving into 2020s: Essential competencies for effective 21st century electrical and computer engineers. In *2020 IEEE Frontiers in Education Conference (FIE)* (pp. 1-9). IEEE.

Rajest, S. S., & Suresh, P. (2018). The "Four Cs" education for 21st century's learners. *Research Guru Online Journal of Multidisciplinary Subjects, XII*, 888–900.

Reid-Griffin, A., Croson, J., Fisher, S., & Lopez, N. (2023). Collaborative partnership: Helping adolescents to develop a STEM mindset. *PDS Partners: Bridging Research to Practice, 18*(1), 43–53. DOI: 10.1108/PDSP-01-2023-0002

Rouvrais, S., & Gaultier Le Bris, S. (2018). Breadth experiential courses to flexibly meet new programme outcomes for engineers. In *Engineering Education for a Smart Society: World Engineering Education Forum & Global Engineering Deans Council* (pp. 326-342). Springer International Publishing. DOI: 10.1007/978-3-319-60937-9_25

Seely, B. E. (2005). Patterns in the history of engineering education reform: A brief essay. In *Educating the engineer of 2020: Adapting engineering education to the new century* (pp. 114–130). National Academic Press.

Shuman, L. J., Besterfield-Sacre, M., & McGourty, J. (2005). The ABET "professional skills"—Can they be taught? Can they be assessed? *Journal of Engineering Education, 94*(1), 41–55. DOI: 10.1002/j.2168-9830.2005.tb00828.x

Skvarenina, T. (2008, June). Incorporating and Assessing ABET "Soft Skills" in the Technical Curriculum. In *2008 Annual Conference & Exposition* (pp. 13-727). DOI: 10.18260/1-2--4089

Succi, C., & Canovi, M. (2019). Soft skills to enhance graduate employability: Comparing students and employers' perceptions. *Studies in Higher Education, 45*(9), 1834–1847. DOI: 10.1080/03075079.2019.1585420

Thornhill-Miller, B., Camarda, A., Mercier, M., Burkhardt, J. M., Morisseau, T., Bourgeois-Bougrine, S., Vinchon, F., El Hayek, S., Augereau-Landais, M., Mourey, F., Feybesse, C., Sundquist, D., & Lubart, T. (2023). Creativity, critical thinking, communication, and collaboration: Assessment, certification, and promotion of 21st century skills for the future of work and education. *Journal of Intelligence, 11*(3), 54. Advance online publication. DOI: 10.3390/jintelligence11030054 PMID: 36976147

Ülker, N., & Otrar, M. (2025). University 4.0 essentials: Influence of industry 4.0 on higher education. *Industry and Higher Education, 39*(5), 528–538. DOI: 10.1177/09504222241295625

UNESCO. 2017. Education for sustainable development goals: Learning objectives. Available at: https://unesdoc.unesco.org/ark:/48223/pf0000247444 (Accessed December 2023)

UNESCO. (2020). *Education for sustainable development. A roadmap*, UNESCO, Paris. Available at: https://unesdoc.unesco.org/ark:/48223/pf0000374802 (Accessed March 2024)

Vithanage, V., & Nakashima, N. (2025) The Role Played by the Student-Centred Approach in the Acquisition and Development of 4 Cs of 21st Century Skills Through a Project-Based STEM Curriculum ISSN: 2186-5892 – The Asian Conference on Education 2024: Official Conference Proceedings (pp. 595-610) DOI: 10.22492/issn.2186-5892.2025.53

White, C., & Hastings, D. (2018). An International Study of Faculty Perceptions on Communication Development in Engineering Education. In Auer, M., & Kim, K. S. (Eds.), *Engineering Education for a Smart Society. GEDC WEEF 2016 2016. Advances in Intelligent Systems and Computing* (Vol. 627). Springer. DOI: 10.1007/978-3-319-60937-9_21

Xu, X., Lu, Y., Vogel-Heuser, B., & Wang, L. (2021). Industry 4.0 and industry 5.0-Inception, conception and perception. *Journal of Manufacturing Systems, 61*, 530–535. DOI: 10.1016/j.jmsy.2021.10.006

ADDITIONAL READINGS

Beagon, U., Carthy, D., & Bowe, B. (2019) Graduate engineering skills a literature review & call for rigorous methodological approaches. Paper presented at the 47th SEFI Annual Conference. Available at: https://arrow.tudublin.ie/engschcivcon/124/

Korte, R., Sheppard, S., & Jordan, W. (2008, June). A qualitative study of the early work experiences of recent graduates in engineering. In *2008 Annual Conference & Exposition* (pp. 13-94). DOI: 10.18260/1-2--3520

Liew, C. P., & Kiew, P. L. (2022). Sustainable assessment: The inevitable future of engineering curriculum. *Asean Journal of Engineering Education*, *6*(1), 23–32. DOI: 10.11113/ajee2022.6n1.74

Passow, H. J. (2012). Which ABET competencies do engineering graduates find most important in their work? *Journal of Engineering Education*, *101*(1), 95–118. DOI: 10.1002/j.2168-9830.2012.tb00043.x

Winberg, C., Bramhall, M., Greenfield, D., Johnson, P., Rowlett, P., Lewis, O., Waldock, J., & Wolff, K. (2020). Developing employability in engineering education: A systematic review of the literature. *European Journal of Engineering Education*, *45*(2), 165–180. DOI: 10.1080/03043797.2018.1534086

KEY TERMS AND DEFINITIONS

ABET EAC: Accreditation Board for Engineering and Technology comprises four accreditation commissions, one of which is Engineering Accreditation Commission (EAC). ABET EAC is a US based agency that accredits undergraduate and graduate level engineering programs across the US and globally.

Accreditation: Accreditation is a quality assurance mechanism that determines standards for educational quality and verifies whether programs and/or institutions meet the previously defined criteria. Accrediting agencies aim to instill a culture of continuous quality improvement in programs and/or institutions mainly through the Plan-Do-Control-Act Cycle and regularly review their quality criteria through feedback from relevant stakeholders.

Engineers Australia: Based in Australia, Engineers Australia is an accrediting agency that specifies the quality criteria for engineering programs and awards accreditation status to those in compliance with previously defined standards. It defines competency standards for Professional Engineer, Engineering Associate and Engineering Technologists.

Engineers Ireland: Engineers Ireland is the body responsible for determining the international quality standards for the accreditation of engineering programs in Ireland. It describes appropriate criteria under three professional categories: Chartered Engineer, Associate Engineer and Engineering Technician.

EUR-ACE: EUR-ACE is the label awarded to engineering degree programs mainly in Europe and globally that meet the quality standards specified by European Network for Accreditation of Engineering Education (ENAAE).

Higher Education 4.0: Higher Education 4.0 reflects the features of the current academic landscape which emerged as a response to changing circumstances brought by the 4th industrial revolution and grew at an accelerating rate due to the influences of the pandemic. It has led to numerous changes in the provision of higher education including but not limited to teaching and learning, assessment, administration and quality assurance practices.

Whole School Approach: Whole School Approach can be defined as the incorporation of Education for Sustainable Development principles into curriculum, research, and campus operations in a holistic manner. It requires reforms in numerous aspects of higher education teaching, learning, and administration including but not limited to learning objectives and outcomes, assessment practices, research focus, and teaching pedagogies as a whole. The aim is to transform the students' learning experiences to prepare them as future-ready graduates.

21st Century Skills: The contemporary professional life requires a mixture of competencies from their employees in line with the requirements of the changing framework. 21st century skills encompass a variety of social skills, also referred to as soft skills or professional skills, which help new generation employees survive and succeed in the 21st century workplace.

4 Cs: 4 Cs, namely communication, collaboration, creativity, and critical thinking, are the core learning skills functioning as a critical constituent of learning and innovation skills domain. Higher education institutions are expected to equip their students with 4 Cs in addition to technical skills to prepare them for a complex and constantly evolving context, which has accelerated in the post-pandemic world.

Chapter 2
Integration of Research Into Undergraduate Curriculum:
A Pathway to Transformative Engineering Education

K. Muthamil Sudar
http://orcid.org/0000-0001-9640-3477
Mepco Schlenk Engineering College, India

P. Nagaraj
http://orcid.org/0000-0003-1803-8544
SRM Institute of Science and Technology, Tiruchirappalli, India

ABSTRACT

When considering the integration of research into undergraduate programs, a pedagogical approach can help students go beyond mere technical competencies and towards a holistic learning experience. Coming from Kolb's Experiential Learning Cycle, learning is a construction process where knowledge is born out of real-life experiences. Concrete experiences come from the fieldwork, and thoughtful self-reflection enables them to critique what they have found and encountered. Bloom's Taxonomy is a hierarchical framework for sharpening critical thinking skills and mental abilities. By applying that, teachers can fine-tune research opportunities that progressively push their students. University professors can be role models, instructors and leaders of research projects, and show their students the ropes of the research process. Successful mentorship is all about being supportive, allowing the

DOI: 10.4018/979-8-2600-2606-9.ch002

students to figure things out for themselves. With respect to engineering programs, the use of research-led curricula showcases a very effective blend of theoretical concepts and mentoring.

INTRODUCTION

The area of engineering education is constantly changing. The rapid development of technology, a broad range of global issues, and critical thinking are transforming the way universities nurture their. In order to solve real-world issues, today's engineers must possess not only technical proficiency but also the capacity for flexibility and interdisciplinary collaboration. Well-known universities are reorganizing their systems and course delivery to respond to this change. Undergraduate engineering curricula have drawn predominantly, for decades, from a model of lecture-based teaching and prescribed laboratory activities. While this approach has produced competency in foundational knowledge, it has not been credited with positively nurturing independent thought, problem solving and creativity. Graduates, oriented around memorized knowledge by rote, may be competent on theory, but are unable to apply same in open-ended or enigmatic contexts; both employers and academics have observed the gap and suggested it was one worthy of attention for reforming curricula graduates (Xu, 2024).

An approach, that appears well suited to address these issues, is the inculcation of research into the undergraduate curriculum. Research in its very essence involves inquiry, exploration and experimentation; it is inherently declaratory and provides the undergraduate with an environment where they are encouraged to ask a question rather than merely provide back or repeat an answer (Dart et al., 2021). When an undergraduate completes a research project, they have experienced what it is to observe a discovery via investigating a specific problem; they have developed a relevant literature review; they have designed experiments or models; they have collected/ taken some significant data from evidence; they have drawn a conclusion on the basis of evidence. These independent and often fictitious experiences ensure the student will be managing and exercising intellectual independence and confidence in their own ability. Integrating research into the undergraduate experience is not a new approach; however, in the past decade or more has gained pace. Many of the world's premier universities understand and now promote the outcome that undergraduate students benefit from early engagement with research at many levels. An undergraduate engaged in research strengthens his or her grasp of discipline content, enhances critical thinking capabilities, develops communication skills, promotes deeper inquiries for undertaking professional degrees and doctoral studies, and will spur attitudes of innovation. In addition, studies at college-level may promote mental toughness. As they encounter many difficulties, students need to develop their abilities in terms of how to be adaptable to situation and solve problems.

In engineering education, this integrative approach is particularly important, as solutions to engineering problems are rarely clear-cut. Some engineering problems are classified as "wicked problems" and time and space each present additional constraint (Liu & Zhou,2025). Often, the constraints also stem from complex interdependencies reflective of the real world, including cost, sustainability and equity issues. Research based learning can provide students with research problems that they must solve without a "solution" in mind. Simulation-based learning, like classroom or textbook exercises cannot fully prepare students for the realities of the workplace, where values constantly evolve and shape normative "problem solving" behaviors. In India, a research-based approach could also help counter many of the longstanding issues. Proficiency of new engineering graduates demands attention, as many graduates do not fulfil industry expectations due, in part, to only limited exposure to authentic problem-solving experiences. Capstone projects, internships (including co-ops) all provide valuable experiences, but they are typically offered toward the end of degree. With a limited time, frame to build on the experience, students miss the opportunity to further develop their research skills. By introducing or integrating research elements into the curriculum early in the degree, students can develop their competencies in layers, with multiple opportunities to develop before responsibility.

There is a cultural component as well. In traditional education, students often keep their thoughts about authority, or going beyond their assigned coursework, to themselves. Research Integration omits this aspect. It allows for an environment of curiosity that encourages students to consider "why" and "how" as worthwhile questions as getting the "correct" answer to the assignment. This cultural shift can change life-long learner attitudes in how students will approach learning (He, 2025). Moreover, undergraduate involvement in research can enhance the faculty-student relationship. Faculty who supervises research involvement report an enhanced satisfaction with teaching, as it separates them from students merely completing a task to see a student intellectually develop and "own" the learning. Mentorship can lead to projects where faculty and student collaborate on publication, presentations at conferences, or perhaps a student receiving a patent that reflects positively on the faculty as well when three respective graduate programs recognize listing each other's' names.

From a mindset of the institution, research-based integration of research within an undergraduate's course of study could enhance stature and competitiveness as an institution of higher learning. Graduate programs and employers seek demonstrated proficiency in research by an institution's graduates. Perceptions made about institutions, based on the reputation of thoroughness and quality of research, add value to a graduate's qualifications (Alam & Mohanty 2024). By reliability, the student establishes a narrative about their time spent at an institution that may lure funding, partnerships and high-ranking faculty and staff. Institutions seeking to establish higher ranks or work to satisfy accreditation needs from accrediting bodies such as NBA or ABET, integration of research led educational undergraduate experiences is certainly a differentiator. When considering the value of research in engineering education, it's not just about the institutional benefits. It's also about giving students the opportunity to take a more active role in the process, from being passive recipients of knowledge to being producers of new insights. This will give them a feeling of control and accountability that goes beyond the classroom and into the world of work life. Well-known global issues such as sustainability and technological advancements have enlarged the need for engineers to contribute to the fight against climate change, renewable energy development, medical breakthroughs and robust infrastructure. But we can't just produce engineers who know what to do. Instead, we need to educate them as professionals who can understand the problems by collecting and analyzing the data, bring in ideas from other fields and portraits the solution for the needy ones. By applying research in different perspective, that is possible.

Although incorporating research into undergraduate programs is not easy because it requires clear goals on the part of the educators, institutions and the availability of resourcesUniversities must strike a balance between staying true to the fundamental theoretical teachings and providing enough flexibility in the course plan to accommodate research. And we also need to make sure that access to research doesn't turn into an extra for the academic elite, but is made available to all. Some new models are being tested to improve the difficulties of updating research into the curriculum. Such as breaking up the research into small segments that are scattered throughout the usual coursework, creating problems that include industry partnerships and connecting life into the curriculum through the use of simulators, virtual labs and technology. Research integration is a way for higher education to further transition to learner-centered approaches to education. When engineering education is the impetus for deeper learning, or a springboard to explore and expand knowledge, the result is that institutions can provide their students not just information, but the tools to be curious, able, and creative problem solvers. From this perspective, they are well positioned to critically question the status quo. The engineering competency of sustainability is an excellent example of this. This approach gives them the capacity to get the best out of their clients in a changing world.

Research Integration and Global Competitiveness

Global competitiveness in higher education is increasingly linked to research strength and institutional visibility (Gazi, 2025). Ranking frameworks emphasize outputs such as publications, citations, academic reputation, and employer perception. Within this environment, integrating research into undergraduate education serves as a strategic driver rather than a purely instructional choice. Early exposure to research strengthens academic ecosystems. Undergraduate participation supports faculty collaboration, improves research indicators, and often encourages progression to innovation-led careers. These outcomes indirectly enhance alumni performance and employer trust. Research-integrated curricula also promote international mobility. Students trained in inquiry adapt more readily to global academic and industrial contexts, while institutions benefit from increased attraction of international faculty, collaborators, and funding. In globally ranked universities, teaching and research operate as complementary functions. Positioning undergraduates as contributors to knowledge creation signals institutional maturity.

Undergraduate Research and Global Rankings

Global university ranking systems increasingly evaluate institutional quality through research-driven indicators rather than teaching inputs alone. Frameworks such as QS World University Rankings, Times Higher Education (THE), and the Academic Ranking of World Universities (ARWU) emphasize research output, citation impact, academic reputation, and international engagement as core measures of global standing (Edu, 2025). Within this evaluative environment, the integration of research into undergraduate education exerts an indirect but meaningful influence. Early undergraduate involvement in research strengthens faculty–student collaboration and sustains research productivity over longer periods. Co-authored publications, conference papers, and project outputs that arise from such engagement add up to the number of citations, which is a key factor in THE and ARWU rankings. Reputation factors, especially in QS and THE rankings, are also influenced by research-active learning environments. Learning environments that make research a norm for undergraduates are likely to produce graduates who can seamlessly move into postgraduate programs, innovation-based jobs, or research-intensive sectors, which in turn sustains employer reputation. International outlook criteria, especially in THE rankings, are also supported by research-led learning environments that attract visiting scholars, international collaborators, and globally mobile students. Undergraduate research projects often serve as a springboard to joint supervision, cross-border projects, and institutional collaborations, which enhance global engagement without necessarily being identified as ranking factors. Taken together, the integration of undergraduate research is highly consistent with the underlying rationale of global ranking systems. Although rarely measured as a discrete parameter, its effects permeate citation performance, reputation surveys, and international collaboration indicators, positioning institutions with research-integrated undergraduate programs more favorably within an increasingly competitive and metrics-driven global higher education landscape.

LITERATURE REVIEW

In relation to undergraduate education, the pathways and traditions that students build are basically the world they'll operate in for the rest of their careers, and Southworth's book in '23 stresses that. Engineering programs, up until recently, have laid out a traditional sequence of lectures, tutorials and hands-on lab work, and then expect students to be perfectly prepared to 'become an engineer'. Employers, research institutions, and society expect graduates to be more than just technically ready workers. Employers increasingly seek out candidates who can examine ideas and processes critically and analytically (Lantada, 2022). They look for candidates who can synthesize information, be aware and adaptable, solve complex problems, and think collaboratively. In the aspect of professional preparation for undergraduate, there is a need to introduce a critical path namely research.

Bridging Theory and Practice

Especially in subjects like math, physics, computer science and engineering design, when research is incorporated into the learning process it really gets students thinking about the practical application based on the theoretical knowledge they gained (Southworth et al., 2023). By theoretical knowledge it's not always helpful to students in scenarios like how it will be used to solve real world problems. This can make the learning process feel bore and unfastening. This can be achieved with the help of integrating research into a curriculum. For example, a civil engineering student learning about structural mechanics will have the opportunity to take part in a research project on building resilience to earthquakes. Through applied experimentation, they begin to see how theoretical equations activate into design approaches for potentially lifesaving strategies. Likewise, a student learning about signal processing in electrical engineering can apply these ideas in a research study on medical imaging systems. In these instances, the classroom serves as a launching point, while any research students do on their own, serves as the connective tissue to applicable, impactful work. The connection between theory and application contributes to an enhanced understanding, and also helps students learn and remember concepts for even longer periods of time. Students are able to see the value in what they are learning and, therefore, learn with more motivation and purposeful learning.

Fostering Critical Thinking

Critical thinking, as a skill, can emerge from questioning, analyzing, and evaluating information from various positions (Das, 2025). In most traditional coursework, students are only focused on solving a problem with a clear solution. Furthermore, with these often-over-rehearsed topics, although students have already learned to re-learn problem solving, it does not lead students to question what assumptions led students to that problem. Nor does it allow for exploration of alternative methods or approaches from a different aspect. In many respects, "research" occupies a domain where "knowledge" is not common, and the "correct" answer is not easily established. It asks students to develop ways to establish data, curate the data, interpret the result, and make the best-informed decisions possible with the incomplete or contradicting evidentiary base they have just established. This causes students to think critically about the methods associated to the output, and acknowledge weaknesses and biases.

For example: A student working on a project related to renewable energy has proposed a respectable initial hypothesis (Hazrat et al., 2023). After having performed experimental observations, there is a disconnect between data and hypothesis. It would seem they were unable to connect the two, and thus be able to discard the project as a failure. Instead, they would have to revisit the project design, working through possible sources of error, only to discover new ways to approach, investigate, redesign, develop, and iterate their understandings. This experience should be seen as a teaching moment for resilience, and for teaching students how to develop an investigative mindset and the associative value that could be utilized academically or professionally.

Enhancing Employability and building innovation culture

When looking for engineers in the market, employers are on the lookout for the next set of graduates who can respond to the rapid evolution of technology and excel in the complexities of a multidisciplinary work environment (Narong & Hallinger, 2024). For instance, these companies started as an attempt to solve a particular technical problem that was extracted during coursework. Institutions now aid these projects through the setup of "research-to-market" ventures like university incubators, assistance in patent applications and early seed funding. An example of this is given in the description of a low-cost water purification scheme developed by a group of university students that now goes through metamorphosis from being a component of environmental engineering research to becoming a financially prosperous product. This helping in large part with the sponsorship of the university. Even more profound is the spirit of inquiry that extends beyond specific tasks, as students are encouraged to seek out, evaluate, and critically assess innovations in terms of their practical value. A mindset of research-based discovery is given to not just the founders of known companies, but to those who can bring ideas to an existing corporation.

A Strategic Imperative

Integration of research into undergraduate is not an improvement activity that can be done by identifying selected group of interested and talented students. Instead, it needs to be a purposeful and integrated priority for all students throughout the curriculum (Kuffuor et al., 2024). Contemporary engineering challenges in energy, healthcare, infrastructure, and digital technologies need problem-solvers who are adept at working with ambiguity and creating novel solutions. By exposing all students systematically to research, institutions can democratize innovation and make talents with different backgrounds have the chance to play a role. It allows more diverse sources of ideas and ideas of various sorts, which can bolster the quality of solutions created.

Theoretical Perspectives Supporting Research Integration

Although Kolb's Experiential Learning Cycle and Bloom's Taxonomy are useful pedagogical frameworks for the integration of undergraduate research, they are not the only conceptual frameworks that can be used to understand these practices (Jamison et al., 2022). Constructivist learning theory is a conceptual framework that focuses on the active and constructive nature of knowledge, which is consistent with research-based learning environments. While Bloom's Taxonomy emphasizes the hierarchical development of cognitive skills, constructivist learning theory emphasizes meaning-making and the social construction of knowledge. Knowledge production and innovation theory is a conceptual framework that not only focuses on learning outcomes but also sees undergraduate research as a contribution to knowledge systems in the early stages. While Kolb's Experiential Learning Cycle emphasizes individual learning transformation, knowledge production and innovation theory emphasizes the role of inquiry-based activities in producing knowledge, research outputs, and problem-solving capabilities that can be transferred and have a wider impact. These conceptual frameworks collectively indicate that undergraduate research is a dual process that is both a learning process and an innovation process.

TRANSFORMATIVE ENGINEERING EDUCATION FRAMEWORK

Embedding research in the undergraduate curriculum is not formulaic. It depends on what models institutions can choose based on their resources, faculty skills, readiness of students, and academic culture (Liu et al., 2025). In most situations, a mixture of methods is most effective, as it exposes students to doing research incrementally throughout their program. The models described below represent plausible routes for incorporating research at the undergraduate level. Figure 1 shows the framework of transformative engineering education

Figure 1. Transformative Engineering Education Framework

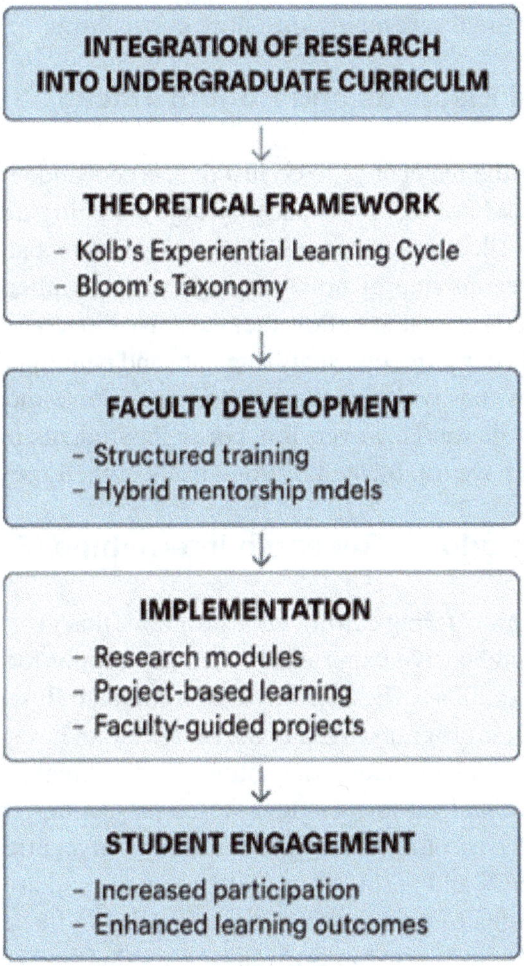

Course-Embedded Research Projects

One of the strongest methods of introducing research is to incorporate it into routine coursework (Rath et al., 2023). In this design, some courses integrate mini-research projects into the grading. The projects are made to fit within the course's learning goals while providing students with autonomy to investigate topics in more depth. For instance, in a "Structural Analysis" course, students may examine the response of various building materials under different load conditions through experiments in the laboratory. For a "Data Science" course, students may analyze open data to identify patterns and make predictions and record their methodology and findings. This model guarantees that all students are exposed to research, whether they enter a specialized research program or not. It also permits faculty members to incorporate research activities without revamping the entire curriculum.

Research-Based Electives and Honors Tracks

Universities offer them a chance to do just that, when students in their junior or senior years of high school discover that they enjoy digging deeper into research (Naixin et al., 2024). Elective courses, or sometimes honors pathways, are the key to unlocking the research side of university education. Rather than a traditional lecture-exam format, these courses allow them to delve into reading journal articles, designing small-scale experiments, analyzing data and penning their findings, and, in some cases, it even ends with a master's thesis or a twelve-month long challenge supervised by an instructor. However, it is better for students to enter these kinds of courses once they have established a strong basis in their subject.

Summer Undergraduate Research Internships (SURI)

Universities are now offering cutting-edge programs that give students a far more interesting and comprehensive experience when they apply for research opportunities (Novawan et al., 2024). The Summer Undergraduate Research Internship, or SURI, is a very popular program in many universities that has gained its fair share of recognition. Here, students spend the entire summer break, instead of juggling classes, completely immersed in a single research project that they get to work on closely with a faculty mentor. Coming from many universities, these programs also come with stipends and partnerships with companies, that make it financially manageable for students to participate. An average day in these programs usually starts with some lab work, a seminar is given by a visiting speaker in the afternoon, and followed up with time to get feedback and review progress, and by the end, students typically submit a report, produce a captivating poster and sometimes can even write an original paper that's strong enough to be presented in a conference. In other cases, universities have started to team up with research labs and start-ups so that students can get a taste of what research outside the classroom is really like.

Faculty-Led Research Groups

With respect to involving undergraduates in research, one of the best ways is to let them join already established research teams (Pacher et al., 2024). In research-oriented universities, professors typically have ongoing projects that are partially funded, and these provide the ideal setting for undergraduates to contribute. From running simulations, gathering data, and writing portions of technical documentation, professors, graduate students, and postdocs can help them get a feel for how actual research team's work. Often, the more that undergraduates contribute, the greater are the chances they'll produce results, and if they do, they may find that they have earned the right to be a co-author on a paper, and in turn become an integral part of the research project.

Hackathons, Innovation Challenges, and Competitions

Not all research training has to happen over months or years. Some of the most energizing experiences come from fast-paced events like hackathons, innovation sprints, or design contests (Zhang et al., 2025). In these settings, students dive into a problem, brainstorm solutions, and build prototypes — all within a day or two. An university ran a 48-hour "Smart City Innovation Challenge," where teams tackled issues such as traffic congestion, waste disposal, and energy use, pitching their results to a panel of judges. When working against a deadline, students can't help but make quick decisions and rely on students team's abilities. Coming through the stages of idea, design, testing and presentation is basically the same as the initial stages of a real research project, and these competitions get the attention of the industry also. Mentors and people with deep knowledge shows up, offering to guide and fund projects that gains their attention.

Community-Engaged Research

Regarding teaching problem-solving, some educational approaches are throwing out the textbooks and teaming students up with the people and companies around them (López, 2025). By this way, students can turn theoretical concepts into real-world challenges. For example, a group of environmental engineering students in a rural village could integrate their skills and build a low-cost, practical water filtration system. Similarly, a team of computer science majors teaming up with local farmers can develop an application that gives them access to up-to-date crop prices and weather updates. These projects not only just give engineering principles a workout, but also really drive home that technical expertise comes with a responsibility to society.

Research Focused Capstone projects

When engineering programs include capstone projects, the experience can be taken to the next level by placing a heavy importance to research activity (Pham et al., 2023). Students who explore into the existing literature, formulate a well-defined research question, collect the required data and present formal results in the capstone, will transform it from being a design into a much more sophisticated analysis, but also contributes to the body of engineering knowledge.

Blended and Progressive Approaches

Undergraduate programs frequently see the best outcomes when research engagement is incrementally layered over the duration of the four years of study, compared to using those models in standalone.

Year 1: Small inquiry-based tasks built into introductory courses.
Year 2: Open-ended problems that push students to think beyond standard solutions.
Year 3: Direct involvement in faculty projects or structured summer internships.
Year 4: A culminating capstone or honors thesis with a strong research component.

This phased approach means that students learn research skills gradually, rather than be swamped by learning about research only in the last year. Table I shows the integration models and its expected outcomes.

Table 1. Research Integration Models

Model	Key Features	Expected Outcomes
Course-Embedded Projects	Mini-projects within courses	Early research exposure
Research-Based Electives/Honors	Thesis, advanced analysis	Deeper research skills
Research Internships	Summer projects, industry ties	Real-world experience
Faculty-Led Groups	Team-based, ongoing research	Collaboration, mentoring
Competitions/Hackathons	Fast-paced, creative problem solving	Innovation, teamwork

continued on following page

Table 1. Continued

Model	Key Features	Expected Outcomes
Community-Engaged Research	Focus on local/regional issues	Social impact, engagement
Capstone Projects	Research-focused final projects	Comprehensive, applied learning
Progressive Models	Stepped, year-wise integration	Incremental skill development

IMPLEMENTATION FRAMEWORK

Implementing research into the undergraduate curriculum takes more than well-intentioned desire. It takes a coherent plan that connects to institutional priorities, allocates resources efficiently, and involves faculty and students. Lacking a shared framework, research initiatives stand the risk of being discreet experiments instead of an integral component of the educational culture (Broo et al., 2022). The below framework provides a realistic approach to integrating research meaningfully into undergraduate teaching in universities and colleges. It is intended to be flexible to suit institutions of different sizes, resources, and academic composition. Table II shows the implementation framework table.

Table 2. Implementation Framework Table

Stage	Activity	Key Stakeholders	Expected Outcomes
1.Strategic Planning	Define research goals, form steering committee	Academic council, HODs, student reps	Clear vision and policy framework
2. Faculty Capacity Building	Workshops, mentoring incentives	Faculty development cell, research office	Skilled faculty mentors, increased buy-in
3.Curriculum Design	Embed projects, research courses, thesis options	BoS, curriculum committee	Structured research pathway
4.Resource Allocation	Labs, databases, funding partnerships	Management, industry partners	Adequate tools and financial support
5.Student Engagement	Research fairs, project portals, guest lectures	Student affairs, faculty mentors	High student participation
6.Assessment & Evaluation	Rubrics, peer review, feedback sessions	Faculty, evaluation committees	Quality and accountability in research outputs
7.Recognition & Dissemination	Awards, publications, media coverage	PR office, research office	Increased visibility and motivation

Implementation Stages

Stage 1: Vision Setting and Strategic Planning

The institution has to form a common vision for undergraduate research prior to any adjustment in the curriculum. It entails:

- Setting clear objectives (e.g., enhancing employability, promoting innovation, building academic reputation).
- Prioritizing research areas based on faculty strengths, industry needs, and social imperatives.
- Aligning the effort with accrediting agency expectations and institutional strategic plans.
- To regulate the process, an advisory committee is formed by comprising faculty mentors, senior administrators and student representatives

Stage 2: Faculty Capacity Building

The hidden key to successful research integration is the faculty. If the faculty is not trained properly, even a well-designed curriculum will fail.

Major actions are:

- Organizing workshops on research mentorship, project supervision, and evaluation.
- Offering incentives such as recognition awards, lightened teaching loads, or research grants for actively mentoring undergraduate projects by faculty
- Encouraging faculty members to work together across disciplines to increase research opportunities.

Stage 3: Curriculum Design

The curriculum has to be reformulated to include research components after the faculty preparation completed.

- Embedding mini-projects within current courses.
- Providing elective research methodology courses in the second or third year.
- Introducing credit-bearing research projects or thesis work in the final year.
- Developing a progression model where research exposure escalates year by year.

There is a need to make sure that research activity is aligned with learning outcomes and does not overwhelm students.

Stage 4: Resource Allocation

To carry out research activities, institutions must provide sufficient resources both digital and physical.

- Provide laboratories with the necessary tools, software, and safety protocols.
- Offer access to academic databases, journals, and simulation software.
- Set budgets for consumables, conference travel, and student stipends.
- Collaborate with industry, research institutions, and funding agencies to increase resources.

Stage 5: Student Engagement and Awareness

Students must be engaged and aware of,

- Annual undergraduate research fairs in which students showcase work under way.
- Establishing web pages to post faculty projects welcoming student participation.
- Arranging guest talks and panel discussions involving researchers and industry professionals.
- Providing initial sessions explaining how to participate in research studies.

Stage 6: Assessment and Evaluation

Assessment is mandatory to ensure quality and credibility. Well defined rubrics must be formulated.

- Problem definition and literature review.
- Methodology and experimental design.
- Data analysis and interpretation.
- Quality of presentation and communication.
- Originality and potential impact.

Peer review processes may also be established, providing students with experience in reviewing research.

Stage 7: Recognition and Dissemination

To stimulate participation and maintain momentum:

- Reward excellent projects through awards, scholarships, or special commendations.
- Support students in publishing their work as articles in journals or as presentations at conferences.
- Highlight research success stories on the institution's website and social media.
- Promote involvement in innovation contests, hackathons, and startup incubators.

CASE STUDIES

When analyzing the success of university research models in different countries, we can get a sense of the real-world challenges and benefits of integrating research into the undergraduate curriculum, with each model tailored to its local resources, culture and policies.

Indian Context

IUCEE's Project-Based Learning Initiatives

Coming from the Indian context, the Indo Universal Collaboration for Engineering Education, IUCEE, is credited with leading project-based and research-based learning in Indian engineering colleges (Sigahi & Sznelwar, 2022). It is essentially through faculty development workshops, knowledge sharing and curriculum counselling that encourage universities to bring real-life projects right into the first year of their courses. Well-known IUCEE participating colleges craft semester-long projects that look at social issues such as the adoption of renewable energy in rural areas, low-cost assistive tools for people with disabilities. It also involves the kind of step-by-step approach, literature reviews, problem formulation, prototype construction and final presentations that impersonates formal research. The students are trained to cut through problems in a systematic way and document the whole process so that it can be evaluated by their professors.

IIT Bombay's UG Research Symposium

The University Grants Commission, IIT Bombay, is also running an undergraduate research symposium that showcases a remarkable display of innovative research at which students projects get presented to panels made up of faculty, industry experts and alumni (Idris et al., 2024). With heavy competition, the projects are picked by a panel of experts. This event helps the students get to a typical conference and may receive practical and constructive feedback. Plenty of these projects go on to become papers in reputable publications or also make entry in innovation competitions. Table III shows the comparative analysis of research integration in UG.

Table 3. Comparative Analysis Of Undergraduate Research Integration Case Studies

Institution / Program	Geographic Context	Core Model	Key Strengths	Contribution to Global Competitiveness	Transferable Lessons
IUCEE – Project-Based Learning Initiatives	India	Course-embedded, project-based research	Early exposure to real-world problems; strong faculty development; structured documentation	Builds foundational research skills at scale; improves graduate readiness and applied innovation capacity	Faculty training is critical; research can be embedded even in resource-constrained institutions
IIT Bombay – UG Research Symposium	India	Competitive research dissemination platform	Peer review, industry interaction, conference-style presentation	Enhances research visibility; strengthens academic reputation and innovation pipelines	Undergraduate research benefits from formal dissemination and competitive evaluation
MIT – Undergraduate Research Opportunities Program (UROP)	USA	Institution-wide, flexible research engagement	High faculty–student collaboration; co-authored publications; flexible credit/pay options	Direct contribution to citation impact, research output, and global reputation	Institutional culture and flexibility sustain long-term research productivity
University of Cambridge – Research Placements	UK	Structured summer research placements	Advanced training; integration with doctoral research; ethics and data skills	Strengthens international outlook, cross-border collaboration, and research excellence	Structured mentorship and formal training enhance global research preparedness

International Context

MIT's Undergraduate Research Opportunities Program (UROP)

It has been offering research experiences to first-year undergraduates and beyond since 1967. Concerning the program's scientific output, the production of co-authored publications in leading journals is the result of its flexibility (Zhang et al., 2025). Students can choose to work for pay, credits or also to earn experience. Well-known for its exceptional institutional culture, the programme makes sure that undergraduate research is at the heart of its learning process.

University of Cambridge's Research Placements

Students enrolled in the natural sciences tripos at the University of Cambridge are eligible for summer research placements in university departments and affiliated research centres, as per the guidelines established by Sigahi in 2022. These placements are often at the forefront of contemporary discoveries, encompassing areas such as sustainable materials and artificial intelligence. This opportunity enables students to collaborate closely with Ph.D. candidates and postdoctoral researchers, thereby mastering advanced experimental techniques. Additionally, the university ensures that these placements are complemented by formal training in data management, research ethics, and academic writing, equipping students with transferable skills applicable in both academia and industry. Table IV shows the assessment of research integration approaches.

Table 4. Assessment Of Research Integration Approaches

Integration Model	Ease of Implementation	Scalability	Depth of Engagement
Course-Embedded Projects	High	High	Moderate
Research-Based Electives/Honors	Moderate	Low-Moderate	High
Summer Research Internships	Low	Low	High
Faculty-Led Research Groups	Low	Low	Very High
Peer-Mentored/Group Research	Moderate	Moderate	Moderate-High
Capstone Thesis/Required Research	Moderate	Moderate	High
Optional Honors Thesis	Low	Low	Very High

FRAMEWORKS AND MENTORSHIP MODELS SUPPORTING UNDERGRADUATE RESEARCH

Kolb's Experiential Learning Cycle is one of the theoretical frameworks that has been frequently discussed when integrating research into undergraduate education (Wan, 2025). The four stages of this cycle—concrete experience, reflective observation, abstract conceptualization, and active experimentation—are where undergraduate research truly shines. Feedback and observations help to simplify the problems that students face, which are then broken down into logical models and finally tested with the help of improved concepts. With this approach, students are brought back to the start and become completely engaged in their education. Bloom's Taxonomy focuses on the high-level thinking that is essentially at the core of research endeavours. Coming heading out of the gate with research tasks, these have a massive impact on the learning process, pushing students away from routine memorization towards more critical and innovative thinking. The undergraduate research program also relies heavily on mentorship, and instructors just knowing their subject isn't enough. Because they need to guide the students through identifying the problems, planning the research and presenting the results in a way that anyone can understand. Lots of universities have developed the necessary infrastructure to get this in place. By training their faculty, cross-departmental collaborations and providing project management and outcome tracking tools. Also, by blending faculty mentorship, help from older students and even industry feedback, to make sure the projects stay challenging, relevant and at the bleeding edge of their fields. A center of excellence can coordinate all this, sorting out seed money, lab space and progress reports (Ngoc et al., 2023). And also knows just how to reward the faculty who are pouring so much time into this sort of thing, through grants, performance reviews and institutional recognition. A comparison of research integration models is provided in Table V.

Table 5. Comparison Of Undergraduate Research Integration Models: Key Attributes, Outcomes, And Limitations

Program Name	Target Student Population	Duration or Timing	Educational Outcomes	Key Mentoring or Curriculum Features
Course-Embedded Project	All enrolled undergraduates	Semester/ Academic year	Improved theory-practice connection, basic research skills	Faculty-guided, group project, embedded in course
Honors Research Thesis	High-achieving students	Final year or multi-year	High innovation, strong grad school prospects	Individual mentorship, advanced methodology
Faculty-Led Research Group	Selected or volunteer students	Year-round or by project	Co-authorship, deep skill building	Close mentorship, peer collaboration
Summer Reserach Internship (SURI)	Juniors/Seniors, diverse pool	Full summer,. intensive	Conference presentations, professional networks	Hands-on, seminar series, stipend support
Capstone Research Project	All (required) or selected	Final year, 1–2 semesters	Problem-solving, applied research, portfolios	Teamwork, guided assessment, formal defense
Community-Engaged Research	Undergraduates/all levels	Variable/project-based	Social impact, soft skills, leadership	Field work, partnership mentoring
Research-Based Elective Course	Upperclassmen, interested	Single semester	Analytical thinking, discipline-specific skills	Topic-driven, focused faculty input

DISCUSSION AND FUTURE WORK

The integration of research into undergraduate engineering education is still evolving, and it still opens for deeper exploration. While current models demonstrate promise, future works should investigate about different institutional contexts, public versus private, regional versus global and shape the outcomes of research-based learning.

Table 6. Comparative Analysis Of Recent (2025) Studies On Research Integration In Engineering Education

Study	Approach / Model	Context	Key Outcomes	Strengths & Limitations	Relevance
Liu et al. (2025)	AI-integrated engineering education framework	Higher education (global)	Improved problem-solving, adaptability, and engagement	Strong empirical validation using large datasets Focus limited to AI-enabled environments	Supports technology-driven research integration and adaptive learning
Zhang et al. (2025)	Digital transformation strategy for universities	China / global institutions	Enhanced institutional research capacity and global competitiveness	Links policy, pedagogy, and research outcomes Context-specific (mainly large institutions)	Aligns with global rankings and institutional competitiveness discussion
Wan (2025)	AI-assisted project-based learning	Engineering classrooms	Increased innovation, creativity, and student participation	Clear measurement of innovation outcomes Limited longitudinal evidence	Supports innovation culture and research-based learning models
He (2025)	AI-supported instructional design	Classroom-level implementation	Improved academic performance and conceptual clarity	Strong evidence on learning outcomes Less focus on research integration explicitly	Validates learning outcome improvements through research-oriented methods
Liu & Zhou (2025)	AI readiness and innovation framework	Software engineering education	Enhanced student readiness for research and innovation	Integrates behavioral and technological factors Early-stage framework (needs further validation)	Supports future work and need for adaptive research ecosystems

In table VI, one can note that although both approaches involving AI technology and project work are efficient in engaging students and encouraging them to innovate, their efficiency largely depends on institutional capacity building and scaling. Research papers such as those by Liu et al. (2025) and Zhang et al. (2025) stress the need for systemic change, while the ones published by Wan (2025) and He (2025) consider the significance of changes in the classroom. Therefore, there is a need for integrating research into education through aligning innovative processes and institutional strategy. Foundational frameworks such as the research–teaching nexus (Healey & Jenkins, 2009) and experiential learning theory (Kolb, 1984) establish the theoretical basis for integrating research into undergraduate education.

Comparative analyses across countries may help to understand whether certain frameworks are more effective in enhancing employability, innovation culture. Another significant step is to collect real evidence instead of only talking about ideas. Currently, most studies highlight benefits like better problem-solving or critical thinking without any proper evidence. To make the case stronger, universities should gather data through graduate surveys, feedback from employers, and by following the students career progress over time. This kind of information would clearly show the impact of research-based learning. In addition, universities could work with ranking bodies to link student research activities directly to measures of reputation, visibility, and international standing. A key point in the discussion is the role of internationalization. Research opportunities should not be limited to activities inside one country. When students take part in collaborative projects, exchange programs, or joint research with abroad universities, they gain valuable global skills. These experiences make learning richer and prepare students to work in diverse environments. At the same time, such collaborations help universities improve their research skill which is an important factor in global rankings. Future studies could look more closely at how these partnerships affect things like shared publications, citation networks, and the overall reputation of institutions worldwide. Considering all, these directions and recommendations highlight that undergraduate research is not simply an academic exercise but a strategic imperative. Graduates are prepared for complex professional landscapes, and the standing of institutions in the competitive global higher education environment is enhanced, when research is successfully integrated into the undergraduate journey.

CONCLUSION

For engineering education, research is no longer an optional add-on, but a strategic necessity, and universities must increasingly consider how to make this a seamless part of the learning process. In a global higher education environment shaped by research output, academic reputation, citation impact, and international outlook, undergraduate research integration also contributes indirectly to institutional competitiveness and visibility. Building on the need for more effective and relevant knowledge that combines theory with real-world problems, engineers today must develop critical thinking while also building capacities that allow even organizations without formal research teams to access innovation-ready graduates. This chapter draws on Kolb's Experiential Learning Cycle and Bloom's Taxonomy to establish a foundation for this transformation and finds that faculty mentorship—supported through formal training programs and hybrid engagement models—is instrumental to successful implementation. At the same time, when viewed through broader knowledge production perspectives, undergraduate research functions not only as a learning mechanism but as a contributor to institutional research ecosystems. Nationwide and international examples demonstrate that earlier and stronger institutional support leads to greater impact, strengthening publication pipelines, alumni outcomes, and employer perception, while also enhancing opportunities for international collaboration.

Undergraduate research should therefore not be treated as an afterthought, a separate extracurricular activity, or an isolated academic exercise. Instead, it must be positioned within coordinated institutional strategies that align curriculum design, faculty incentives, resource allocation, and global partnerships. Practical measures such as dedicated research units, funding mechanisms, platforms for disseminating student outcomes, and recognition for mentors help sustain momentum and reinforce research culture. These efforts also support accreditation objectives and respond to ranking-driven expectations increasingly faced by universities worldwide. Importantly, institutions that embed research experiences early tend to cultivate graduates who are more analytically capable, professionally adaptable, and globally mobile. Such attributes resonate across academia and industry, strengthening institutional identity and long-term reputation. Whether acting as job creators or research centers, universities succeed when theory-driven courses, strong mentorship, and structured self-assessment frameworks operate together to monitor impact and guide continuous improvement. Ultimately, reforming undergraduate engineering education toward research-led learning represents a long-term investment in innovation capacity, global relevance, and competitive positioning, enabling institutions to respond effectively to societal needs while sustaining excellence in an increasingly metrics-driven higher education landscape.

REFERENCES

Alam, A., & Mohanty, A. (2024). Integrated constructive robotics in education (ICRE) model: A paradigmatic framework for transformative learning in educational ecosystem. *Cogent Education, 11*(1), 2324487. DOI: 10.1080/2331186X.2024.2324487

Broo, D. G., Kaynak, O., & Sait, S. M. (2022). Rethinking engineering education at the age of industry 5.0. *Journal of Industrial Information Integration, 25*, 100311. DOI: 10.1016/j.jii.2021.100311

Dart, S., Trad, S., & Blackmore, K. (2021). Navigating the path from technical engineering to engineering education research: A conceptual model of the transition process. *European Journal of Engineering Education, 46*(6), 1076–1091. DOI: 10.1080/03043797.2021.1992609

Das, D. K. (2025). *Problem-based learning for engineering education: Developing the engineers of the future*. Routledge., DOI: 10.1201/9781003529743

Edu, N. (2025). The influence of international rankings on higher education reforms and institutional strategies. *International Journal of Innovative Social Sciences & Humanities Research, 13*(1), 273–280. DOI: 10.1201/9781351182003-6

Gazi, A. I. (2025). AI Meets Academia: How Machine Learning is Transforming Higher Education in China. *Journal of Educational Studies, 3*(3), 1–13. DOI: 10.1108/EMJB-03-2024-0055

Hazrat, M. A., Hassan, N. M. S., Chowdhury, A. A., Rasul, M. G., & Taylor, B. A. (2023). Developing a skilled workforce for future industry demand: The potential of digital twin-based teaching and learning practices in engineering education. *Sustainability (Basel), 15*(23), 16433. DOI: 10.3390/su152316433

He, X. (2025). Practical Research on Classroom Teaching Reform Based on AI-Assisted Instructional Design. *IJLAI Transactions on Science and Engineering, 3*(4), 13–20. DOI: 10.12677/ae.2025.155750

Healey, M., & Jenkins, A. (2009). *Developing undergraduate research and inquiry*. Higher Education Academy.

Idris, M. D., Feng, X., & Dyo, V. (2024). Revolutionizing higher education: Unleashing the potential of large language models for strategic transformation. *IEEE Access : Practical Innovations, Open Solutions, 12*, 67738–67757. DOI: 10.1109/ACCESS.2024.3400164

Jamison, C. S. E., Fuher, J., Wang, A., & Huang-Saad, A. (2022). Experiential learning implementation in undergraduate engineering education: A systematic search and review. *European Journal of Engineering Education, 47*(6), 1356–1379. DOI: 10.1080/03043797.2022.2031895

Kolb, D. A. (1984). *Experiential learning: Experience as the source of learning and development*. Prentice-Hall.

Kuffuor, O., Aggrawal, S., Jaiswal, A., Smith, R. J., & Morris, P. V. (2024). Transformative pathways: Implementing intercultural competence development in higher education using Kotter's change model. *Education Sciences, 14*(7), 686. DOI: 10.3390/educsci14070686

Lantada, A. D. (2022). Engineering education 5.0: Strategies for a successful transformative project-based learning. *Insights into Global Engineering Education after the Birth of Industry 5*, 19. DOI: DOI: 10.5772/intechopen.102844

Liu, C., Wang, G. C., & Wang, H. F. (2025). The application of artificial intelligence in engineering education: A systematic review. *IEEE Access : Practical Innovations, Open Solutions, 13*, 17895–17910. DOI: 10.1109/ACCESS.2025.3532595

Liu, C., & Zhou, D. (2025). AI Integration in Higher Education: A Software Engineering Perspective on Readiness, Anxiety, and Innovation. *International Journal of Software Engineering and Knowledge Engineering*. Advance online publication. DOI: 10.1142/S0218194025501116

López, M. B. (2025). Evolving pedagogy in digital signal processing education: AI-assisted review and analysis. *IEEE Access : Practical Innovations, Open Solutions, 13*, 45559–45567. DOI: 10.1109/ACCESS.2025.3549477

Naixin, Z., Wai Yie, L., Tong, Z., & Changqing, W. (2024). Artificial intelligence in engineering education: A review of pedagogical innovations. *INTI Journal, 2024*(46), 1–10. DOI: 10.61453/INTIj.202446

Narong, D. K., & Hallinger, P. (2024). Traversing the evolution of research on engineering education for sustainability: A bibliometric review (1991–2022). *Sustainability (Basel), 16*(2), 641. DOI: 10.3390/su16020641

Ngoc, T. N., Tran, Q. N., Tang, A., Nguyen, B., Nguyen, T., & Pham, T. (2023). AI-assisted learning for electronic engineering courses in higher education. *arXiv preprint arXiv:2311.01048. DOI: https://doi.org/*DOI: 10.3102/2198146

Novawan, A., Ismailia, T., Zuhro, C., Utami, L. D., Pratama, M. R., Karimah, K., & Haq, R. N. (2024). Design thinking approach to powerful material development in educational contexts: From theory to practice. [IJOSSH]. *International Journal of Studies in Social Sciences and Humanities, 1*(2), 125–145. DOI: 10.25047/ijossh.v1i2.5571

Pacher, C., Woschank, M., Zunk, B. M., & Gruber, E. (2024). Engineering education 5.0: A systematic literature review on competence-based education in the industrial engineering and management discipline. *Production & Manufacturing Research, 12*(1), 2337224. DOI: 10.1080/21693277.2024.2337224

Pham, T., Nguyen, T. B., Ha, S., & Ngoc, N. T. N. (2023). Digital transformation in engineering education: Exploring the potential of AI-assisted learning. *Australasian Journal of Educational Technology, 39*(5), 1–19. DOI: 10.14742/ajet.8825

Rath, K. C., Senapati, A. K., Dalla, V. K., Kumar, A., Sahu, S., & Das, R. P. (2023). Growing role of AI towards digital transformation in higher education systems. In *Advancements in Artificial Intelligence, Blockchain Technology, and IoT in Higher Education* (pp. 3–26). Apple Academic Press., DOI: 10.1201/9781003300458-2

Sigahi, T. F., & Sznelwar, L. I. (2022). Exploring applications of complexity theory in engineering education research: A systematic literature review. *Journal of Engineering Education, 111*(1), 232–260. DOI: 10.1002/jee.20438

Southworth, J., Migliaccio, K., Glover, J., Glover, J. N., Reed, D., McCarty, C., Brendemuhl, J., & Thomas, A. (2023). Developing a model for AI across the curriculum: Transforming the higher education landscape via innovation in AI literacy. *Computers and Education: Artificial Intelligence, 4*, 100127. DOI: 10.1016/j.caeai.2023.100127

Wan, Y. (2025). A study on the impact of AI-assisted project-based learning design on innovation ability. *Frontiers in Interdisciplinary Educational Methodology, 2*(3), 210–223. DOI: 10.1109/ICEIB53692.2021.9686424

Xu, L. (2024). Innovative interdisciplinary models in engineering education: Transforming practices across global universities. *Engineering Education Review, 2*(3), 129–144. DOI: 10.54844/eer.2024.0846

Zhang, Y., Zhang, M., Wu, L., & Li, J. (2025). Digital transition framework for higher education in AI-assisted engineering teaching: Challenge, strategy, and initiatives in China. *Science & Education, 34*(2), 933–954. DOI: 10.1007/s11191-024-00575-3

Chapter 3
Embedding Social-Emotional Competency and Well-Being in Curriculum Planning:
A Future-Focused Strategy for Resilient Higher Education

Priyal Malhotra
http://orcid.org/0009-0005-1120-146X
Christ (Deemed to be) University, Delhi-NCR, India

Sneha Saha
http://orcid.org/0000-0002-8521-5224
Christ (Deemed to be) University, Delhi-NCR, India

ABSTRACT

This chapter advances a future-focused framework for embedding social-emotional competency and well-being into curriculum planning. Drawing on social-emotional learning theory, positive psychology, and curriculum as lived experience, it conceptualizes human flourishing as both a moral imperative and a strategic indicator of institutional quality. Through narrative inquiry, the chapter presents composite cases from international, interdisciplinary, and blended-learning contexts to illustrate how SEC-informed practices emerge, evolve, and encounter resistance in real settings. Building on these accounts, it proposes a multi-level strategic framework encompassing guiding principles, a cyclical planning process, curriculum and assessment design, faculty, and staff development, and enabling institutional structures. Policy and practice implications are outlined for institutional leaders, program

DOI: 10.4018/979-8-2600-2606-9.ch003

teams, educators, and external stakeholders, arguing that resilient, equitable higher education systems must treat SEC and well-being as central design criteria rather than peripheral concerns

INTRODUCTION

Across the globe, higher education systems are navigating an era of profound volatility characterized by demographic shifts, fluctuating enrollment patterns, unstable funding structures, tightening visa regimes, geopolitical tensions, and rapid technological disruption. These transformations have intensified long-standing pressures on universities to demonstrate accountability, efficiency, and global competitiveness while simultaneously expanding participation and responding to increasingly diverse student populations (OECD, 2022; UNESCO, 2023). As institutions confront these intersecting challenges, the need for future-focused educational planning that strengthens institutional resilience and sustainability has become increasingly urgent.

Within contemporary policy and institutional discourse, resilience is frequently pursued through mechanisms such as data analytics, market responsiveness, and technological innovation. While these approaches play an important role in strategic planning, they can inadvertently overshadow the human dimensions of higher education, particularly the social-emotional well-being of students and faculty and the relational conditions that sustain meaningful learning communities. A growing body of scholarship highlights rising levels of loneliness, anxiety, stress, and burnout across academic communities, suggesting that the emotional and psychological landscape of higher education warrants greater institutional attention (Ryff, 2014; Seligman, 2018; OECD, 2021). These concerns have been further intensified by global crises, including the COVID-19 pandemic, climate-related disruptions, and geopolitical conflicts, all of which have heightened uncertainty and vulnerability among learners and educators (UNESCO, 2023; World Health Organization, 2022).

The pressures associated with these developments are particularly acute for students navigating multiple structural and social challenges. First-generation learners, international students, and individuals experiencing intersecting forms of marginalization often confront complex financial pressures, cultural transitions, family expectations, and precarious migration conditions alongside demanding academic environments. These intersecting pressures can significantly affect students' emotional well-being, sense of belonging, and persistence in higher education. Despite increasing recognition of these challenges, institutional responses frequently remain reactive, focusing on individualized interventions such as counselling services or short-term well-being initiatives. While valuable, such responses often address symptoms rather than the broader systemic conditions that shape student flourishing and educational engagement.

This chapter seeks to address this gap by positioning well-being and social-emotional competency (SEC) as central pillars of institutional sustainability and future-focused curriculum planning in higher education. Drawing on insights from positive psychology, social-emotional learning (SEL), and humanistic perspectives that conceptualize curriculum as lived experience, the chapter argues that competencies such as resilience, empathy, self-regulation, ethical decision-making, and adaptability can no longer be treated as peripheral "soft skills." Instead, they must be intentionally integrated across curriculum design, assessment practices, faculty development, and institutional policy as strategic mechanisms for enhancing student engagement, retention, and academic success within complex and uncertain educational environments (CASEL, 2023; Immordino-Yang & Darling-Hammond, 2021).

Within this framework, human flourishing is understood both as a measurable indicator of institutional effectiveness and as a normative commitment guiding educational practice. When higher education planning deliberately foregrounds social-emotional well-being and competency development, institutions are better positioned to cultivate learning ecosystems that are adaptive, inclusive, and resilient. This perspective aligns closely with the aims of the edited volume *Future-Focused Educational Planning Strategies in Diverse Higher Education Institutions*, which seeks to sustain quality, innovation, and inclusion by reimagining institutional planning processes. By reframing curriculum planning as a form of institutional care, this chapter situates social-emotional well-being as a core dimension of strategic governance and quality assurance rather than as a peripheral or optional enhancement.

The chapter proceeds in six sections. Following this introduction, the second section outlines the conceptual and theoretical foundations of the argument, drawing on social-emotional learning theory, psychological well-being frameworks, and perspectives that conceptualize curriculum as lived experience. The third section presents narrative reflections and illustrative cases drawn from diverse higher education contexts, demonstrating how educators and curriculum designers have integrated social-emotional competencies and well-being considerations into program design and pedagogical practice. The fourth section proposes a strategic framework for future-focused curriculum planning that embeds SEL principles across multiple layers of institutional practice. The fifth section examines policy and leadership implications for institutional leaders, accreditation bodies, and policymakers, particularly in diverse or resource-constrained contexts. The concluding section reframes conventional indicators of educational success through the lens of well-being and social-emotional resilience while outlining priorities for future research and institutional practice.

The central argument advanced in this chapter reflects broader shifts within global educational policy agendas. International organizations increasingly emphasize the role of higher education in fostering social cohesion, sustainable development, and responsible global citizenship (OECD, 2021; UNESCO, 2020). Addressing complex global challenges requires graduates who can collaborate across cultural and ideological differences, engage constructively with uncertainty, and navigate complex problems that have no simple solutions. Such capabilities are inherently social-emotional in nature. When institutions prioritize narrowly defined cognitive or technical indicators of performance, they risk underpreparing graduates for these broader societal roles and responsibilities (UNESCO, 2023).

Empirical research increasingly supports the strategic value of integrating social-emotional competencies into educational systems. While early research on SEL focused primarily on primary and secondary education, recent studies demonstrate its relevance within higher education contexts. Large-scale analyses indicate that SEL initiatives contribute to improved learning environments, enhanced academic performance, and reduced emotional and behavioural challenges (Taylor et al., 2017; Cipriano et al., 2023). Emerging research in tertiary settings similarly suggests that supportive and relational learning environments strengthen students' sense of belonging, emotional regulation, and persistence, particularly during the critical transition into first-year university study (Felten & Lambert, 2020; Bond et al., 2023).

The COVID-19 pandemic further underscored the importance of integrating social-emotional considerations into institutional planning. Rapid transitions to remote learning, disruptions to mobility, and prolonged social isolation placed unprecedented strain on students and faculty members (Crawford et al., 2020; UNESCO, 2021). Institutions that had invested in relational pedagogies, advising systems, and cultures of care were generally better positioned to sustain engagement and student support during these disruptions. At the same time, the growing integration of digital technologies and artificial intelligence within education introduces new opportunities as well as challenges related to digital fatigue, algorithmic bias, and the potential erosion of meaningful human interaction in learning environments (Holmes et al., 2022; UNESCO, 2023).

By offering both conceptual insight and practice-oriented guidance for integrating well-being and social-emotional competency into curriculum design, this chapter contributes to ongoing debates concerning retention, equity, and institutional resilience within contemporary higher education. Ultimately, it argues that genuinely future-focused educational planning must place the flourishing of students and faculty at the centre of institutional strategy, recognizing that resilient universities are sustained not only through technological innovation or managerial efficiency, but through sustained investment in the well-being of the people who constitute them.

2. THEORETICAL FOUNDATIONS

The integration of social-emotional competency (SEC) and well-being into higher education planning is grounded in three interrelated theoretical perspectives: social-emotional learning (SEL), positive psychology and psychological well-being, and curriculum as lived experience. Together, these frameworks provide a human-centered understanding of educational quality that moves beyond technocratic models of planning focused primarily on efficiency, performance indicators, and market responsiveness. They offer conceptual tools for designing curriculum, pedagogy, and institutional structures that foster flourishing among students and staff in diverse higher education contexts. Recent scholarship further highlights how these perspectives remain particularly relevant in post-pandemic universities navigating digital transformation, hybrid learning, and changing student needs (OECD, 2021; UNESCO, 2021).

2.1 Social-Emotional Learning and Competency Development

Social-emotional learning (SEL) has emerged as a widely recognized framework for understanding the attitudes, skills, and dispositions that enable individuals to manage emotions, build relationships, and make responsible decisions (CASEL, 2023). The SEL framework identifies five core competencies: self-awareness, self-management, social awareness, relationship skills, and responsible decision-making.

Self-awareness refers to individuals' capacity to recognize their emotions, values, strengths, and limitations and understand how these influence behavior and learning. Self-management involves regulating emotions, managing stress, sustaining motivation, and setting goals. Social awareness encompasses empathy, perspective-taking, and sensitivity to diverse cultural contexts. Relationship skills involve communication, collaboration, and conflict resolution. Responsible decision-making refers to evaluating consequences and making ethical choices that consider individual and collective well-being (CASEL, 2023).

Research across educational settings demonstrates that SEL interventions contribute to improved academic outcomes, stronger classroom climates, and better mental health (Durlak et al., 2011; Taylor et al., 2017; Cipriano et al., 2023). Although much early evidence emerged from school environments, these competencies are increasingly recognized as essential within higher education. University students often face significant academic pressures, complex social transitions, and uncertain career pathways, making emotional regulation, resilience, and collaboration crucial capabilities for navigating higher education successfully.

The relevance of SEL is particularly evident within internationalized and diverse universities. Students frequently encounter challenges related to cultural adaptation, identity formation, and belonging within unfamiliar academic environments. Competencies such as empathy and perspective-taking enable students to negotiate differences in language, epistemology, and academic culture. Similarly, self-management and resilience are essential for managing financial pressures, demanding assessment regimes, and family expectations.

In this chapter, the concept of social-emotional competency (SEC) emphasizes the developmental nature of these capacities. SECs are not fixed traits but learnable abilities that can be cultivated through intentional pedagogical practices and supportive institutional environments. Embedding SEC development in higher education therefore requires deliberate curriculum design, collaborative learning experiences, reflective activities, and assessment practices that recognize growth and process rather than solely performance outcomes.

Faculty development is also central to this framework. Educators shape classroom climate and relational learning environments through their pedagogical approaches, communication practices, and feedback styles. Research indicates that educators' own social-emotional competencies significantly influence psychological safety and student engagement within classrooms (Immordino-Yang & Darling-Hammond, 2021). Institutions that invest in faculty development related to relational pedagogy and emotional awareness are therefore better positioned to cultivate inclusive and supportive learning cultures.

From a planning perspective, SEL provides a practical framework for translating institutional aspirations into concrete pedagogical strategies. When strategic plans and quality assurance frameworks incorporate SEC-related objectives, they legitimize practices that promote well-being and inclusive learning environments. Conversely, the absence of such priorities often results in fragmented initiatives that lack institutional support and sustainability.

2.2 Positive Psychology and Psychological Well-Being

Positive psychology offers a complementary theoretical lens by focusing on the conditions that enable individuals and communities to flourish rather than concentrating solely on psychological distress (Ryff, 1989; Seligman, 2011). Within this perspective, psychological well-being is conceptualized as multidimensional, encompassing self-acceptance, personal growth, purpose in life, autonomy, environmental mastery, and positive relationships (Ryff, 2014).

Seligman's PERMA model further conceptualizes well-being through five interrelated dimensions: positive emotion, engagement, relationships, meaning, and accomplishment (Seligman, 2011). These constructs resonate strongly with the broader mission of higher education institutions, which frequently aspire to cultivate intellectual development, personal growth, and civic responsibility.

Despite these aspirations, institutional evaluation systems often prioritize narrow performance indicators such as grade point averages, completion rates, and employment statistics. While important, such metrics capture only a partial picture of educational quality and may inadvertently reinforce competitive cultures that undermine well-being.

Positive psychology encourages a broader perspective on student development. Flourishing students are those who engage deeply with learning, develop supportive relationships with peers and mentors, and cultivate a sense of purpose that connects academic learning to personal aspirations and societal challenges. Recent research demonstrates that these dimensions of well-being are strongly associated with academic persistence, motivation, and long-term success (Kern et al., 2022; OECD, 2021).

Integrating positive psychology into higher education planning therefore requires conceptual and practical shifts. Conceptually, institutions must recognize that student well-being is shaped not only by counselling services but also by curriculum design, pedagogical approaches, and institutional culture. Practically, this may involve creating learning experiences that encourage students to identify their strengths, engage in meaningful inquiry, and connect disciplinary knowledge to real-world challenges.

For example, reflective assignments can support students in linking academic learning with personal values, while interdisciplinary or capstone projects can address complex societal problems. Such approaches foster meaning and engagement—central dimensions of psychological flourishing.

Positive psychology also provides tools for measuring well-being as an institutional outcome. Universities increasingly incorporate well-being indicators into institutional surveys, strategic plans, and research agendas (Kern et al., 2022; OECD, 2021). Recognizing flourishing as an institutional goal signals that educational success encompasses both intellectual development and human well-being.

2.3 Curriculum as Lived Experience

A third theoretical perspective conceptualizes curriculum not merely as a technical blueprint but as a lived, relational, and affective experience (Aoki, 1993). From this perspective, curriculum exists simultaneously in three forms: the official curriculum documented in institutional plans, the hidden curriculum embedded within institutional norms and power relations, and the lived curriculum experienced by students and educators in everyday educational practice.

This perspective challenges instrumental understandings of curriculum focused primarily on content delivery. Instead, it foregrounds the relational and experiential dimensions of learning that shape students' intellectual and emotional engagement.

Understanding curriculum as lived experience has important implications for student well-being. Institutional practices such as lecture-dominated pedagogies, competitive grading systems, and high-stakes assessment regimes shape students' emotional landscapes and influence their sense of belonging and agency.

Equally significant are everyday pedagogical interactions. Feedback practices, classroom dialogue, and collaborative learning activities can either foster curiosity and psychological safety or reinforce anxiety and disengagement. The hidden curriculum also raises questions about whose knowledge, experiences, and identities are recognized within academic environments—issues particularly relevant for students from marginalized backgrounds (Biesta, 2015).

Viewing curriculum through this lens reframes curriculum planning as a form of institutional care. Educational design decisions—including assessment structures, program organization, and pedagogical practices—should be evaluated not only for compliance with external standards but also for their effects on the lived experiences of students and faculty.

For instance, shifting from predominantly high-stakes summative assessment toward greater use of formative feedback and collaborative learning can reduce stress while promoting deeper engagement. Similarly, integrating discussion-based seminars within large programs can strengthen relational learning and intellectual dialogue. Reflective pedagogies may also help students integrate disciplinary knowledge with personal identity and lived experience.

2.4 Theoretical Synthesis and Implications

Synthesizing SEL, positive psychology, and curriculum as lived experience provides a comprehensive framework for reimagining curriculum planning as a driver of institutional care and resilience.

SEL offers a structured set of competencies that can be translated into learning outcomes, pedagogical strategies, and assessment practices (CASEL, 2023). Positive psychology contributes conceptual models and empirical measures of flourishing, emphasizing meaning, engagement, and relationships (Kern et al., 2022). The lived curriculum perspective situates these ideas within everyday educational practice, highlighting how institutional cultures and power relations shape learning experiences (Aoki, 1993; Biesta, 2015).

Together, these perspectives encourage institutions to move beyond narrow planning concerns such as market positioning or regulatory compliance. Instead, they prompt deeper questions about the types of learners and communities that curricula cultivate and the ways in which institutional practices shape student well-being.

Research across SEL and positive psychology consistently demonstrates that well-being is relational and ecological, emerging from the environments in which individuals learn and interact (Cipriano et al., 2023; OECD, 2021). Viewing curriculum as lived experience reinforces this insight by emphasizing that classrooms and programs are key contexts through which belonging and recognition are experienced.

For institutions serving diverse student populations, these insights are particularly significant. Supporting student well-being requires addressing systemic issues related to inclusion, representation, and psychological safety (Thomas, 2012). In practice, this involves aligning SEC initiatives with broader equity and inclusion strategies within institutional planning.

This theoretical synthesis also highlights the importance of shared responsibility. If curriculum is understood as lived and co-constructed, educators, administrators, and students all play roles in shaping the relational climate of higher education. Faculty development programs can strengthen educators' capacities in relational pedagogy and emotional awareness, while participatory approaches that engage students as partners in curriculum design can make planning more responsive and inclusive.

2.5 AI, Digital Well-Being, and Post-COVID Higher Education

The rapid digital transformation of higher education following the COVID-19 pandemic has intensified scholarly attention toward artificial intelligence (AI), digital well-being, and technology-mediated learning environments. Universities increasingly rely on AI-enabled tools, virtual learning platforms, and learning analytics to support personalized learning, assessment, and student support (OECD, 2023).

While these technologies offer opportunities for adaptive instruction and self-regulated learning, they also raise concerns regarding digital overload, cognitive dependency, and the erosion of authentic learning practices (Chan & Hu, 2023). Generative AI tools can assist students with brainstorming, research, and writing support; however, their effective use requires AI literacy, self-regulation, and ethical awareness (Dagtekin & Erkalkan, 2025).

Research suggests that students' trust in AI systems, perceived usefulness, and digital competence significantly influence learning outcomes when using AI tools (Dagtekin & Erkalkan, 2025). Consequently, higher education institutions increasingly emphasize AI literacy as an essential graduate capability.

Alongside these developments, scholars have highlighted the concept of digital well-being, defined as maintaining a balanced and healthy relationship with technology in digitally mediated environments. Excessive screen time and constant connectivity have been linked to digital fatigue, distraction, and mental health challenges among university students, particularly following extended periods of remote learning during the pandemic (Pérez-Juárez et al., 2024; Uslu, 2025).

At the same time, responsible integration of digital tools—combined with SEL-informed pedagogies—can enhance collaboration, reflection, and digital citizenship

(OECD, 2023). Emerging research emphasizes the importance of designing educational technologies that support both learning outcomes and student well-being.

Within post-pandemic higher education systems, AI and digital technologies therefore represent a double-edged phenomenon. While they can enhance personalized and flexible learning experiences, poorly designed digital environments may intensify distraction, academic dependency, and stress (Vehrer & Pálfalusi, 2025).

Contemporary educational planning increasingly recognizes the need to integrate AI literacy, digital well-being, and social-emotional competencies as complementary dimensions of educational quality. Embedding these elements within curriculum design supports a human-centered approach to digital transformation—one that balances technological innovation with the psychological, relational, and ethical dimensions of learning (OECD, 2023; Uslu, 2025.

3. NARRATIVE REFLECTIONS: LIVED EXPERIENCES OF EMBEDDING SOCIAL-EMOTIONAL COMPETENCY IN HIGHER EDUCATION

Narrative inquiry provides a valuable lens for understanding how social-emotional competency (SEC) and well-being are enacted within everyday practices of higher education. Rather than viewing curriculum planning solely as a technical or managerial process, narrative perspectives illuminate how educators, students, and institutional leaders experience efforts to integrate social-emotional learning (SEL) into academic cultures and pedagogical practices (Clandinin, 2013). Through lived stories, narrative inquiry reveals dimensions of educational change often overlooked in policy discourse or quantitative indicators, including emotions, relationships, identity formation, and institutional culture (Riessman, 2008).

This section presents composite and anonymized narratives drawn from recurring experiences across diverse higher-education contexts, including international colleges, interdisciplinary programs, and blended learning environments. These narratives synthesize patterns observed across multiple initiatives rather than representing single case studies. Such narrative synthesis allows exploration of the complex ways SEC and well-being become embedded in institutional life while highlighting tensions, possibilities, and unintended consequences.

Recent research suggests that post-pandemic higher education must move beyond narrow academic performance metrics toward more holistic models of student development and digital well-being (OECD, 2021; UNESCO, 2023). Universities worldwide are therefore reconsidering curriculum design, teaching practices, and institutional support structures to address the emotional and relational realities of learning in uncertain times (Crawford et al., 2020; Zhai & Du, 2022). Narrative accounts provide insight into how such transformations unfold in practice.

3.1 Beginning with the Classroom: A Psychology Lecturer in an International College

The first narrative centers on a psychology lecturer, Dr. K, teaching introductory psychology at an international college enrolling student from more than twenty countries. Many students are studying abroad for the first time and navigating academic work in a second or third language. Although motivation is typically high at the beginning of the semester, recurring patterns emerge over time: students report academic anxiety, uncertainty regarding expectations, and feelings of disconnection.

During office hours, students frequently disclose challenges related to homesickness, financial pressures, family obligations, or immigration concerns. Several students who eventually withdraw attribute their difficulties primarily to emotional and social stress rather than academic ability. These experiences echo research indicating that international students often face significant psychological strain while adapting to unfamiliar academic and cultural environments (Glass et al., 2021; Marginson, 2022).

Recognizing these patterns, Dr. K introduces small pedagogical adjustments designed to support students' social-emotional awareness without formally restructuring the curriculum. Classes occasionally begin with brief emotional "check-ins," such as anonymous stress polls or one-word reflections capturing students' current state of mind. These activities normalize emotional experiences within academic spaces while providing the lecturer with insight into students' evolving needs.

Over time, these practices reveal recurring stress points, including assessment periods, visa renewal deadlines, and geopolitical crises affecting students' home regions. In response, Dr. K integrates short psychoeducational segments into lectures connecting psychological theories—such as emotion regulation and resilience—to strategies students can apply in daily life.

Group discussions invite students to share culturally situated approaches to managing stress and uncertainty. These exchanges challenge deficit narratives about international students while validating diverse emotional practices. Alongside conventional assessments, students complete reflective journals linking psychological concepts to personal experiences of transition, identity formation, and belonging. Reflective learning practices have been shown to deepen conceptual understanding while enhancing emotional awareness (Moon, 2013; Felten & Lambert, 2020).

Several outcomes emerge from this course-level initiative. Students report feeling more recognized within the classroom environment, and peer dialogue becomes richer as theoretical concepts connect with lived experiences. While institutional factors make causal claims difficult, modest declines in course failure and withdrawal rates are observed across subsequent cohorts.

Nevertheless, tensions arise. Some colleagues question whether reflective activities detract from disciplinary content, while others worry about blurring boundaries between teaching and counseling roles. Dr. K addresses these concerns by emphasizing that the goal is not therapeutic intervention but rather creating pedagogical conditions that support students' development of competencies necessary for academic success.

This narrative illustrates how SEC integration often begins with individual educators experimenting within their immediate teaching contexts. At the same time, it highlights the need for institutional recognition if such practices are to become sustainable components of curriculum design.

3.2 Program-Level Reform: Reimagining Outcomes in an Interdisciplinary Degree

The second narrative shifts from classroom innovation to program-level reform within an interdisciplinary undergraduate degree integrating social sciences, environmental studies, and innovation studies. Despite its ambitious mission of preparing students to address global challenges, an internal review reveals concerning trends, including elevated attrition and reports of emotional exhaustion among students.

Many students describe feeling overwhelmed by exposure to complex global crises without opportunities to process emotional responses or sustain long-term engagement. In response, program leaders initiate a participatory curriculum review grounded in narrative inquiry. Faculty, students, and professional staff share "moments that mattered," recounting experiences when the program felt aligned—or misaligned—with its stated mission.

Through these reflections, a shared vision emerges of graduates capable of navigating uncertainty, collaborating across cultures and disciplines, and sustaining ethical commitment to societal challenges. These aspirations reveal that many desired graduate capabilities are fundamentally social-emotional rather than purely cognitive (Biesta, 2015; Nussbaum, 2010).

Curriculum mapping subsequently reveals uneven integration of these capacities across courses. While some classes incorporate reflective learning and community engagement, others rely heavily on dense content coverage and high-stakes assessment.

Students' narratives reinforce these inconsistencies. Although they value opportunities to explore global issues, many report emotional fatigue and limited support for processing distress. Recent research suggests that engagement with complex societal challenges can generate both motivation and emotional strain, particularly when students feel powerless to enact change (Leal Filho et al., 2023).

In response, the program undertakes a multi-year reform process. First, program-level learning outcomes are revised to include competencies such as reflective self-awareness, ethical collaboration, and adaptive engagement with uncertainty. Embedding these outcomes in official documentation signals institutional commitment to SEC development (OECD, 2021; UNESCO, 2023).

Second, a first-year course titled *Learning for an Uncertain Future* is introduced. Drawing on SEL and positive psychology, the course explores well-being as a resource for sustained engagement with global challenges. Reflective writing, experiential learning, and collaborative projects encourage students to examine emotional responses to societal issues while developing strategies for resilience and collective action.

Third, group assignments across the program are redesigned to explicitly teach collaboration skills. Assessment rubrics evaluate both project outcomes and teamwork processes, reinforcing the value of relational learning.

Early feedback suggests improvements in student engagement and reflective capacity. Students report greater confidence in managing emotional responses to challenging material, while faculty observe deeper classroom discussions. Preliminary retention data also indicate improved first-year progression.

However, these reforms also require substantial faculty engagement and professional development. Many instructors must reconsider traditional disciplinary roles and adapt to pedagogies that foreground emotional engagement alongside intellectual inquiry.

3.3 Blended Learning and the Challenge of Connection

The third narrative examines an institution that rapidly expanded blended and online learning following the COVID-19 pandemic. Initial institutional discourse emphasized flexibility and technological innovation, with quality assurance processes focusing on accessibility and content alignment.

However, student and faculty narratives increasingly highlight experiences of isolation and digital fatigue during prolonged remote learning. These experiences reflect broader findings that online education can weaken students' sense of belonging when relational dimensions of learning are neglected (Bond et al., 2021; Zhai & Du, 2022).

In response, the university's teaching and learning center launches a faculty initiative titled *Designing for Presence, Connection, and Well-Being Online*. Rather than focusing solely on technology, the program invites instructors to reflect on the emotional dimensions of digital pedagogy.

Workshops and peer-learning circles encourage educators to share experiences of connection and disconnection in online teaching. One engineering lecturer describes initially interpreting silent online classes as disengagement before learning that many students were coping with caregiving responsibilities, unstable internet access, or crowded living environments.

This insight prompts course redesign emphasizing diverse forms of participation, including discussion forums, collaborative breakout sessions, and multimedia reflections. Across disciplines, faculty experiment with similar approaches, such as grounding exercises and collaborative communication norms.

These practices enhance student engagement while strengthening instructors' sense of connection in digital environments. At the same time, concerns remain regarding increased workload and emotional labor, particularly when institutional reward structures continue to prioritize traditional productivity metrics.

3.4 Student Voices: Belonging, Agency, and Emotional Labor

Student perspectives highlight the lived significance of SEC initiatives. Across contexts, narratives emphasize the importance of recognition by faculty, the emotional challenges of navigating unfamiliar academic cultures, and the tension between gratitude for educational opportunity and pressure to succeed.

For example, an international business student describes initially feeling lost within large lectures until a lecturer introduces structured discussions addressing cultural communication differences. This intervention fosters a renewed sense of belonging and agency.

Similarly, a first-generation STEM student recounts avoiding help-seeking due to fear of disappointing family expectations. Participation in a peer mentoring program—where senior students openly discuss academic struggles—helps normalize vulnerability and encourages engagement with support services.

These narratives suggest that SEC initiatives function not merely as skill-development programs but also as expressions of institutional values. When universities acknowledge students' emotional realities, learners often interpret this as recognition of their full personhood rather than solely their academic performance.

3.5 Cross-Cutting Themes and Lessons for Future-Focused Planning

Several themes emerge across these narratives with implications for curriculum planning and institutional strategy.

First, educational change frequently begins with individual educators who identify gaps between institutional rhetoric and everyday student experiences. Through small-scale innovations—such as reflective assignments or relational pedagogies—these educators create experimental spaces for integrating SEC within existing structures.

Second, sustainable SEC integration requires alignment between micro-level pedagogical practices and macro-level institutional frameworks. Classroom initiatives gain greater legitimacy when embedded within program outcomes, faculty development strategies, and quality-assurance mechanisms valuing holistic student development.

Third, diversity, equity, and inclusion remain central considerations. International students, first-generation learners, and marginalized groups often shoulder disproportionate emotional burdens when navigating unfamiliar academic environments. Effective SEC initiatives must therefore address structural inequities rather than focusing solely on individual coping strategies.

Finally, engagement with SEL concepts can transform educators' professional identities. Many faculty involved in these initiatives describe shifting from viewing themselves primarily as content experts toward seeing their roles as relational facilitators of learning. Institutions that acknowledge and support this dimension of academic labor may be better equipped to navigate the ongoing volatility of contemporary higher education.

Together, these narrative reflections highlight both the challenges and possibilities of embedding social-emotional competencies within curriculum planning. They illustrate how lived experiences—across classrooms, programs, and digital environments—can inform more holistic approaches to educational design. The following section builds upon these insights to outline a strategic framework for systematically integrating SEC and well-being within diverse higher-education contexts.

4. STRATEGIC FRAMEWORK FOR FUTURE-FOCUSED, SEL-INFUSED CURRICULUM PLANNING

Building on the theoretical foundations and narrative reflections presented earlier, this section proposes a strategic framework for integrating social-emotional competency (SEC) and well-being into curriculum planning within diverse higher-education institutions. The framework is intentionally designed to remain adaptable across institutional contexts, recognizing that universities differ considerably in their missions, governance structures, student populations, and regulatory environments. Nevertheless, it is grounded in shared conceptual foundations derived from social-emotional learning (SEL), positive psychology, and the notion of curriculum as lived experience (Aoki, 1993; CASEL, 2023; Ryff, 2014; Seligman, 2011).

Recent scholarship increasingly emphasizes that higher education must adopt human-centered planning models that prioritize relational learning, holistic student development, and digital well-being in response to the profound transformations affecting contemporary universities (Bond et al., 2021; OECD, 2021; UNESCO,

2023). In the wake of the COVID-19 pandemic, institutions across the globe have reported growing concerns related to student anxiety, disengagement, and emotional exhaustion, alongside the rapid expansion of blended and online learning environments. These developments highlight the limitations of traditional planning models that focus primarily on technological innovation, market responsiveness, or institutional competitiveness while overlooking the relational and emotional dimensions of learning.

Within this changing landscape, the integration of SEC and well-being into curriculum planning represents an important strategic response. Social-emotional competencies—including self-awareness, empathy, collaboration, emotional regulation, and responsible decision-making—support students' capacity to navigate academic challenges while engaging constructively with complex societal issues. Research indicates that these competencies contribute not only to improved learning outcomes but also to stronger engagement, resilience, and persistence within higher education (Durlak et al., 2011; Taylor et al., 2017).

The framework presented in this section therefore aims to translate the conceptual insights discussed earlier into actionable strategies for curriculum planning. Rather than proposing a single prescriptive model, the framework identifies a set of guiding principles, planning processes, pedagogical approaches, and institutional mechanisms that can support contextually responsive implementation. Drawing on both theoretical perspectives and the narrative insights explored in previous sections, the framework seeks to balance aspirational goals with the practical realities of institutional change.

4.1 Guiding Principles for SEL-Oriented Planning

A future-focused framework for embedding SEC within higher education rests upon four mutually reinforcing principles: human flourishing, equity and inclusion, coherence and integration, and shared responsibility. These principles provide normative guidance for decision-making at multiple levels of institutional planning, from strategic leadership to program design and classroom practice.

The first principle positions human flourishing as a central objective of higher education. Universities have traditionally been regarded as institutions dedicated to the production and transmission of knowledge. However, contemporary perspectives increasingly emphasize their broader role in supporting the development of individuals capable of leading meaningful and socially responsible lives. Within positive psychology, flourishing is conceptualized as a multidimensional state that includes autonomy, competence, purpose, positive relationships, and personal growth (Ryff, 2014; Seligman, 2011).

When institutions explicitly foreground flourishing within mission statements, graduate attribute frameworks, and strategic plans, the development of socially and emotionally capable graduates becomes an integral element of educational purpose rather than an ancillary concern. This perspective challenges narrow, performance-driven conceptions of educational success that prioritize measurable outputs such as grades, publication counts, or employment outcomes while overlooking broader dimensions of student development.

Global policy agendas increasingly reinforce the importance of human-centered educational goals. Organizations such as the OECD and UNESCO highlight the need for higher education to prepare graduates capable of navigating uncertainty, addressing global challenges, and contributing ethically to complex societies (OECD, 2021; UNESCO, 2023). By recognizing flourishing as a strategic objective, universities can expand the scope of quality indicators to include belonging, engagement, and well-being alongside academic achievement.

The second principle emphasizes equity and inclusion. Social-emotional experiences in higher education are not distributed evenly; rather, they are shaped by broader structural conditions such as socioeconomic inequality, migration status, linguistic diversity, and cultural marginalization. Research demonstrates that international students, first-generation learners, and students from historically underrepresented backgrounds often experience heightened emotional pressures as they navigate unfamiliar academic environments (Felten & Lambert, 2020; Marginson, 2022).

An equity-oriented approach to SEL therefore avoids framing social-emotional competencies solely as individual traits that students must develop independently. Instead, it recognizes that institutional structures—including curriculum design, pedagogical practices, and administrative policies—play critical roles in shaping experiences of recognition, belonging, and participation. SEL initiatives must consequently remain culturally responsive and contextually sensitive, rather than imposing universal expectations regarding emotional expression or interpersonal communication (Biesta, 2015; CASEL, 2023).

The third principle focuses on coherence and systemic integration. In many institutions, well-being initiatives are implemented through isolated programs, optional workshops, or short-term projects. Although these initiatives can provide valuable support, their impact is often limited when they are not integrated into broader institutional strategies. A coherent approach aligns program-level learning outcomes, curriculum structures, pedagogical practices, faculty development initiatives, and student-support services around a shared vision for SEC development.

Such alignment ensures that relational pedagogies introduced within individual classrooms are reinforced by program expectations and institutional policies. It also acknowledges the emotional and temporal labor required for implementing socially responsive teaching practices. Contemporary research on institutional resilience suggests that universities capable of integrating relational and academic priorities across organizational levels are better positioned to respond effectively to disruption and uncertainty (OECD, 2021; Zhai & Du, 2022).

The final guiding principle, shared responsibility, highlights that fostering SEC and well-being is not solely the domain of counseling services or student-affairs units. Although mental-health professionals play essential roles in institutional support systems, the everyday interactions among faculty members, administrative staff, and students collectively shape the emotional climate of universities. Teaching practices, advising relationships, administrative procedures, and peer cultures all contribute to students' experiences of belonging and engagement (Felten & Lambert, 2020).

Future-focused curriculum planning therefore requires distributed leadership and cross-institutional collaboration. Engaging diverse stakeholders—including students, educators, professional staff, and institutional leaders—in the design and implementation of SEC initiatives strengthens collective ownership and increases the likelihood of sustained institutional change.

4.2 A Cyclical Process for SEC Integration

Translating these guiding principles into practice requires a structured yet flexible planning process. The framework proposed here outlines a cyclical pathway consisting of six interconnected phases: (1) inquiry and assessment, (2) co-creation of vision and goals, (3) curriculum and assessment alignment, (4) capacity building, (5) implementation and adaptation, and (6) evaluation and learning. Although presented sequentially for conceptual clarity, these phases are iterative and frequently overlap as institutions refine their strategies through ongoing reflection and evidence-based learning.

The first phase, inquiry and assessment, focuses on developing a comprehensive understanding of the current state of SEC and well-being within the institution or program. Mixed-method approaches—including surveys, focus groups, narrative interviews, and analysis of retention, progression, and engagement data—enable planners to identify both strengths and areas requiring attention (Clandinin, 2013; Riessman, 2008). Central questions guiding this phase include: How do students and staff experience the emotional dimensions of learning and work? Which contexts generate stress, exclusion, or burnout? Where do individuals experience belonging, connection, and growth? What informal SEL practices already exist within the institution?

This exploratory phase is crucial for building upon existing strengths while avoiding deficit-oriented narratives that frame students or educators as lacking resilience. Instead, it highlights institutional resources and practices that can serve as foundations for further development.

The second phase involves the co-creation of a shared vision and goals for SEC integration. Participatory planning processes—such as design workshops, dialogue forums, and collaborative reflection sessions—enable institutions to engage stakeholders in articulating the qualities they seek to cultivate in graduates and learning communities (Felten & Lambert, 2020). These conversations often highlight competencies such as resilience, ethical reasoning, intercultural understanding, and collaborative problem-solving.

Translating these aspirations into clearly articulated graduate attributes and strategic priorities strengthens alignment between curriculum planning and institutional mission statements. Linking these goals to broader global frameworks, including the United Nations Sustainable Development Goals, can further reinforce institutional commitment to socially responsible education (OECD, 2021; UNESCO, 2023).

The third phase focuses on curriculum and assessment alignment. Curriculum mapping allows educators to examine where existing courses already support social-emotional development and where gaps remain. Program teams may revise learning outcomes to include competencies such as reflective self-awareness, empathy, ethical decision-making, and collaborative engagement.

The fourth phase, capacity building, acknowledges that educators and professional staff require institutional support to implement SEC-oriented curriculum effectively. Professional development initiatives may include workshops on SEL principles, culturally responsive pedagogy, trauma-informed teaching, and relational classroom practices (CASEL, 2023).

The fifth phase involves implementation and adaptation. Pilot initiatives, such as redesigned courses or new program modules, allow institutions to test innovative practices before scaling them more broadly.

The final phase, evaluation, and learning, closes the planning cycle through systematic assessment of outcomes and experiences. Effective evaluation combines quantitative indicators, such as retention rates and engagement metrics, with qualitative evidence derived from reflective portfolios, interviews, and narrative accounts (Taylor et al., 2017).

4.3 Curriculum and Assessment Design for SEC and Well-Being

Within this planning framework, curriculum, and assessment function as primary mechanisms through which SEC becomes embedded within everyday learning experiences. One foundational strategy involves articulating explicit SEC-related learning outcomes at both program and course levels.

A second strategy centers on learning activities that cultivate relational and reflective engagement. Practices such as structured dialogue, reflective journaling, collaborative projects, and community-engaged learning encourage students to connect disciplinary knowledge with lived experience (Aoki, 1993; Moon, 2013).

Assessment design also plays a critical role. SEC-aligned assessment often incorporates reflective and formative components alongside traditional summative tasks, enabling students to analyze how they develop collaboration, empathy, and resilience.

4.4 Faculty and Staff Development for SEC-Informed Practice

Educators' own social-emotional competencies and well-being significantly influence the success of SEC initiatives. Faculty and staff model empathy, communication, and emotional regulation through everyday interactions with students (Felten & Lambert, 2020).

Professional development initiatives should therefore move beyond isolated workshops to create communities of reflective practice where educators share experiences and experiment with new pedagogical approaches (Clandinin, 2013). Institutional policies must also acknowledge the emotional labor associated with teaching and advising, ensuring that relational contributions are recognized within promotion and workload frameworks (Crawford et al., 2020).

4.5 Institutional and Policy Levers

Sustainable integration of SEC ultimately depends on alignment with institutional governance structures and policy frameworks. Universities can embed SEC and well-being within strategic plans, graduate-attribute frameworks, and quality assurance processes, thereby signaling a commitment to human-centered education (OECD, 2021; UNESCO, 2023).

Resource allocation further reinforces institutional priorities. Investments in teaching-and-learning centers, faculty development programs, and student-support services expand institutional capacity to implement SEC-informed curricula.

Finally, student participation in governance remains essential. Mechanisms such as student-staff partnership initiatives and participatory curriculum design processes ensure that SEC initiatives remain responsive to lived experiences.

Collectively, these principles, planning processes, pedagogical strategies, and institutional mechanisms form a coherent framework for embedding SEC and well-being within future-focused higher education planning. The following section examines the broader policy and leadership implications of this framework for institutions seeking to cultivate resilient, equitable, and human-centered learning ecosystems.

5. POLICY AND PRACTICE IMPLICATIONS

The strategic framework outlined in Section 4 carries significant implications for policy and practice across the higher education ecosystem. While social-emotional competency (SEC) and student well-being are often implemented through localized initiatives, the conceptual and empirical discussions developed throughout this chapter suggest that meaningful and sustainable integration requires system-wide alignment. Institutional strategy, curriculum design, professional practice, and the broader policy and funding environment must function coherently if SEC development is to move beyond fragmented or symbolic efforts (OECD, 2021; UNESCO, 2021; O'Dea & Stern, 2023).

The rapid digital transformation of universities following the COVID-19 pandemic has further amplified the relevance of SEC and well-being. Hybrid learning environments, increased reliance on artificial intelligence and digital platforms, and rising student mental-health concerns have prompted renewed calls for institutions to adopt more holistic models of educational success (Williamson, Bayne & Shay, 2020; Zawacki-Richter, Marín & Bond, 2022; UNESCO, 2023). Consequently, SEC development must be conceptualized not as an auxiliary concern but as a strategic dimension of institutional quality and future readiness.

This section translates the conceptual framework into practical implications for institutional leaders and senior managers, curriculum and program teams, educators and support professionals, and external stakeholders such as policymakers and accreditation bodies. It concludes with a conceptual "map" illustrating the dynamic relationships among these levels of action.

5.1 Implications for Institutional Leaders and Senior Management

For senior institutional leaders—including presidents, vice-chancellors, provosts, deans, and directors—the central implication is the need to reposition social-emotional competency and well-being from peripheral concerns to core institutional priorities. As emphasized within the literature on positive psychology and flourishing, human well-being constitutes not only a moral imperative but also a measurable dimension of institutional effectiveness and educational quality (Ryff, 1989; Seligman, 2011; Kern et al., 2022).

To achieve this repositioning, SEC and well-being must be explicitly embedded within institutional mission statements, strategic plans, and graduate attribute frameworks. Importantly, such integration should move beyond aspirational language describing "supportive environments" toward clearly articulated commitments accompanied by accountability mechanisms and evaluative indicators (OECD, 2021).

In practical terms, institutional leaders can take several steps.

First, strategic planning and performance frameworks should incorporate SEC and well-being objectives alongside conventional metrics such as enrolment growth, completion rates, research productivity, and employability outcomes. Emerging research increasingly demonstrates that students' emotional resilience, belonging, and psychological well-being are strongly associated with retention, academic persistence, and long-term professional adaptability (Kahu & Nelson, 2022; OECD, 2023).

Second, institutions should allocate dedicated resources to support SEC-oriented initiatives. These may include funding for curriculum innovation, specialist leadership roles focused on student well-being and inclusive pedagogy, and institutional support for research and evaluation of effective practices (Felten & Lambert, 2020; Kern et al., 2022). Without sustained resource allocation, SEC initiatives risk remaining symbolic rather than transformative.

Third, quality assurance processes should be recalibrated to incorporate SEC priorities. Program review processes, accreditation self-studies, and internal evaluation mechanisms can require departments to articulate how their curricula foster social-emotional development and student well-being. Such alignment ensures that SEC is embedded within existing governance structures rather than treated as an optional add-on (Durlak et al., 2011; OECD, 2021).

Leadership practice also plays a critical symbolic role. Institutional leaders communicate values through everyday decision-making, communication, and engagement with staff and students. A future-focused approach to well-being therefore requires leadership styles characterized by transparency, empathy, and attentiveness to institutional emotional climates, particularly during periods of uncertainty and rapid technological change (Crawford et al., 2020; Williamson et al., 2020).

Participatory practices such as listening forums, collaborative planning processes, and narrative-based consultation can help ensure that institutional strategies reflect diverse perspectives and lived experiences (Biesta, 2015; O'Dea & Stern, 2023).

Finally, leaders must remain attentive to the risk of initiative fatigue. SEC and well-being initiatives are most effective when embedded within existing institutional priorities—such as equity, diversity and inclusion (EDI), digital transformation, and graduate employability—rather than implemented as separate agendas. For example, professional development programs focused on relational online teaching can simultaneously advance digital innovation, inclusive pedagogy, and student well-being.

5.2 Implications for Program and Curriculum Design

At the program level, the framework implies a significant shift in how SEC and well-being are conceptualized within curriculum design. Rather than being treated as optional enhancements or co-curricular activities, SEC development should be integrated into core curriculum structures and learning pathways.

Program teams therefore play a crucial role in translating institutional commitments into meaningful educational experiences. As the narrative analysis in Section 3 suggests, this work is both generative and complex, requiring deliberate reflection on curriculum coherence, assessment design, and student experience.

A key strategy involves systematic curriculum mapping in relation to SEC-related learning outcomes (Moon, 2013). Mapping exercises allow program teams to identify where competencies such as collaboration, ethical reasoning, resilience, and reflective practice are already embedded within courses. At the same time, they help reveal areas where students may experience fragmentation, excessive stress, or misalignment between intended learning outcomes and assessment practices.

Importantly, curriculum mapping should extend beyond formal documentation to incorporate student and staff narratives, enabling teams to understand the curriculum not only as planned but also as experienced.

Second, programs may adopt a spiral model of SEC development, in which competencies are introduced, revisited, and deepened throughout the course of study (CASEL, 2020; Felten & Lambert, 2020). Early-stage courses might prioritize self-awareness and support for academic transition, while intermediate courses emphasize collaboration, communication, and engagement with complexity. Capstone experiences can then focus on ethical decision-making, leadership, and sustained engagement with professional challenges.

Such developmental approaches avoid positioning SEC as a discrete intervention and instead situate it within students' broader intellectual and professional growth.

Third, assessment practices should be examined through a well-being lens. Overreliance on high-stakes, summative assessment can undermine motivation and increase anxiety, whereas balanced approaches that incorporate formative feedback, authentic tasks, and reflective components promote deeper engagement and resilience (Thomas, 2012; Kahu & Nelson, 2022).

Program-level reforms may therefore include diversifying assessment formats, reducing clustering of deadlines, and recognizing reflective and collaborative processes alongside final outcomes.

Finally, program teams should actively involve students as partners in the design and evaluation of SEC-oriented curricula. Student–staff partnership initiatives, curriculum co-design workshops, and participatory evaluation methods allow institutions to draw upon students' lived expertise (Felten & Lambert, 2020; Healey, Flint & Harrington, 2021). These collaborations help identify unintended consequences of institutional policies and ensure that curricula remain responsive to diverse student needs.

5.3 Implications for Teaching, Advising, and Support Practice

While institutional and programmatic structures establish enabling conditions, SEC and well-being ultimately become visible through everyday interactions between educators, advisors, and students. Classrooms, laboratories, advising sessions, and virtual learning environments constitute the spaces where students most directly experience institutional values.

Educators can integrate SEC-informed practices through relatively small but consistent strategies. These include brief reflective activities, structured check-ins, and opportunities for students to connect course content with personal or professional experiences (Felten & Lambert, 2020). Such practices help cultivate self-awareness and foster a sense of belonging within learning communities.

Collaborative learning activities should also be carefully scaffolded to promote equitable participation, perspective-taking, and collective problem-solving—particularly within diverse and international student cohorts (CASEL, 2020; Thomas, 2012).

Feedback practices likewise play an important role. Research in motivational psychology indicates that feedback emphasizing growth, effort, and learning strategies supports resilience and self-efficacy more effectively than feedback focused solely on outcomes (Dweck, 2006; Kern et al., 2022).

Advisors and student-support professionals contribute by helping students reframe challenges, normalize help-seeking behaviours, and connect with relevant resources. However, such relational work must be supported by clear institutional guidelines regarding role boundaries and referral pathways to specialized mental-health services (Gelso & Lent, 2000).

Professional development initiatives—including training in trauma-informed and culturally responsive communication—can further equip staff to respond sensitively to student needs while maintaining appropriate professional scope (UNESCO, 2023).

The narrative reflections presented earlier in this chapter also highlight the emotional labour inherent in relational pedagogical work. Institutions should therefore recognize and support this labour by incorporating SEC-related competencies into professional development frameworks, workload models, and performance evaluation systems (Felten & Lambert, 2020).

Without such recognition, caring roles may disproportionately fall on women and staff from marginalized backgrounds—a pattern documented in recent research on academic labour and student support responsibilities.

5.4 Implications for Policymakers and Accreditation Bodies

Beyond individual institutions, **policymakers, funding agencies, and accreditation bodies** play a decisive role in shaping the conditions under which SEC and well-being initiatives emerge.

Policy frameworks that emphasize metrics such as completion rates, graduate employment, and research productivity can unintentionally discourage investment in SEC initiatives by reinforcing the perception that they lie outside universities' core missions (OECD, 2021).

Conversely, regulatory frameworks that explicitly recognize well-being, inclusion, and social-emotional competencies as indicators of educational quality can provide powerful incentives for institutional innovation.

Accreditation bodies may support this shift by embedding criteria related to learning environments, student flourishing, and non-cognitive competencies within institutional review processes (Taylor et al., 2017; OECD, 2023). Self-study guidelines can also encourage institutions to examine how curricula, pedagogy, and support services collectively foster student development.

Importantly, accrediting agencies should recognize diverse forms of evidence, including qualitative narratives, student feedback, and mixed-method evaluations alongside traditional quantitative indicators.

Policymakers and funding bodies can further strengthen SEC integration by supporting targeted funding initiatives linking well-being with strategic priorities such as widening participation, digital innovation, and sustainable development (UNESCO, 2023).

Additionally, investment in longitudinal research examining relationships between SEC development, well-being, academic success, and career outcomes would help strengthen the empirical case for policy reform.

Cross-institutional networks and communities of practice can also facilitate knowledge sharing and innovation across the sector.

5.5 A Textual "Map" of SEC-Oriented Policy and Practice

To synthesize these implications, the framework can be visualized through a simplified "map-like" structure illustrating how multiple levels of the higher education system interact in relation to SEC and well-being.

Layer 1: Global and National Policy Environment.

This layer includes international agendas—such as the Sustainable Development Goals—as well as national higher education policies and accreditation frameworks that increasingly emphasize inclusion, well-being, and graduate capabilities (OECD, 2021; UNESCO, 2023).

Layer 2: Institutional Strategy and Governance.

At this level, mission statements, strategic plans, governance structures, and resource allocation decisions determine whether SEC and well-being are prioritized within institutional agendas (Felten & Lambert, 2020).

Layer 3: Program and Curriculum Design.

Program-level learning outcomes, curriculum mapping processes, and assessment strategies embed SEC development within the planned curriculum (Moon, 2013; Thomas, 2012).

Layer 4: Lived Pedagogy and Student Experience.

Finally, classroom interactions, advising encounters, peer relationships, and digital learning environments constitute the lived curriculum shaping students' everyday experiences (Aoki, 1993; Clandinin, 2013).

These layers are mutually constitutive. Policy frameworks influence institutional priorities, which shape curriculum design and pedagogical practice. At the same time, innovations emerging from classrooms and programs can inform institutional reforms and contribute to broader policy conversations.

Sustainable transformation therefore depends on both top-down and bottom-up dynamics, rather than relying on either approach alone.

In sum, embedding social-emotional competency and well-being within higher education requires coherent, multi-level strategies that align institutional leadership, curriculum design, professional practice, and policy frameworks. When these elements operate in concert, universities are better positioned to cultivate resilience, ethical awareness, and collaborative capacity among graduates, qualities increasingly essential for navigating complex and uncertain futures.

CONCLUSION

This chapter has argued that integrating social-emotional competency (SEC) and well-being into curriculum planning is not a peripheral enhancement but a future-focused strategy for fostering resilient, equitable, and high-quality higher education systems. In an era characterized by demographic change, financial pressures, geopolitical instability, and accelerated digital transformation, traditional planning approaches that prioritize technological innovation and narrow performance metrics are increasingly insufficient (OECD, 2021; UNESCO, 2020). A human-centered planning approach that foregrounds social-emotional competencies, including self-awareness, emotional regulation, empathy, collaboration, and responsible decision-making. positions human flourishing as both a moral imperative and a measurable dimension of institutional effectiveness.

Section 1 established the rationale for this shift by highlighting the growing emotional and relational pressures experienced by students and staff across diverse higher education contexts. The COVID-19 pandemic intensified mental-health challenges, social isolation, and academic disruption across global universities, underscoring the limitations of planning models that overlook the social and emotional conditions of learning. Research on pandemic-era education shows that institutions capable of integrating relational and social-emotional approaches were better positioned to sustain engagement and support students during periods of remote and hybrid learning. These challenges are particularly acute for international and first-generation students navigating unfamiliar academic systems, financial pressures, and cultural transitions. Reframing well-being as central to educational quality therefore aligns with global policy agendas calling on higher education to prepare graduates capable of addressing complex societal challenges and uncertainty (OECD, 2021; UNESCO, 2020).

Section 2 developed the conceptual foundation for this argument by integrating three complementary theoretical perspectives: social-emotional learning (SEL), positive psychology, and the notion of curriculum as lived experience. SEL frameworks conceptualize social-emotional competencies as learnable capacities that can be intentionally cultivated through curriculum design and pedagogical practice. Recent systematic reviews demonstrate increasing interest in technology supported SEL approaches within higher education, highlighting how digital tools and online environments can support emotional regulation, reflective learning, and relational engagement among educators and students.

Positive psychology further reframes educational success beyond the absence of distress toward multidimensional flourishing, encompassing meaning, relationships, engagement, and achievement.

Section 3 translated these conceptual insights into narrative accounts drawn from diverse teaching contexts, including international classrooms and blended learning environments. These narratives revealed both the possibilities and tensions of embedding SEC-oriented practices within higher education. Even modest pedagogical interventions, such as reflective exercises, emotional check-ins, and collaborative learning structures, can enhance belonging and student engagement when grounded in social-emotional learning principles. At the same time, student narratives highlight that the recognition of emotional realities signals institutional commitment to seeing learners as whole persons rather than merely academic performers.

Section 4 advanced a strategic framework for future-focused curriculum planning, emphasizing guiding principles of human flourishing, equity and inclusion, coherence, and shared responsibility. The framework proposed an iterative planning cycle encompassing inquiry, co-creation, alignment, implementation, and evaluation. Importantly, the framework situates SEC integration within institutional systems such as professional development, quality assurance processes, and governance structures. Emerging research also suggests that digital and AI-enabled learning environments can influence both academic performance and students' psychological well-being, highlighting the need to integrate technological innovation with social-emotional development in curriculum design.

Section 5 translated this framework into actionable implications for institutional leaders, curriculum teams, educators, and policymakers. Sustainable SEC integration requires alignment between institutional strategy, curriculum design, teaching practice, and policy frameworks. In contemporary digital learning environments, this alignment is increasingly important, as the growing use of generative AI and digital tools raises new questions regarding cognitive engagement, ethical decision-making, and student well-being. Emerging evidence suggests that excessive reliance on AI technologies may influence critical thinking, interpersonal skills, and emotional development, reinforcing the importance of balancing technological advancement with human-centered educational design.

Taken together, the chapter demonstrates that future-focused educational planning must position SEC and well-being as foundational design principles rather than supplementary concerns. While institutions will implement these principles in context-specific ways, the overarching objective remains consistent: to cultivate learning environments that support both intellectual growth and human flourishing. For higher education leaders, educators, and researchers, these reframing positions curriculum planning as a fundamentally human endeavor—one that evaluates success not only through academic outcomes but through the capacity of students and educators to engage with uncertainty, complexity, and social responsibility with resilience, empathy, and purpose.

REFERENCES

Aoki, T. T. (1993). Legitimating lived curriculum: Toward a curricular landscape of multiplicity. *Journal of Curriculum and Supervision, 8*(3), 255–268.

Biesta, G. (2015). *The beautiful risk of education.* Routledge. DOI: 10.4324/9781315635866

Bond, M., Bedenlier, S., Marín, V. I., & Händel, M. (2021). Emergency remote teaching in higher education: Mapping the first global online semester. *International Journal of Educational Technology in Higher Education, 18*(1), 50. DOI: 10.1186/s41239-021-00282-x PMID: 34778537

Bond, M., Khosravi, H., De Laat, M., Bergdahl, N., & Gašević, D. (2023). A meta-analysis of student engagement in online learning. *Educational Psychology Review, 35*(2), 1–29.

CASEL. (2023). *What is the CASEL framework?* Collaborative for Academic, Social, and Emotional Learning. https://casel.org

Chan, C. K. Y., & Hu, W. (2023). Students' voices on generative AI: Perceptions, benefits, and challenges in higher education. *International Journal of Educational Technology in Higher Education, 4*(1), 100129. DOI: 10.1186/s41239-023-00411-8

Cipriano, C., Tominey, S. L., & Rivera, M. C. (2023). Supporting social and emotional learning in higher education: A review of emerging evidence. *Educational Psychologist, 58*(1), 1–18.

Clandinin, D. J. (2013). *Engaging in narrative inquiry.* Routledge.

Crawford, J., Butler-Henderson, K., Rudolph, J., Malkawi, B., Glowatz, M., Burton, R., Magni, P., & Lam, S. (2020). COVID-19: 20 countries' higher education intra-period digital pedagogy responses. *Journal of Applied Learning & Teaching, 3*(1), 1–20.

Dagtekin, M., & Erkalkan, H. (2025). Artificial intelligence literacy and student engagement in higher education: Implications for responsible AI use in learning environments. *Computers and Education: Artificial Intelligence, 6*, 100223.

Durlak, J. A., Weissberg, R. P., Dymnicki, A. B., Taylor, R. D., & Schellinger, K. B. (2011). The impact of enhancing students' social and emotional learning: A meta-analysis of school-based universal interventions. *Child Development, 82*(1), 405–432. DOI: 10.1111/j.1467-8624.2010.01564.x PMID: 21291449

Dweck, C. S. (2006). *Mindset: The new psychology of success.* Random House.

Felten, P., & Lambert, L. M. (2020). *Relationship-rich education: How human connections drive success in college*. Johns Hopkins University Press. DOI: 10.1353/book.78561

Gelso, C. J., & Lent, R. W. (2000). Scientific training and professional practice in counseling psychology. In S. D. Brown & R. W. Lent (Eds.), *Handbook of counseling psychology* (3rd ed., pp. 117–132). Wiley.

Glass, C. R., Kociolek, E., Wongtrirat, R., Lynch, R., & Cong, S. (2021). Uneven experiences: The impact of student-faculty interactions on international students' sense of belonging. *Journal of International Students, 11*(2), 1–20.

Healey, M., Flint, A., & Harrington, K. (2021). *Students as partners guide: Student engagement through partnership*. Advance HE.

Holmes, W., Bialik, M., & Fadel, C. (2022). *Artificial intelligence in education: Promises and implications for teaching and learning*. Center for Curriculum Redesign.

Immordino-Yang, M. H., & Darling-Hammond, L. (2021). *The brain basis for integrated social, emotional, and academic development*. Aspen Institute.

Kahu, E. R., & Nelson, K. (2022). Student engagement in the educational interface: Understanding the mechanisms of student success. *Higher Education Research & Development, 41*(5), 1467–1480.

Kern, M. L., Waters, L., Adler, A., & White, M. (2022). A multidimensional approach to measuring well-being in education. *Educational Psychology Review, 34*(1), 1–25. PMID: 34226808

Leal Filho, W., Wall, T., Rayman-Bacchus, L., Mifsud, M., Pritchard, D., & Lovren, V. (2023). Impacts of climate change education on student awareness and emotional engagement. *International Journal of Sustainability in Higher Education, 24*(2), 295–310.

Marginson, S. (2022). Global student mobility and inequality in higher education. *Higher Education, 84*(1), 1–18. DOI: 10.1007/s10734-004-7649-x PMID: 34584277

Moon, J. A. (2013). *Reflection in learning and professional development: Theory and practice*. Routledge. DOI: 10.4324/9780203822296

Nussbaum, M. C. (2010). *Not for profit: Why democracy needs the humanities*. Princeton University Press.

O'Dea, R., & Stern, N. (2023). Reimagining the civic role of universities in the twenty-first century. *Higher Education Quarterly, 77*(2), 243–259.

OECD. (2021). *OECD skills outlook 2021: Learning for life*. OECD Publishing.

OECD. (2022). *Education at a glance 2022: OECD indicators*. OECD Publishing.

OECD. (2023). *OECD digital education outlook 2023: Towards an effective digital education ecosystem*. OECD Publishing.

Pérez-Juárez, M., Serrano-López, A. E., & García-Martínez, I. (2024). Digital well-being and university students: The role of screen time, stress, and academic engagement. *Computers & Education, 203*, 104828.

Riessman, C. K. (2008). Narrative methods for the human sciences. *Sage (Atlanta, Ga.).*

Ryff, C. D. (1989). Happiness is everything, or is it? Explorations on the meaning of psychological well-being. *Journal of Personality and Social Psychology, 57*(6), 1069–1081. DOI: 10.1037/0022-3514.57.6.1069

Ryff, C. D. (2014). Psychological well-being revisited: Advances in the science and practice of eudaimonia. *Psychotherapy and Psychosomatics, 83*(1), 10–28. DOI: 10.1159/000353263 PMID: 24281296

Seligman, M. E. P. (2011). *Flourish: A visionary new understanding of happiness and well-being*. Free Press.

Seligman, M. E. P. (2018). PERMA and the building blocks of well-being. *The Journal of Positive Psychology, 13*(4), 333–335. DOI: 10.1080/17439760.2018.1437466

Taylor, R. D., Oberle, E., Durlak, J. A., & Weissberg, R. P. (2017). Promoting positive youth development through school-based social and emotional learning interventions: A meta-analysis. *Child Development, 88*(4), 1156–1171. DOI: 10.1111/cdev.12864 PMID: 28685826

Thomas, L. (2012). *Building student engagement and belonging in higher education*. Higher Education Academy.

UNESCO. (2020). *Education for sustainable development: A roadmap*. UNESCO.

UNESCO. (2021). *Reimagining our futures together: A new social contract for education*. UNESCO.

UNESCO. (2023). *Higher education in a time of global disruption: Policy perspectives*. UNESCO.

Uslu, N. (2025). Digital well-being and self-regulation in higher education learning environments. *Education and Information Technologies, 30*(1), 1–18.

Vehrer, A., & Pálfalusi, N. (2025). Artificial intelligence in higher education: Opportunities and risks for academic integrity and student learning. *Higher Education Policy*, *38*(2), 1–20.

Williamson, B., Bayne, S., & Shay, S. (2020). The datafication of teaching in higher education: Critical issues and perspectives. *Teaching in Higher Education*, *25*(4), 351–365. DOI: 10.1080/13562517.2020.1748811

Zawacki-Richter, O., Marín, V. I., & Bond, M. (2022). Systematic review of research on artificial intelligence applications in higher education. *International Journal of Educational Technology in Higher Education*, *19*(1), 1–23. PMID: 35013716

Zhai, X., & Du, X. (2022). Digital resilience and well-being in higher education during COVID-19. *Computers & Education*, *179*, 104410.

Chapter 4
Curriculum Design and Development in Higher Education:
Frameworks, Innovations, and Future Directions for Quality Education (SDG 4)

Tarana Afrin Chandel
http://orcid.org/0000-0002-8605-6018
Integral University, India

ABSTRACT

The curriculum is the core of quality education, guiding what students learn to prepare them for societal and global challenges. A well-designed curriculum and its development are essential for building a strong educational foundation. It not only frames the knowledge and skills to be imparted but also highlights the socio-economic condition of the country. Thus, the curriculum designed plays a vital role in shaping the professional and ethical capacities of learners. Curriculum frameworks must adapt to address evolving global challenges and promote sustainable learning. This chapter explores the theoretical concept of curriculum design and evaluates the trend of digital pedagogy, competency-based education, and outcome-based education The study outlines a global and Indian strategy for higher education institutions, using the National Education Policy 2020 as a guide to help them become more relevant, adaptable, and excellent in their teaching and learning through integration of digital technologies and alignment with Sustainable Development Goal 4.

DOI: 10.4018/979-8-2600-2606-9.ch004

1 INTRODUCTION

Education plays an important part in building human personality and societal growth. In this regards, knowledge based employment has made education very critical than previous. The methodology that the students use to learn and engage with the content is followed by high educational practitioners to gain more knowledge and develop creative approach towards social challenges. The basic concept of curriculum design at university level or higher education institute is based on the strategic framework of what and how students learn, and how their outcomes are assessed? The development of study program, teaching and learning resources, lesson plans, assessments are based on curriculum. Basically, curriculum is a Latin word, which mean the content or material that is to be taught to students (Adagale, 2015). Curriculum designing is a process that is used to design academic programs from primary to higher education. It is a guideline, how to connect each element to prepare the educational goals (Huck, 2025). Every book, projects, related to professional education is chosen to construct a coherent learning journey, aiming from today and where is expected for tomorrow. The process of feedback draws the insights from research, industry and students to assure that the programs are intellectually relevant and rigorous. The curriculum also helps to analyse the standards for the knowledge they acquired in the classrooms. Basically the curriculum refers as a structured learning in an academic session in schools, college and higher education. The curriculum has everything organised, such as lesson plan, study materials for the educators or tutors to follow and assess the learning outcomes that are set for the student's leaning outcomes. A curriculum not only for academic subjects, but it also takes into consideration about the skill and extracurricular activities so that students are enriched at the end for lifelong and skilled based learning and other socio-development programs. The framework set is educators as well as students. The educators design the structure and the students follow it to gain the objectives ensuring their holistic growth and developments. The framework should be systematically aligned with the overall developments of the students with the predefined standard set for them. Curriculum design at university level or higher education institute reflects a strategic framework for what and how students learn how their outcomes are assessed. In this regard globalization, digitization, sustainability imperatives; curriculum development has evolved beyond traditional content delivery to skills, attitudes, and values essential for lifelong learning.

The 21st-century university faces complex challenges, including technological change, employability gaps, and the urgent need for sustainable development competencies. A vital challenge for higher education is the integration of sustainability into curricula and the development of sustainable competencies in students (Nahia I.M., 2023). Higher Education Institutions (HEIs) play a significant role in serving society through research, teaching, and leadership; furthermore, none of the SDGs are achievable without the contribution of academia (Nahia I.M., 2023). ES aims to empower future professionals with the systemic knowledge and actionable skills required to foster a sustainable and just society (Nahia I.M., 2023).To fulfill this mission, universities must broaden their existing education efforts and adopt pioneering approaches that deviate from traditional methods. These all-encompassing programs should build the necessary sustainability skills across all student levels (undergraduate, graduate, doctoral, and executive). Consequently, universities need to innovate with transformative teaching approaches that train students to analyse global challenges from multiple perspectives through action-based, collaborative, and stakeholder-involved methods—approaches that are not yet standard practice. Since the adoption of the SDGs in 2015, the significance of sustainable development education for all students has become increasingly recognized. Within today's convoluted global environment, universities hold immense, untapped capacity to foster global sustainability. Despite this, higher education still needs significant improvement to fully realize its capacity in attaining the 2030 goals. A critical area requiring immediate, faster implementation is the provision of sustainability-focused education. ES is vital for fostering an integrated understanding of core sustainability issues, along with the necessary capabilities and competencies. The role of HEI in upgrading the regional development towards SDG is using AI tools and shaping with great impact (Borsatto et al., 2024). Filho et al. (2021) stress the need for a framework to facilitate holistic SDG inclusion in academic curricula, complementing Valdez et al.'s (2024) investigation into how three Mexican HEIs incorporated the 17 SDGs into institutional strategies and their respective contributions to sustainable development.

1.1 Curriculum Designing in Higher education

Course planning in higher education is a strategic process of structuring learning experiences, focusing on aligning learning outcomes, content, and pedagogy with industry needs and 21st-century skills. Effective design integrates student-centric approaches, formative assessments, and technological tools to bridge the academic-industry gap. Key phases include need analysis, mapping learning outcomes, and continuous evaluation to ensure relevance.

1.1.1 Theoretical Foundations of Curriculum Design

According to Saylor, curriculum is a systematic process designed to offer a set of educational experiences, for individuals undergoing education [Lyall, 2025]. Education is shaped not only by textbooks but also by the playground, library, laboratory, reading rooms, extracurricular activities, the overall educational setting and numerous other factors. Within the school context/ higher education, both the educator and the learner constitute essential components of the curriculum, as they form part of the learning environment. The curriculum represents a systematically organized body of subject matter, specifically designed to address the needs of students. Consequently, the modern concept of curriculum encompasses the experiences and activities that equip students with the knowledge and skills required to face with diverse real-life situations. The student should be offered subjects that are balanced and harmoniously integrated. These subjects should be carefully selected and organized to help Learners Bridge the gap between educational life and experiences beyond the classroom. The upgradation of democratic values such as equality, liberty, and fraternity is necessary for learners to develop into responsible democratic citizens. Therefore, the curriculum should also aim to cultivate a spirit of nationalism among students. It is observed that learners exhibit a wide range of interests, skills, and aptitudes. Student satisfaction is very important therefore, the curriculum should be designed to address both the general and specific needs of the learners. Basic motive of education is the development of character, which requires fostering in learners a strong commitment to desirable values. The development of educational frameworks is often centered on the accumulation of subject matter and cognitive content. Admittedly, this represents a core objective; however, it is not the only goal of the curriculum.

1.1.2 Evolution of Curriculum Design (From Traditional to Learner-centric approach)

Curriculum development is the systematic process of generating, arranging, and upgrading educational resources within an organized learning framework. This process necessitates developing a structured scheme for the curriculum, including teaching methodology and expected learning goals. Curriculum action plan is a recurrent and emerging field of pedagogical study, heavily influenced by socio-political, traditional, and technological shifts. The transformation from conventional instructor-led pattern based on established customs to contemporary student-centric and capability models frameworks illustrates a growing societal grasp of knowledge construction, cognitive engagement, and human development (Judijanto et al., 2025). Initially, the curriculum was primarily authoritarian, rigid, or normative focusing on the transfer of customary, conventional information. Historically, curricula were predominantly didactic, focusing on passing down fixed knowledge and ethical standards, frequently geared toward state-sponsored ideologies or theological beliefs (Kelly, 2009). The essential input of pioneers like Ralph Tyler and Hilda Taba established the basis for curriculum studies, emphasizing the necessity of learning goals, organized content choices, and assessment procedures. The syllabus acts as the central pillar directing both educators and pupils by providing a structured framework that allows teachers to create cohesive instruction, meaningful educational experiences, and results aligned with established educational standards.

Conventional, face-to-face curricula fell short in digital settings, forcing a swift evolution in Indian online education through the demand for tailored virtual curricula. In traditional classrooms, the teacher serves as the primary authority figure, and learning follows a linear and structured approach. Focus is heavily on memorization, knowledge accumulation, and uniform testing.

In conventional classrooms, the teacher serves as the primary authority figure, and learning follows a linear and structured approach. Emphasis is placed on content acquisition, rote learning, and standardized forms of assessment. Characteristics of conventional pedagogy is given below

- Instructor-centered modes of teaching
- Limited student participation
- Strong reliance on lectures and prescribed textbooks
- Structured curricula with predetermined learning outcomes
- Homogeneous instructional approaches for diverse learners

From the early twentieth century onward, educational theorists such as John Dewey and Jean Piaget began to question traditional pedagogical practices. Their work built the bedrock for socio-constructivist approaches in which learning is understood as dynamic, interactive, and individual-driven key to the following transformations:

- Active learning facilitated through discussion, problem-solving, and project-based activities
- Greater emphasis on learners' experiences and prior knowledge
- Learning conceptualized as a process of inquiry and reflective practice
- Focus on the development of skills in addition to factual knowledge

The transition from conventional to transformative pedagogical approaches reflects a fundamental shift in conceptions of learning and the professional role of educators. Modern pedagogical standards prioritize learner-focused, accessible, tech-enhanced, and socially conscious teaching methods. Instructors who constantly evolve their teaching techniques to meet the changing demands of today's students achieve superior teaching efficacy and wider educational influence.

Modern pedagogical approaches prioritize student-focused, accessible, tech-enabled, and community-aware teaching strategies. Educators who perpetually modify their instructional techniques to cater to modern learners' changing needs demonstrate enhanced teaching efficiency and wider academic impact. Effective educational reform requires both a respect for foundational historical principles and the adoption of progressive teaching methodologies across curriculum design, professional development, and classroom instruction.

1.3 Curriculum Aims, Goals, and Objectives

The syllabus's targets, purposes, and learning outcomes map out the designed path of the academic program. They clarify goals by outlining anticipated results, operational strategy, and core pedagogical beliefs. Methods for checking student progress, academic achievement audits, learning assessments, and learner evaluation procedures are outlined below.

- **Course Content:** The educational framework offers a methodical plan detailing learning objectives, competency levels, and key concepts for mastery. Education holds a core responsibility to deliver categorized knowledge to learners in a methodical way. Organized curriculum planning ensures fluid movement across educational stages and averts knowledge gaps.
- **Learning Activities:** Pedagogical techniques and classroom design, which form the heart of the curriculum, dictate the educational experiences of students. Such instructional methods convert learning goals into action, utilizing course material to achieve precise targets. Skilled implementation converts the written syllabus into impactful teaching.
- **Educational Assessment:** Evaluating academic curricula is an essential part of an effective teaching program. It assesses the quality, value, relevance, and impact of teaching strategies, learning materials, and academic outcomes. Assessment measures how well intended learning objectives have been met. Delivering a curriculum fails to produce results without precise learning targets and adequate support materials

2 CURRICULUM DEVELOPMENTS (CD) IN HIGHER EDUCATION

It is the method of mapping out, executing and analysing the course of study to assure efficient student learning, aligning it with standards and social relevance. At first glance, curriculum and curriculum development appear to be primary concerns for educators, administrators, and parents alike, as both hold significant utility for community development and prosperity. It identifies the gap and defines the purpose, including analysing stakeholder requirements and institutional goals. Planning the structure of study programs, learning and teaching resources, lesson plans and evaluation, and even teacher education are all dependent on curriculum. It is concerned with both content and process. Course content is what students are expected to know or be able to do by the end of a lesson or course and process is a step-by-step progression of tasks. It must be organized in a logical and sequential manner to develop interest. It must promote critical thinking and provide opportunities to the students to develop the ability to make question judgmental. The process of CD in India lies between the two extremes of centralization and decentralization. From time to time, the national government formulates the National Policy on Education which includes broad guidelines regarding content and process of education at different stages (Adagale, 2015). Curriculum development involves a variety of activities namely the creation of planned curriculum, pedagogy, instructional material, delivery methods and evaluation for making the student learning process effective.

The global digitization has brought principal changes to the education sector. It has changed the roles and priorities of educators—previously the sole source of content knowledge—as well as those of students, who were once told to listen. Technology has enabled both teachers and students to search for new, more accessible, and reliable sources of knowledge. Innovative methods and models of learning, creativity and collaboration for both domestic and global are enabled through innovative technological advancement.

Curriculum is an active process of teaching- learning process. This is a dynamic programme that must evolve because the amount of knowledge across all fields is growing rapidly, along with the quality of instructional tools and methods. The curriculum is undergoing continuous re-engineering regarding learning outcomes, content, pedagogical practices, and assessment techniques. It needs to be structured, rolled out, modified, and redirected periodically. Consequently, several key principles must be considered when designing and implementing a curriculum for any group of learners

Vision and Mission: Without well-defined goals, curriculum development and implementation are impossible for any group; for instance, planning for a typically developing child requires establishing goals that provide knowledge and subject competency based on established norms. As a result, the curriculum focuses on subject mastery. The goal determines the direction in which curriculum is to be shaped. The following are the parameters kept in mind while making vision and mission.

Needs-driven: Because learners possess diverse needs and abilities, the curriculum must offer a broad spectrum of classroom experiences addressing personal, social, vocational, and recreational facets. It is a learner-centered approach that aligns educational programs with societal, industry, and student needs to bridge competency gaps.

Adequate level: The educational framework should suit the student's development, with curriculum content and feedback in conventional schools organized according to their grade placement. Systematic curriculum development involves a four-step, recursive process: needs analysis, design, implementation, and evaluation. Quality assurance in university programming necessitates repetitive framework: identifying needs, planning, implementing, and reviewing.

State-of-the-art: In the current era, the field of education and special education is witnessing numerous transformations and innovations driven by empirical research and experimentation. The educational program must be regularly updated and aligned to integrate current subject matter, pedagogical approaches, resources, and assessment strategies. The educator must offer learner a modern learning space and current curriculum.

Innovative: Every student deserves the chance to foster creativity and innovation through their learning journey. The curriculum must inspire students to resolve complex problems, generate innovative concepts, and address the demands of contemporary life. Students should be prompted to try new things in the learning environment. This principle is equally applicable to students with intellectual disabilities, who display creative potential when provided with appropriate stimulation and guidance. The modern integration of Activity-Based Learning (ABL) into mainstream curricula offers avenues for boosting student creativity.

Interdisciplinary: At every stage, the curriculum should be holistic and interconnected, featuring a well-ordered progression of learning experiences. It should be directly tied to routines that support a learner's independence, regardless of their developmental level. Consequently, the curriculum must be practical and actionable for students.

Comprehensive: Curriculum serves as the comprehensive framework of learning opportunities—including co-curricular and social activities—that facilitates student development, rather than just a list of subject areas. Curriculum refers to the integrated roadmap of instruction and learning—including classroom and non-classroom activities—aimed at achieving holistic student development, rather than just listing subject matter. It must be designed broad enough to encompass a wide spectrum of co-curricular activities, including arts, crafts, music, yoga, exercise, excursions, performances, and cultural events. The same principle applies to programming for students with intellectual disabilities, who engage more effectively in concrete, engaging activities rather than abstract, challenging academic tasks.

2.1 Role of Regulatory Bodies in Higher Education

The primary authority ruling the Indian education are the Ministry of Education (previously MHRD) which holds responsibility for the entire education system for school education and higher-level technical as well as academic institutions (Shree Adhitya education, 2026). They frame policies, which are essential for HEIs to maintain quality and continuity. The supervision of the education sector is vital, especially for emerging nations attempting to balance widespread access with rigorous quality standards and long-term societal sustainability. Policy guidelines create the base for educational institutions, fostering balanced access, effective administration of resources, and conformity to excellence standards (Ilawagbon, 2025). Educational policies establish the organizational framework for institutions, guaranteeing inclusive access, efficient resource allocation, and adherence to quality standards. They tackle fundamental issues, including corruption, inefficiency, and disparity, which are endemic to many educational systems, particularly within emerging nations, in addition to adhering to educational benchmarks. UGC is an authorized organization accountable for regulating higher education in India. It was first formed in 1945 to manage and supervise three Central Universities Aligarh, Banaras and Delhi. Its responsibility was extended in 1947 to cover all Indian universities. The University Grants Committee was inaugurated in 1945 to monitor the three central universities of Aligarh, Banaras, and Delhi, and its jurisdiction was expanded in 1947 to encompass all Indian universities (Wikipedia). A recommendation in August 1949 urged the reorganization of the UGC modelled on the British University Grants Committee. The University Grants Commission (UGC) was formally inaugurated on December 28, 1953, and later became a statutory body of the Government of India in 1956 following an Act of Parliament. The commission chaired by S. Radhakrishnan was appointed in the year 1948–49, to report on Indian University Education and suggest improvements and extensions that may be desirable to suit present and future requirements of the country (Wikipedia). Their focus was to modernize and reform higher education to meet the needs of a newly independent nation, focusing on scientific, technical, and democratic needs. Over time, its mandate has expanded to encompass certifying academic programs, ensuring minimum standards are met, and fostering innovation and research within the higher education sector (Wikipedia). The MoE is the apex body regulating and financing the development of higher education, ensuring policy implementation and standards (Shree Adhitya education, 2026). It is as follows;

2.1.1 Policy Making

Policymaking involves government bodies, ministries, regulatory bodies, and increasingly diverse actors that influence the higher education sector. Policies are increasingly shaped by the need for international competitiveness and the integration of technology and research. Educational planning must consider the social, political, and economic conditions of the society. The policies implemented by Indian government are as follows

- Design National Education policy (NEP 2020)
- Set frameworks for curriculum research and skill development
- Ensure inclusion, innovation and quality in education

2.1.1.1 National Education policy (NEP 2020)

: Education is essential for realizing complete human capability, fostering a fair and balanced community, and driving the progress of the nation. Ensuring comprehensive, high-quality education for all is crucial for India for sustained growth and international leadership regarding financial prosperity, egalitarianism, heritage protection, national solidarity and technological advancement. India's 2015 commitment to SDG4 strives to guarantee universal access to high-quality, fair education and long lasting development opportunities by 2030. Such an ambitious goal requires restructuring the education system to foster learning to achieve the 2030 Agenda for Sustainable Development targets. The National Education Policy prioritizes the cultivation of every student's innovative capabilities. (NEP, 2020). The strategy is based on the concept that education should enhance not only cognitive abilities—spanning from fundamental literacy and numeracy to high-level critical thinking—but also social, ethical, and emotional characteristics.

2.1.1.2 Vision of this Policy

NEP 2020 visualizes an education system embedded in Indian ethos that contributes directly to transforming India sustainably into an equitable and vibrant knowledge society, by providing high-quality education to all, and thereby making India a global knowledge superpower.

2.1.1.3 Holistic development of learners

The primary aim of reforming educational methods and content across all stages is to shift the system from memorization-based learning to conceptual understanding and self-reflective learning (NEP, 2020). The objective is to foster holistic development—bridging academic learning with emotional and social growth—to produce well-rounded individuals equipped with 21st-century competencies. To meet essential educational goals, both the content taught and the way it is delivered will be fundamentally revamped. From preschool to university, the educational process will embed essential values and practical skills across all disciplines (Borkar, 2023).

2.1.1.4 Reduce Curriculum Content to Improve Critical Thinking and Essential Learning

By focusing on core concepts and practical application, this curriculum streamlines content to foster analytical thinking, inquiry, and discovery-based learning.

The educational environment is characterized by collaborative, exploratory projects, ensuring that student questions guide the curriculum. Learning is made interactive and engaging, designed to deepen comprehension through active, joyful participation (Borkar, 2023).

2.1.1.5 Integrate Experimentation Learning

Immersive, interdisciplinary, and active learning will be implemented across all educational levels, featuring practical experiences, arts-integrated and sports-integrated education, and narrative-based pedagogy. Experiential learning—encompassing hands-on, arts-integrated, sports-integrated, and story-telling-based pedagogy—will be adopted across all academic levels (Borkar, 2023). Proficiency-based learning approaches will increasingly define classroom settings, aiming to close the achievement gap (Borkar, 2023). Art-integrated learning is an interdisciplinary pedagogical approach that utilizes diverse facets of arts and culture to anchor conceptual understanding across disciplines.

2.1.1.6 Choice-Based Credit System (CBCS)

Students will enjoy greater flexibility and a wider range of subject choices, including physical education, arts and crafts, and vocational training, enabling them to design their own educational paths and future plans. There will be no rigid separation between academic, vocational, curricular, extracurricular, arts, humanities, and sciences

2.1.1.7 Linguistic Diversity

Scientific evidence shows that foundational learning is most effective in a child's home language. Therefore, the curriculum should be taught in the child's native tongue until at least Grade 5, but ideally through Grade 8. Recognizing that young children (ages 2-8) learn languages quickly, the curriculum emphasizes early immersion in multiple languages, anchored by the mother tongue, to drive cognitive growth. The Three-Language Formula is maintained to honour constitutional obligations and regional needs while fostering unity. The policy is adaptable, ensuring flexibility for states rather than enforcing a specific language (NEP, 2020; Borkar, 2023).

Efforts will be made to produce top-tier bilingual learning materials, enabling students to communicate in science and math in both their native language and English. Additionally, regional languages—along with their rich literature—will be available as school options, including online options, to preserve their importance. In addition to strong English and Indian language programs, secondary students will have the opportunity to learn international languages such as Korean, Japanese, and Mandarin to increase their global awareness and personal opportunities. The instruction of all languages will be enhanced through innovative and experiential methods—including gamification and mobile apps—by weaving in cultural components like film, theatre, literature, and music, alongside connecting learners with relevant subjects through personal experiences

2.1.1.8 21st Century Skills/Competencies

While fostering curricular choice, education must ensure students acquire essential skills—scientific reasoning, problem-solving, creativity, aesthetic appreciation, communication, and physical fitness—to thrive as productive, innovative citizens in a rapidly evolving world. Multiple state-led programs and frameworks are managing the profound transformation of the workforce caused by artificial intelligence. NEP 2020 identifies artificial intelligence as a key driver for financial prosperity, overcoming learning hurdles, empowering educators, and tailoring instruction to individual needs and stresses, the necessity of integrating AI education at every stage of the schooling system. Established in March 2024, the IndiaAI Mission seeks to position the nation as a worldwide authority in AI by promoting creative development among state bodies, businesses, and research centres. Government offers AI-courses for students and educators at the following platform.

DIKSHA Platform: Developed by the Ministry of Education, DIKSHA acts as a digital knowledge-sharing framework, utilizing AI to enhance accessibility through video search functionalities and audio aids for visually impaired learners. The app offers mobile accessibility on Google Play Store to users, including educators, students, and families (PIB, GoI, 2026). This application is packed with interactive educational content aligned with the mandated academic syllabus, notes (PIB, GoI, 2026).

SOAR Initiative: The Ministry of Skill Development and Entrepreneurship launched SOAR (Skilling for AI Readiness) to build AI awareness and skills for classes 6 –12 students and educators. Program

Includes three 15 -hour student modules and one 45 -hour "AI for Educators" teacher module.

This program equips educators with the skills to understand AI curriculum and pedagogy, apply AI tools effectively in teaching, ensure inclusivity for varied learners, design AI-based projects, and teach ethical AI practices.

SWAYAM Platform: The Ministry of Education's SWAYAM portal offers over 110 free AI courses from top institutions like IITs and IISc, with 41.2 lakh students enrolled. This initiative aims to provide quality, accessible, and high-level digital skills training to learners across the country.

The objective of NEP 2020 is to cultivate ethical individuals while simultaneously transforming them into responsible members of the international community. A primary emphasis of the policy is on the foundational development and strengthening of the country. Integrating skill-based training into the course of study allows learners to follow their passions and enhances their marketability to future employers. This initiative seeks to implement a technology-driven framework to modernize the Indian learning landscape. Software providers for educational management are now tasked with upholding the standards of NEP 2020 by supporting schools in reorganizing their academic content and instructional methods (MHRD, GoI, 2020)

2.2.2 Regulatory Bodies in Higher Education

India possesses an immense higher education system, largely managed by private entities holding 60% of colleges and hosting 64% of student enrolment (Shah, 2015). The Indian tertiary sector is structured in three layers, consisting of universities, colleges, and specific academic courses (Shah, 2015). This setup interacts directly with regulatory authorities, while accreditation bodies are essential in maintaining sector standards and quality. Higher learning institutions serve as the primary catalyst for developing a nation's intellectual capacity and economic competitiveness (edutiip, 2026). Statutory bodies under India's Ministry of Education define academic benchmarks, extend financial assistance, and oversee quality standards across tertiary and professional institutions. Types of Regulatory Bodies in Higher Education:

Apex Regulatory Bodies (General/Overall Control):

- The UGC is a statutory organization, founded via a 1956 Act of Parliament, charged with overseeing academic quality, facilitating higher education, and disbursing grants.
- Department of Higher Education (Ministry of Education): Oversees overall policy-making and governmental regulation.

Technical Education Bodies:

- All India Council for Technical Education (AICTE): Sets standards and approves courses in technical and management fields, functioning as a statutory body since 1987.

Professional Councils (Field-Specific Regulations): These bodies set standards for specific professional courses, such as:

- National Council for Teacher Education (NCTE): Oversees teacher training.
- Medical Council of India (MCI): Regulates medical education (now replaced by NMC).
- Bar Council of India (BCI): Regulates legal education.

- Pharmacy Council of India (PCI): Sets standards for pharmacy education.
- Council of Architecture (COA): Regulates architectural education.

Accreditation Bodies (Quality Assurance):

- National Assessment and Accreditation Council (NAAC): Assesses and accredits universities and colleges to maintain quality.
- National Board of Accreditation (NBA): Focuses specifically on the accreditation of technical and professional programs.

Research & Professional Specialized Councils:

- ICSSR (Social Science), CSIR (Science), ICHR (Historical Research): Promote and fund research in specialized fields.

State-Level Regulators:

- State Councils for Higher Education (SCHE): Coordinate and plan higher education within state jurisdictions.

UCG (University Grants Commission: UGC is a statutory body dedicated to coordinating, defining, and upholding academic standards within university education. It is key to developing higher education; therefore, understanding this body is very important. In 1944, the Sargent Report suggested creating the University Grants Commission (Yoshida, 2025). Consequently, in 1945, the Central Government established the University Grants Committee. At first, the committee operated in a purely advisory capacity, lacking financial authority (Yoshida, 2025). Subsequently, acting on the 1949 University Education Commission's advice, Parliament passed the UGC Act of 1956, granting it proper funding and authority. Besides distributing funds to qualified institutions, the UGC guides Central and State governments on initiatives essential for improving tertiary education (DHE MoR GoI, 2016) . The commission operates from its New Delhi headquarters and through six regional branches in Bhopal, Pune, Bangalore, Kolkata, Guwahati, and Hyderabad (DHE MoR GoI, 2016; edutiip, 2026). The function of UGC in Higher education are as follows (edutiip, 2026);

- Regulation, establishment, and upholding of academic quality in tertiary institutions
- Upholds academic integrity, fairness, and progress in higher education institutions.

- Allocate funding to universities.
- Approves universities in India and maintains a database of accredited institutions.
- Issues regulations on minimum standards of education, appointment of teachers, PhD procedures, and open/distance learning.
- It nurtures academic research by awarding funding, fellowships, and scholarships to educators and students.
- It actively encourages partnerships between Indian and foreign universities to support collaborative research and exchange initiatives.
- To confirm eligibility for JRF and lectureship positions, the UGC conducts the NET exam.

AICTE (All India Council for Technical Education): Established in 1945 and granted statutory authority in 1987, the All-India Council for Technical Education (AICTE) is the premier national advisory body for regulating technical education (DHE MoR GoI, 2016; edutiip, 2026). It oversees, plans, maintains standards, and regulates technical education, encompassing fields like engineering, technology, management, pharmacy, and architecture (DHE MoR GoI, 2016; edutiip, 2026). AICTE's head office is based in New Delhi, operating seven regional offices in Kolkata, Chennai, Kanpur, Mumbai, Chandigarh, Bhopal, and Bangalore (DHE MoR GoI, 2016; edutiip, 2026). Eight primary bureaus function under the AICTE umbrella (edutiip, 2026), these are as follows;

- Research
- Institutional and Faculty Development Bureau
- Planning and Coordination Bureau
- Academic Bureau
- University Bureau
- Administration Bureau
- Approval Bureau
- Finance Bureau
- Governance Bureau

NAAC (National Assessment and Accreditation Council): Founded in September 1994, the National Assessment and Accreditation Council is an independent entity supported by the UGC (edutiip, 2026). Originating from the 1986 National Policy on Education's directives, this initiative heavily emphasized maintaining the caliber of Indian higher education (edutiip, 2026). NAAC represents a significant type of regulatory body in higher education. Indian Higher Educational Institutions (HEIs) undergo assessment and accreditation by the NAAC. To evaluate educational quality and institutional effectiveness, NAAC reviews and grades institutions of higher learning—including universities, colleges, and recognized organizations, to determine their quality status. Functions of NAAC in Higher Education are

- Regular evaluations of the teaching-learning strategies
- Encourage learning through research and tried-and-true teaching methods.
- To encourage self-evaluation, accountability, autonomy and innovations in higher education.
- Making quality assurance a crucial component of higher education institutions' (HEIs') operations is its stated objective.
- Encourage the academic environment in order to improve the calibre of research and teaching-learning in institutions of higher learning.

NCTE (National Council for Teachers Education): Established in 1973, the National Council for Teacher Education formerly functioned as a consultative body (edutiip, 2026). NCTE is a crucial regulatory authority operating within higher education. As the foremost institution, the NCTE regulates all teacher education programs in India (edutiip, 2026). This legally established body regulates teacher training, defining standards and policy frameworks nationally (edutiip, 2026). NCTE's core purpose is to formulate norms for teacher training and to foster planned, uniform development of the education system across the country.

3 MODELS OF CURRICULUM DEVELOPMENT

Curriculum studies are a deeply rooted area of educational inquiry, and extensive literature exists on theoretical curricula, as well as how educational philosophies and theory intersect with the realities of classroom instruction. A CD model acts as a structured blueprint for designing, delivering, and evaluating educational programs, methodically outlining learning goals, subject matter, teaching strategies, and evaluation methods (Hurixdigital, 2026). These structured plans guide crucial pedagogical decisions by solving core questions about what to teach, how to deliver content, and how to measure success. By following a rigorous, orderly process, these frameworks ensure the consistency, precision, and quality of educational materials. These instructional frameworks are applied in various sectors, including schooling (K–12), universities, professional corporate training, and virtual learning environments. Some models prioritize results-focused planning and evaluation, while others emphasize instructor participation, student requirements, or continuous refinement. The best model is selected based on key factors like learner's profiles, content complexity and organizational objectives. Comprehending curriculum design approaches.

Instructional design frameworks facilitate the systematic development of tailored, high-impact training materials. These frameworks help professionals build adaptable educational content that prioritizes the student experience. Educational models facilitate the creation of personalized, effective, and flexible curriculum pathways.

Administrative model of curriculum: This model was adopted from the beginning of education. Administrators, having analyzed relevant information and set objectives, create or choose a structured pattern—a curriculum design—to outline learning experiences. As the most enduring and utilized approach, the Administrative Model centers on a top-down, expert-driven process for creating curriculum. The widely used Administrative Model is fundamentally a top-down, authority-driven process for crafting the curriculum. The major 5 types of curriculum design model are given below (Neendoor, 2026; Evelyn, 2023; Pressbook, 2026)

- Tyler's Curriculum Model
- Hilda Taba's Grassroots Model
- John Goodlad's Curriculum Model
- Wheeler's Curriculum Model
- Kerr's Curriculum Model

3.1. Tyler's Curriculum Model

This model was developed by American educator Ralph W. Tyler in 1949, known as the objective Model. This model is also referred as *Best for Outcome-Driven Learning*. It is a widely recognized curriculum model. This approach champions education as a tool for developing practical skills and meaningful understanding. It aligns with a pragmatic view, centring education on useful, life-relevant knowledge. This model is completely dependent upon planning. At the same time, it ensures coherence between goals, learning outcomes, and educational experiences. It is a systematic, four-step curriculum development model comprising the definition of objectives, selection of learning experiences, organization of content, and evaluation including the following steps

i. Aiming to achieve educational aim, learning goal, pedagogical aim, instructional goal, academic goal and educational aspiration.
ii. Instruction needed to satisfy the learning objective.
iii. By the end of this module, the learning outcome for the student is to recognize.
iv. Appraising educational opportunities.

This model's effectiveness stems from its organized, streamlined framework, while offering sufficient adaptability. Its versatile design allows educators to readily implement it across diverse educational levels and subjects. By prioritizing curricular evaluation, Tyler's model allows educators to analyse the effectiveness of their plans and implement necessary improvements. Tyler's framework has drawbacks; it downplays social learning and critical thinking, which may not adequately address the diverse needs of all students. Therefore, teachers can enhance this approach by incorporating more holistic, student-centered methodologies.

3.2 Hilda Taba's Grassroots Model

The interactive Model, or Taba's Model, prioritizes the deliberate organization of teaching methods. It is also referred as *Teacher-Led Curriculum Design.* Created by educational reformer Hilda Taba in 1962, this framework focuses on a flexible, learner-centered process for designing curriculum. This model is a teacher-driven, inductive framework designed to enhance curriculum flexibility and respond directly to student needs. This model utilizes a bottom-up methodology, placing educators at the centre of the curriculum design process. The framework comprises seven interconnected stages that make up the instructional and learning process. These are given below

i. Identifying learning requirements
ii. Establishing objectives/targets/goals
iii. Collection of content
iv. Content management, content curation, data governance
v. Designing appropriate learning activities
vi. Coordination of instructional activities
vii. Formal measurement/ assessment

This framework fosters open-ended inquiry rather than focusing on binary right/ wrong answers. A key advantage is that it enables profound conceptual exploration through analytical reasoning.

3.3. John Goodlad's Curriculum Model

John Goodlad, an educational expert and theorist from Canada, developed the framework known as Goodlad's Model. This unique curriculum approach is founded on the primary conviction that goals and values must be the fundamental catalysts for all school systems. While Goodlad treated values as primary data sources in curriculum development, he contrasted this with Tyler's approach of using them only as a screening device. Goodlad's curriculum model is built upon four primary data inputs: values, funded knowledge, conventional wisdom, and student needs

- Value orientations
- Research-based (scientific) knowledge
- Conventional wisdom
- Teaching prerequisites

Goodlad maintains that explicit values and goals ought to steer educational systems, employing them to direct content choices and instruction while Tyler utilizes values solely as a filter for evaluating objectives. A primary difference is that Goodlad's model integrates scientific knowledge stemming from research. The model's data sources depend upon explicitly stated value judgments. The model supports ongoing and thorough evaluation across all stages of the curriculum.

3.4 Wheeler's Curriculum Model

Wheeler's model utilizes a coherent, five-step cyclical process of curriculum development, guaranteeing that instructional design is constantly adapted and improved based on evaluation. This strategy utilizes a systematic, structured approach to planning and executing the curriculum, ensuring continuous refinement and adaptation. This framework supports teachers in designing and executing an engaging, practical, and highly functional curriculum. Wheeler's framework consists of five interrelated stages of curriculum planning, namely

- Establishment of goals and purposes
- Learning Opportunity Curation
- Content selection
- Systematic planning of educational experiences
- Curriculum Assessment and Review

Wheeler created his framework to rectify the limitations found in Tyler's approach to curriculum design. Because Tyler's model follows a straight, linear path, it fails to connect the key elements of curriculum construction. Consequently, Wheeler introduced this cyclical model. This approach emphasizes the holistic connection between different elements of the curriculum. This framework allows developers to start the design process from any phase. It emphasizes assessing the specific context of the school and its community. Nevertheless, this framework requires significant time and can be challenging to put into practice.

3.5 Kerr's Curriculum Model

Developed by British specialist John Kerr, this model mirrors Tyler and Wheeler, yet distinguishes itself by highlighting the interconnected nature of its components through direct and indirect data flow. John Kerr proposed four components for his curriculum development model (Jugessur, 2023).

- *Goals/Aims:* The intended outcomes of education, which Kerr categorized into cognitive, affective, and psychomotor domains
- *Content:* The subject matter, facts, and concepts that are to be taught, which should be organized, sequenced, and integrated.
- *Process/Method*: The activities and methods employed by the school to facilitate learning, influenced by pupil-teacher relationships and the learning environment.
- Assessment/Review: The continuous, systemic collection of information to determine curriculum efficiency and whether objectives have been met.

Kerr's Model recommends sorting objectives as cognitive, psychomotor, and effective. Furthermore, it emphasizes the necessity of structuring, uniting, sequencing, and reinforcing knowledge. This approach highlights student needs, interests, social conditions, and maturity, yet it lacks emphasis on teacher input.

3.6 Application of these Models in Real Classrooms

The Director of education institutes can utilize established models to enhance program quality through the following ways (Snehnath Neendoor, 2026)

Framework Development: Leverage these organized frameworks to guide the educational design process through all its stages. Implement structured methodologies to ensure thorough preparation and implementation.

***Foster stakeholder collaboration*:** This educational structure motivated the involvement of teachers, students, alumni and parents in designing curriculum, fostering collaboration between content creators, enabling curriculum designers, educational publishers, and educators to provide a cohesive and high-impact learning journey.

Optimize learning outcomes: Educators can select premium, relevant materials to design innovative learning trajectories tailored to diverse student needs. Moreover, employing diverse teaching strategies and promoting critical reasoning fosters a captivating, interactive learning environment, productive classroom which fosters high academic achievement and nurtures a commitment to continuous education.

***Skills Training/Dev*elopment**: Providing sector expertise and training to empower educators in mastering and implementing the curriculum. This ensures teachers have the skills to deliver the curriculum effectively and align with modern pedagogical approaches

Integrate innovative technology: Train educators to synchronize assessment methods with institutional objectives, utilizing instructional design frameworks to select and adopt digital tools for curriculum integration.

4 APPROACHES TO CURRICULUM DESIGN AND DEVELOPMENT

Curriculum frameworks constitute the structured, orderly organization of instructional components within a course of study. It represents the educational journey, embodied in instructor lesson plans and active experiential learning. In building an educational blueprint, instructors curate course content, manage operational controls, and determine implementation timelines.

4.1 Purpose of Curriculum Design

Curricula that fail to bridge academic gaps significantly disrupt daily routines and academic progression. Beyond its core function, curriculum planning acts as a strategic blueprint for realizing further goals. Synchronizing middle school curriculum with lower and higher levels ensures seamless transitions and conceptual cohesion. Such alignment ensures learning targets are organized to build knowledge cumulatively over time. Educational plans that do not remediate learning disparities substantially disrupt students' lives or scholastic achievement. The three primary methodologies for designing curricula include subject-centered, learner-centered, and problem-centered approaches

4.1.1 Subject-centered Curriculum Design (SCCD): (focus on content)

Subject-centered curriculum design is organized (Prezi, 2015) and structured (Exceed, 2025) within a specific discipline or area of study rather than individual learners. For instance, such a curriculum may emphasize subjects like mathematics (Exceed, 2025) or biology (Prezi, 2015), outlining both the content to be covered and the methods through which it should be taught. The core curriculum represents a common form of subject-centered design that can be standardized across schools, states, and even at the national level. In this model, teachers are provided with a predetermined set of topics and instructional guidelines that specify what should be taught and how it should be delivered. A primary drawback of subject-centered curriculum design is its neglect of the learner's individual needs and experiences. As a result, this can diminish student engagement and motivation, and at times, lead to academic underachievement.

4.1.2 Learner-centered Curriculum Design (LCCD): (focus on student needs)

Learner-centered education prioritizes the individual needs (Exceed, 2025), goals, and ambitions of pupils [Prezi, 2015]. This model aims to build student competence by offering diverse learning avenues, including active projects, visual aids, and interactive tasks. Versatility helps increase enthusiasm and foster ongoing dedication to the material. Nevertheless, this strategy poses significant difficulties. Implementing differentiated instruction is a time-intensive process that places a high demand on teachers to curate or develop materials tailored to diverse learning profiles. Instructors often face constraints in time, expertise to deploy these pedagogical approaches successfully. Furthermore, designing learner-centered curriculum requires a difficult balance between catering to student interests and achieving key learning outcomes (Prezi, 2015).

4.1.3 Problem-Centered Curriculum Design (PCCD): (focus on real-world application)

Likewise, learner-centered designs, problem-centered curriculum is also a form of student-centric education. This method instructs students in critical analysis and solution development by engaging with authentic, real-world challenges (Exceed, 2025). PCCD promotes creative thinking and educational relevance; however, it fails to consistently accommodate individual learning styles.

5 MICRO-CREDENTIALS: INNOVATION IN HIGHER EDUCATION

Surpassing conventional diplomas, modern certifications are necessary to differentiate oneself in the current cutthroat employment landscape. Micro-credentials are concise certifications, provide a direct alternative to university degrees, focusing specifically on industry-recognized competencies. These courses are offered in virtual, hybrid, remote, or in-person formats, and span proficiency levels from foundational to expert (Singh, 2024). Targeting a broad audience from students to the unemployed, this program aligns with the shift toward skills-based hiring, as employers increasingly favour demonstrated competence over formal education. It is structured as four-credit modules, one credit equates to one hour of instruction or two hours of laboratory work, whereas conventional education credits are determined by contact hours, such as lectures or lab sessions (Kumar, 2024).

5.1 Vision Behind Micro-credentials

According to Prof. M. Jagadesh Kumar, UGC Chairman, these guidelines are essential for facilitating industry-aligned skill acquisition and enhancing academic progress (Jacob, 2025). He contends that India's young population boom offers significant capacity for international and economic dominance. Modernizing the university system is essential to align with evolving job markets and societal needs. These specialized, concise courses envisioned by the UGC seek to enhance employability and provide niche skill development.

5.2 Importance of Micro-credential

It is essential for higher education institutions to actively cultivate employability skills in students. A disparity exists between academic learning and the competencies needed for the workforce. Tackling the talent shortage, micro-credentials are transforming education by allowing students to fast-track the acquisition of industry-relevant skills. Owing to their adaptable and reachable format, these specialized credentials are quickly becoming a staple in higher learning (Bhargava, 2022).

5.3 Benefits of Micro-Credentials

Micro-credentials facilitate accessible, budget-friendly educational trajectories that particularly benefit post-traditional students and individuals with constrained access to traditional university settings. These certifications increase the worth of post-secondary education by facilitating the acquisition of focused competencies, leading to improved job prospects and immediate industry application. Additionally, these flexible certifications boost tailored education, enabling self-directed progression and personalized curriculum choices. These certifications prompt major employers to build local training hubs, strengthening national infrastructure and boosting the practical value of modern education. These certifications drive non-academic organizations to build local training centres, which strengthens the national education ecosystem and boosts the practical application of modern training programs

5.4 India's approach to Micro-Credential

The adoption of micro-credentials into higher education signifies transformation toward accessible, skill-driven, and flexible learning environments. Combining academic knowledge with real-world application, these initiatives equip students to excel as future leaders and innovators in a rapidly evolving global landscape (Jacob, 2025). This innovative endeavour underscores the promise to make India's universities hubs of holistic, career-ready education, preparing students with distinct, market-ready skills. The approach for HEI in India (Singh, 2024; Forum IAS, 2024) is as follows:

- **Alignment with National Education Policy (NEP) 2020:** Aligning with the demand for micro-credentials, NEP 2020 pushes for skill-centric education, ensuring hands-on proficiency training from the school level up to university.
- **National Credit Framework (NCrF) Integration**: The NCrF incorporates micro-credentials by standardizing their credits and outcomes to match traditional academic qualifications. The NCrF, act as an overarching structure National School Education Qualification Framework (NSEQF), National Higher Education Qualification Framework (NHEQF), and National Skills Qualification Framework (NSQF) to facilitate credit integration, echoing micro-credential principles (Drishti IAS, 2026).
- **Academic Bank of Credits (ABC):** It is mandatory for learners to establish an Academic Bank of Credits (ABC) account to store credits earned from digital macro or micro-credentials. Students are required to register for an Academic Bank of Credit account using their Aadhaar card.
- **Study Webs of Active-Learning for Young Aspiring Minds (SWAYAM):** The Indian Ministry of Education initiated the SWAYAM program. By offering open-access online courses encompassing higher education, secondary schooling, and vocational training, it promotes the notion of micro-credentials. The SWAYAM website now hosts in excess of 4,400 online classes. The site is open to all at no cost, featuring curricula spanning from ninth grade to higher education
- **Market Demand and Employability**: As firms demand more skilled young workers, micro-credentials are increasingly valued as a supplement to traditional education that accelerates job readiness.

6 FUTURE DIRECTIONS IN HIGHER EDUCATION

Universities are moving away from traditional degrees, pivoting instead toward personalized, tech-enabled, and industry-aligned frameworks that prioritize lifelong learning, AI, and modular, competency-based credentials. Major shifts redefining the future of university education are as follows;

- AI-Powered Personalization
- Sustainability and Digitalization
- Employability and Career-Aligned Curricula
- Data-Driven Decision Making
- Boom Taxonomy

6.1 AI-Powered Personalization

AI-powered tools are transitioning away from repetitive chores toward developing customized learning routes, adjusting material complexity, and providing personal feedback to boost academic result. Technologies powered by AI—specifically Machine Learning, Natural Language Processing, and intelligent tutoring systems—customize learning by developing flexible educational pathways designed to meet the specific needs of each learner (Lai, 2025; Chandel, 2024). Machine learning aids in examining educational data to detect student behavioural trends, while natural language processing allows for natural communication in AI-based tutoring systems

6.2 Digitalization and Sustainability

Although digital technology is deeply embedded in university operations, its significant contribution to sustainability is overlooked, despite its alignment with 'smart university' research which emphasizes using digital tools for resource efficiency and data-driven decision-making (Hopping, 2025). The seamless integration of technology makes environmentally friendly practices a standard part of daily campus operations, all while preserving the main purpose of academic learning. Higher Education Institutions play a critical role in advancing the UN 2030 Agenda by fostering societal digitization and creating innovative, sustainable technological solutions (Trevisan et al., 2024).

6.3 Employability and Career-Aligned Curricula

Numerous strategies can narrow the divide between university curricula and workplace requirements, largely through leveraging corporate insights and evaluations to maintain updated syllabi, as emphasized by Bridgstock in 2009. Furthermore, Jackson in 2015 proposes that embedding hands-on vocational training—like work placements and traineeships—improves students' immersion in authentic workplace settings. Implementing a skill-focused framework acts as an effective method, concentrating on acquiring bespoke abilities required by organizations (Nondumiso Shabangu, 2024). This model provides improved pedagogical adaptability and accommodates diverse corporate requirements. Furthermore, encouraging partnerships between academia and the corporate sector facilitates information sharing and elevates academic standards

6.4 Data-Driven Decision Making

With higher education becoming increasingly competitive, universities are under growing pressure to justify the effectiveness of their staff, academic programs, and assets. The shifting landscape necessitates enhanced transparency, driving schools to address logistical challenges, forecast industry trends, and collaborate to encourage development and innovation (Mahajan, 2024). Relying on evidence is essential for universities to raise academic results, better manage resources, and remain leaders in the sector (Vyas, 2024). Through the use of sophisticated data collection and analysis, colleges can launch a new phase of fact-based decision-making, which is critical for securing a competitive edge (Gaftandzhieva et al., 2024).

6.5 Boom's Taxonomy

Higher Education Institutions (HEIs) realize that while course (CLOs) and program learning outcomes (PLOs) appear well-structured on paper, demonstrating their alignment often reveals a significant gap between curricular theory and actual evidence during accreditation reviews. Bloom's Taxonomy is a hierarchical classification of pedagogical objectives and competencies, often referred to as learning outcomes, acting as a layered framework to foster critical thinking in educational settings

(Parker, 2025). Teachers frequently adopt this structure to build lesson plans that encourage critical thinking and create tests that measure a range of intellectual skills. It categorizes cognitive skills to direct the creation of educational goals and learning tasks. It encourages progressing from simple factual recall to complex analytical and innovative thought.

Mapping Course Learning Outcomes (CLOs) to Program Learning Outcomes (PLOs) is easy in theory, but generating the necessary documentation to prove this alignment for accreditation purposes remains a significant challenge (Team Creatrix, 2026). Throughout tertiary education, Bloom's taxonomy endures as the standard framework for structuring cognitive levels, defining learning objectives, and guiding assessment methods. To meet higher administrative demands, Bloom's Taxonomy must shift from a classroom tool to an AI-driven strategic framework, using systems that turn learning objectives into measurable, audit-ready evidence (Team Creatrix, 2026).

7 QUALITY EDUCATIONS SHAPING FUTURE LEADER

Boosting learning standards serves as a cornerstone for shaping versatile people and promoting effective leadership. Excellent schooling goes beyond academic knowledge to nurture critical analysis and communication skills required for future success. Exceptional learning builds a strong base for heightened professional success and individual progress. It advances logical thinking, creativity, and lifelong learning, providing people with the essential skills and values needed for productive economic and civic engagement.

7.1 Role of Quality Education in Leadership Development

Leadership qualities often get entrenched during schooling. They strengthen their skills in clear expression, attentive listening, and teamwork through group exercises and dialogue" (Coach Space, 2024). Such core experiences cultivate empathy and agility, which are the mainstays of strong leadership. Elite schooling acts as a vital tool, empowering students to pursue leadership positions while bolstering self-confidence (IFIM Institute, 2026; Chandel, 2024). Superior education imparts essential skills, fostering well-rounded individuals capable of analytical thinking, addressing intricate challenges, navigating choices wisely, and acting with accountability (Mayberry, 2023). Such specialized instruction is indispensable for equipping prospective leaders, providing equitable access to education that matches various industry demands (IFIM Institute, 2026). STEM instruction cultivates the next generation of innovators by instructing pupils in analytical reasoning, inventive troubleshooting, and imaginative techniques (Chandel, 2025). Science and technology education fosters essential leadership skills by combining academic principles with practical, hands-on application (Coach Space, 2024).

7.2 Higher Education: Bridging Knowledge with Strategy

As students advance in their education, gaining knowledge becomes essential. At universities and colleges, students face a wide variety of viewpoints and complicated concepts. This phase is vital in forming the viewpoints of future leaders and broadening their comprehension. Business, management, and communication programs provide students with insights into organizational behavior, negotiation skills, and strategic thinking. Leveraging these key leadership skills empowers us to facilitate fully immersive learning initiatives. Academic institutions offer a base structure for fostering core leadership abilities. Leadership skills are nurtured by many through self-guided learning, practical experience, and taking initiative in professional growth. For sustained effectiveness, leaders must pledge to continuous education, broadening their proficiency through seminars, professional workshops, mentorship, and individual research (Coach Space, 2024). Adopting lifelong learning helps leaders develop a developmental perspective, which improves personal performance and empowers teams for excellence. Excellent training fosters superior moral principles, responsibility, and both practical and strategic capabilities. Universities and advisors hold a vital position in promoting these values via focused studies in moral philosophy and civic duty. Executives trained in ethics are more prepared to reconcile public responsibility, environmental viability, and financial gain. This empowers them to resolve conflicts honestly, promoting confidence among interested parties and the community. Moral conduct can be cultivated via education, mentorship, and diverse perspectives.

CONCLUSION

We conclude that the curriculum design and development is the foundation of quality education, contributing a structured framework that nurtures the professional standards and ethical conducts, essential for the students to deal with global challenges. In view of the changing education scenario, conventional teaching is being replaced by student-centred strategies that focuses on hands-on-training experience and distinctive competence. Educational goals are achieved through engaged pedagogy, structured within the framework of the Tyler and Taba curriculum development model. The Viksit Bharat Shiksha Adhishthan Act, 2025 is designed to implement NEP 2020 by replacing UGC and AICTE. These two regulatory bodies assure quality and tech-innovation in higher education institutes. Micro credentials certification requires AI personalization and sustainability education for filling the gap between theoretical education and employability requirement. Quality education is also the foundation for moulding future leaders with critical thinking, moral integrity and instructing them to handle challenges, preparing then for the 2030 Aganda, i.e. 2030 Sustainable Development Goals (SDG-4)

REFERENCES

Adagale, A. S. (2015). Curriculum development in higher education. *International Journal of Applied Research*, *1*(11), 602–605. https://www.allresearchjournal.com/archives/2015/vol1issue11/PartI/1-11-80.pdf

Bhargava, P. (2022, October 20). The increasing importance of micro-credentials on your international college applications. The Economic Times. https://economictimes.indiatimes.com/nri/study/the-increasing-importance-of-micro-credentials-on-your-international-college-applications/articleshow/94989354.cms

Borkar, P. (2023). NEP 2020: New structural changes in curriculum and pedagogy in education. https://www.iitms.co.in/blog/new-structural-changes-in-curriculum-and-pedagogy-in-education.html

Borsatto, J. M. L. S., Marcolin, C. B., Abdalla, E. C., & Amaral, F. D. (2024). Aligning community outreach initiatives with SDGs in a higher education institution with artificial intelligence. *Cleaner and Responsible Consumption*, *12*, 100160. Advance online publication. DOI: 10.1016/j.clrc.2023.100160

Chandel, T. A. (2024). Emerging technology: Present and future generation leadership. In *Impact of new technology on next-generation leadership* (pp. 1–28). IGI Global., DOI: 10.4018/979-8-3693-1946-8.ch001

Chandel, T. A. (2024). Artificial intelligence in the workplace: The future of learning and developments. In *Gaming, wellness, and technology in the bold global workforce* (pp. 203–234). IGI Global., DOI: 10.4018/979-8-3373-5322-7.ch007

Chandel, T. A. (2025). E-collaboration technologies with generative AI tools. In *Humans and generative AI tools for collaborative* (pp. 369–402). IGI Global., DOI: 10.4018/979-8-3693-8332-2.ch016

Coach Space. (2024). The role of the right education in helping leaders succeed. https://thecoachspace.com/blog/role-of-education-in-helping-leaders-succeed/

Drishti, I. A. S. (2026). National credit framework. https://www.drishtiias.com/daily-updates/daily-news-analysis/national-credit-framework-1

edutiip. (2026). Types of regulatory bodies of higher education in India. https://english.edutiips.com/regulatory-bodies-of-higher-education/

Evelyn, L. (2023). Curriculum development models. https://www.evelynlearning.com/blog/curriculum-development-models

Exceed, C. (2025). Types, principles & process of curriculum development. https://exeedcollege.com/blog/principles-and-process-of-curriculum-development/

Forum, I. A. S. (2024, February 5). Micro-credentials and higher education in India. https://forumias.com/blog/micro-credentials-and-higher-education-in-india/

Gaftandzhieva, S., Hussain, S., Hilcenko, S., Doneva, R., & Boykova, K. (2023). Data-driven decision making in higher education institutions: State-of-play. *International Journal of Advanced Computer Science and Applications, 14*(6). Advance online publication. DOI: 10.14569/IJACSA.2023.0140642

Hopping, D. (2025). Digitalisation in sustainable higher education campuses. Sustainability Magazine. https://sustainabilitymag.com/articles/digitalisation-in-sustainable-higher-education-campuses

Huck, C. (2025). How does curriculum development in higher education work? American College of Education. https://ace.edu/blog/how-does-curriculum-development-in-higher-education-work/

IFIM Institute. (2026). How quality education shapes future leaders. https://ifim.edu.in/how-quality-education-shapes-future-leaders/

Ilawagbon, O. (2025). The role of regulatory bodies in sustaining educational development in Nigeria: An assessment of the National Universities Commission. *International Journal of Research and Innovation in Social Science, 9*(4), 2664–2681. DOI: 10.47772/IJRISS.2025.90400198

Jacob, M. (2025). Micro-credentials in Indian higher education institutions. https://ipsrsolutions.com/academix/micro-credentials-in-indian-higher-education-institutions/

Judijanto, L., Jata, W., & Istiarsyah, I. (2025). Evolution of curriculum design approaches in education studies. *The Eastasouth Journal of Learning and Educations, 3*(3), 294–308. DOI: 10.58812/esle.v3i03.801

Jugessur, Y. S. M. F. (2023). Kerr's model of curriculum design and curriculum development in education. *International Journal of Humanities and Social Science Invention, 12*(4), 105–107. DOI: 10.35629/7722-1204105107

Kelly, A. V. (2009). *The curriculum: Theory and practice* (6th ed.). SAGE Publications Ltd.

Kumar, M. J. (2024, February 4). Micro-credentials, the next chapter in higher education. The Hindu. https://www.thehindu.com/opinion/op-ed/micro-credentials-the-next-chapter-in-higher-

Lai, M. K. (2025). *AI-personalised learning in higher education: A study on learning outcomes and motivation among university students*. International Journal of Research and Innovation in Social Science., DOI: 10.47772/IJRISS.2025.905000473

Lyall, A. (2025). Theoretical foundation of curriculum. https://itcollege.ac.in/itdc/assets/images/econtant/Dr-A.Lyl_.pdf

Mahajan, H. (2024). The power of data-driven decision making in higher education. https://www.academiaerp.com/blog/the-power-of-data-driven-decision-making-in-higher-education/

Mayberry, M. (2023, February). You don't need to be "the boss" to be a leader. Harvard Business Review. https://hbr.org/2023/02/you-dont-need-to-be-the-boss-to-be-a-leader

Ministry of Human Resource Development, Government of India. (2020). National education policy 2020. https://www.education.gov.in/sites/upload_files/mhrd/files/NEP_Final_English_0.pdf

Neendoor, S. (2026). 5 popular curriculum development models you should know. https://www.hurix.com/blogs/popular-curriculum-development-models-you-should-know/

Nondumiso Shabangu., & Madondo, N. E. (2024). Addressing graduate unemployment: Aligning higher education curricula with labour market demands. In Proceedings of the Focus Conference (TFC 2024). Atlantis Press. https://doi.org/ DOI: 10.2991/978-94-6463-630-7_5

Parker, J. (2025). Bloom's taxonomy. Center for Teaching Excellence, University of Florida. https://teach.ufl.edu/resource-libraryold/blooms-taxonomy/

Press Information Bureau, Government of India. (2026). AI in education: Building India's talent pipeline for global leadership.

Pressbooks. (2026). Curriculum design, development and models: Planning for student learning. https://oer.pressbooks.pub/curriculumessentials/chapter/curriculum-design-development-and-models-planning-for-student-learning-there-is-always-a-need-for-newly-formulated-curriculum-models-that-address-contemporary-circumstance-an/

Prezi. (2015). Approaches to curriculum design. https://prezi.com/rka1dtoahbpr/approaches-to-curriculum-designing/

Shah, P. J. (2015). Regulatory structure of higher education in India (Working paper). International Growth Centre. https://www.theigc.org/sites/default/files/2015/11/Shah-2015-Working-paper.pdf

Short, E. (2025). Curriculum design, development and models: Planning for student learning. In Curriculum essentials. Pressbooks. https://oer.pressbooks.pub/curriculumessentials/chapter/curriculum-designdevelopment-and-models-planning-for-student-learning-there-is-always-a-need-for-newlyformulated-curriculum-models-that-address-contemporary-circumstance-an/

Shree Adhitya Education. (2026). Shaping the future: How Ministry of Education powers higher education in India. https://touchcampus.in/blog/shaping-the-future-how-the-ministry-of-education-powers-higher-education-in-india

Singh, S. (2024, February 14). Micro credentials: An innovation in Indian higher education institutes.

Team Creatrix. (2026). Bloom's taxonomy: The dean's guide to curriculum design. https://www.creatrixcampus.com/blog/blooms-taxonomy-in-higher-education

Trevisan, L. V., Eustachio, J. H. P. P., Dias, B. G., Filho, W. L., & Pedrozo, E. Á. (2024). Digital transformation towards sustainability in higher education: State-of-the-art and future research insights. *Environmental Science and Pollution Research International*, *26*, 2789–2810.

Vyas, K. (2024). Data-driven decision-making in higher education. https://www.sogolytics.com/blog/data-driven-decisions-higher-education/

Yoshida, H. (2025). Regulatory bodies in higher education. https://www.scribd.com/document/846820711/Regulatory-bodies-in-education

Section 2
Learning Theories and Knowledge Acquisition

Chapter 5
Embedding Learning to Earn Pedagogies in Future-Focused Higher Education: A Conceptual Framework for Strengthening Employability and Work Transition

Preet Kanwal
http://orcid.org/0009-0006-5114-8381
Lovely Professional University, India

Anjali Sharma
http://orcid.org/0000-0002-4497-5489
Lovely Professional University, India

ABSTRACT

The education systems of higher education globally experience the growing pressure to address the continuing mismatch between academic qualifications and the labour market demands. This chapter presents a conceptual framework of integration of learning-to-earn pedagogies, educational strategies that formally integrate academic learning with earning opportunities, into a future-oriented higher education. In the chapter, it determines five fundamental dimensions of such pedagogies including experiential and project-based learning, work-integrated learning, entrepreneurship and innovation, digital and platform-based earning, and community engagement. It follows their conceptual roots in the experiential learning theory, human capital

DOI: 10.4018/979-8-2600-2606-9.ch005

theory, constructivism, and work-integrated learning scholarship. The proposed framework theorizes the curriculum design, institutional strategy, industry collaboration, and student agency as four symbiotic supports that jointly make a dynamic learning bionetwork.

1. INTRODUCTION

The systems of higher education around the world are confronted with a double-edged problem: the quantity of graduates has increased dramatically, and the labour market has become both more challenging at the same time and less predictable. Structural, rather than intermittent, elements of graduate experience are skills incompatibility, underemployment, and the duration of the university-to-work transition in the OECD economies (OECD, 2019; World Economic Forum, 2020). The predictability of linear careers, based on the pattern of skill acquisition, is depreciated by automation, platform economies, gig-based work arrangements, and the foresight of the requirement of graduates with flexibility, entrepreneurial literacy, and the capacity to acquire new skills continuously (Sanyal and Kumar, 2025; Idhalama and Makori, 2024).

Although there is increased awareness of these trends, most institutions of higher learning still view employment as an after-graduation event, and not as an aspect of the learning process. Career services are still fragmented in relation to academic programs, internships and placements are extrinsic and not intrinsic, and evaluation is still based on theoretical reproduction as opposed to applied competence. The consequence of such structural mislike is the production of graduates with credentialled qualifications who are not ready to work in the profession, which brings about dissatisfaction among employers, underemployment among graduates, and irrelevance of the institution in an ever-changing economy (Monteiro et al., 2025; Jackson, 2015).

This gap is filled in this chapter by the creation of an idea to implement learning-to-earn pedagogies in higher education in the future. Learning-to-earn pedagogies are defined as education practices that strategically integrate earning experiences, paid internship, entrepreneurial projects, digital freelancing, consultancy and community enterprise into the formal academic programme in ways that enable students to achieve professional competence and economic agency along with academic qualifications. Unlike traditional employability programs, which superimpose career preparation onto established curricula, learning-to-earn pedagogies re-conceptualize the curriculum as such, as a site of professional practice, and economic interaction.

There are two research objectives in the chapter: (1) to theorize learning-to-earn pedagogies as a coherent and unique pedagogical orientation, based on the well-established educational and economic theory; and (2) to suggest an integrative conceptual framework that outlines how institutions can systematically incorporate these pedagogies in order to enhance graduate employability and facilitate work transition in diverse higher education settings.

The chapter is organized in the following way. Section 2 places the argument in the context of the evolving nature of work and the strains that this exerts on higher education. Section 3 theorizes learning-to-earn pedagogies and their theory. The five fundamental dimensions are given in Section 4. In section 5, the integrative conceptual framework is presented. Section 6 deals with the implementation in different institutional settings. Section 7 talks about critical perspectives and limitations. Section 8 concludes.

2. FUTURE OF WORK AND HIGHER EDUCATION TRANSFORMATION

Three overlapping forces, which include technological disruption, the introduction of flexible employment ecosystems, and the sustainability transition drive the transformation of work in the twenty-first century. Both execute exclusive requirements on graduate groundwork, which traditional higher education models fails to meet.

Occupational landscapes are being reorganized by automation and artificial intelligence, which replaces everyday cognitive and manual work with a higher-order analytical and creative work, and demands more sophisticated analytical and interpersonal skills (Sanyal and Kumar, 2025). It is not a single change but the continuous disruption cycle that makes the acquisition of skills in static form too limited. The higher education implication is that higher education graduates need to acquire the ability to engage in lifelong reskilling, rather than simply the attainment of a technical qualification at graduation (OECD, 2019; Murphy, 2025).

The second structural change is the expansion of platform-based and gig employment (Peng and Mun, 2025; Arora, 2025). The flexible, project-oriented, and freelance employment systems are growing in most sectors virtually. These arrangements provide freedom and access, but also demand that graduates have developed self-management capacity, financial literacy, entrepreneurial orientation, and can develop and sustain professional networks without organizational employment (Gazi et al., 2025). These abilities need to be instilled in students in higher education, rather than presumed to be provided by organizational jobs.

The third driver is sustainability transition-structural change of economic activity forced by climate demands, resource limitations, and demands of social equity (Park & Bishara, 2023). New professional jobs in renewable energy, circular economies, and social entrepreneurship mandate graduates to be technologically competent, morally judgmental, and systems-thinkers. Incorporating sustainability in curricula, however, not solely in specialist courses, is thus an aspect of future-focused employability training (Almasyhari et al., 2025).

The second structural alteration is the extension of gig and platform-based engagement. Over a third of workers in developed economies now perform some type of freelance, contract, or platform-mediated labor (World Economic Forum, 2020). Digital media have enabled people to sell professional services around the world without the need to have an employment relationship, allowing them to diversify their income stream and be flexible in geography. The flexibility, however, has its weaknesses: the instability of incomes, the lack of training funded by the employer, and the necessity to constantly sell professional skills. Graduates who move into gig-related professions requires financial literacy, self-marketing skills, professional portfolio management, and the entrepreneurial resilience to grip uneven earnings streams - skills that traditional degree programs typically teach in a piecemeal manner (Gazi et al., 2025; Peng and Mun, 2025). Without actively developing these abilities, higher education institutions are predisposing students to become casualised by the platform economy, instead of becoming empowered.

The fourth dimension that is influencing the future work is the growing significance of interdisciplinary knowledge and cross-cutting competence. Modern workplaces are defined by issues that cannot be addressed in one area: product design needs technical, aesthetic and commercial expertise, environmental consulting needs scientific, regulatory and communication skills, social enterprise needs business, community development and policy expertise. As it is revealed by Anand and Singh (2025), interdisciplinary learning, organized interaction with problems in disciplinary terms, builds more adaptive competence than instruction in one discipline. Colleges and universities organized around disciplinary silos are graduating students, with knowledge frameworks that are poorly allied with the integrative demands of real-world professional environments.

Graduate employability crisis offers the immediate incentive to learning-to-earn innovation. Employers unswervingly contend that graduates are not work ready, lacks practical skills and the professional attitude required for entry-level roles. The graduates, in turn, oppose that their educational programs have not adequately prepared them for the realities of the professional world (Monteiro et al., 2025; Jackson & Li, 2022).This collective discontent is not the failure of individual performance but rather a case of structural misfit: academic curricula that are best geared towards knowledge delivery, and academic test performance, give rise to graduates who are highly proficient in one form of academic performance, but who have little time to learn the kinds of practical judgment, professional communication, and group problem solving that the working world demands. Instead of creating more vocational in this, more limited, sense of academic programs, that is, replacing theory with technique, the solution is to design the conditions under which theory and practice grow together, each enriching the other, by the deliberate design of the curriculum learning-to-earn.

The institutional strategy inferences are profound. Higher education should also be transformed by a provision logic, whereby, institutions provide standardized academic material and students take it, to an ecosystem logic, where institutions deliver dynamic ecosystems where learning, earning, professional development and civic engagement are reinforcing endeavors. This change is less of a pedagogical change than an architectural one: It demands the reformulation of the structures, incentives, partnerships, and assessment systems in which the students interact with their learning. Collectively, these forces validate a distinguished institutional void. The capability necessities of the current labour market, as Table 1 demonstrates, are suggestively dissimilar to the outputs of outdated degree-based higher education, which creates an environment, where employability-focused education provides a remedial structural reply.

Table 1. Labour Market Demand vs. Conventional Higher Education Output

Dimension	Labour Market Demand	Conventional HE Output
Skills type	Transferable, adaptive, digital	Disciplinary, theoretical
Work model	Flexible, project-based, gig	Preparation for stable employment
Assessment mode	Portfolio, performance, outcomes	Examinations, essays, grades
Earning timing	Concurrent with learning	Post-graduation
Entrepreneurship	Integral competency	Optional add-on
Industry linkage	Embedded in curriculum	Peripheral internships

Source: Authors' synthesis based on OECD (2019), World Economic Forum (2020), and Jackson (2015).

3. THEORIZING LEARNING-TO-EARN PEDAGOGIES

3.1 Definition and distinguishing features

Learning-to-earn pedagogies can be described as purposeful pedagogical approaches that formally incorporate earning opportunities, in whatever form they come, that generate income, professional capital or entrepreneurial experience, into the academic curriculum as a structural component and not an extraneous addition. The difference is that it is simultaneous: the learning and earning are not done in sequence (learning, earning) but simultaneously in the academic program. This coexistence changes the attitude of the student towards his or her own study:

it obtains direct professional sense and economic sense, maintaining the motivation and supporting the topicality of the educational material.

Learning-to-earn is not a completely new idea. Cooperative education models established at the University of Cincinnati in the initial twentieth century, and then protracted to other countries, combined paid work placements as a structural feature, not elective, of academic programs. Work-integrated learning scholarship later evolved a strong evidence base that proved that combined academic-workplace experience is better as compared to academic-only preparation (Billett, 2011; Ferns et al., 2014). In the recent understanding of learning-to-earn pedagogies, the earning modality is extended past the traditional employer placements to include the digital freelancing, platform work, entrepreneurial projects, and community enterprise, which are forms of economic activity that indicate the gig-based, digitally mediated, and socially entrepreneurial nature of the current working life. This broadened understanding makes sure that learning-to-earn models are not obsolete in a labour market that is more and more outside of the conventional employer-employee relationship.

This is a critical variance between learning-to-earn models and traditional work-integrated learning. Work-integrated learning (WIL) programs are usually interruptions of academic learning with formal placements in the workplace. Learning-to-earn pedagogies extend: earning activities are part of the curriculum, graded as academic work and are created to produce simultaneous academic and professional learning outcomes (Koseda et al., 2025). They also expand WIL by including digital and platform-based earning, entrepreneurial ventures, and community enterprise as valid locations of professional learning along with conventional employer placements.

3.2 Theoretical Foundations

There are four convergent theoretical traditions upon which learning-to-earn pedagogies are based. Experiential learning theory, linked with Kolb (1984), is based on the idea that learning is best achieved when it is cycled around the experience of concrete event, reflective observation, abstract conceptualization, and active experimentation. It is precisely these cycles that are offered by learning-to-earn environments: students get to participate in real professional activity, reflect on their performance, abstract principles, and apply them in the next round. Such cyclical design enriches the learning process, going beyond the passive reception of knowledge. Human capital theory (Becker, 1993) establishes the conceptual link between learning-to-earn pedagogies and economic outcomes. Training and education enhance personal productivity, income-earning power, and financial stability. Institutions are able to create human capital more effectively by integrating earning into the learning process than sequential degree-then-employment models, and can transfer those advantages to economically disadvantaged students who cannot meet the temporal and financial cost of the unpaid post-graduation skill development.

Constructivist theory of learning (Dewey, 1938) is based on the idea that knowledge is constructed in the process of meaningful interaction with problems in real-life situations. This constitutes a radical shift in the model of transmission that structures much traditional higher education: instead of absorbing knowledge via authoritative sources and regurgitating it in tests, learners in constructivist contexts build up knowledge by disciplined inquiry into real problems that lack predetermined solutions. These have far-reaching implications on assessment- when knowledge is constructed through participation in real problems, then assessment of learning should measure the quality of that participation and the learning that it produces, rather than the learning that is produced by information received. Learning-to-earn pedagogies adopt this constructivist logic of assessment: professional project deliverables, reflective journals, portfolio assessments substitute or supplement traditional exams, and the quality of professional performance is an academically valid kind of evidence.

According to constructivist learning theory (Dewey, 1938), the process of knowledge construction is based on the active involvement in the process of meaningful problems in real-life situations. Learning-to-earn environments offer the real worlds of professional work which constructivism recommends: Learning-to-earn environments offer the real worlds of professional work which constructivism recommends: students learn by doing the work of the profession, not by receiving information about it. Anand and Singh (2025) develop this point in interdisciplinary settings, showing that knowledge built across disciplinary boundaries, as is typically needed in learning-to-earn programs, results in adaptive competence, compared to single-discipline learning.

The graduate career management skills framework offered by Bridgstock (2009) contributes an additional theoretical level, defining the meta-competencies that allow graduates to take charge of their careers throughout a life of lifelong change: career self-management, professional networking and the orientation to continuous learning. These meta-competencies cannot be developed merely by studying academic material; they have to be exercised in the real life of the professional situations as time goes. The learning-to-earn pedagogies are in a unique position to teach career management skills since they entail students undertaking exactly the kinds of activities, such as professional networking, work performance, self-marketing, feedback management, where such skills are constructed. The career management competence in a graduate who has gone through three professional earning experiences in the course of his undergraduate study cannot be matched by a graduate who has gone through the career management theory but never exercised it.

The empirical and practical basis of the institutionalisation of learning-to-earn approaches is the work-integrated learning scholarship (Billett, 2011; Ferns et al., 2014; Jackson, 2015). Decades of WIL research establish that systematic combination of workplace and academic learning produces greater effects of employability than do academic-only preparation and the institutional contexts in which such combination succeeds through alignment of curricula, training of mentors, reflection, and industrial collaboration.

The fifth theory tradition pertinent is the graduate capital model put forward by Tomlinson (2017), which theorizes graduate employability as the stocking of various types of capital, including human capital (skills and knowledge), social capital (professional networks), cultural capital (professional norms and identity), psychological capital (confidence and resilience), and identity capital (a coherent professional self-concept). It is an especially helpful framework to design learning-to-earn pedagogy, since it clarifies that employability cannot be distilled to skill acquisition: graduates with technical skills who have not achieved the network capital, cultural literacy, and professional identity that perpetuate employability will not succeed in labour markets increasingly discriminating on cultural fit and professional confidence as well as on technical expertise. When properly designed, learning-to-earn pedagogies build all five kinds of capital concomitantly: human capital in the form of project-based learning, social capital in the form of industry experience and peer learning, cultural capital in the form of socialization into professional worlds, psychological capital in the form of the experience of overcoming professional challenges, and identity capital in the form of progressive development of a professional self-concept based on real achievement as opposed to The four theoretical traditions collectively lead to a basic argument, namely that the best way to prepare to live professionally is to base learning on meaningful, authentic practice with an economic dimension and not to precede such practice. These convergence models are operationalized in learning-to-earn pedagogies that structure the academic programs in a way that the professional practice including the economic activity that it produces are not an outcome that comes after the completion of the academic programs. The conceptual consistency of this methodology in the experiential, economic, constructivist, and work-integrated traditions offers a solid foundation to institutional advocacy and program design.

4. MAINSTREAMS OF LEARNING-TO-EARN PEDAGOGIES

Learning-to-earn pedagogies are poly dimensional. A learning-to-earn curriculum ecosystem encompasses in one or more core dimensions summarized in Table 2.

Table 2. Core Dimensions of Learning-to-Earn Pedagogies

Dimension	Description	Example Institutional Activity
Experiential & project-based learning	Real-world problems as curriculum content; paid consultancy and design work	Paid industry client projects embedded in course assessments
Work-integrated learning	Formal academic–workplace integration; internships, apprenticeships, co-op education	Assessed paid internship with reflective academic portfolio
Entrepreneurship & innovation	Startup incubation, enterprise development; entrepreneurial skills curriculum	University incubator with course credit for startup development
Digital & platform earning	Freelancing, e-commerce, digital content; online professional identity	Supervised digital freelancing projects linked to program learning outcomes
Community & social enterprise	Community-based projects; social ventures; civic earning	Community organization partnerships generating co-designed services

Source: Authors' synthesis.

Learning-to-earn embedding has the least institutionally accessible entry point of the experiential and project-based learning dimension since real-world projects can be commissioned to local businesses, non-governmental organizations or public sector bodies on relatively modest or no-cost terms, and the value exchange is professional work done by students in exchange of real problems and real feedback. The challenge in pedagogical design is to make the projects challenging and open-ended enough to involve the use of authentic professional judgment, not only task performance, and to have systematic processes of reflection, so that the students can draw transferable learning out of local project experiences. Evaluation of project-based earning work should consider both quality of the deliverable (professional standard) and quality of the learning (academic standard) which entails faculty gaining new assessment competencies in addition to new facilitation skills.

The work-integrated learning dimension, which includes formal internships, apprenticeships, and cooperative education arrangements, has the strongest evidence base and the most well-developed institutional infrastructure (Billett, 2011; Ferns et al., 2014). The learning-to-earn embedding challenge is to make placements truly earning experiences: that students are justly remunerated in their work, that quality of placements is observed and controlled as opposed to being assumed, and that academic integration of workplace learning- through reflective journals, workplace mentor appraisal and submission of academic portfolios- ensures that professional experience produces academic learning instead of just an employment entry on the resume of a student. The institutions need to invest in placement officer capacity, mentor training and academic as well as industry communication systems to ensure the quality and equity of work-integrated learning aspects of learning-to-earn programs.

There are institutional enablers necessary in each dimension. Learning through experience and projects necessitates faculty training in facilitative pedagogy and management of relationships with the industry. Work integrated learning involves formal partnership agreements, training of mentors and structures of academic credit of workplace learning. Entrepreneurship and innovation ecosystems demand physical and digital infrastructure, such as incubators, seed funding, legal and accounting assistance, and curricula that cultivate opportunity recognition, risk management, and venture development. Online and platform-based income demands that institutions make technology accessible, train on digital literacy and guide on exposure to online professional markets. The community engagement and social enterprise demand community development relationships, social impact assessment frameworks and combination of civic education and professional development.

The community engagement and social enterprise aspect is an under-exploited area of learning-to-earn opportunity that should be given special attention. Combining the earning aspect (revenue-generating activity) with the civic aspect (social purpose) in such a way that is highly appealing to the values orientation of modern graduates, many of whom are driven by purpose rather than income, social enterprise organizations that achieve their social or environmental goals by commercial activity are particularly attractive to the values orientation of the modern graduate. The unique strengths of universities in social enterprise creation are that they are closer to communities, convening, and because they can bring students of various disciplines together to solve complex social issues. Students can be exposed to truly complex professional problems of market analysis, stakeholder management, financial planning, impact measurement, in social enterprise projects integrated into academic programs, and it can create economic and social value to communities that would otherwise have no access to professional expertise. In this aspect, the learning-to-earn model is multifaceted in that it deals with graduate employability, community development, and the civic mission of higher education simultaneously.

The dimensions are not exclusive of one another but complementary. The experience of an experiential learning project can result in an internship, and this can prompt entrepreneurial aspirations or digital freelance work, which subsequently can be developed into community enterprise. The most extensive and sustainable employability outcomes are produced in institutions that plan their learning-to-earn ecosystems to support these transitions, and not to see each dimension as a program on its own. The most intricate institutional applications apply a scaffolded approach: first-year students participate mostly in experiential learning and structured peer and industry mentoring; second-year students undertake the work-integrated learning placements and introductory entrepreneurship courses; third and final-year students are offered an option to create digital earning portfolios, start social enterprises, or take up advanced industry placements. This is a staged method of acquiring competence in the profession through progressively retaining academic rigor throughout the stages.

5. AN INTEGRATIVE CONCEPTUAL FRAMEWORK

5.1 Framework Overview

The conceptual framework suggested in the chapter structures the embedding of the learning-to-earn pedagogies in four mutually reinforcing parts and is based on the theoretical underpinnings and core dimensions developed in the previous sections. The framework is integrative in both senses: it brings together the knowledge of the organizational theory, educational psychology, labour economics, and institutional management; and it brings together the various levels, such as individual student, classroom, department, institution, industry, and policy, at which learning-to-earn embedding needs to be undertaken simultaneously to be sustainable and equitable. It is also contextual in nature: the framework does not dictate the particular institutional form but offers an architectural framework that institutions can tailor to their particular resources, partnerships, student bodies, and strategic priorities without violating the main design principles.

The theoretical framework suggested by this chapter systematizes the incorporation of learning-to-earn pedagogies in four mutually supportive elements; Curriculum Integration, Institutional Strategy, Industry and Community Engagement, and Student Agency. The Figure 1 shows the structure and relations of these components.

Figure 1. Integrative Conceptual Framework for Learning-to-Earn Pedagogies

CURRICULUM INTEGRATION	**INSTITUTIONAL STRATEGY**
Experiential learning · WIL · Entrepreneurship · Digital earning · Community enterprise	Leadership · Policy alignment · Faculty development · Infrastructure
INDUSTRY & COMMUNITY ENGAGEMENT	**STUDENT AGENCY**
Curriculum co-design · Placements · Mentorship · Social enterprise	Autonomy · Entrepreneurial identity · Reflective practice · Economic confidence
OUTCOMES: Enhanced Employability · Smoother Work Transition · Economic Inclusion · Graduate Resilience	

Note: Arrows between components represent continuous feedback loops. Outcomes feed back into curriculum and strategy revision.

5.2 Component Descriptions

Three design principles distinguish the framework as compared to the current models of employability enhancement. To begin with, integration and not supplementation: the earning activities are not an extracurricular addition to the formal curriculum, but a subject of academic credit. Second, a concurrence and not a sequence: professional earning is not a transition after graduation, but a co-occurring activity with academic study during the program. Third, reflexivity instead of passivity: students are supposed to do structured critical reflection about their earning experiences as an academic work and create learning out of practice, rather than simply accrue practice hours. These three principles make learning-to-earn ecosystems unique to traditional internship programs, career fairs, and employability skills modules that maintain the degree-first, employment-second order of sequence.

The frame work is operationalized by Curriculum Integration. It mandates that earning opportunities be institutionally infused in academic curricula, not provided as an extracurricular option, and with specific credit, evaluation, and reflective learning demands. Redesign of assessment is essential: traditional tests should be accompanied by portfolio assessment, work-industry-evaluated project work, reflective journals that reflect professional learning and the academic content (Knight and Yorke, 2003; Yorke, 2006).

Curriculum Integration is made sustainable through the conditions of Institutional Strategy. This amalgamation, involve leadership perseverance to employability as a tactical objective, policy frameworks that enable the design of flexible curriculum, faculty development initiatives that create capacity towards project-based and industry-facing pedagogics, and infrastructure investment in innovation labs, digital platforms, and career mentoring systems. The absence of leadership alignment makes learning-to-earn initiatives pilot programs that do not scale (Fullan, 2016; Kezar and Eckel, 2002).

The external aspect of the framework is Industry and Community Engagement. Sustainable learning-to-earn models use formal, two-way collaborations with employers, start-ups, social enterprises and community organizations. These associations offer the practical projects, mentors, placement, and employment opportunities that make the curriculum practical. Co-designing curriculum with industry guarantees that academic programs will be dynamically aligned to the ever-changing workforce needs and not as a reaction to the previous skills demand (Tomlinson, 2017; Jackson, 2015).

The motivational and affective aspect of the framework is Student Agency. When students are active participants in their learning and earning pathways as opposed to passive consumers of institutional provision, learning-to-earn pedagogies work best. Growing entrepreneurial identity, financial literacy, professional self-confidence and technical skills can help graduates to overcome career uncertainty in a resilient way (Yorke and Knight, 2006). The agentic alignments shaped by mentoring, peer learning societies, and structured echo practices are what enable employability to be maintained throughout a career, not just in graduate labor market.

These four ingredients will be weighted differently depending on institutional setting, student body and discipline. Student agency and industry participation in entrepreneurially oriented business programs may be the prevailing elements, curriculum integration with formal work-integrated learning requirements in professionally regulated sectors like law, medicine, or engineering, and community and social enterprise in community-engaged liberal arts institutions may be the primary earning context. The framework itself is not prescriptive regarding the most prominent components, but regarding the necessity of having all of the four components and the necessity of their mutual support. An institution that creates good industry relationships, but does not create student agency will generate graduates who can work in settings that they have been exposed to, but have, in terms of career sustainability, over a lifetime, no adaptive resilience. A school developing good student agency by educating about entrepreneurship will not have any real industry involvement and will end up with students with entrepreneurial confidence and little knowledge of the market to apply that confidence to real economic activity.

The four components work in continuous feedback loops which are equally significant as the components. The student experiences of industry partnerships produce insights that inform curriculum revision; curriculum revision informs the type of industry engagement desired; better institutional strategy makes the conditions of stronger student agency; and student agency produces entrepreneurial and professional outcomes that create the conditions of new industry partners. This is what makes the difference between a dynamic learning-to-earn ecosystem and an unresponsive program: the former becomes more refined as it goes on with the information that it generates, whereas the latter provides a fixed experience no matter the circumstances. Institutions thus need to invest in the initial design of every component, but in the governance and communication systems that ensure feedback loops are both active and responsive.

5.3 Implementation Pathway

An effective implementation of the learning-to-earn framework must take into consideration the sequencing and interdependence of the four elements of the framework. Those institutions that fail to establish sufficient infrastructure, develop partnerships and prepare faculty before introducing all four components of the framework often end up with piecemeal programs that do not last long and create frustration on the part of the students and resistance to change on the part of the faculty instead of the transformative results that the framework promises. The recommended pathway of phased implementation suggested here will be aimed at developing institutional capacity gradually, establishing initial evidence of value that will sustain leadership commitment, and the environment that will allow the full-scale embedding before it requires full-scale investment.

This can be applied to institutions in phases. Phase 1 (Assessment and Design) encompasses auditing current curricula, partnerships and student support systems to find points of integration and gaps in resources. Phase 2 (Pilot Implementation) integrates learning-to-earn elements in chosen courses or departments, where there is a strong assessment and student feedback in place. Phase 3 (Institutionalization and Scaling) institutionalizes successful pilots, with policy reform, revision of strategic plan, and resource reallocation. Adaptive improvement throughout all the phases is ensured by continuous monitoring, with the help of indicators described in Table 3.

Table 3. Monitoring and Evaluation Indicators for Learning-to-Earn Programs

Indicator Category	Sample Measures	Data Source
Participation	% students in earning activities; earning type distribution	Institutional records
Skill acquisition	Self-reported competency gains; employer assessments	Surveys; placement feedback
Employment outcomes	Graduate employment rate; time-to-employment; job relevance	Graduate destination surveys
Income generation	Average student earnings during study; financial self-sufficiency	Student financial records
Equity	Participation rates by socio-economic background, gender, location	Disaggregated institutional data
Student wellbeing	Academic-work balance; stress levels; dropout rates	Student wellbeing surveys

Source: Authors' synthesis.

The monitoring framework Table 3 is developed with the following dual purpose: accountability (proving the value of the program to institutional leaders, funders, and accreditors) and improvement (discovering which practices and conditions produce the most significant results with the greatest variety of students). The equity indicator category is especially important: the aggregate employment rate data may be misleading to hide high inequalities in the outcomes based on student background, gender, or location that will show that learning-to-earn benefits are not being fairly distributed. By disaggregating all outcome indicators based on student demographic characteristics, since the start of the program implementation, the institution will be able to detect and intervene on equity gaps before they become ingrained elements of program design.

6. APPLICATION IN A VARIETY OF INSTITUTIONAL SETTINGS

Learning-to-earn pedagogies are systematically applicable to different institutions, geographic locations, and socio-economic settings. It must be context-sensitive: one model cannot be completely generalized without taking into consideration the unique opportunities and limitations of any given institutional context.

Large, socio-economically diverse student populations in public universities can use scale to develop wide-ranging community partnerships and government-funded internship programs. The difficulty is in the regulatory restrictions and bureaucracy that restricts curricular flexibility. Institutional leaders usually need to advocate strategically in order to gain the support of the policy and safe curriculum space by framing learning-to-earn initiatives as equity and retention interventions (Tilak, 2015; McCowan, 2016).

More commonly in private institutions, the curriculums are more autonomous and better-established relationships within an industry, which can allow the quicker implementation of employer-co-designed programs. The equity risk is that commercially oriented learning-to-earn models might prefer students who already have a professional or financial means to have access to opportunities offered without pay or low pay. Learning-to-earn initiatives should be designed to be inclusive and financial support, mentoring, and program design must be entrenched in institutions (Johnstone and Marcucci, 2010).

The geographically distant and rural institutions have infrastructure limitations, poor local industry presence, and professional networks. Nevertheless, there are also some unique opportunities in these settings: community-based enterprise, local economic development partnerships, agricultural and environmental entrepreneurship, and digital freelancing, which does not depend on geographical restrictions. Rural students can contribute to global earning ecosystems without having to move to urban areas through digital platforms, and local partnerships can produce locally embedded learning-to-earn experiences that cannot be recreated by urban institutions (Roberts and Green, 2013; Hodgkinson-Williams and Trotter, 2018).

In economies with high graduate unemployment, in particular developing ones, the learning-to-earn pedagogies can offer a huge potential to broaden graduate economic opportunities by means of entrepreneurship, involvement in informal economy, and earning via platforms (International Labour Organization, 2020). The limitations that appear critical are digital infrastructure disconnects, insufficient institutional capacity, and inadequate links between industry and academic. Enabling conditions (international collaboration, open educational resources, and government funding of digital infrastructure) can be provided in ways that institutions in developing settings cannot provide in isolation (Van Dijk, 2020).

Practical guidance is provided by the experience of successful attempts by institutions to implement learning-to-earn approaches. Cities with well-established industry city relationships: technology hubs, financial centres, creative districts can use their proximity to create dense networks of micro-placement and consultancy opportunities so that students in any programme can have access to professional earning contexts without necessarily taking formal semester-long placements. Social enterprise ecosystems provide institutions with an opportunity to co-design service-learning programs with community organizations that will both generate income to students and social value to communities. With good alumni networks, institutions can establish a formal mentoring and micro-commissioning relationship where alumni contract student work on commercially viable projects, and integrate mentoring with actual professional experience. The common characteristic of these various models is that an institutional decision was made to make earning a curriculum feature instead of a student initiative, in other words, eliminating the inequalities of access that would otherwise substitute when only well-networked or highly motivated students discover their own careers.

Policy alignment is an essential enabling condition in all institutional settings. The accreditation models that accept only the traditional credit-based academic activities can have to be changed to include the experiential earning credits. The quality assurance systems need to establish evaluation procedures of professional and entrepreneurial learning that are in addition to the current academic quality systems. Models of funding that incentivize graduation rates and research output and do not incentivize graduate employment outcomes or quality of professional development present perverse incentives that deter learning-to-earn integration. Policymakers nationally and regionally concerned about graduate employability should thus consider the regulatory and funding framework of higher education in such a way that it facilitates and does not hinder the institutional transformation that learning-to-earn embedding necessitates.

Systems of support of students have to be re-engineered to follow learning-to-earn embedding. Traditional academic advising based on course choice and graduation criteria is ineffective with students who have the added complexity of working concurrently. Advisors will need to build an ability to assist professional decision-making, work-study balance, and career-trajectory planning with academic advice. The support mechanism that is most cost-effective: peer mentoring by more senior students who have already successfully completed learning-to-earn combinations: peer mentoring is able to offer role modelling, pragmatic advice, and social demonstration that concurrent learning and earning is a viable student activity, which first-generation students will find especially useful since their family has no experience of professional work as a student activity. Mental health and wellbeing services should also be sensitive to the extra demands that learning-to-earn participation can create, especially in programs where earning is required as opposed to voluntary and in which failure to get professional offerings may create academic disadvantage.

Micro-level capacity and motivation of the faculty are equally important. Implementing learning-to-earn pedagogies necessitates faculty to acquire new skills, such as managing relationships in industry, facilitating projects, mentoring entrepreneurs, and literate in digital platforms, which they are not usually taught in their own academic degree programs. These competencies can be developed through professional development programs, industry secondments and collaborative curriculum design processes but only to the extent that institutional incentive structures appreciate them. Faculty will logically devote their discretionary time to research, where the promotion and recognition systems are based on research productivity rather than on teaching and industry involvement. The leaders of the institutions should thus make sure that learning-to-earn engagement is directly identified in the appraisal, promotion and rewards system not as a supplementary expectation but as a prized and appreciated aspect of academic professional identity.

7. CRITICAL APPROACHES AND SHORTCOMINGS

The limitations and risks of learning-to-earn pedagogies need to be engaged with, as well as their potential, to warrant a comprehensive assessment. There are three important issues which should be mentioned. To start with, labor exploitation is a threat. In the context of earning experiences as part of academic programs, the power imbalance between students (who must work and get the experience) and employers or clients (who get the work) can lead to an unpaid or low-paid work in the name of educational experience. It is the moral responsibility of institutions to make sure that the earning activities comply with fair labor practices, that the students are not exploited as a source of inexpensive professional labor and that the commercial value created by the student work is fairly distributed. The minimum is strong institutional control, partnership policies in the industry that outline equitable pay, and student involvement in program management.

The conflict between democratizing learning-to-earn potential and its equity risks is especially acute in the aspect of digital earning. Freelancing on a platform provides a global access to professional marketplaces to scholars who are economically or geographically deprived without the need to physically travel or be funded by an employer. In a developing economy, a country-based, rural student with good digital abilities can develop an international client base through freelancing sites in ways that would have been unattainable in a pre-digital economy. Nonetheless, it is also important that digital earning needs a good internet connection, proper equipment, digital literacy and cultural trust to work in global professional markets, which are not equally distributed among the student populations that most need the economic opportunities of learning-to-earn engagement. Those institutions that establish digital earning aspects of learning-to-earn programs without providing equitable access to the facilitating conditions will discover that it is their most privileged students who will gain most by these programs, the very last thing they set out to do.

Second, educational and commercial goals are in structural struggle. When learning-to-earn programs are highly motivated by industry needs, there is a threat that the curricula will become highly vocational at the cost of critical thinking, civic education, and intellectual breadth. Learning-to-earn pedagogies should be conceptualized within a comprehensive vision of the purposes of higher education the production of critical, ethical, democratically engaged citizens as well as employable workers rather than merely as a supply chain to industry labor needs (Marginson, 2016; Kucukuncular, 2026).

Third, the design of the programs does not guarantee equity of access to earning opportunity. Students with disadvantaged socio-economic background, students with disabilities, students with care giving commitments, and students in poorly connected locations might have structural barriers to their participation in learning-to-earn programs that institutions ought to address proactively through offering financial support, flexible working hours, distance learning, and special mentoring. Learning-to-earn programs without intentional equity structure will recreate and magnify the professional network benefits of already-privileged students (Doyle, 2011; Chesters, 2020).

There is a certain equity issue in the evaluation of learning-to-earn experiences. The assessment of professional earning activities as academic work provides an intrinsic assessment advantage to students who obtain high-quality, well-mentored placements in high-profile organizations in contrast to students whose earning prospects are less high-profile or not as well-supported. Institutions need to create evaluation systems that measure the quality of student learning and student reflection instead of the status of the earning context- so that a student who learns and earns in a community organization does not face systematic disadvantage when compared to a student who learns and earns in a multinational corporation. This necessitates the creation of subtle professional judgment of learning quality in a variety of earning contexts by faculty assessors aided by explicit assessment rubrics and moderation procedures. Learning-to-earn Assessment equity is not just an equity issue but an integrity issue: it is whether outcomes of such a program truly represent the quality of student learning or whether they simply represent the quality of student access to prestigious opportunities.

A fourth limitation is related to the outcome measurements. Learning-to-earn pedagogies produce learning outcomes that are intricate, multiple-dimensional and hard to quantify using traditional academic evaluation. The most evident results are employment rates and income generation which do not capture all the benefits of professional identity formation, network capital formation, entrepreneurial orientation and capacity to engage in civic activities that well-designed learning-to-earn programs can produce. To prove the worth of these programs to accreditors, funders, and policymakers, institutions need multi-method evaluation frameworks, such as quantitative outcome tracking and qualitative measures of professional development and student agency. Table 3 shows the monitoring indicators that are a starting point of such frameworks, and institutional research capacity should be dedicated towards the development and validation of these methods in different contexts.

Such constraints do not invalidate the argument of learning-to-earn pedagogies; they outline the circumstances in which the argument can be put forward in a responsible manner. To be implemented effectively, it is critical that institutions should not treat these programs as market-responsiveness mechanisms, but as equity and quality interventions, which are open to the same ethical and evaluative scrutiny as any other aspect of academic provision. The question of whether learning-to-earn is a way to democratize the experience of professional life and whether it entails the danger of perpetuating existing disparities by offering unequal opportunities is, after all, a question of political and organizational, rather than pedagogical, concern. It must be resolved through an institutional governance that is both equity aware and evidence-based and dedicated to the educational, not just the commercial aspects of the learning-to-earn business.

8. CONCLUSION

The swing of higher education to learning-to-earn models is not purely a change of pedagogical direction. It is a re-conceptualization of the purpose and social contract of universities and colleges in the twenty-first century. When higher education is interpreted as delivery of disciplinary knowledge, employability is consequent and can be met by career services on the periphery. However, when higher education is perceived as the production of competent, self-confident, economically independent individuals who are able to negotiate in a multifaceted and fast-evolving society, then the merging of learning and earning is not an appendage that can be added to the institution but a fundamental institutional task. The operational manifestation of this reconceptualization are learning-to-earn pedagogies: that place the professional world inside the academic one; not in concession to the market, but as an acknowledgement that the lives of graduates are lived in the professional world and that training them to live well in that professional world is an irreducibly educational goal.

The chapter has created a conceptual framework of integrating learning-to-earn pedagogies in the future-oriented higher education systems. It has theorized that the modern labour market, that is technically disruptive, platform-based, and driven by sustainability desires, requires a structural re-conception of the connection between higher education and employment, not as a sequence (education, then work), but as a simultaneity (learning through earning).

The suggested model incorporates four components that are reinforcing, such as curriculum integration, institutional strategy, industry and community engagement, and student agency, into a dynamic learning ecosystem that builds academic competency, professional identity, and economic capability simultaneously. This ecosystem is practically implemented through the five central dimensions of learning-to-earn pedagogies (experiential learning, work-integrated learning, entrepreneurship, digital earning, and community enterprise) that offer the practical content of this ecosystem in various institutional contexts.

It has also critically discussed the dangers and limits of learning-to-earn strategies, which encompasses labor abuse, curriculum watering down, equity design and complexity of measuring, and asserted that active institutional governance, equity design and ongoing monitoring with authenticated outcome pointers are needed to carry out such strategies responsibly. Unless these dimensions are given attention, the learning-to-earn programs will end up being labor market commodification tools as opposed to educational transformation tools. The skepticism expressed in Section 7 is not an injunction against education as a means to make a living but a narrowing down of the circumstances in which these pedagogies will be effective instead of reproducing the inequalities they are intended to combat. Those institutions that are serious about such conditions, that develop strong governance, authentic equity design and deep assessment into their learning-to-earn programs at the beginning, are doing truly transformative educational practice.

The chapter contributions are primarily conceptual and normative. Empirical research into the future should test the framework by using longitudinal institutional research, cross-context comparative studies and qualitative study of the lived experience of learning-to-earn participation, by students themselves. Studies that trace the long-term career paths of learning-to-earn graduates versus those with conventional programs, adjusting (or conditioning) on institutional type and student background are particularly and especially desired. The analytical policy of the regulatory and funding contexts that facilitate or limit institutional adoption in various national systems such as accreditation reform, quality assurance adaptation, and revision of the funding model would also contribute greatly to the field. To make sure that these pedagogies serve their democratizing purpose instead of reproducing existing educational inequalities, research on the equity effects of programs to learn to earn, including tracking the disparities in participation and benefit across socio-economic backgrounds, gender, disability status and geographic location, is crucial. The outline suggests the conceptual framework within the context of which such work on experience and policy can be developed productively.

It is also notable that learning-to-earn pedagogies are not. Neither of them is a privatization of higher education nor a resignation of its academic freedom to the market. They do not assert that learning must be economically productive, or that the humanities, the arts, and the pure sciences must not be included in future-oriented curricula. They are not an assurance that all students who work to study will graduate to gain high paying and professionally fulfilling jobs. They are an acknowledgment that the better equipped graduates who have engaged in some professional work in the course of their academic formation are than their less engaged counterparts; and that the preparation advantage is presently uneven, with those with social capital and access to financial resources benefiting more than those without. In this less ambitious, yet more justifiable assertion, learning-to-earn pedagogies are a valuable and viable addition to a more equitable and more effective system of higher education.

The expediency of this change cannot be overestimated. At a time when automation is reshaping the occupational terrain, platform economies are increasing the variety of forms of work graduates need to move through, and sustainability demands are establishing new professional practices and eliminating old ones, institutions of higher education that are still structured around the sharing of proven disciplinary knowledge are not just failing their students—they are becoming unnecessary to the societies that support them and fund them. Issues around whether learning to earn transformation is desirable or not are irrelevant but rather whether institutions have the leadership aspiration, policy support and organizational capability to do so at the magnitude and rate at which the labour market is changing.

Its practical meaning is obvious: graduate employability cannot be realized by institutions of higher learning that make it a priority but only use superficial career services or extracurricular activities that are optional. A systemic implementation of earning opportunities into the academic curriculum, coupled with institutional strategy, industry partnership, and student agency development, is the key to sustainable, equitable increase in graduate employment outcomes, and a true learning-to-earn ecosystem. This chapter provides a logical, evidence-based basis of that change in the form of the model.

REFERENCES

Almasyhari, A. K., Rachmadani, W. S., Sari, Y. P., & Basrowi, . (2025). Strategic decision-making: Linking corporate choices, social responsibility, and environmental accounting in waste management. *Social Sciences & Humanities Open*, *11*, 101404. DOI: 10.1016/j.ssaho.2025.101404

Anand, A., & Singh, P. (2025). Interdisciplinary studies: Issues, perspectives, and challenges from National Education Program 2020. In *Integrating personalized learning methods into STEAM education* (pp. 233–260). IGI Global. DOI: 10.4018/979-8-3693-7718-5.ch011

Arora, V. (2025). Shifting employment paradigms: Role of the gig economy in transforming traditional jobs. *Indian Journal of Accounting*, *57*(1), 38–50. DOI: 10.63637/ija.v57i1.38-50

Becker, G. S. (1993). *The economic way of looking at life* [Nobel Prize lecture]. University of Chicago.

Billett, S. (2011). Integrating experiences in workplace and university settings: A conceptual perspective. In *Developing learning professionals: Integrating experiences in university and practice settings* (pp. 21–40). Springer. DOI: 10.1007/978-90-481-3937-8_2

Bridgstock, R. (2009). The graduate attributes we've overlooked: Enhancing graduate employability through career management skills. *Higher Education Research & Development*, *28*(1), 31–44. DOI: 10.1080/07294360802444347

Chesters, J. (2020). Preparing for successful transitions between education and employment in the twenty-first century. *Journal of Applied Youth Studies*, *3*(2), 133–151. DOI: 10.1007/s43151-020-00002-8

Dewey, J. (1938). *Experience and education*. Macmillan.

Doyle, E. (2011). Career development needs of low socio-economic status university students. *Australian Journal of Career Development*, *20*(3), 56–65. DOI: 10.1177/103841621102000309

European Commission. (2020). *A new skills agenda for Europe*. Publications Office of the European Union.

Ferns, S., Campbell, M., & Zegwaard, K. E. (2014). *Work integrated learning. Higher Education Research and Development Society of Australia*. HERDSA Inc.

Fullan, M. (2016). *The new meaning of educational change* (5th ed.). Teachers College Press.

Gazi, M. A. I., Mim, A. T., Masud, A. A., Rahman, M. K. H., Amin, M. B., Senathirajah, A. R. B. S., & Oláh, J. (2025). Paving the way of entrepreneurship for university students: The role of innovativeness, technological adaptability, and self-management. *Cogent Education, 12*(1), 2455230. Advance online publication. DOI: 10.1080/2331186X.2025.2455230

Hodgkinson-Williams, C., & Trotter, H. (2018). A social justice framework for understanding open educational resources and practices in the global south. *Journal of Learning for Development*, *5*(3), 204–224. DOI: 10.56059/jl4d.v5i3.312

Idhalama, O. U., & Makori, E. O. (2024). Artificial intelligence, deep learning, machine learning, robotics and digital transformation: Applications, implications and future. *Ukrainian Journal of Educational Studies and Information Technology*, *12*(3), 1–21. DOI: 10.32919/uesit.2024.03.01

International Labour Organization. (2020). *Global employment trends for youth 2020*. ILO.

Jackson, D. (2015). Employability skill development in work-integrated learning: Barriers and best practice. *Studies in Higher Education*, *40*(2), 350–372. DOI: 10.1080/03075079.2013.842221

Jackson, D., & Li, I. (2022). Transition to work, mismatch and underemployment among graduates: An Australian longitudinal study. *International Journal of Manpower*, *43*(7), 1516–1539. DOI: 10.1108/IJM-03-2021-0195

Kezar, A., & Eckel, P. D. (2002). The effect of institutional culture on change strategies in higher education. *The Journal of Higher Education*, *73*(4), 435–460. DOI: 10.1080/00221546.2002.11777159

Knight, P. T., & Yorke, M. (2003). *Assessment, learning and employability*. Open University Press.

Kolb, D. A. (1984). *Experiential learning: Experience as the source of learning and development*. Prentice-Hall.

Koseda, E., Cohen, I. K., Cooper, J., & McIntosh, B. (2025). Embedding employability into curriculum design: The impact of education 4.0. *Policy Futures in Education*, *23*(3), 676–688. DOI: 10.1177/14782103241282121

Küçükuncular, A. (2026). Dehumanising education: AI and the capitalist capture of teaching. *AI and Ethics*, *6*(1), 123. DOI: 10.1007/s43681-026-01006-5

Marginson, S. (2016). *Higher education and the common good.* Melbourne University Publishing.

McCowan, T. (2016). Universities and the post-2015 development agenda: An analytical framework. *Higher Education, 72*(4), 505–523. DOI: 10.1007/s10734-016-0035-7

Monteiro, S., Santos, S., Teixeira, J. N., Torres, L., & Palhares, J. (2025). Determinants of higher education graduates' employability: A scoping review. *Education + Training, 67*(1), 56–74. DOI: 10.1108/ET-04-2024-0190

Murphy, L. (2025). The productivity dilemma: Examining the truth behind automation's impact on employment. *The International Journal of Organizational Analysis, 33*(3), 622–644. DOI: 10.1108/IJOA-04-2024-4430

OECD. (2019). *OECD future of education and skills 2030: Conceptual learning framework.* OECD Publishing.

Park, S. K., & Bishara, N. D. (2023). Climate change and a just transition to the future of work. *American Business Law Journal, 60*(4), 701–748. DOI: 10.1111/ablj.12235

Peng, L. M., & Mun, B. W. K. (2025). Understanding gig work in paving towards gig economy sustainability: Insights from platform-based companies. *Malaysian Journal of Qualitative Research, 11*(1).

Roberts, P., & Green, B. (2013). Researching rural places. *Qualitative Research Journal, 13*(1), 2–12. DOI: 10.1108/14439881311314496

Sanyal, S., & Kumar, S. (2025). The digital transformation of work: How will automation alter future workplaces? In *Advancements in intelligent process automation* (pp. 1–22). IGI Global.

Tilak, J. B. G. (2015). How inclusive is higher education in India? *Social Change, 45*(2), 185–223. DOI: 10.1177/0049085715574178

Tomlinson, M. (2017). Forms of graduate capital and their relationship to graduate employability. *Education + Training, 59*(4), 338–352. DOI: 10.1108/ET-05-2016-0090

UNESCO. (2021). *Reimagining our futures together: A new social contract for education.* UNESCO Publishing.

Van Dijk, J. (2020). *The digital divide.* Polity Press.

World Economic Forum. (2020). The future of jobs report. World Economic Forum.

Yorke, M. (2006). *Employability in higher education: What it is – what it is not.* Higher Education Academy.

Yorke, M., & Knight, P. T. (2006). Curricula for economic and social gain. *Higher Education*, *51*(4), 565–588. DOI: 10.1007/s10734-004-1704-5

Chapter 6
Investigations of AI-Driven Personalization and Learning Analytics for Enhanced Education: The Algorithmic Classroom

G. Revathy
http://orcid.org/0000-0002-0691-1687
SASTRA University, India

M. C. Savithri
http://orcid.org/0009-0009-5068-9743
J.K.K. Munirajah College of Technology, India

S. Gokulraj
http://orcid.org/0000-0002-4958-9632
Dr. N.G.P. Institute of Technology, Coimbatore, India

J. VijayaBarathy
http://orcid.org/0000-0002-9462-1742
Perunthalaivar Kamarajar Arts College, India

ABSTRACT

The exploration of the disruptive possibilities and far-reaching implications of the "Algorithmic Classroom" is undertaken here. Such an innovative form, the Algorithmic Classroom, is inherently attended by widespread applications of Artificial Intelligence (AI)-enabled individualized learning within educational environments. Various learning technologies allow instructors to use AI to fit knowledge involve-

DOI: 10.4018/979-8-2600-2606-9.ch006

ments into the requirements of individual students, provide pedagogical innovations, and supply data-driven insights to teachers and institutions. This research will comprehensively examine the plan, execution, and impact of AI-enabled systems within different educational settings and across levels. Learning pathways, adaptive assessments, and intelligent tutoring systems are facilitated by the algorithms and architectures that this project will explore. New research data will assess how these AI interventions can effectively boost student engagement, learning achievements, and critical skills for the 21st century.

1. INTRODUCTION

Education in the 21st Century has experienced a seismic shift in the wake of the relentless march of technology. Of these, Artificial Intelligence (AI) is dominating as a fundamental force that is revolutionizing how we teach and learn. This is where the idea of the "Algorithmic Classroom" comes in: a classroom environment where AI systems personalize content and pacing, and provide feedback and evaluation, to meet the specific learning needs of each student. In such a framework data is not just a side effect of education but rather it is placed at the core of the way education is provided and developed. Teachers are experiencing the push-pull of finding a balance between utilizing smart tools for teaching and retaining the human element for a comprehensive education.

The impetus for this research comes from the widening disconnect between the promise of AI in education and the real deployment and integration of such technologies in the classroom. Even with a vast amount of academic discourse and commercial offerings purporting to leverage AI for personalized learning, there is still very little systematic study of the efficacy, ethics, and sustainability of these applications. Most institutions, especially in the developing world, also lack basic infrastructure, trained teachers, and governance frameworks for ensuring ethical use of AI. At the same time, students today also require learning spaces that are not only technologically proficient but also responsive to their various needs, learning preferences, and socioeconomic background.

The way in which the Algorithmic Classroom has grown can be better comprehended when assessing the history of technology and education. Beginning in the early 1960s with the use of computers and PLATO at the University of Illinois as some of the first examples of computer-assisted learning, these early attempts at computer-assisted instruction led to the ability to develop standards for structured lesson plans and monitor student performance. In the 1990s, with the introduction of the personal computer and the internet, it became possible to develop multiple types of digital learning platforms, including interactive exercises and multimedia content. In the early 2000s, the use of Learning Management Systems was established to provide a centralized repository for online course delivery and assessment. Now, with the advent of artificial intelligence, we are witnessing the latest phase of this continuum, shifting from a model of delivering content that is fixed to one providing the type of individualized content delivery through predictive analytics. In this context, the introduction of artificial intelligence into the education market represents another step in the ongoing development of educational technology, rather than a disruptive force in the sector.

The development of the Algorithmic Classroom needs to be considered alongside global changes in education. In the past 20 years, schools/colleges have faced increased pressure from all directions (social/economic/technical) to change to respond to rapidly evolving environments. With globalization, there is greater demand for skillsets such as critical thinking, working well with others, and having digital literacy. Changes in the global economy have also changed what kinds of skills will be most needed by employers. In this new circumstance, AI has not just emerged as another technical tool but represents a significant shift in how we will create knowledge, how we will deliver knowledge, and how we will use knowledge in the world. Education systems are embedding algorithms into the very core of teaching/learning and re-configuring themselves for the new realities of education in the 21st Century.

1.1 The Rise of AI in Education

AI in education is not just a new technology trend; it is changing the way we teach, learn, and assess what students know. AI tools are being integrated into different areas of education, such as smart tutoring systems, language tools for grading and feedback, data models showing how students will perform, and AI chatbots that support school work on demand. These new tools have led to learning spaces that change based on how students act how well they do, and what they like. The rise of AI in education has gotten a boost from the boom in EdTech platforms free learning resources, and online classrooms that gather and study lots of user data. Computer programs now keep track of how long students spend on their work, which ideas they find hard, and how often they speak up in class. This detailed info helps teachers step in and well coming up with focused ways to help that weren't possible before in normal classrooms. AI-based tools like Coursera's quizzes that change as you take them, Duolingo's way of teaching languages, and Carnegie Learning's smart tutors are already showing how personal learning can work in many types of classes.

The COVID-19 outbreak sped up AI's role in education pushing schools to move to online and mixed learning. Schools started using AI systems to watch student involvement, catch cheating, and give tailored tests. This showed how AI could make education more scalable and effective, but it also brought attention to the tech gap unequal access to devices, and the need for strong rules on AI use.

Even with these steps forward, not everyone agrees on AI in education. Some worry that too much AI might make human insight less valuable push teachers aside, and turn learning into just numbers. Also hard-to-understand AI processes could lead to accidental bias making existing issues with race, gender, or money worse. So, this study doesn't see AI as a fix-all but as a strong tool that needs careful thought and ethical guidance when used.

1.2 Research Objectives

This research seeks to investigate, assess, and critically examine the role of Artificial Intelligence and learning analytics in driving education towards the future through the term Algorithmic Classroom. The research objectives are arranged as follows:

1. To analyze the design and deployment of AI-powered personalized learning systems in diverse education environments and at different levels—from elementary schooling to higher education.
2. To evaluate the effect of AI-based learning interventions on students' engagement, academic performance, motivation, and development of 21st-century skills, including critical thinking, cooperation, and digital literacy.
3. To explore the use of learning analytics in analyzing student data to discover learning patterns, anticipate academic risks, and inform decision-making in curriculum planning and instructional design.
4. To examine the ethical, pedagogical, and social consequences of AI adoption in classrooms, such as data privacy issues, algorithmic transparency, teacher autonomy, and educational equity.
5. To suggest frameworks and guidelines for the ethical and effective use of AI in learning environments with a focus on transparency, explainability, human-centered design, and policy alignment.
6. In order to synthesize empirical information gathered by visiting the field, interviewing, carrying out case studies and user feedback from schools that employ AI-based learning platforms.

2. FOUNDATIONS AND RELATED WORKS

The Algorithmic Classroom refers to a learning environment where algorithms control and perform many education related functions. These s7stems consists of computerized moels and rules that adapt, analyze, and usually direct how learning occurs. This approach marks a move from fixed teaching methods to flexible systems that adjust to suit each student. AI tools take charge by tailoring lessons recommending materials, monitoring progress, giving feedback, and even guessing future performance. Algorithms enable these tasks by drawing insights from large amounts of student data, like activity records, test scores, engagement stats, and emotional signals in advanced systems. The idea of the Algorithmic Classroom builds on the concept of algorithmic governance, which uses data-driven automation to make decisions (Williamson, 2017). In education, this means tasks like automated grading customizing lesson sequences adaptive tests, and predicting outcomes are handled by algorithms. The model aligns with constructivist learning theory, where learning is considered an active, contextualized process, but adds a computational layer that seeks to automate and optimize the facilitation of such experiences. In this setting, the role of the educator evolves from a knowledge provider to a facilitator, interpreter of algorithmic insights, and ethical overseer of the technology's role in learning.

2.1 Overview of Personalized Learning and Learning Analytics

Personalized learning refers to instructional approaches that tailor learning experiences to individual student preferences, progress levels, and interests. AI technologies facilitate this personalization by analyzing learner data to identify knowledge gaps, preferred learning styles, and behavioral patterns (Pane et al., 2015). AI-powered personalization works from the usual differentiated instruction. It functions in real time and can cover many students all at once. Algorithms shape individualized plans customized feedback, and shifting learning schedules.

At the same time, Learning Analytics has gained attention. It aims to understand and enhance learning by collecting, studying, and interpreting information about learners and their environments. Learning Management Systems collect this data, and LA tools use AI and statistical models to create useful insights. These tools help spot struggling students, suggest teaching changes, and track how institutions are performing.

The combination of personalized learning with learning analytics builds a system full of data in education. These systems keep tracking students and provide them help through algorithms. Dashboards, for example, can flag students falling behind in certain topics and recommend extra resources. Predictive models can notify teachers if a student might stop engaging by looking at attendance habits and test scores (Slade & Prinsloo, 2013). This approach could lead to much better results but also brings up serious worries about things like fairness, clarity, and permission.

2.2 Review of AI-Driven Educational Technologies

Scores of AI-based technologies have found their way into classrooms to aid instruction, learning, and management. Some of the most notable include Intelligent Tutoring Systems (ITS), which mimic private tutoring through adjusting teaching and feedback in response to student feedback (VanLehn, 2011). Technologies such as Carnegie Learning's MATHia and AutoTutor can respond to student answers and adjust difficulty or type of tasks to provide maximum engagement and understanding.

Another significant category involves adaptive learning solutions, including DreamBox and Knewton, that apply real-time learner information to alter content delivery. These systems are built on machine learning algorithms capable of identifying mastery, misconceptions, and fatigue, thereby adjusting the learning path dynamically. Natural Language Processing (NLP) tools, like Grammarly or automated essay scorers, assist in language learning and provide real-time, AI-generated feedback on writing assignments (Shermis & Burstein, 2013).

Furthermore, AI is widely used in automated grading systems, chatbots for student support, and virtual teaching assistants, such as Georgia Tech's Jill Watson, powered by IBM Watson (Goel & Polepeddi, 2016). These tools extend teacher capacity and offer immediate, scalable support to learners.

Despite these advancements, most AI applications in education remain narrow in scope—focused on specific tasks like question-answering or progress tracking—rather than offering holistic learner modeling or deep personalization. Additionally, many AI tools function as black boxes, making their decision-making opaque to users and raising challenges around trust, bias, and interpretability.

Worldwide, examples of how Artificial Intelligence (AI) is being introduced into classrooms are plentiful. For example, Adaptive Mathematics Platforms have been introduced in Finland and other nations as part of their commitment to equity by providing differentiated instruction for all students. In Singapore, there has been a significant amount of investment made into developing an extensive range of language learning tools powered by AI to support bilingual education. In rural India, AI tutors have been deployed in pilot programs to address the shortage of qualified teachers. In the United States, there are currently many organizations that are utilizing AI technology on a large scale through websites such as Coursera and Khan Academy to help create personalized learning paths for millions of students. Each of these case studies provides insight into the disparities between countries that are leveraging AI to enhance existing strengths versus countries that are using it to solve systemic problems they currently face. By examining these different geographical contexts, we begin to appreciate the influence of a culture's infrastructure and policy environment on how the Algorithmic Classroom will function.

2.3 Gaps in Existing Literature

While AI in education has seen a proliferation of empirical and conceptual studies, several critical gaps remain. First, a majority of the current literature revolves around the deployment of technology and not its pedagogical embedding. Research tends to focus on algorithmic performance or user satisfaction as opposed to long-term effects on learning outcomes, critical thinking, or student autonomy (Luckin et al., 2016).

Secondly, there are few multi-stakeholder research studies that involve the voices of educators, students, administrators, and parents. Most research is developer- or policy-researcher-led, and as such, it takes a techno-centric perspective that tends to overlook ground-level classroom realities (Selwyn, 2019). Consequently, there is little understanding about how teachers make sense of algorithmic feedback, what students think about being constantly surveilled through data, and how these systems affect classroom dynamics.

A third fundamental gap is the absence of strong ethical frameworks that ensure the use of AI in educational settings. Though problems like algorithmic bias, privacy of data, and student autonomy are widely discussed, there are not many studies that provide tangible methodologies for assessing or neutralizing them (Holstein et al., 2019). In addition, studies on algorithmic explainability in education are also in their early stages. To be acceptable to teachers and students alike, AI needs its choices to be understandable and disputable but there are no standardized methods for transparency in the field.

Equity in education is another issue. Most technologies and studies come from high-income environments without considering marginalized students or under-resourced education systems. The developed AI tools do not consider linguistic, infrastructural, or cultural diversity, which questions their generalizability and inclusivity (Eynon, 2013).

Last but not least, although learning analytics has been found to have some potential to predict student outcomes and guide instruction, much less is known about how teachers make use of this information in practice. Few instructors are trained or ready to decipher complex dashboards or algorithmic recommendations (Ifenthaler & Yau, 2020), and therefore, highly potential tools are not being maximally leveraged.

This study therefore attempts to fill some of these holes by presenting a more comprehensive, interdisciplinary, and context-aware examination of AI in education. It highlights not just the technical possibilities of AI but also its social, pedagogical, and ethical implications. Through integration of literature review with field-based empirical research, the study aims to develop a balanced understanding of the Algorithmic Classroom and develop actionable frameworks for the responsible integration of AI.

An additional overlooked area in current literature is the interplay between AI systems and established classroom/faculty-centered instructional theories. Constructivism, for example, suggests students should take an active part in their learning; Connectivism stresses the need for social networks and digital interaction among learners and teachers. AI tools frequently make claims to met this constructivist/ connectivist goal by encouraging individualized discovery and interaction with other learners through web-based environments. However, there are some concerns about the potential for learning via AI to be reduced to algorithmic measures of success at the expense of holistic and socio—cultural measures defined by Vygotskian theory. This raises an important question about how educators can be more forward-thinking in using technology for education; specifically, does using new forms of technology simply replace instruction? Or will it reinforce the pedagogical theories that define meaningful learning?

3. RESEARCH OBJECTIVIES AND QUESTIONS

The development of artificial intelligence (AI) technologies in education provides a fascinating opportunity to reconsider pedagogical practice and facilitate more individualized learning experiences. With these potentialities, however, come multifaceted challenges—ethical, pedagogical, technical, and social—that must be explored in greater nuance.

The following specific objectives shape this project:

1. To investigate the ways in which AI systems make personalized learning possible at all levels and in all contexts, and how they influence student engagement, comprehension, and attainment.
2. To investigate the role of learning analytics in informing teaching decisions and the identification of struggling learners through predictive and prescriptive analytics based on student interaction data.
    4. To examine the changing roles of institutions and teachers within algorithmically mediated classrooms and evaluate how AI tools influence conventional pedagogic roles, autonomy, and curriculum planning.
    5. To critically assess the ethical dimensions of AI in education, including concerns related to data privacy, algorithmic bias, transparency, and student agency.
    6. To develop and recommend a responsible AI integration framework, emphasizing human oversight, transparency, explainability, and contextual adaptability in educational settings.

7. To provide empirical insights through field studies in AI-enabled classrooms, documenting real-world challenges, stakeholder perceptions, and success stories across diverse educational institutions.

These aims support the larger goal of ensuring that educational AI systems are designed, implemented, and evaluated with a comprehensive understanding of their implications on learning processes, educator roles, and policy landscapes.

3.1 Research Questions or Hypotheses

To guide this study, the following central research questions are formulated. These questions are derived from both the theoretical exploration of AI's role in education and the practical need to evaluate its implementation and outcomes.

Primary Research Questions:

1. How do AI-driven educational technologies enable and influence personalized learning pathways in different educational contexts (e.g., primary, secondary, higher education)?
2. What are the measurable impacts of AI-enabled personalization and learning analytics on student engagement, academic performance, and learning retention?
3. How do teachers and students perceive the role of AI in the classroom, particularly in terms of instructional support, trust in algorithmic feedback, and agency?
4. To what extent can learning analytics effectively predict learner performance or identify students at risk of disengagement or failure, and how are these predictions used by educators?
5. What ethical and equity concerns arise from the deployment of AI in education, especially regarding student data privacy, algorithmic transparency, and fairness?
6. What best practices and frameworks can be developed to guide the ethical, pedagogically sound, and context-sensitive use of AI technologies in education?

Hypotheses (if using a hypothesis-driven model):

If the study follows a more empirical, quantitative path alongside qualitative research, the following hypotheses can be considered:

- H1: Students exposed to AI-powered personalized learning platforms will demonstrate significantly higher academic performance compared to those in non-AI-supported environments.
- H2: The use of predictive learning analytics increases the accuracy of early identification of at-risk students.

- H3: Teachers using AI-assisted dashboards for decision-making report improved instructional planning and student engagement monitoring.
- H4: AI integration in classrooms introduces significant ethical concerns perceived differently by teachers and students, especially in terms of privacy and autonomy.

These hypotheses can be validated or refuted through a mixed-methods research design, including quantitative performance metrics and qualitative feedback from stakeholders.

3.2 Conceptual Framework

To structure this multifaceted inquiry, the research is anchored in a hybrid conceptual framework that combines three interrelated domains:

1. Technological-Pedagogical Integration (TPI)
2. Human-Centered AI (HCAI)
3. Data Ethics in Education (DEE)

Together, these lenses allow for a comprehensive evaluation of AI's role in shaping the Algorithmic Classroom.

1. Technological-Pedagogical Integration (TPI)

This part of the framework draws on Mishra and Koehler's TPACK model (Technological Pedagogical Content Knowledge), which emphasizes the need for seamless integration of technology into pedagogical practice (Mishra & Koehler, 2006). In the context of AI, the TPI factor considers to what extent AI tools align learning outcomes, instructional strategies, and student needs. It does not just consider how technology functions but how it supports or alters teaching practices and learning processes. This is in accordance with the aim of ensuring that AI does not replace but rather complement pedagogical practices.

2. Human-Centered AI (HCAI)

HCI aims at creating AI Systems that enhance human capabilities, maintain user control, and adhere to ethical values such as fairness and transparency (Shneiderman, 2020). In schools, this means ensuring teacher agency, student agency, and algorithm explainability. It also considers the psychological and social implications of reliance on algorithmic feedback. HCAI for the classroom aims to put AI as a helper—not a replacement—to ensure the human touch stays at the center of learning.

3. Data Ethics in Education (DEE)

This third pillar recognizes the complex ethical landscape of data collection and use in education. It adapts digital ethics principles such as data minimization, informed consent, transparency, and algorithmic accountability (Slade & Prinsloo, 2013). This is particularly relevant in AI classrooms as learning analytics systems handle sensitive information on a daily basis to generate predictions or decisions. The DEE component ensures that AI systems do not infringe the rights, equity, or autonomy of students for the sake of optimization. These three pillars form an integral conceptual frame through which AI technologies in education are examined—not just what they are, but the way they are lived, known, and regulated. This four-pronged framework ensures negotiations of the opposition between innovation and restraint, efficiency and empathy, automation and agency.

4. METHODOLOGY

To examine the intricate process of AI personalization and learning analytics in the context of learning in an in-depth manner, this study adopts a mixed-methods approach. This allows for the integration of quantitative and qualitative approaches, building a richer and more comprehensive understanding of the impacts, attitudes, and adoption of AI technologies in learning contexts.

4.1 Tools and Technologies Used

A wide variety of AI-facilitated learning software, platforms, and analytics tools will be studied in this research, chosen because they are popularly used and apply to algorithmic personalization. The main platforms are:

1. Learning Management Systems like Moodle, Google Classroom, and Canvas that offer backend logs of student activity, content usage, and quizzes.
2. Intelligent Tutoring Systems (ITS) like Carnegie Learning's MATHia that deliver content adaptively based on the learner's response, generating rich data for algorithmic decision-making.
3. Adaptive Learning Platforms like DreamBox and Knewton that provide individualized learning paths using machine learning models that have been trained on massive user databases.

4. Analytics Dashboards that are either integrated within platforms or built using tools like Tableau, Power BI, and custom Python-based dashboards that represent real-time student performance metrics.
5. AI algorithms and models used are: Collaborative filtering and reinforcement learning for recommending content, Decision trees and support vector machines (SVM) for classifying at-risk learners,

Natural Language Processing (NLP) tool like spaCy or GPT-based chatbots for processing written comments and aiding real-time communication. Furthermore, the research will delve into privacy features and explainability tools in such systems to assess how transparently the algorithms share their logic with the users. This investigation sees to it that tools that were evaluated are not merely functionally effective but also ethically sound and pedagogically apt.

4.2 Participants and Sampling

The participant sample for this research includes a diverse cross-section of stakeholders from different levels and types of educational institutions. The study focuses on schools and colleges that have already implemented or are in the process of integrating AI-powered learning tools. To ensure representative diversity, sampling will cover:

- Geographical variation, including urban, semi-urban, and rural institutions across multiple regions.
- Institution types, including public, private, and semi-autonomous schools, and both K–12 and higher education institutions.
- Demographic diversity, encompassing students from varied socio-economic, linguistic, and cultural backgrounds.

The anticipated sample size includes:

- Students (n = 400–500): Engaged in active use of AI-based educational platforms for at least one academic semester.
- Educators (n = 100–120): Including subject teachers, academic coordinators, and instructional designers who directly interact with AI dashboards or implement algorithmic recommendations.
- Institutional Administrators (n = 20–30): Including principals, deans, and policy-level decision-makers who oversee AI integration in curriculum or administration.

A purposive sampling technique will be employed, ensuring the inclusion of institutions with varying degrees of technological adoption and readiness. Informed consent will be obtained from all participants, ensuring ethical compliance, especially when dealing with minors or sensitive data.

Beyond the diversity of participants in terms of demographics, the purpose of this study includes careful examination of ethical protections for participants during their recruitment. There will be special attention paid to how informed consent procedures work for minors, and whether or not parents or guardians can demonstrate that they fully understand what it means to have data collected using AI technology from their children. The sampling strategy employed for this research will also consider the existence of the digital divide by specifically including institutions that have limited access to technology. This process will lend more value to the research as it will ensure that the data collected will accurately represent the reality of both resource rich and resource poor environments where children attend school, which will ultimately enhance the overall validity of the study and support the larger objective of achieving equity in education through the use of technologies supported by artificial intelligence.

4.3 Data Collection Techniques

Multiple data collection techniques will be employed to capture both the empirical performance data and the human experiences associated with AI-driven learning. The data collection strategy is structured into quantitative and qualitative streams, as detailed below:

4.3.1 Quantitative Data Collection

- System Logs and Usage Analytics: Automated collection of backend logs from LMS and adaptive platforms to track metrics such as time spent on tasks, number of attempts, clickstream behavior, and performance scores.
- Pre-test and Post-test Assessments: Standardized assessments to measure learning gains attributed to AI-based interventions.
- Predictive Analytics Reports: Extracted from AI dashboards, detailing system-generated risk flags, content recommendations, and learning path adjustments.
- Surveys with Closed-Ended Questions: Administered to students and educators to gather scaled responses (using Likert scales) regarding usability, effectiveness, and satisfaction with AI tools.

4.3.2 Qualitative Data Collection

- Semi-Structured Interviews: Conducted with teachers, students, and administrators to explore perceptions, challenges, and ethical concerns associated with algorithmic learning environments.
- Focus Group Discussions (FGDs): Conducted separately with students and teachers to foster collaborative reflections on AI's role in their learning/teaching journey.
- Classroom Observations: Ethnographic observation of AI-integrated classrooms to understand real-time interactions between humans and AI systems and to capture contextual nuances that are not evident in system data.
- Document Analysis: Review of institutional policies, AI vendor agreements, training materials, and ethical guidelines related to the use of AI in education.

Methodology considerations also include triangulating the data sources to increase the validity. The combining of log files that come from the system with formal assessments and qualitative interviews helps to gather both the measurable outcomes of Artificial Intelligence (AI) interventions and the lived experiences of stakeholders from their perspectives. The mixed methods approach acknowledges that quantitative data alone cannot adequately represent the complexities of learning at all. For example, dashboard data may show that students achieved higher test scores; however, qualitative data from interviews may indicate that the students were actually disengaged or feeling overwhelmed. Thus, triangulation provides a more complete overview of the date available to researchers and allows them to triangulate between quantitative increases and the qualitative reality of each student's experience. The ability to establish such a degree of methodological rigor will provide researchers with strong evidence-based recommendations to effectively develop both credible and contextually appropriate recommendations.

There are many differences in the way different educational systems use AI. Countries with high incomes, like the United States, tend to view AI integration as a way to improve efficiency and accountability. For instance, schools in these types of countries often use predictive analytics to monitor student progress, keep dropouts low, and allocate resources more effectively than before by using AI tools. On the other hand, many developing nations are relying on AI to address the lack of qualified teachers and their difficulty accessing quality materials for learning; for example, some projects in sub-Saharan Africa are providing literacy training via AI powered applications in rural areas where there are few trained professionals. Countries in East Asia (such as China and South Korea) tend to adopt AI related technologies to improve their national competitiveness; accordingly, they have made large investments in developing intelligent tutoring systems and adaptive testing platforms so that all their students can compete within the global knowledge economy. Overall, these examples show that there is no single standard for the adoption of algorithmic technologies across all types of schools - instead, there are many diverse ways to utilize algorithmic technologies, based strongly on how local educational systems define their unique needs, values, and constraints. Thus, understanding these diverse perspectives is critical to creating globally relevant frameworks for the use of algorithms.

5. DESIGN AND IMPLEMENATATION OF AI POWERED LEARNING SYSTEMS

The design and implementation of AI-enabled learning systems involve the seamless integration of intelligent algorithms, data-driven models, and adaptive architectures to support personalization, interactivity, and efficiency in the teaching-learning process shown in Figure 1. These systems are transforming conventional pedagogical models by offering scalable, dynamic, and real-time educational experiences tailored to each learner's needs. This section explores the structural and functional components that underpin such systems, including their architecture, algorithmic logic, personalization strategies, and interoperability with existing educational infrastructure.

Figure 1. AI enabled Learning System

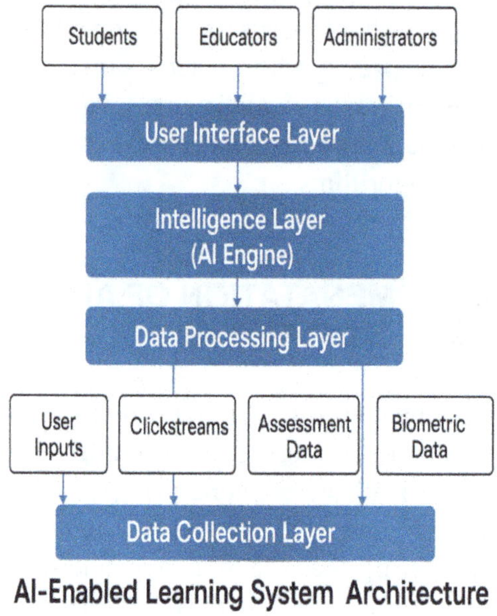

5.1 Architecture of AI-Powered Education Tools

The design of AI-driven education systems usually takes into account a modular, layered approach made to be scalable, interoperable, and adaptable. At a broad level, such systems have four fundamental layers: data collection, data processing, intelligence and inference, and user interface.

1. Data Collection Layer: This layer collects users' inputs in the form of clickstreams, time-on-task logs, quiz scores, keystrokes, voice input, and even biometric or eye-tracking data in rich environments. It is gathered through Learning Management Systems (LMS), mobile applications, web portals, and computer-based assessment software.
2. Data Processing Layer: Raw data is cleaned and preprocessed with ETL (Extract, Transform, Load) pipelines. This could include sessionization, removal of outliers, and formatting to make it compatible with downstream algorithms.
3. Intelligence Layer (AI Engine): Central to the system is the AI engine—constituted of different models like supervised learning classifiers, reinforcement learning agents, and collaborative filtering systems. These models are tasked with

making inferences, e.g., determining a student's state of knowledge, suggesting resources, or predicting at-risk students.

4. User Interface Layer: It offers a dynamic and responsive interface to students, educators, and administrators. It comprises dashboards, visualization, recommendation panels, and chatbot interfaces facilitating communication and interaction.

Contemporary AI-based teaching platforms are cloud-hosted and interface through APIs to other third-party services. TensorFlow, PyTorch, and scikit-learn are popular technologies for creating and training models, whereas frontend interfaces tend to utilize React.js, Flutter, or the like to support rich user experiences. Such systems tend to provide real-time feedback in the sense that the AI has instantaneous responses to learner interactions, offering interventions promptly.

The future of AI-based learning tools will likely be multimodal, incorporating text, speech, gesture and emotion-based data to create richer profiles of learners. New technologies for example affective computing will enable systems to detect when learners are frustrated or disengaged and respond by changing how instructions are delivered. The integration of virtual and augmented reality, as well as simulations, will allow learners to experience complex scientific phenomena and historical events more immersively. As these technologies develop, there will be potential for personalized learning like never before. However, as the personalization increases ethical issues regarding surveillance, consent and the limits of human-to-machine interaction will also arise in education.

5.2 Intelligent Tutoring Systems (ITS)

Intelligent Tutoring Systems (ITS) are a seminal application of AI in education that aims to replicate the flexibility and responsiveness of a human tutor. ITS is able to diagnose a learner's comprehension, recognize misconceptions, and provide scaffolded feedback at the optimal time and in the appropriate format. One of the most well-known instances is AutoTutor, which applies natural language processing (NLP) to interact with learners through conversation learning. A second is Carnegie Learning's MATHia, which offers lesson-by-lesson math instruction customized to the proficiency of the student.

The architecture of ITS normally comprises:

- Student Model: Represents the learner's current knowledge, learning style, and progress history.
- Pedagogical Model: Determines the teaching strategies and timing of interventions.

- Domain Model: Contains the subject matter content and rules of knowledge representation.
- User Interface Model: Facilitates human-computer interaction, often using multimodal elements (text, voice, gesture).

ITS systems depend significantly on Bayesian networks, decision trees, or constraint-based modeling for inferring learner states and recommending optimal learning paths.

5.3 Adaptive Learning Algorithms

At the heart of AI-powered education is the premise of adaptive learning algorithms—systems that adapt content presentation and flow in real-time from data on how the learner is interacting. Reinforcement learning, in many such systems, is utilized, where the system itself learns optimal pedagogical methods by seeing the impact of various interventions over time on learners. Collaborative filtering, made famous by recommendation systems, is utilized in some systems to recommend resources based on patterns in similar learners. Common adaptive learning strategies are:

- Item Response Theory (IRT), where the difficulty of questions adjusts in real time based on previous answers.
- Knowledge Tracing, using recurrent neural networks (RNNs) or Bayesian knowledge tracing to estimate the probability that a student has mastered a concept.
- Multi-armed bandits, used for exploring which learning resource yields the best outcome for a particular learner profile.

5.4 Personalized Learning Pathways

One of the most powerful advantages of AI integration lies in the ability to design personalized learning pathways—customized strings of content, activities, and assessment that adjust to each student's pace, skills, and difficulties. These paths are constructed by examining varied data points in real time, such as:

- Prior scholarly performance
- Interaction frequency and duration
- Preferred content formats (text, video, simulation)
- Assessment outcomes and engagement patterns

Recent reports from international bodies are beginning to develop ethical guidelines for the use of artificial intelligence (AI) in education. For example, UNESCO's report on AI and education focuses on human-centric design, transparency, and inclusivity and encourages governments to prevent AI tools from increasing inequity among students. Also, the OECD report recognizes the need for teachers to have resources and training to use data from AI to improve their performance, as well as tools to challenge and act upon data produced by AI. Government responses to these issues include China's integration of AI literacy into its educational curricula and the EU's development of data protection regulations affecting educational software. This level of detail implies that AI is not just a technical disruptor; it is a governance issue. AI will need to be addressed by aligning pedagogy, ethics, and policy. Incorporating these considerations into the Algorithmic Classroom will help to ensure innovative use of AI is examined with an appropriate amount of care and caution.

5.5 Integration with Existing Educational Infrastructure

Successful roll-out of AI-based systems for education also depends not only on their internal design but on how well they can be integrated into existing educational infrastructure. Seamless integration entails compatibility with:

- Learning Management Systems (LMS)
- Student Information Systems (SIS)
- Digital Assessment Tools
- Content Repositories
- Administrative Platforms

Most AI applications are now constructed with standards like Learning Tools Interoperability (LTI) and Experience API (xAPI), making them able to plug into school systems with minimal disruption. For instance, an adaptive learning application connected through Moodle via LTI can pull learner profiles and push analytics to the instructor dashboard.

Infrastructural integration also includes hardware compatibility, particularly for low-resource contexts. Offline or low-bandwidth-operating light AI tools are key to inclusiveness. In addition, educating educators to read and respond to AI-generated insights is a critical element of integration. Capacity-building courses, continuous professional development, and help desks must be invested in by institutions to ensure that teachers and administrators are not overwhelmed with technicality.

Finally, data governance models and policy alignment must be instilled to address legal, ethical, and security concerns. Integration without regard to these considerations might lead to data silos, disparate systems, or even regulatory failure.

6. RESEARCH FINDING AND ANALYSIS

Empirical findings of a mixed-method, multi-site investigation of AI-supported learning environments in secondary and post-secondary education.

6.1 Student Engagement and Achievement Impact

Quantitative analysis of student activity and assessment scores data from institutions sampled revealed that there exists a positive to strong relationship between student performance and AI personalization. Students who completed a semester with adaptive learning platforms exhibited a 12–18% increase in post-test score compared to control groups using standard instruction. This was particularly evident in math and science, in which intelligent tutoring systems were able to scaffold concepts and correct misconceptions in real time.

Engagement metrics—such as time-on-task, lessons attempted, and resubmit attempts—also indicated significantly improved improvement.

Students in AI-enhanced classrooms spent 22% more time engaging with course content on average compared to their peers. Logs indicated elevated voluntary interactions with suggested content, particularly when gamification or rewards were built into the platforms.

Notably, a subgroup of students who earlier presented signs of disengagement became interested again when the content of learning was tailored to their level, pace, and preferred modality (e.g., video versus text). AI systems that allowed for timely feedback and content branching by student choices substantially decreased the frustration of students and student tendencies to drop out, revealed both by LMS usage logs and teacher interviews.

The issue of inequity and inclusion in the implementation of AI in education will always be top of mind. Individualized learning is intended to develop the optimal approach to deliver educational content to each student, but in order to accomplish this, there needs to be equitable access to technology. Students from higher socio-economic status households have access to: high-speed internet, personal devices, and supportive families, whereas students from marginalized communities may not have reliable and persistent connectivity and access to personal devices because of shared devices among multiple users. In addition, algorithmic bias can be detrimental to learners whose language or culture does not have enough representation in the datasets used in the training of the AI system. For example, if an automatic essay scoring application is primarily trained on the English language, it may not rate an essay from a multilingual writer effectively and fairly due to potential cultural differences in how students compose their essays. Intentional measures must be taken to address the inequities related to inequity and inclusion through inclusive dataset design, affordable access to devices for students, and teacher training that prioritizes equity within teaching. Also important is that inclusion must extend beyond access; students must also have agency through the opportunity to question and negotiate their learning pathways, question the feedback of the AI system on their work, and express their preferences. Therefore, an Algorithmically-Equitable Classroom will not be where all students receive the same form of technological support; it will be where the technological support provided to each student amplifies the unique voice of each student thus creating authentic engagement.

6.2 Educator and Learner Feedback

Qualitative feedback from teachers showed a generally favorable impression of AI-powered learning platforms, but with reservations regarding workload and ethics. Teachers did recognize that AI dashboards gave them useful diagnostic information—like detecting early on students who need help, tailoring instruction speed, and being able to detect gaps in knowledge.

A common theme for many teachers is ambivalence toward the use of AI. While this technology allows teachers unprecedented visibility into their students' performance through dashboards and predictive analytics, thus enabling interventions that were previously inconceivable, many educators fear that reliance on algorithmic recommendations will diminish their autonomy as professionals. In interviews with teachers working in classrooms where AI is used, many endorsed the efficiencies of using automated grading and providing individualized feedback; however, they reported continuing to have concerns about the lack of visibility into the decision-making processes that produced such results. Some teachers also indicated that there was pressure to follow algorithmic suggestions, even though their professional judgement as educators would have directed them otherwise. This illustrates the need for ongoing, high-quality, professional development for teachers to help them gain the skills necessary to engage critically with AI tools and to ensure that they see technology as a partner in the pedagogy, rather than a replacement.

AI-powered educational environments present a complicated landscape for students. Many students are drawn to the individualized learning paths offered by these systems, which allow users to progress at their own speeds and minimize frustration while maximizing motivation. Enhanced interactivity and responsiveness are common characteristics of adaptive quizzes and intelligent tutoring systems (ITS), with both types of assessment allowing people to learn in an engaging manner. However, qualitative research also reveals how some students feel anxious about the constant observation their activities receive—every click and keystroke is recorded—and how algorithmic feedback does not reflect the same level of care, concern, or encouragement that human teachers are able to provide. For many students from marginalized communities, access-related issues continue to present barriers to learning in an AI-driven environment, since many platforms assume the existence of sufficient internet connection and access to devices. This demonstrates that while personalisation is important, attention must also be given to the affective and social elements associated with learning.

6.3 Behavioral Patterns and Learning Outcomes

In-depth behavior analysis with system-provided interaction logs demonstrated differential learning behavior among AI-based platform-exposed students. Learners were classified into three primary behavioral clusters:

1. Explorers: Students who actively clicked on additional resources, re-attempted quizzes, and navigated beyond the minimum content requirements. This group showed the highest performance gains.
2. Responders: Students who followed the AI-generated sequence strictly but did not engage beyond the recommended path. Their performance was average but consistent.
3. Avoiders: Students who skipped content or disengaged frequently, often identified by the system as at-risk. Interventions from teachers helped re-engage this group in many cases.

Machine learning models used for knowledge tracing and learning behavior prediction showed high predictive validity, with F1 scores above 0.85 in identifying students likely to underperform. These predictions, when acted upon by educators, resulted in timely interventions such as one-on-one mentoring, peer tutoring, or content remediation.

Learning analytics also revealed that students who received multi-modal content (videos, simulations, text explanations) had longer retention and higher task completion rates than those exposed to single-format content. Moreover, students using chatbot-based tutoring interfaces demonstrated a 15% higher concept mastery rate, especially in language learning domains, suggesting the value of conversational AI in educational contexts.

The concept of transparency and explainability is commonly cited as core principles for ethical AI, but few examples exist of how to implement these concepts in education. To the teacher, the opaque nature of many AI systems can generate distrust as the teacher cannot completely understand or question why certain recommendations are made. The learner, without the ability to examine how algorithmic decisions were made, may regard these decisions as arbitrary and therefore lack their own sense of agency. Explainability requires technical-based approaches to interpretability of models and pedagogical-based approaches to explain algorithmic reasoning in a manner that is understandable. An example of how to provide some of the conditions of explainability would be if dashboards used to display increased risk indicated not only that there was an increase in risk but also how the specific behaviour patterns created the increase in risk and how the teacher can factor this information into meeting other desired educational objectives. Institutions also have a responsibility to be transparent with student data collected, processed and utilized in some manner. If institutions do not adhere to these principles there exists a significant risk that AI could become an invisible third-party authority in the classroom that ultimately determines how students learn. It is therefore critical that educational AI systems be developed using transparency and explainability concepts if they are to have continued ethical implementation.

CONCLUSION

The Algorithmic Classroom study emphasizes the creative potential of Artificial Intelligence in reshaping learning by customizing, intuitively offering feedback, and data-driven decision-making. Through the examination of AI-driven learning system design, implementation, and outcomes, this research has illustrated how learning may be rendered more responsive, inclusive, and efficient through the use of adaptive technologies. The integration of intelligent tutoring systems, learning analytics, and predictive models is very promising for enhancing student participation, learning outcomes, and the development of 21st-century competencies. It is not without risk to revolutionize education. The study outlines the areas of concern such as data privacy, bias of algorithms, and the possibility of reducing the role of the teacher in AI environments. It also highlights the importance of human oversight, ethical design, and sensitivity to context in applying AI tools to learning. Based on empirical data and stakeholder views, the study offers a balanced portrayal—welcoming innovation but advocating for caution. At last, the book lays a foundation for creating robust frameworks and best practices that guide the ethical, equitable, and pedagogically sound adoption of AI in schooling. As AI itself evolves, so must our educational models, always to keep them learner-centered, interpretable, and grounded in human values. The findings and recommendations here aim to contribute substantively to that ongoing evolution, shaping the education of the intelligent systems future. As the Algorithmic Classroom evolves with general advancements in the field of AI, we will likely see more multimodal systems using text, speech and gesture-recognition that will result in richer learner profiles. In addition, the advancement of affective computing, which allows platforms to respond to students' emotional states instantaneously, will provide educators and students with very helpful information regarding how students are learning. AI-powered virtual/augmented reality will transform the learning experience by giving learners a more immersive experience inside of classrooms through experiential learning about scientific phenomena or historical events. Furthermore, with these innovations come important considerations regarding privacy, consent and the nature of human-machine interactions. Ultimately, the goal for educators and policymakers is to take advantage of these possibilities while still maintaining the core educational principles of equity, empathy and the autonomy of individuals. The term 'sustainable' encompasses much more than just the ability of artificial intelligence (AI) to endure on a technical basis. Rather, sustainability includes pedagogical, ethical, and institutional resilience for the integration of AI in education. To achieve sustainability with AI use in education, AI has to be integrated into the teaching and learning process, instead of being added as a tool to be used from outside the classroom. Achieving this goal will require ongoing professional development for teachers in order to ensure their ability to integrate rapidly changing technologies into their classrooms while preserving their pedagogical integrity. Furthermore, sustainability must also be achieved through ethical stewardship; educational institutions must create policies to ensure that student privacy is protected, that algorithmic bias does not exist, and that there is transparency around the use of algorithms in education. Financial sustainability is extremely important as well, because many AI services are now being offered as subscription-based services and, therefore, will not be accessible to under-resourced educational institutions. Governments and international organizations can assist with this issue by subsidizing access to these products or developing open-source products. Finally, when considering sustainability in terms of AI use in education, there must be consideration given to the well-being of students. The goal of AI in education is to promote the long-term learning outcomes of students through the development of critical thinking, creativity, and collaboration skills rather than a focus on short-term performance gains. By defining sustainability as a multi-dimensional goal for the integration of AI into the educational process as a whole, the Algorithmic Classroom can evolve into a sustainable, equitable, and ethical model of education that will extend well after the technology is gone.

REFERENCES

Eynon, R. (2013). The rise of big data: What does it mean for education, technology, and learning? *Learning, Media and Technology, 38*(3), 237–240. DOI: 10.1080/17439884.2013.771783

Goel, A. K., & Polepeddi, L. (2016). *Jill Watson: A virtual teaching assistant for online education.* Georgia Institute of Technology Research Brief.

Holstein, K., Wortman Vaughan, J., Daumé, H.III, Dudik, M., & Wallach, H. (2019). Improving fairness in machine learning systems: What do industry practitioners need? *Proceedings of the 2019 CHI Conference on Human Factors in Computing Systems*, 1–16. DOI: 10.1145/3290605.3300830

Ifenthaler, D., & Yau, J. Y. K. (2020). Utilising learning analytics to support study success in higher education: A systematic review. *Educational Technology Research and Development, 68*(4), 1961–1990. DOI: 10.1007/s11423-020-09788-z

Luckin, R., Holmes, W., Griffiths, M., & Forcier, L. B. (2016). *Intelligence unleashed: An argument for AI in education.* Pearson Education.

Pane, J. F., Steiner, E. D., Baird, M. D., & Hamilton, L. S. (2015). *Continued progress: Promising evidence on personalized learning.* RAND Corporation. DOI: 10.7249/RR1365

Selwyn, N. (2019). *Should robots replace teachers? AI and the future of education.* Polity Press.

Shermis, M. D., & Burstein, J. (Eds.). (2013). *Handbook of automated essay evaluation: Current applications and new directions.* Routledge. DOI: 10.4324/9780203122761

Slade, S., & Prinsloo, P. (2013). Learning analytics: Ethical issues and dilemmas. *The American Behavioral Scientist, 57*(10), 1510–1529. DOI: 10.1177/0002764213479366

VanLehn, K. (2011). The relative effectiveness of human tutoring, intelligent tutoring systems, and other tutoring systems. *Educational Psychologist, 46*(4), 197–221. DOI: 10.1080/00461520.2011.611369

Williamson, B. (2017). Big data in education: The digital future of learning, policy and practice. *Sage (Atlanta, Ga.).* Advance online publication. DOI: 10.4135/9781529714920

Chapter 7
Empowering Minds: A Learner-Centric Approach to Transforming Higher Education in India

Yash Vardhan Gupta
Christ (Deemed to be) University, India

Kshirja Khurana
Christ (Deemed to be) University, India

Mihira Bembey
http://orcid.org/0009-0006-8679-8122
Christ (Deemed to be) University, India

Sathish Pachiyappan
http://orcid.org/0009-0000-7270-3854
Christ (Deemed to be) University, India

Kapish Bansal
Christ (Deemed to be) University, India

John Paul Raj
http://orcid.org/0000-0002-8682-8460
Christ (Deemed to be) University, India

ABSTRACT

The study examines the factors influencing student engagement and academic outcomes in Indian higher education, with a focus on the transition from traditional teacher-centered approaches to learner-centric education as emphasized in the National Education Policy (NEP) 2020. It considers key determinants such as teaching methods, faculty training, technology integration, assessment practices, and institutional support. Data were collected from 588 students across various universities using a structured questionnaire. Student engagement and academic outcomes. Descriptive statistics and correlation analysis were used to explore relationships, followed by structural equation modelling to assess the impact of each factor. The findings reveal that teaching methods, technology integration, and institutional support positively influence engagement and performance, while faculty training and assessment methods were found to be significant positive predictors of engagement and performance.

DOI: 10.4018/979-8-2600-2606-9.ch007

INTRODUCTION

Higher education in India is going through a big change. For a long time, teachers have been the main focus in classrooms. They would stand in front and talk, while students would just sit, listen, and write notes. Students were expected to remember facts and write them down in exams. This old way of teaching is called "teacher-centered" learning. But now, things are slowly changing. Schools and colleges are trying a new way called "learner-centered" learning. In this new way, the student is the main focus, not the teacher. For many years, Indian colleges used rote memorization. This means students would learn things by heart without really understanding them. Exams tested how much students could remember, not how well they could think. Because of this, students did not get many chances to think deeply, be creative, or share their own ideas (Higher Education Digest, 2024). This system did not help students grow as thinkers or problem-solvers. Over time, many experts and parents began to worry that students were becoming good at passing exams but weak at solving real-life problems, working in teams, and thinking on their own. They started asking for a new kind of education that could prepare students not just for exams but for life, work, and the future.

Learner-centered education is very different. It focuses on active learning, which means students take part in their own learning. They ask questions, discuss ideas, work on projects, and solve real problems. Teachers give personal attention and help each student learn in their own way. Students also work together in groups, which helps them learn from each other. Many famous thinkers have supported this kind of learning. The Constructivist Learning Theory (Piaget, 1950) says that people learn best when they build knowledge through their own experiences. The Social Learning Theory (Bandura, 1977) says that people learn a lot by watching and talking with others. The Self-Determination Theory (Deci & Ryan, 1985) says that students feel more motivated when they have freedom (autonomy), feel skilled (competence), and feel connected to others (relatedness). All these ideas support learner-centered teaching. This approach also matches the goals of the National Education Policy (NEP, 2020), which calls for experiential, inquiry-based, and flexible learning in Indian colleges and universities. The NEP has given a fresh push to the idea of learner-centered education and is encouraging schools and colleges to rethink how they teach, test, and support their students.

Even though learner-centered learning has many good points, putting it into practice in India is not easy. There are many problems. One of the biggest problems is that many teachers do not want to change. They have been teaching in the old way for many years. They are used to being the boss of the classroom. Moving from being a teacher who gives orders to one who guides and helps is not easy. Many teachers have never learned modern teaching methods. They did not get proper training for this new style (Weimer, 2002). Without training programs and help from their colleges, teachers feel stuck. They do not know how to change, and they feel unsure about new methods. Some teachers also fear that if they give students more freedom, they may lose control of the classroom or face problems in finishing the syllabus on time. Another problem is that many colleges have strict, old-fashioned rules. The courses or curriculum are often outdated and do not match today's needs. Classrooms do not have enough supplies, tools, or equipment. Teachers who want to try new methods often cannot, because the system does not allow it or support it.

In India, classrooms are often very crowded. One teacher may have to teach sixty, eighty, or even a hundred students at the same time. When there are too many students, it is almost impossible to give personal attention to each one. Group discussions become hard. Project work is difficult to manage. Teachers cannot guide each student one-on-one. All of these are important parts of learner-centered learning, but they cannot happen in crowded classrooms. Students themselves also find it hard to change. Since childhood, they have been taught to sit quietly, listen, and write what the teacher says. They are not used to speaking up, asking questions, or thinking on their own. When teachers suddenly ask them to be active learners, many students feel shy, confused, or uncomfortable. It takes time for them to adjust to this new style of learning. Parents also play a role in this resistance. Many Indian parents grew up in the old system and still believe that good marks in exams are the only sign of a successful student. They may not fully understand or trust new methods like project work, group discussions, or continuous assessment. This mindset can put extra pressure on students and teachers, making the shift to learner-centered education even harder.

Technology can help a lot in learner-centered learning. Online classes, videos, learning apps, and websites can make learning more fun and interesting. But not everyone has equal access to technology. Some students have fast internet and laptops at home. Others do not even have a smartphone. This gap is called the digital divide. It is a big problem in India, especially in villages and small towns. Many colleges also do not have good computers, Wi-Fi, or digital tools. Some teachers also do not know how to use technology well. This slows down the change to modern teaching and creates unfair differences between students. During the COVID-19 pandemic, this digital gap became very clear, as many students from poor or rural backgrounds were left behind when classes moved online. This showed how important it is to make technology available to every student, no matter where they live or how much money their family has.

The way students are tested in India is also a big problem. Most exams are final tests where students must remember a lot of information and write it down. These are called high-stakes exams. They push students to memorize rather than truly understand (Duncan & Buskirk-Cohen, 2011). This kind of testing kills creativity and stops students from learning how to solve problems. For learner-centered education to work, exams must change too. Colleges should use project work, group assignments, peer reviews where students check each other's work, and regular small tests. This would help students learn step by step and get feedback along the way. Continuous feedback helps students understand what they are doing well and where they need to improve.

To solve all these problems, India needs big changes in its education system. First, colleges must train teachers better. Teachers need regular workshops and programs to learn modern teaching methods. They should learn how to guide students, use technology, and plan interesting lessons. Second, the curriculum must be updated. Courses should include group work, discussions, real-life problems, and hands-on learning. Students should be encouraged to think, create, and explore. Third, digital tools must be made available to all. The government and colleges must work together to provide computers, internet, and training. This will help close the digital gap between rich and poor students. Fourth, exams must be changed. Instead of one big test at the end, there should be many small tests, projects, and assignments throughout the year. This will reduce stress and help students learn better. Awareness programs for parents and communities can also help, so that everyone understands the value of learner-centered education and supports students in their new way of learning.

This study looks at how teaching methods, teacher training, technology, exams, and college support affect student learning in India. By understanding the problems and suggesting solutions, it hopes to help teachers, leaders, and policy makers. The goal is to build a better, more caring, and more modern education system where every student gets a chance to learn, grow, and succeed in their own way. When students are placed at the center of learning, they develop not only knowledge but also important life skills like thinking, creativity, teamwork, and confidence. These are the skills they need to succeed in the real world and to help build a stronger and better India in the future.

THEORIES AND LITERATURE REVIEW

The learner-centered approach to education is built on strong ideas given by many great thinkers over the years. These thinkers spent their lives studying how people learn, why they learn, and what makes them enjoy learning. Their ideas help us understand why putting students at the centre of education works so well. Three main theories form the base of learner-centered learning. These are the Constructivist Learning Theory, the Flow Theory, and the Self-Determination Theory. Each of these theories looks at learning from a different angle, but together they give us a full picture of how students can learn in the best way possible.

The first and most important theory is the Constructivist Learning Theory (Piaget, 1950). Piaget was a famous thinker from Switzerland who studied how children learn and grow. He said that learning is not something that is simply poured into a student's mind by a teacher. Instead, students build their own knowledge through their own experiences. This is why the theory is called “constructivist,” because students construct or build their understanding step by step. According to Piaget (1950), a learner is not an empty pot that the teacher fills with facts. Rather, the learner is an active builder. When a student meets new information, they think about it, connect it to what they already know, and slowly create meaning from it. This process happens through active participation, where students do things, try things, and reflect on what they have done. Later thinkers built upon Piaget's work to make it even stronger. Vygotsky (1978) added that learning is not just something that happens inside one student's mind. It also happens through talking, working, and sharing ideas with other people. He gave the idea of the Zone of Proximal Development, which means the gap between what a student can do alone and what they can do with a little help. Bruner (1961) also supported this idea by saying that students learn best through discovery, when they find answers on their own rather than being told. Jonassen (1999) later said that teachers should design learning environments where students face real problems, work with real cases, and use real tools to build their own understanding. Reflection is very important in this theory. It means thinking back on an experience and asking questions like “What did I learn?” and “How does this connect to what I knew before?” Without this active building and reflecting, real learning does not happen. Recent studies also support these ideas. Almulla (2023) found that constructivist classrooms help students grow in critical thinking, creativity, and problem-solving, which then improve academic performance. This theory is the strong foundation of the learner-centered approach because it reminds us that the student, not the teacher, is the true builder of knowledge.

The second important theory is the Flow Theory (Csikszentmihalyi, 1990). Csikszentmihalyi was a psychologist who wanted to know why people sometimes become so deeply involved in what they are doing that they forget about time and everything else around them. He called this special state of mind “flow.” Flow happens when a person is fully focused, feels good, and is enjoying the task at the same time. In this state, learning becomes natural and powerful. Csikszentmihalyi (1990) said that students experience flow when they are given tasks that are just right for them. The tasks should not be too easy, because easy tasks make students bored. The tasks should also not be too hard, because very hard tasks make students feel stressed and give up. Instead, the tasks must be meaningful and match the student's skill level with just enough challenge to keep them interested. When students feel this balance, they fall into a state of deep involvement where they learn the most. They enjoy what they are doing, they feel proud of their work, and they want to keep going. Shernoff et al. (2003) tested this idea with real students and found that engagement was highest when lessons were challenging, relevant, and gave students some freedom to choose. Shernoff (2013) further explained that optimal learning environments need clear goals, quick feedback, and strong support to help students reach this state of flow. Buil et al. (2019) also showed that when university students used classroom tools that gave them instant feedback and the right level of challenge, they experienced more flow, and their learning and satisfaction improved. This is why teachers who follow a learner-centered approach try to design lessons that are interesting, meaningful, and well-matched to each student. When this happens, learning stops feeling like hard work and starts feeling like a joyful journey.

The third main theory is the Self-Determination Theory (Deci & Ryan, 1985). These two researchers studied human motivation for many years. They wanted to understand what makes people truly want to do something, rather than being forced to do it. Their answer was that people have three basic needs, and when these needs are met, people feel motivated from inside themselves. This inner motivation is called "intrinsic motivation," and it is much stronger and longer-lasting than being motivated by rewards or fear of punishment. The three needs they talked about are autonomy, competence, and relatedness. Autonomy means having some freedom and choice. When students are allowed to make their own decisions about what and how they learn, they feel more interested and responsible. Competence means feeling skilled and capable. When students can see that they are learning and improving, they feel proud and want to keep working. Relatedness means feeling connected to others. When students feel cared for by their teachers and feel like they belong in a group of classmates, they feel safe and happy, and they learn better. Deci and Ryan (1985) showed that when all three of these needs are met, students become truly engaged in their learning. Later work by Ryan and Deci (2000, 2020) has further proven that meeting these three needs helps students in classrooms all over the world. Reeve (2006) showed that teachers who support student autonomy, by giving reasons for tasks, listening to students, and using kind language, help their students become more motivated and engaged. Niemiec and Ryan (2009) also explained that when these needs are met, students do better in their studies and feel happier in school. A meta-analysis by Howard et al. (2021), which combined the results of hundreds of studies, proved that intrinsic motivation is the strongest predictor of academic success and student well-being. These students do not need to be pushed or forced. They want to learn because it feels good and meaningful to them.

When we look at all three theories together, we can clearly see why the learner-centered approach is so powerful. Piaget (1950) reminds us that students must actively build their own knowledge. Csikszentmihalyi (1990) tells us that students learn best when they are deeply involved in meaningful tasks that match their skills. Deci and Ryan (1985) explain that students need freedom, a sense of ability, and connection with others to stay motivated. All of these ideas point to the same truth. Students are not machines that simply store information. They are thinking, feeling human beings who learn best when they are respected, supported, and challenged in the right way. McCombs and Whisler (1997) also supported this view by giving the Learner-Centered Psychological Principles, which remind us that good teaching must focus on both the individual learner and the science of how people learn. Traditional teaching methods, which focus only on memorizing facts and passing exams, often ignore these truths. They treat students as passive receivers and rely on outside pressure, like exams and grades, to make them study. This kind of learning may bring short-term results, but it does not create deep understanding or a love for learning.

In contrast, the learner-centered approach uses the lessons from these three theories to create classrooms where students enjoy learning, feel motivated, and grow as thinkers. In such classrooms, teachers act as guides rather than bosses. They give students interesting tasks, allow them some choice, encourage them to reflect on their learning, and build warm relationships with them. Weimer (2013) explained that this change means shifting the balance of power, the role of the teacher, and the way students are tested, so that students take more responsibility for their own learning. Freeman et al. (2014), in a large study of over 200 research papers, found that active learning methods improved student performance by a big margin and reduced failure rates by more than half compared to lecture-based teaching. Fredricks et al. (2004) also showed that student engagement has three parts: doing the work (behavioural), enjoying the work (emotional), and thinking deeply about the work (cognitive), and that all three can be improved through learner-centered teaching. As a result, students become confident, creative, and curious learners. They develop not only knowledge but also important life skills like problem-solving, teamwork, and self-discipline. For India, where the education system has relied on old methods for many years, these theories offer a clear path forward. The National Education Policy (NEP, 2020) has also pushed for this change, calling for experiential, inquiry-based, and learner-centered teaching at all levels of education. Kulal et al. (2024) studied how well NEP 2020 is being put into practice and found that students and teachers both support its learner-centered vision, but teachers still need a lot of training and digital skills to make it work. Brinkmann (2019) also pointed out that changing teaching methods in India is not just about rules or tools. It is about changing the deep beliefs that teachers hold about teaching and learning. These studies show that changing teaching methods is not just about using new tools or new technology. It is about understanding students as human beings and creating an environment where they can truly grow. By building on the ideas of Piaget (1950), Csikszentmihalyi

(1990), and Deci and Ryan (1985), along with the work of many other researchers, Indian colleges and universities can slowly move toward a better, more caring, and more effective system of higher education. This new system will prepare students not just for exams, but for life itself.

TEACHING METHODS: STUDENT ENGAGEMENT & ACADEMIC OUTCOMES

Learner-centred teaching represents a transition from traditional instructor-led approaches to methods that actively involve students in the learning process. Early work by Weimer (2002) explains that this approach includes sharing classroom responsibility, encouraging reflection, and promoting independent learning. Such strategies create an environment where students participate more actively and develop critical thinking skills. More recent research also shows that approaches such as problem-based and project-based learning significantly improve student involvement and understanding by encouraging autonomy and participation (Goodwin, 2024; Bhuttah et al., 2024). By aligning instructional practices with intended learning outcomes, these methods contribute to improved academic Outcome and skill development. Based on the above discussion, the following hypotheses are formulated:

H_1: Teaching methods have a significant influence on Student Engagement.

H_6: Teaching methods have a significant influence on Academic Outcome.

FACULTY TRAINING: STUDENT ENGAGEMENT & ACADEMIC OUTCOMES

The effectiveness of learner-centred education largely depends on the readiness and capability of faculty members. Blumberg (2009) emphasizes that instructors need to redesign course structures and adopt active learning strategies to support student-centred environments. Previous studies (Trigwell et al., 2005; O Neill & McMahon, 2017) indicate that trained educators are more likely to encourage student responsibility and deeper learning. Recent findings further highlight that continuous professional development, including digital skills and pedagogical adaptability, plays a crucial role in enhancing both student engagement and academic success (An & Mindrila, 2020). Thus, faculty training strengthens instructional quality and learning outcomes. Based on the above discussion, the following hypotheses are formulated:

H_2: Faculty training has a significant influence on Student Engagement.

H_7: Faculty training has a significant influence on Academic Outcome.

TECHNOLOGY INTEGRATION: STUDENT ENGAGEMENT & ACADEMIC OUTCOMES

The use of technology in education supports learner-centred practices by enabling flexible, interactive, and personalized learning experiences. Earlier studies (Harrell & Wendt, 2016) highlight the importance of digital tools in promoting student participation and independent learning. Recent research further demonstrates that technology-enhanced learning environments increase student engagement by supporting collaboration, interaction, and accessibility (Godsk & Møller, 2024). Additionally, blended learning models have been found to positively impact both engagement and academic achievement by addressing different dimensions of learning (De Bruijn-Smolders & Prinsen, 2024). These developments help students acquire relevant skills and improve their overall performance. Based on the above discussion, the following hypotheses are formulated:

H_3: Technology integration has a significant influence on Student Engagement.

H_8: Technology integration has a significant influence on Academic Outcome.

ASSESSMENT METHODS: STUDENT ENGAGEMENT & ACADEMIC OUTCOMES

Assessment practices play a vital role in shaping how students approach learning. Duncan and Buskirk-Cohen (2011) suggest that assessment methods focusing on continuous feedback and application of knowledge promote active participation and critical thinking. The National Education Policy (2020) also emphasizes the need to move beyond rote-based evaluation towards conceptual understanding. Recent studies indicate that learner-focused assessment methods, including peer evaluation and constructive feedback, improve student involvement and learning effectiveness. These practices support skill development and lead to better academic outcomes by encouraging continuous improvement. Based on the above discussion, the following hypotheses are formulated:

H_4: Assessment methods have a significant influence on Student Engagement.

H_9: Assessment methods have a significant influence on Academic Outcome.

INSTITUTIONAL SUPPORT → STUDENT ENGAGEMENT & ACADEMIC OUTCOMES

Institutional support is a key factor in successfully implementing learner-centred approaches. Brinkmann (2015) highlights that aligning institutional policies and teaching beliefs is essential for promoting such practices. Support mechanisms such as faculty development programs and infrastructure improvements enable educators to adopt effective teaching strategies (An & Mindrila, 2020). Recent research also shows that institutions providing strong technological and pedagogical support systems contribute to higher levels of student engagement and improved academic Outcome (De Bruijn-Smolders & Prinsen, 2024). Therefore, institutional involvement is critical for sustaining quality education. Based on the above discussion, the following hypotheses are formulated:

H_5: Institutional support has a significant influence on Student Engagement.

H_{10}: Institutional support has a significant influence on Academic Outcome.

RESEARCH GAP

Even though there is growing interest in learner-centered approaches in the Indian education system, there are still many important gaps in research that make it hard to put these methods into practice and judge how well they work. Over the past few years, policy documents like the National Education Policy (NEP, 2020) have strongly pushed for a shift toward student-centered teaching, and many colleges have started experimenting with new methods. However, the excitement around these changes has not been matched by strong, high-quality research that can guide their proper implementation. Most of the studies done so far focus only on theoretical frameworks and case studies. They talk about ideas and give examples, but they do not provide strong, real-world evidence on how these methods actually work across India's very different educational settings. While theoretical work is important for building a foundation, it is not enough on its own. Without empirical studies that test these ideas with real students and real teachers, it is difficult to know whether the theories truly work in practice or whether they need to be changed to fit the Indian context. India is a huge country with many types of colleges, from big city universities to small rural institutions, and each one faces its own set of problems. A college in Bengaluru or Mumbai may have modern classrooms, strong internet, and well-trained teachers, while a college in a small town may struggle with basic facilities, limited faculty, and students from diverse economic backgrounds. Without proper empirical evidence from all these different places, it is difficult to truly understand whether learner-centered methods are working or not. A teaching method that succeeds in one setting may completely fail in another, and only careful, context-sensitive research can reveal these differences.

Another big gap is that the challenges faced by teachers and colleges in adopting these new methods have not been studied enough. This is especially true for rural areas and under-resourced institutions, where traditional teaching methods still dominate. Teachers in these places often lack the training, tools, and support they need to change their teaching style, but their struggles are rarely discussed in research. Many rural colleges still rely on chalk-and-talk methods, outdated syllabi, and one-size-fits-all exams, not because the teachers are unwilling to change but because they simply do not have access to modern resources or proper training. The voices of these teachers, who often work under very difficult conditions, are missing from most research on learner-centered education. Another important gap lies in the area of technology integration. Although some studies have looked at how technology affects student engagement, there is very little research on how to use different technological tools in the right way within learner-centered frameworks in Indian higher education. Simply giving students access to computers or online platforms does not automatically lead to better learning. What matters is how these tools are used, how well they are connected to the lesson goals, and how students and teachers are trained to use them effectively. Research that looks at the smart and thoughtful use of technology in Indian classrooms is still rare.

Similarly, the role of institutional support and faculty training in helping colleges move toward learner-centered teaching has not been studied deeply enough. Institutional support includes everything from good infrastructure and clear policies to leadership that encourages innovation and a culture that values student learning. Without strong support from college administration, even the best-trained teachers cannot bring lasting change. Faculty training is another critical area that needs more attention. Most colleges in India do not have regular, structured programs to help teachers learn and apply modern teaching methods. When such training is offered, it is often short, one-time, and too general to make a real difference. Research that examines what kinds of training programs truly work, how long they should last, and how they should be designed is still very limited. Another important missing piece is the voice of the students themselves. Most existing studies do not include students' own views and experiences with these new methods, even though their feedback is essential. Students are the ones who actually sit in classrooms, complete assignments, and take exams, so their perceptions are crucial for understanding whether a teaching method is truly effective. Ignoring student voices can lead to reforms that look good on paper but fail in real life. Some students may find certain methods exciting and helpful, while others may feel lost or overwhelmed, and only direct feedback from students can reveal these differences. In addition, there is a lack of research that looks at how different groups of students, such as those from different genders, economic backgrounds, regions, or learning abilities, experience learner-centered teaching differently. A truly inclusive education system must understand and respond to the needs of all its students, not just a few.

This study fills these gaps by giving a complete look at learner-centered approaches in Indian higher education, focusing on real challenges, institutional support, and student feedback to improve engagement and academic outcomes. By collecting empirical data from a large and diverse sample of students, this research goes beyond theory and provides clear, evidence-based insights that can guide teachers, college leaders, and policymakers. It also brings student voices to the center of the discussion, making sure that the views of the learners themselves are heard and respected. In doing so, this study contributes to a more practical, balanced, and grounded understanding of learner-centered education in India, helping to close the gap between policy, research, and classroom practice.

OBJECTIVES

1. To understand the influence of teaching methods on student engagement and outcomes.
2. To find the relationship among teaching methods, technology integration, institutional support, assessment methods, faculty training, academic outcomes and Students engagement.
3. To find the influence of teaching methods, technology integration, institutional support, assessment methods on faculty training, academic outcomes as well as students engagement

RESEARCH MODEL

Figure 1. Research Model

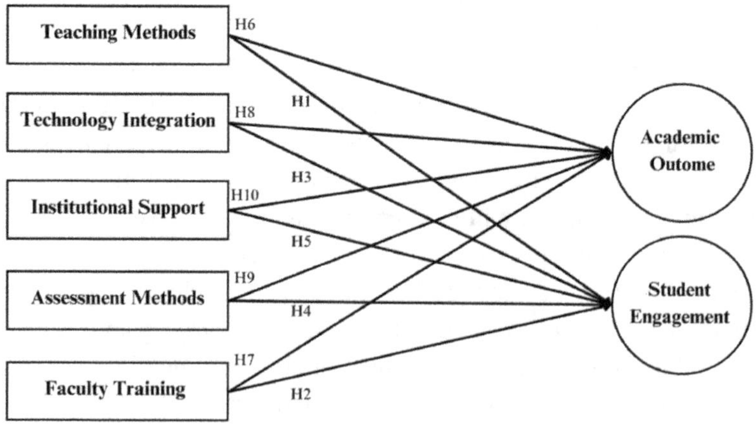

METHODOLOGY

This study uses a quantitative, cross-sectional research design to examine the relationship between teaching methods, faculty training, technology integration, assessment methods, and institutional support with student engagement and academic outcomes within the context of learner-centered education in Indian higher education. A quantitative approach was chosen because it allows the researcher to collect numerical data from a large number of students and use statistical tools to measure the strength of different relationships. A cross-sectional design means that the data were collected at one single point in time, giving a clear picture of student experiences during that period. The target population for this research consists of private university students in Bengaluru, which is estimated at around 180,000 based on extrapolations from the All India Survey on Higher Education (AISHE) 2021-22 data. Bengaluru was chosen because it is one of India's biggest education hubs, with a wide mix of private universities offering different courses to students from many backgrounds. This makes it a good place to study learner-centered education in a diverse setting. To select the sample in a fair and balanced way, the study used stratified random sampling. This method ensures proportional representation across different universities, academic disciplines, and years of study, so that no single group is over-represented or left out. The minimum sample size required for the study was 384, which was calculated using Cochran's formula at a 95% confidence level with a 5% margin of error. However, to make the statistical analysis stronger and more reliable, the researcher collected 588 valid responses, which is well above the required minimum. A structured survey was used to systematically measure student perceptions in a clear and organized way. The survey was distributed through institutional networks, email, and social media platforms, making it easy for students to access and respond. The questionnaire was carefully divided into three main parts. The first part included demographic variables such as age, gender, and year of study. The second part covered the explanatory variables, namely teaching methods, faculty training, technology integration, assessment methods, and institutional support. The third part measured the outcome variables, which are student engagement and academic outcomes. All items were assessed on a 5-point Likert scale, allowing students to show the strength of their agreement or disagreement with each statement. Table 1 presents detailed information on the constructs, their measurement scales, and the sources from which the items were adapted.

Table 1. Construct, Scales and Sources

Construct	Items	Adapted from
Teaching Methods	5	Weimer (2002)
Faculty Training	5	Blumberg (2009); Trigwell et al. (2005)
Technology Integration	5	Harrell & Wendt (2016)
Assessment Methods	5	Duncan & Buskirk-Cohen (2011)
Institutional Support	5	An and Mindrila (2020)
Student Engagement	5	Fredricks et al. (2004)
Academic Outcome	6	Kuh (2009)

Source: Author's own work

Prior to analysis, the collected data underwent cleaning and editing to remove inconsistencies. Reliability analysis was conducted to assess internal consistency, followed by descriptive statistics to outline respondent characteristics. The study employed Spearman's rank correlation to test hypotheses and structural equation modelling (SEM) to examine the relationships among variables, ensuring a comprehensive analysis of the factors influencing student engagement and academic outcomes.

ANALYSIS AND INTERPRETATION

Demographic Profile of Respondents

Table 2 shows the demographic Profile of the respondents which includes age group, gender, current academic level, access to technology for learning, group-based projects and Mode of Learning.

Table 2. Demographic Profile of Respondents

Demographic Variable	Category	Frequency	Percentage
Age Group	18-21	349	59.4%
	22-25	239	40.6%
Gender	Male	219	37.2%
	Female	220	37.4%
	Prefer Not to Say	149	25.3%
Current Academic Level	Under graduation	282	48.0%
	Postgraduation	157	26.6%

continued on following page

Table 2. Continued

Demographic Variable	Category	Frequency	Percentage
	Others	149	25.3%
Access to Technology for Learning	Excellent	237	40.3%
	Good	133	22.6%
	Average	103	17.5%
	Poor	115	19.6%
Group-Based Projects	Very Frequent	237	40.3%
	Frequent	120	20.4%
	Occasional	112	19.0%
	Rare	119	20.2%
Mode of Learning	Traditional Classroom	292	49.7%
	Hybrid	141	24.0%
	Online	155	26.4%

Source: Author's own work

The demographic profile of respondents provides insights into their age, gender, academic level, access to technology for learning, participation in group-based projects, and mode of learning. The majority of respondents (59.4%) belong to the 18-21 age group, while 40.6% fall within the 22-25 age group, indicating that the sample primarily consists of younger individuals, likely undergraduate students. In terms of gender distribution, 37.2% of respondents are male, while 37.4% are female, showing a balanced representation. However, a significant 25.3% preferred not to disclose their gender, which underscores the importance of inclusivity and privacy in demographic surveys. Regarding academic level, 48.0% of respondents are undergraduates, while 26.6% are postgraduates. Additionally, 25.3% fall under the "Others" category, which may include diploma or certificate students, as well as those in non-traditional education programs.

Access to technology for learning varies among respondents. 40.3% reported having excellent access, while 22.6% described their access as good. However, a notable proportion has average (17.5%) or poor (19.6%) access, suggesting that some students face technological barriers in their learning experience. When it comes to group-based projects, 40.3% of respondents engage in them very frequently, while 20.4% do so frequently. A smaller percentage, 19.0%, participate occasionally, and 20.2% rarely engage in group projects, indicating a mix of collaborative and independent learning approaches.

Finally, the mode of learning among respondents is diverse. 49.7% prefer traditional classroom learning, making it the most common mode. Meanwhile, 24.0% engage in hybrid learning, combining both in-person and online elements, and 26.4% rely entirely on online learning, reflecting the growing shift towards digital education. This variation highlights the evolving nature of learning preferences and the need for institutions to offer flexible learning models.

Reliability Analysis

Cronbach's alpha was calculated to test the reliability of the scale used for each variable. A threshold of 0.70 was set to confirm acceptable internal consistency (Nunnally, 1978).

Table 3. Reliability Analysis

Variable	No. of Items	Cronbach's Alpha
Teaching Methods	5	0.81
Technology Integration	5	0.85
Faculty Training	5	0.79
Institutional Support	5	0.82
Assessment Methods	5	0.79
Student Engagement	5	0.81
Academic Outcome	6	0.83

Table 4. Reliability Analysis (Overall)

Scale Reliability Statistics	Cronbach's Alpha
Scale	0.87

Source: Author's own work

The reliability analysis presented evaluates the internal consistency of various variables using Cronbach's Alpha, a widely used reliability coefficient. Table 3 provides the reliability values for different constructs, while Table 4 presents the overall scale reliability.

The overall Cronbach's Alpha for the entire scale as 0.87, which indicates excellent reliability. Generally, a Cronbach's Alpha value above 0.70 is considered acceptable, and values above 0.80 indicate strong reliability. Since all individual variables have reliability values above 0.75, the dataset is considered highly reliable, demonstrating that the responses used in each construct consistently measure the intended factors. These results suggest that the measurement tool used in this study is statistically reliable.

Descriptive Statistics

Descriptive Statistics were used to provide a summary of the data for each variable, including the mean, median and standard deviation in Table 5.

Table 5. Descriptive Statistics

Variable	Mean	Median	Standard Deviation	Shapiro-Wik W	Shapiro-Wik p
Teaching Methods	3.30	3.20	0.82	0.92	< 0.001
Technology Integration	3.39	3.20	0.86	0.93	< 0.001
Faculty Training	3.23	3.20	0.79	0.92	< 0.001
Institutional Support	3.24	3.20	0.71	0.93	< 0.001
Assessment Methods	3.38	3.20	0.81	0.90	< 0.001
Student Engagement	3.43	3.40	0.87	0.92	< 0.001
Academic Outcome	3.22	3.17	0.77	0.94	< 0.001

Source: Author's own work

The above descriptive statistics provide a comprehensive overview of the distribution, central tendency, and variability of the measured variables. The mean values range from 3.22 to 3.43, suggesting that, on average, participants responded at a moderate to slightly high level across all variables. The median values, which are very close to their respective means (ranging from 3.17 to 3.40), indicate that the distributions of responses are relatively symmetric with minimal skewness. The standard deviation values, which range from 0.71 to 0.87, provide insights into the variability of responses. Among independent variables, Institutional Support (0.71) exhibits the least variation, suggesting a consensus on its impact. In contrast, Technology Integration (0.86) and Student Engagement (0.87) show higher variability, indicating differing perceptions. The dependent variable Academic Outcome (0.77) suggests moderate variability, reflecting diverse academic outcomes. The Shapiro-Wilk test results, with W values between 0.90 and 0.94 and p-values consistently < 0.001, indicate significant deviations from normality for all variables. This means the data does not follow a normal distribution, which has important implications for statistical analysis. Hence, the study has used non-parametric test for statistical analysis.

Correlation Analysis

Spearman's rank correlation coefficients (rho) analysis was conducted to examine the relationship between Student Engagement and Academic Outcomes with respect to independent variables. A significance level of 0.05 was used for all tests.

Table 6. Summary of Correlation Matrix

	Teaching Methods	Technology Integration	Faculty Training	Institutional Support	Assessment Methods	Students Engagement	Academic Outcomes
Teaching Methods	-						
Technology Integration	0.534**	-					
Faculty Training	0.496**	0.448**	-				
Institutional Support	0.453**	0.443**	0.365**	-			
Assessment Methods	0.525**	0.527**	0.523**	0.488**	-		
Student Engagement	0.540**	0.555**	0.514**	0.498**	0.561**	-	
Academic Outcome	0.460**	0.502**	0.448**	0.451**	0.478**	0.488**	-

Note: * & ** indicates 1 and 5 percent significance level
Source: Author's own work

Table 6 presents Spearman's rank correlation coefficients (rho), which measure the strength and direction of the relationships between the given variables. The correlation values range from 0.365 to 0.561, indicating moderate to strong positive correlations among the variables. Importantly, all correlations are statistically significant ($p < .001$), meaning these relationships are unlikely to be due to chance. A significant positive correlation between student engagement and assessment methods ($r=0.561$, $p<0.05$) suggests that well-structured assessments enhance student involvement in learning. Similarly, technology integration ($r=0.555$, $p<0.05$) and teaching methods ($r=0.540$, $p<0.05$) are strongly associated with student engagement, indicating that modernized teaching approaches and the integration of technology contribute to higher levels of active participation. Faculty training ($r=0.514$, $p<0.05$) and institutional support ($r=0.498$, $p<0.05$) also show a positive relationship with engagement, suggesting that well-trained faculty and a supportive academic environment are essential for fostering student involvement.

Academic Outcome is significantly correlated with technology integration ($r=0.502$, $p<0.05$) and assessment methods ($r=0.478$, $p<0.05$), indicating that students benefit from digital learning tools and well-structured evaluation systems. Additionally, institutional support ($r=0.451$, $p<0.05$) and faculty training ($r=0.448$, $p<0.05$) contribute positively to academic success, reinforcing the importance of strong faculty development programs and administrative backing. Furthermore, institutional support is moderately correlated with faculty training ($r=0.365$, $p<0.05$), assessment methods ($r=0.488$, $p<0.05$), and student engagement ($r=0.498$, $p<0.05$), suggesting that a well-supported academic structure enhances teaching quality and student involvement. Teaching methods ($r=0.534$, $p<0.05$) and faculty training ($r=0.496$, $p<0.05$) also show a strong association, emphasizing that professional development programs for educators improve instructional effectiveness. These findings highlight the critical role of technology integration, assessment methods, and institutional support in enhancing both student engagement and academic outcome. Institutions should invest in faculty training, modern teaching strategies, and digital learning tools to create an enriched learning environment. Additionally, structured assessments and administrative support play a vital role in improving student outcomes, underscoring the need for a holistic, student-centric educational approach.

Structural Equation Modelling

This Structural Equation Model (SEM) diagram presents an analytical framework evaluating the influence of learner-centric educational approaches on Student Engagement (SE) and Academic Outcomes (AO). The Structural Equation Modelling (SEM) results indicate that student engagement (SE) and academic outcomes (AO) are influenced by teaching methods (TM), technology integration (TI), faculty training (FT), institutional support (IS), and assessment methods (AM). The model successfully converged with 22 iterations, confirming its stability. SE is primarily shaped by TM, TI, FT, IS, and AM, while AO is affected by the same factors, highlighting the strong role of institutional and pedagogical strategies in shaping both engagement and academic outcome. The use of Maximum Likelihood (ML) estimation in this study is appropriate despite deviations from normality. Although ML assumes multivariate normality, it is robust to moderate violations, particularly with a large sample size. With 588 responses, its asymptotic properties ensure consistent and efficient parameter estimates even under non-normal conditions. Moreover, ML facilitates the calculation of widely accepted model fit indices such as χ^2, RMSEA, and SRMR, which are essential for assessing model adequacy. The satisfactory fit indices obtained further support the suitability of ML estimation for this analysis.

Table 7. Model Tests

Label	x^2	df	p
User Model	13.7	5	0.017
Baseline Model	1044.3	10	<0.001

Table 8. Fit Indices

SRMR	RMSEA	Lower	Upper	RMSEA p
0.018	0.054	0.021	0.090	0.360

Source: Author's own work

Table 7 and 8 presents the model fit indices which indicate a good fit of the Structural Equation Model (SEM) to the data. The chi-square test ($\chi^2 = 13.7$, df = 5, p = 0.017) suggests a statistically significant difference, but chi-square is sensitive to sample size. The Standardized Root Mean Square Residual (SRMR = 0.018) is well below the 0.08 threshold, indicating an excellent fit. The Root Mean Square Error of Approximation (RMSEA = 0.054) falls within the acceptable range (0.05–0.08), with confidence intervals (0.021–0.090) supporting the model's robustness. The RMSEA p-value (0.360) further confirms that the model does not exhibit poor fit.

Table 9. User Model Versus Baseline Model

Indicators	Model
Comparative Fit Index (CFI)	0.992
Tucker-Lewis Index (TLI)	0.983
Bentler-Bonett Non-normed Fit Index (NNFI)	0.983
Relative Noncentrality Index (RNI)	0.992
Bentler-Bonett Normed Fit Index (NFI)	0.987
Bollen's Relative Fit Index (RFI)	0.974
Bollen's Incremental Fit Index (IFI)	0.992
Parsimony Normed Fit Index (PNFI)	0.493

Source: Author's own work

Table 9 presents the model fit indices which strongly support the robustness of the structural equation model, indicating a well-fitting model. The Comparative Fit Index (CFI = 0.992), Tucker-Lewis Index (TLI = 0.983), and Bentler-Bonett Non-Normed Fit Index (NNFI = 0.983) all exceed the recommended threshold of 0.90, demonstrating strong comparative and incremental fit. Similarly, the Relative Noncentrality Index (RNI = 0.992) and Bollen's Incremental Fit Index (IFI = 0.992) reinforce the model's excellent alignment with the observed data. While the Parsimony Normed Fit Index (PNFI = 0.493) is lower, this does not undermine the model's validity, as higher fit indices suggest strong theoretical and empirical alignment. Collectively, these results affirm that the proposed model provides a robust representation of the relationships within the dataset, making it suitable for in-depth academic analysis.

Table 10. Summary of Measurement Model

Endogenous Variable: Academic Outcome								
Latent	**Observed**	**Estimate**	**Standard Error**	**Lower**	**Upper**	**β**	**z**	**p**
AO	TM_AVG	1.000	0.0000	1.000	1.000	0.740		
	TI_AVG	1.048	0.0633	0.924	1.172	0.735	16.6	<.001
	FT_AVG	0.701	0.0506	0.602	0.800	0.614	13.9	<.001
	IS_AVG	0.683	0.0524	0.580	0.785	0.578	13.0	<.001
	AM_AVG	1.313	0.0716	1.173	1.453	0.843	18.3	<.001

Source: Author's own work

Table 10 shows the measurement model results which indicate strong factor loadings for the observed variables. The standardized estimate for TM_AVG is fixed at 1.000 for scaling purposes. TI_AVG has a strong estimate of 1.048 (Standard Error = 0.0633), with a confidence interval of [0.924, 1.172] and a significant z-score of 16.6 ($p < .001$), indicating a robust contribution to the latent factor. FT_AVG has a moderate loading (Estimate = 0.701, Standard Error = 0.0506), with a confidence interval of [0.602, 0.800] and a strong z-score of 13.9 ($p < .001$). IS_AVG also contributes significantly (Estimate = 0.683, Standard Error = 0.0524), confidence interval [0.580, 0.785], $z = 13.0$ ($p < .001$). AM_AVG has the highest estimate (1.313, Standard Error = 0.0716), with a confidence interval of [1.173, 1.453] and the strongest z-score of 18.3 ($p < .001$), indicating a dominant role in defining the AO construct. All estimates are statistically significant, reinforcing the reliability of the construct.

Table 11. Summary of Measurement Model

Endogenous Variable: Students Engagement								
Latent	**Observed**	**Estimate**	**Standard Error**	**Lower**	**Upper**	**β**	**z**	**p**
SE	TM_AVG	1.000	0.0000	1.000	1.000	0.740		
	TI_AVG	1.048	0.0633	0.924	1.172	0.735	16.6	<.001
	FT_AVG	0.701	0.0506	0.602	0.800	0.614	13.9	<.001
	IS_AVG	0.683	0.0524	0.580	0.785	0.578	13.0	<.001
	AM_AVG	1.313	0.0716	1.173	1.453	0.843	18.3	<.001

Source: Author's own work

Table 11 presents measurement model results which reflect similar strong factor loadings. The standardized estimate for TM_AVG is fixed at 1.000. TI_AVG exhibits a strong estimate of 1.048 (Standard Error = 0.0633), with a confidence interval of [0.924, 1.172] and a significant z-score of 16.6 ($p < .001$), suggesting a meaningful association with SE. FT_AVG has a moderate estimate of 0.701 (Standard Error = 0.0506), with a confidence interval of [0.602, 0.800] and a significant z-score of 13.9 ($p < .001$). Similarly, IS_AVG demonstrates a substantial loading (Estimate = 0.683, Standard Error = 0.0524), confidence interval [0.580, 0.785], and a z-score of 13.0 ($p < .001$). AM_AVG remains the most influential observed variable, with an estimate of 1.313 (Standard Error = 0.0716), confidence interval [1.173, 1.453], and the highest z-score of 18.3 ($p < .001$). These results confirm the strong contribution of the observed variables to the SE construct, reinforcing its validity and reliability.

Figure 2. SEM Model

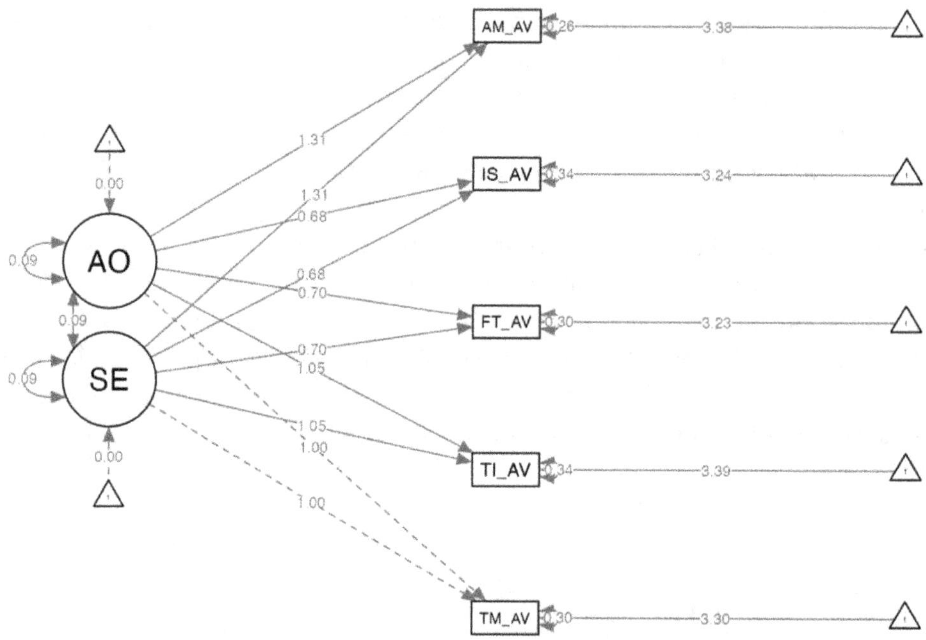

Figure 2 shows the Structural Equation Model (SEM) provides a robust statistical foundation for this research, demonstrating an exceptional fit with the observed data collected from 588 respondents. The model's validity is confirmed by a Comparative Fit Index (CFI) of 0.992 and a Tucker-Lewis Index (TLI) of 0.983, both significantly exceeding the 0.90 threshold for an excellent fit. Furthermore, the Standardized Root Mean Square Residual (SRMR) of 0.018 and an RMSEA of 0.054 (90% CI: 0.021-0.090) indicate minimal residual error and high predictive accuracy. Analysis of the standardized path coefficients (β) identifies Assessment Methods (AM) as the most influential driver for both Student Engagement (SE) and Academic Outcomes (AO) ($\beta = 0.843$, $p < .001$). This is followed by Teaching Methods (TM) ($\beta = 0.740$)

and Technology Integration (TI) ($\beta = 0.735$), which underscore the critical role of interactive pedagogy and digital resources in the learner-centric transition. Faculty Training (FT) ($\beta = 0.614$) and Institutional Support (IS) ($\beta = 0.578$) also provide significant positive contributions to student success. A pivotal revelation is the weak covariance (0.09) between SE and AO, suggesting that while engagement enriches the learning experience, it does not automatically guarantee superior grades, which remain influenced by external institutional constraints and assessment rigor. The model converged successfully in 22 iterations, confirming that all ten hypotheses (H1–H10) are accepted with high statistical significance ($p < .001$).

RESULT AND DISCUSSION

The results indicate that teaching methods, technology integration, and institutional support are significantly associated with enhanced student engagement and improved academic outcomes in Indian higher education. In contrast, insufficient faculty training and ineffective assessment methods hinder these outcomes. These findings support the notion that a learner-centric approach, one that emphasizes active student involvement rather than traditional teacher-centered delivery, can drive deeper learning and critical thinking (Weimer, 2002; Trigwell et al., 2005). For example, Weimer (2002) argued that shifting responsibility from the teacher to the learner fosters self-directed learning, while Trigwell et al. (2005) demonstrated that learner-centric strategies correlate with superior academic outcomes. Our study also aligns with recent research showing that effective technology integration enhances interactive learning environments, facilitating flexible and engaging digital learning experiences (Harrell & Wendt, 2016). When students have access to good digital tools, they can explore topics at their own pace, revisit difficult concepts, and connect with learning materials in ways that traditional classrooms cannot offer. The findings also echo the meta-analysis by Freeman et al. (2014), which showed that active learning methods significantly improve student performance and reduce failure rates in higher education. Furthermore, the observed negative impact of inadequate faculty training echoes Blumberg's (2009) emphasis on robust professional development to successfully implement learner-centric approaches. Teachers are at the heart of any educational change, and without proper training, even the best policies and tools cannot bring the desired results. The study also supports the ideas of Reeve and Cheon (2021), who showed that when teachers are trained in autonomy-supportive teaching, their students become more engaged, motivated, and successful. Institutional support, as highlighted by Brinkmann (2015), plays a similar role, because colleges must align their policies, culture, and resources with learner-centered goals. Overall, the evidence suggests that implementing comprehensive pedagogical reforms, including targeted faculty training, innovative teaching practices, and strategic technology integration, is essential for promoting a learner-centric approach that substantially benefits student engagement and academic achievement. These findings also match the goals of the National Education Policy (NEP, 2020), which calls for a complete shift toward experiential, inquiry-based, and learner-centered teaching in Indian higher education.

MANAGERIAL IMPLICATIONS

The findings emphasize the need for higher education institutions to adopt a more holistic learner-centric approach by strengthening both teaching practices and institutional systems. A primary focus should be on continuous faculty development, where educators are trained in modern pedagogical approaches such as active learning, flipped classrooms, and problem-based teaching. Such training enhances instructional quality and helps create more engaging and interactive learning environments. Faculty development should not be a one-time event but an ongoing process that includes workshops, peer learning sessions, mentoring, and regular refresher courses. Colleges can also encourage faculty members to attend national and international conferences, publish research on teaching methods, and collaborate with other institutions to share best practices. In addition, institutions must invest in robust technological infrastructure, including digital platforms and learning management systems, while ensuring equitable access for all students. This is especially important in India, where the digital divide remains a serious challenge. Colleges should provide free or low-cost laptops, strong Wi-Fi connections, and digital skill-building programs so that no student is left behind because of financial or technical reasons. Thoughtful integration of technology can support personalized learning and improve overall engagement when aligned with instructional objectives. Tools like learning management systems, video lectures, interactive apps, and virtual labs can make learning more flexible, accessible, and enjoyable. However, technology alone cannot replace good teaching; it must be used as a support rather than as a substitute.

Equally important is the reform of assessment practices and institutional support mechanisms. Institutions should move beyond traditional examination systems and adopt a balanced mix of formative and summative assessments that provide continuous feedback and encourage application-based learning. Formative assessments such as quizzes, short projects, class presentations, and peer reviews help students understand their progress and identify areas for improvement throughout the term. Summative assessments, while still important, should not be the only way to judge a student's learning. Project-based evaluations, case studies, group assignments, and real-world problem-solving tasks can better measure a student's ability to apply knowledge in practical situations. These methods also reduce exam-related stress and promote deeper, more meaningful learning. Strengthening support structures, such as mentorship programs, academic counselling, and manageable class sizes, can further enhance the learning experience and student well-being. Smaller class sizes allow teachers to give personal attention to each student, build stronger relationships, and respond to individual learning needs. Mentorship programs, where senior faculty or older students guide newcomers, can also help students feel more connected and supported. Mental health counseling services and career guidance cells are equally important in making sure that students feel emotionally and professionally prepared for life beyond college. Together, these measures contribute to improved academic outcomes and sustained student engagement, enabling institutions to align with the evolving demands of modern higher education. Indian colleges and universities that commit to these reforms will not only improve their rankings and reputation but also create a new generation of confident, skilled, and thoughtful graduates.

CONCLUSION

This study reinforces the transformative potential of a learner-centered approach in higher education and clearly shows how powerful it can be in improving student learning. The findings prove that this modern way of teaching helps students become more engaged, more motivated, and more successful in their academic outcomes. When students are placed at the centre of learning, they do not just memorize facts but truly understand what they are studying. They start to enjoy the learning process, ask more questions, and take ownership of their education. They become independent thinkers who are not afraid to challenge old ideas, explore new ones, and find creative solutions to real problems. The study shows that several important things come together to make learner-centered education work well. Active learning strategies, where students take part in discussions, group work, and real problem-solving, help them learn more deeply. Personalized instruction, where teachers pay attention to each student's needs and pace, makes learning more effective. Every student is different, with unique strengths, weaknesses, interests, and learning styles, and a one-size-fits-all approach can never meet the needs of all learners. Technology integration also plays a big role, as it brings lessons to life through videos, online tools, and interactive platforms. Digital tools can make learning more fun, flexible, and accessible, especially for students who cannot always attend physical classes or who need extra help outside of regular hours. All of these together lead to deeper conceptual understanding and much better learning outcomes. Besides teaching methods, other important factors also shape student success. Faculty training is very important, because even the best teaching methods fail if teachers are not trained to use them. Institutional support, which includes good infrastructure, clear policies, and encouragement from college leaders, also matters a lot. A supportive institutional culture makes teachers feel confident to try new methods and students feel safe to take risks in their learning. Well-structured assessment methods, which test students through projects, continuous feedback, and practical tasks instead of just final exams, help students learn in a more meaningful way. Of course, moving from traditional teaching to learner-centered teaching is not easy. There are real challenges such as faculty resistance, limited resources, crowded classrooms, and the digital divide. Many teachers feel unsure about giving up their old ways, and many colleges struggle to find the money or manpower to make big changes. But with careful planning and strong commitment, these challenges can be overcome. Step-by-step reforms, strong leadership, and the involvement of all stakeholders, including teachers, students, parents, and policymakers, can make this transformation possible. To fully enjoy the benefits of learner-centered education, colleges and universities must adopt policies that support innovative teaching practices, give equal access to digital tools, and offer continuous faculty development programs. A holistic approach, which includes adaptive learning techniques and collaborative instructional strategies, will ensure that students are well prepared for both academic and professional success. Future research should explore the long-term impact of these strategies across different educational contexts so that best practices can be refined over time. By embracing a learner-centered framework, educational institutions can create meaningful, student-driven learning experiences that match the changing needs of the modern academic and professional world. In doing so, they will not only shape better students but also build a stronger, wiser, and more caring society for the future.

LIMITATIONS AND SCOPE FOR FURTHER STUDY

While this study provides valuable insights into the impact of a learner-centered approach on student engagement and academic outcomes, it also has certain limitations that must be acknowledged honestly. Every research study has its boundaries, and being open about these limits helps other researchers and readers judge the findings more fairly. One key limitation is the reliance on self-reported data. Since the information was collected from students through a questionnaire, their answers may have been influenced by their own subjective perceptions and personal biases. Some students may have answered in a way they thought was expected, rather than how they truly felt. Others may have misunderstood certain questions or given quick answers without thinking deeply. Although the questionnaire was carefully designed to reduce such problems, self-reported data can never fully capture the true experiences of every student. Another limitation is that the study is context-specific. It focused on a particular educational setting, mainly private universities in Bengaluru. This means the findings may not fully apply to all other institutions, academic disciplines, or cultural contexts across India or other countries. India is a vast and diverse country, with huge differences between urban and rural colleges, government and private institutions, and different regional cultures. A finding that holds true in Bengaluru may not apply in the same way in smaller cities or villages. The research also does not capture the long-term effects of learner-centered education, because it mainly looked at short-term improvements in student engagement and academic outcomes. A learning approach that shows strong short-term results may or may not bring the same benefits over several years. Some effects of learner-centered teaching, such as improved critical thinking, lifelong learning habits, and professional success, can only be seen many years after graduation. In addition, while technology integration was studied, the differences in digital literacy among students and teachers were not deeply explored. These differences can greatly affect how well technology-based learning strategies actually work in real classrooms. A student who is comfortable with digital tools will benefit much more from online learning than one who struggles even to use basic software.

Future research should focus on longitudinal studies that follow students over many years to assess the lasting impact of learner-centered methodologies on academic performance and career readiness. Such studies can show whether students who experienced learner-centered education become more successful in their jobs, more confident in their skills, and more satisfied with their lives compared to those who studied in traditional settings. Expanding the study to include more diverse educational institutions, public universities, rural colleges, and different academic disciplines would make the findings more widely applicable. Including students from different economic backgrounds, regions, and language groups would also give a richer and more complete picture of how learner-centered education works in varied settings. Further research could also explore the role of digital literacy in making the most of technology-driven learning and study how different learner-centered models affect various groups of students from different backgrounds, genders, and financial conditions. Understanding these differences will help colleges design more inclusive and fair teaching practices that work for everyone, not just a few. Comparative studies between traditional and learner-centered approaches across different education systems would also give deeper insights into what truly works best. Research could also look at how teacher attitudes, leadership styles, and institutional culture shape the success of learner-centered reforms. Additionally, qualitative studies, including interviews, focus groups, and classroom observations, can add depth to the numerical findings by capturing the real voices, feelings, and struggles of students and teachers. Addressing these areas will help build a more complete understanding of learner-centered education and its real power to transform academic experiences globally, creating a brighter future for students everywhere.

REFERENCES

An, Y., & Mindrila, D. (2020). Strategies and tools used for learner-centered instruction. *International Journal of Technology in Education and Science*, *4*(2), 133–143. https://ijtes.net/index.php/ijtes/article/view/1595. DOI: 10.46328/ijtes.v4i2.74

Bandura, A. (1977). *Social learning theory*. Prentice Hall.

Bhuttah, T. M., Xusheng, Q., Abid, M. N., & Sharma, S. (2024). Enhancing student critical thinking and learning outcomes through innovative pedagogical approaches in higher education: The mediating role of inclusive leadership. *Scientific Reports*, *14*(1), 24362. https://www.nature.com/articles/s41598-024-75379-0. DOI: 10.1038/s41598-024-75379-0 PMID: 39420057

Blumberg, P. (2009). *Developing learner-centered teaching: A practical guide for faculty*. Jossey-Bass.

Brinkmann, S. (2015). Learner-centred education reforms in India: The missing piece of teachers' beliefs. *Policy Futures in Education*, *13*(3), 342–359. https://journals.sagepub.com/doi/10.1177/1478210315569038. DOI: 10.1177/1478210315569038

Csikszentmihalyi, M. (1990). *Flow: The psychology of optimal experience*. Harper & Row.

De Bruijn-Smolders, M., & Prinsen, F. R. (2024). Effective student engagement with blended learning: A systematic review. *Heliyon*, *10*(23), e39439. https://linkinghub.elsevier.com/retrieve/pii/S2405844024154709. DOI: 10.1016/j.heliyon.2024.e39439 PMID: 39687123

Deci, E. L., & Ryan, R. M. (1985). Intrinsic motivation and self-determination in human behavior. Springer. https://link.springer.com/book/10.1007/978-1-4899-2271-7

Duncan, T., & Buskirk-Cohen, A. A. (2011). Exploring learner-centered assessment: A cross-disciplinary approach. *International Journal on Teaching and Learning in Higher Education*, *23*(2), 246–259. https://eric.ed.gov/?id=EJ946150

Fredricks, J. A., Blumenfeld, P. C., & Paris, A. H. (2004). School Engagement: Potential of the Concept, State of the Evidence. *Review of Educational Research*, *74*(1), 59–109. https://journals.sagepub.com/doi/10.3102/00346543074001059. DOI: 10.3102/00346543074001059

Godsk, M., & Møller, K. L. (2024). Engaging students in higher education with educational technology. *Education and Information Technologies, 30*(3), 2941–2976. https://link.springer.com/article/10.1007/s10639-024-12901-x. DOI: 10.1007/s10639-024-12901-x

Goodwin, J. R. (2024). What's the difference? A comparison of student-centered teaching methods. *Education Sciences, 14*(7), 736. https://www.mdpi.com/2227-7102/14/7/736. DOI: 10.3390/educsci14070736

Harrell, P. E., & Wendt, J. L. (2016). A learner-centered approach to technology integration. In Keengwe, J., & Onchwari, G. (Eds.), *Handbook of research on learner-centered pedagogy in teacher education and professional development* (pp. 1–22). IGI Global., https://www.igi-global.com/gateway/chapter/163484

Higher Education Digest. (2024). Revolutionizing higher education: The role of technology in enhancing student engagement and learning outcomes. https://www.highereducationdigest.com/revolutionizing-higher-education-the-role-of-technology-in-enhancing-student-engagement-and-learning-outcomes/

Kuh, G. D. (2009). The national survey of student engagement: Conceptual and empirical foundations. *New Directions for Institutional Research, 141*(141), 5–20. https://onlinelibrary.wiley.com/doi/10.1002/ir.283. DOI: 10.1002/ir.283

Nunnally, J. C. (1978). *Psychometric theory* (2nd ed.). McGraw-Hill.

Piaget, J. (1950). *The psychology of intelligence*. Routledge.

Trigwell, K., Prosser, M., & Ginns, P. (2005). Phenomenographic pedagogy and a revised approaches to teaching inventory. *Higher Education Research & Development, 24*(4), 349–360. https://www.tandfonline.com/doi/abs/10.1080/07294360500284730. DOI: 10.1080/07294360500284730

Weimer, M. (2002). *Learner-centered teaching: Five key changes to practice*. Jossey-Bass.

Chapter 8
Developing an International Entrepreneurship Mindset in University Students Through Strategies:
Barriers, Facilitators, and Interdisciplinary Scenarios

Josue Aaron Lopez-Leyva
http://orcid.org/0000-0002-3004-5686
School of Engineering, CETyS University, Mexico

Sialia Karina Mellink-Méndez
http://orcid.org/0000-0002-0629-0227
School of Business and Administration, CETyS University, Mexico

Gloria Janeth Murillo-Aviña
http://orcid.org/0000-0003-3488-6420
School of Business and Administration, CETyS University, Mexico

Diana Esther Woolfolk-Ruiz
http://orcid.org/0000-0002-2949-488X
School of Business and Administration, CETyS University, Mexico

ABSTRACT

This chapter addresses the above situation from a university context intending to promote the international entrepreneurial mindset of future entrepreneurs. First, the

DOI: 10.4018/979-8-2600-2606-9.ch008

evolution of the entrepreneur concept and the types of entrepreneurial mindset are addressed through the entrepreneurial matrix diagram. Then, the scenarios that need to be considered in order to create policies that support the training of international entrepreneurs are described, emphasizing the VUCA and BANI frameworks. The barriers and facilitators in the university environment for promoting international entrepreneurship are then analyzed. Next, some interdisciplinary strategies that could be developed to improve the impact on the international entrepreneurship mindset in the university environment are mentioned. Finally, conclusions and limitations of the research are presented. In this way, this research can help universities establish a starting point for proposing short-, medium-, and long-term roadmaps to enhance their impact on the international entrepreneurial mindset of students.

1 INTRODUCTION

Human beings have long found ways to develop and realize their ideas as part of the solution to difficult social and natural contexts, but sometimes in an unexpected way. In this sense, entrepreneurship is one of how individuals materialize their ideas in order to generate value and economic profit, taking into account some of the needs of people. In this way, the concept of the entrepreneur has evolved based on different philosophical and social aspects. In particular, for Cantillon and Higgs (1932), the entrepreneur is a person who is characterized by buying products at known prices to sell them at unknown prices. Nevertheless, this definition presents some difficulties and contradictions with the current reality. Afterward, the entrepreneur is represented as a risk-taker with an outstanding level of intelligence (Rodríguez, 2009). In this way, the concept of the entrepreneur has been transformed, concluding that the entrepreneur is a person who takes risks based on a high level of creativity and innovation to create a value proposition focused on a product, service, or experience for a particular market segment and, finally, to create an organizational structure that supports the aforementioned intellectual and productive process, i.e. a company (De Vries, 1977; Baumol, 1968; Baumol, 2018; Hisrich et al., 2005; Howorth et al., 2005).

An entrepreneur faces diverse challenges beyond the variable term, including gender, cultural, and personal health pressures, as well as prejudices, fiscal considerations, and aspects related to the location of the company and the market target (Siddegowda, 2020; Zimmerman, 2013; Suvarna et al., 2019; Fernández-Bedoya et al., 2023; Reeves et al., 2019). In this way, and under many considerations, it is possible to classify the entrepreneur concerning the physical scope of the economic activity, whether locally, regionally, nationally, or internationally. To clarify the above, the local entrepreneur is a person who carries out a business activity with creativity and innovation to offer a product, service, or experience that satisfies the needs of a local market segment. However, the value chain and logistical aspects involve local, regional, national, and international stakeholders. Assuming the same rule, it is possible to define the other types of ventures according to the physical scope, i.e., local, regional, national, and international entrepreneurs. In this way, each type of entrepreneurship, based on the classification according to its scope, presents various opportunities and challenges.

In particular, international entrepreneurship is a highly demanding and risky economic activity, especially for those companies with few employees and reduced installed capacity. The high risk and requirements mentioned lie in the fact that this type of venture must have the ability to propose and operate a business model that considers that its end customer is located in a country (or region) different from the origin country of the company. For instance, concerning the components of the business model put forward by Osterwalder and Pigneur, which include key activities, key partners, key resources, cost, value proposition, customer relationships, customers, revenue, and channels (Osterwalde, 2004), an international undertaking should, from its project planning stages to the operational stages, consider aspects of an international nature that could affect each element of its business model, such as language, acculturation, export logistics, and cost structure, among others. Together with the business model of Osterwalder and Pigneur, a PESTEL analysis is recommended. The PESTEL analysis considers the evaluation of external factors concerning the business situation, such as political, economic, social, technological, legal, and environmental aspects. The analysis examines opportunities and threats arising from these factors. The aforementioned can be related to the "Think Globally, Act Locally" strategy. But it has to be considering a lot of variables, especially for emerging markets.

Furthermore, the business model, according to its definition, should act as an interdisciplinary tool, yet this approach is largely absent from the general training of entrepreneurs. In the same sense, the Global Entrepreneurship Monitor (GEM) 2022-2023 Global Report analyses the social, cultural, political, and economic context of entrepreneurship worldwide and notes the impact of various factors on entrepreneurial activity and intention. According to GEM 2022-2023, globally, three in ten people have started a business at some point, while 29% expect to do so shortly. On the other hand, Saudi Arabia, Colombia, and Mexico have the highest percentage of adults who expressed that they are likely to start a business in the future, who are more than half of those surveyed. In contrast, countries such as Belgium (13%), the Netherlands (11%), and Japan (8%) have the lowest rates of people planning to start a business. Although the GEM 2022-2023 is not clear regarding international entrepreneurship, it does provide a transversal exploratory analysis that allows for analyzing various approaches to improve entrepreneurship indicators at a global level through various strategies (Hill et al., 2023).

Intending to clarify the definition of international entrepreneurship, Figure 1 shows the entrepreneur matrix diagram divided into three dimensions: 1) Management skill & business know-how level, 2) Creativity & innovation level, and 3) Internationalization level. As can be seen, international entrepreneurship requires the highest level of business ability, creativity, and innovation, as well as aspects of internationalization. In the same sense, an entrepreneur who has a high capacity for making business, as well as creativity and innovation, but with a low level in aspects of internationalization, could be considered a local or regional entrepreneur. Thus, Figure 1 does not consider the level of collaboration between different knowledge disciplines (e.g., business, humanities, social sciences, and natural and applied sciences) as part of the process of developing the entrepreneurial mentality; rather, it stipulates a particular goal for each dimension.

Figure 1. Entrepreneur matrix diagram.

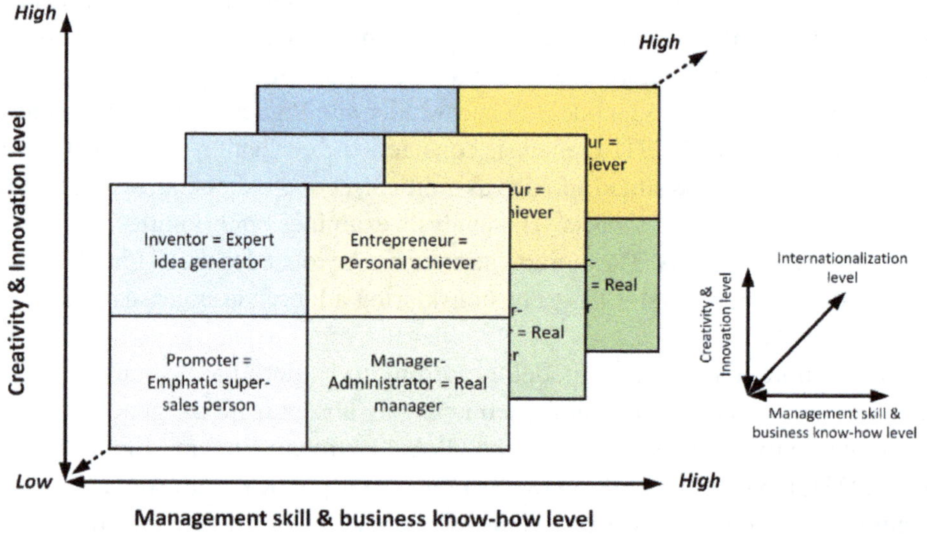

In this fashion, the problem arises regarding the increase in the number of companies related to international entrepreneurship, as well as improving the competitiveness of international entrepreneurship, from the early stages of the entrepreneur as an individual, in our case, from university training. This research problem can be addressed through the following research questions, such as: What are the distinctive characteristics of the international entrepreneurship mentality (mindset) with conventional entrepreneurship? Emphasizing conventional entrepreneurship as that developed for local, regional, and national markets, what are the barriers and facilitators for international entrepreneurship in the university context? And finally, what are the strategies developed in an interdisciplinary way for the development of international entrepreneurship in the university context?

2 SCENARIOS FOR DESIGNING POLICIES AND STRATEGIES TO SUPPORT AND DEVELOP ENTREPRENEURSHIP

Various strategies have been proposed globally to aid in the development of entrepreneurs, addressing the specific conditions and scenarios in each region by mitigating the problems and barriers typically encountered when engaging in entrepreneurial activities. This is the central concept behind implementing strategies that stimulate entrepreneurial activities by identifying and solving barriers and challenges to such activity, through specific actions outlined in a strategic plan. Although there are many complex scenarios for the development of entrepreneurship, below are described some fundamental scenarios, which can also be perceived as barriers.

Although there are many complex scenarios for the development of entrepreneurship, below are described some fundamental scenarios, which can also be perceived as barriers. To clarify, establishing individual strategies for the promotion and development of entrepreneurship is an almost impossible task, but it is possible to generalize their bases. Considering the above, Figure 2 shows the relationship of the various adverse scenarios for the development of entrepreneurship, as well as the direct relationship with each strategy that responds to each scenario. It is important to consider a starting point that describes the reality of entrepreneurship and concludes with a real objective. It is understood that sometimes the strategies do not directly meet the developing entrepreneurship objectives, but there may be an adjustment to the mentioned objectives, as is the case of scenario 5 and strategy 5.

Figure 2. Relation of the strategies and scenarios for developing entrepreneurship.

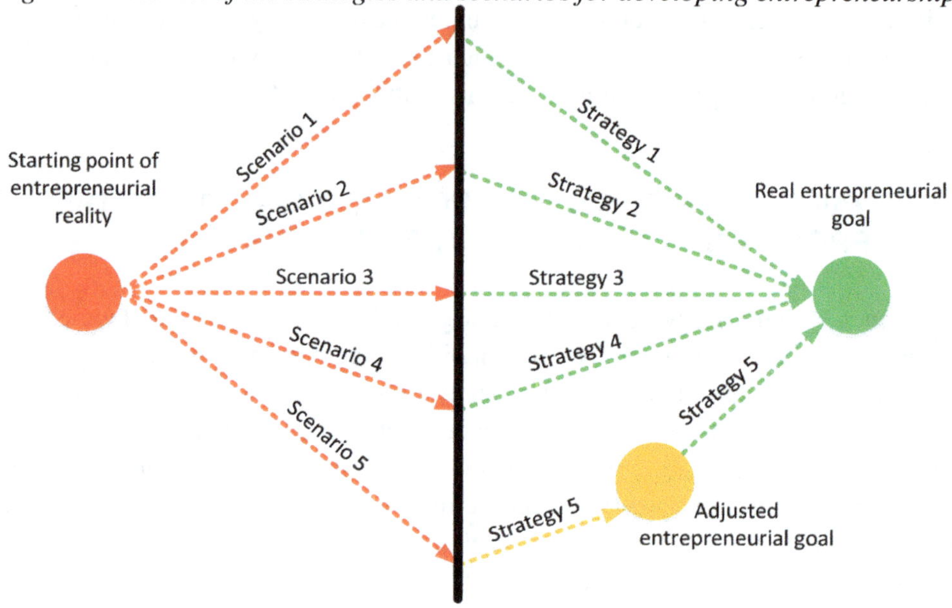

2.1 Gender Equality and Women's Empowerment (Scenario 1)

Considerable strategies have been developed to promote entrepreneurship within the gender equality framework, especially for the development of women in the business field. As general results in terms of strategies, cooperation with other companies is a priority strategy for women to increase their innovation and business capacity (Pitaloka et al., 2021; Al-Qahtani et al., 2022). In the same sense, strategies for women's business development focus on the elimination of social and cultural barriers that limit women's empowerment (Setyaningrum et al., 2023; Ziyae et al., 2021). In addition, strategies related to training in Science, Technology, Engineering, and Mathematics (STEM) have also demonstrated a positive impact on female empowerment in entrepreneurship and increased the possibility that a woman who is in her academic training will undertake at short, medium, or long term (Sharma, 2022; Bernard, 2015). Considering the aforementioned, the keys to creating strategies for the development of entrepreneurship in women are based on research on female references, the design of training programs, the creation of entrepreneurship communication, and the strengthening of hard and soft skills in the business field.

2.2 Sustainable Development (Scenario 2)

The entrepreneurial intention can have various origins and reasons, i.e., different causes or personal scenarios may exist behind the business vision. In this sense, the strategy of raising awareness of global problems as a starting point for a potential solution proposal that involves the creation and innovation of a product and service is highly attractive (Dhanabhakyam, 2021; Hassan et al., 2022; Gifford & McKelvey, 2019; Amir & Prabawani, B2023). For example, based on the 2030 Agenda for Sustainable Development (ASD), there are 17 Sustainable Development Goals (SDGs), which can be starting points for the development of creativity and innovation of entrepreneurial ideas. In particular, the 17 SDGs are 1) No poverty, 2) Zero hunger, 3) Good health and well-being, 4) Quality education, 5) Gender equality, 6) Clean water and sanitation, 7) Affordable and clean energy, 8) Decent work and economic growth, 9) Industry, innovation and infrastructure, 10) Reduced inequalities, 11) Sustainable cities and communities, 12) Responsible consumption and production, 13) Climate action, 14) Life below the water, 15) Life on land, 16) Peace, justice and strong institutions and, 17) Partnerships (Anderson et al., 2022). In this way, a person may conceive a business idea based on the sensitivity of some of the aforementioned SDGs.

2.3 Open Innovation and Entrepreneurial Ecosystem (Scenario 3)

In general, there are two types of innovation according to the interaction between the industrial and academic sectors: Open Innovation (OI) and Closed Innovation (CI). In particular, the distinction between open innovation and closed innovation is determined by the processes with which the innovation is created. For instance, CI is developed in an independent business environment (i.e., at the company's location and with its tangible and intangible resources), while OI incorporates external resources to the management of innovation, such as the exchange of ideas beyond the limits of the company, active co-innovators, high mobility of employees and collaborators, among others. Considering the aforementioned, after the literature review, it was found that the creation of public and private sectors allows an ecosystem for the development of entrepreneurship projects (Liu et al., 2021; Angrisani et al., 2022; Eckhardt et al., 2018; De Brito & Leitão, 2021).

2.4 Organizational Culture (Scenario 4)

Typically, organizational culture refers to the psychological nature of a company. This nature is constituted by the values and attitudes of its employees and managers, the social perception of the company, the quality of direct and indirect processes, social responsibility, and commitment to innovation, among others. In this way, an already established company, with a consolidated organizational culture in all aspects, will seek in some way to influence creativity and innovation within the organization, but without having the obligation to promote entrepreneurship, since there may exist conflicts of interest. Nonetheless, an entrepreneurial intention, which seeks to strengthen itself to the point of creating a formal company, will also seek to strengthen the organizational culture of the newly created company. The above is because the competitiveness of a company has a strong relationship with its organizational culture (Nguyen et al., 2020; Kalamaki et al., 2021; Jufriyono et al., 2017).

2.5 Formal, Non-Formal, And Informal Education (Scenario 5)

A fundamental scenario for the development of entrepreneurship is a well-structured education scheme in the discipline. In general, formal, non-formal, and informal education activities are required that contribute to local, regional, national, and international entrepreneurial. In particular, formal education provides a solid academic foundation, since it is required to be intentional, it is based on a system to achieve achievable pedagogical objectives promptly, which allows one to level up in the discipline. Non-formal education allows the acquisition of practical skills necessary for professional success through structured training programs that are not part of the conventional educational system (i.e., formal model), but that bring the potential entrepreneur closer to real problems of the discipline. Next, informal education provides a general understanding of local conditions and cultures through daily and everyday actions, without the need to have a pedagogical structure or be supported by any organization. For these reasons, there is no documentary evidence (e.g. certificate) that accredits the training level. Considering the above, precisely the lack of some type of education, or the inadequate design of the strategy, is what does not allow the development of entrepreneurs, that is, sometimes public policies focus only on formal education, without considering the advantages of non-formal and informal education (Yasa et al., 2022; Utama, 2021; Usup et al., 2020; Bezanilla et al., 2020; Mei & Symaco, 2022; Sigüenza-Orellana et al., 2022; Nambisan et al., 2018; Bozorgi et al., 2021; Yu, 2018). However, it is necessary to mention that all types of education have their benefits and weaknesses, which is why an exhaustive analysis is needed so that the viability and feasibility of the strategy are adequate.

3 ENTREPRENEURSHIP FIXED AND GROWTH MINDSETS

The description of the concept of mindset is a complex one. Generally, it is more than the conventional definition of a person's mentality in many contexts. In particular, it is a mental process based on beliefs, thoughts, values, and traditions that have an impact on a person's way of being, day-to-day behavior, and decision-making. In this way, mindset influences both the personal and professional development of people, and in the context of entrepreneurship it is no exception. The literature suggests several types of entrepreneurial mindsets, depending on different aspects and situations. For example, three types of entrepreneurial leadership mindsets, such as purpose-oriented, people-oriented, and learning-oriented, have been proposed by Subramaniam and Shankar (2020). Each of these mindsets, or a combination of them, is the basis of the mental programming for the development of all the activities that are both directly and indirectly related to an entrepreneurial leader. More generally, two entrepreneurial mindsets are proposed: the fixed and the growth mindset. The fixed mindset is based on the idea that people's abilities cannot be increased or improved. Therefore, they must work with their intellectual abilities. Instead, a growth mindset is based on the idea that new skills and talents can be cultivated over time through unwavering determination, commitment, and hard work (Dweck, 2015; Glenn, 2010). Given the above and based on a view of local entrepreneurship, a specific mindset or a combination of different mindsets is required for this type of entrepreneurship. The latter takes account of aspects of local enterprises, such as the fact that they generally focus only on one commercial activity, they are micro or small enterprises and are usually managed by a single owner, their income is moderate, their place of operation is a city or a region and, above all, they only influence their economic sector if they are considered as an organization of several enterprises located in the same economic sector. In this way, the fixed mindset may be the one that is most congruent with the context described above. However, to increase the competitiveness of international companies (related to international entrepreneurship), other mindsets will be needed, such as the growth mindset.

4 INTERNATIONAL ENTREPRENEURSHIP MINDSET & VUCA AND BANI FRAMEWORKS

In the context of business strategy and business models, the VUCA (Volatility, Uncertainty, Complexity, and Ambiguity) environment has been widely used to promote business competitiveness. This term dates back to the 1990s and the post-Cold War geopolitical context that encompasses all the terms that make up the acronym

VUCA. Thus, in a VUCA environment, companies aim to thrive even though their context is highly unpredictable and changing. However, this conceptualization of the VUCA environment has been tested by the COVID-19 pandemic and other global changes, so a new environment has emerged, the BANI environment (Brittle, Anxious, Non-linear, and Incomprehensible), which refers to the brittle, anxious, non-linear and incomprehensible moments, in our case in business. In particular, the VUCA environment is pre-pandemic and the BANI environment is post-pandemic. Considering the above, the business mindset of both local and international nature is subject to VUCA and/or BANI environments (Zakharov, 2022; Hierro, 2020; Grabmeier, 2020). Furthermore, there are specific differences between the VUCA and BANI frameworks. In terms of approach, the VUCA framework focuses on the factors that create uncertainty and complexity in the business environment, while the BANI focuses on the impact of these factors on organizations. In terms of the nature of change, VUCA analysis focuses on an environment that is changing rapidly but has a degree of uncertainty (or predictability) and can therefore be analyzed. Next, BANI analysis focuses on an environment that is increasingly difficult to understand and that changes in a non-linear and disruptive manner. In addition, VUCA analysis suggests that organizations need to develop the ability to adapt and respond quickly to changes in the environment, while BANI analysis suggests that organizations need to be more flexible and resilient to survive and thrive in an increasingly uncertain environment (Baskoro, 2023; Peñalver Martínez, 2022). In this way, doing business internationally requires a growth mindset that takes into account some of the environments mentioned above. In our case, we consider the BANI environment. Thus, the international entrepreneur who has a growth mindset that considers the BANI environment will be able to see the challenges and opportunities, focus on the processes and not the results, learn and grow quickly from his personal and business mistakes, take risks, step out of his comfort zone, accept constructive feedback, consider the success of other entrepreneurs and believe that can always improve the skills. The above will enable the entrepreneur to make intelligent decisions that will help maintain and increase the competitiveness business. Consider, for example, local entrepreneurs who want to expand the supply of a product to another country by collaborating with an international company. If these people have a fixed entrepreneurial mindset and their soft skills are nil, weak, and limiting, the international business venture is unlikely to be successful. However, if these entrepreneurs have an entrepreneurial growth mindset and analyze the BANI environment involved in the business, they will surely look for the best ways to reduce or eliminate business risks such as cultural differences, language, and business regulations, among others (Tsyfra et al., 2022; Bushuyev et al., 2023).

Figure 3. Relation between the entrepreneurship mindset and life span and scope of the company.

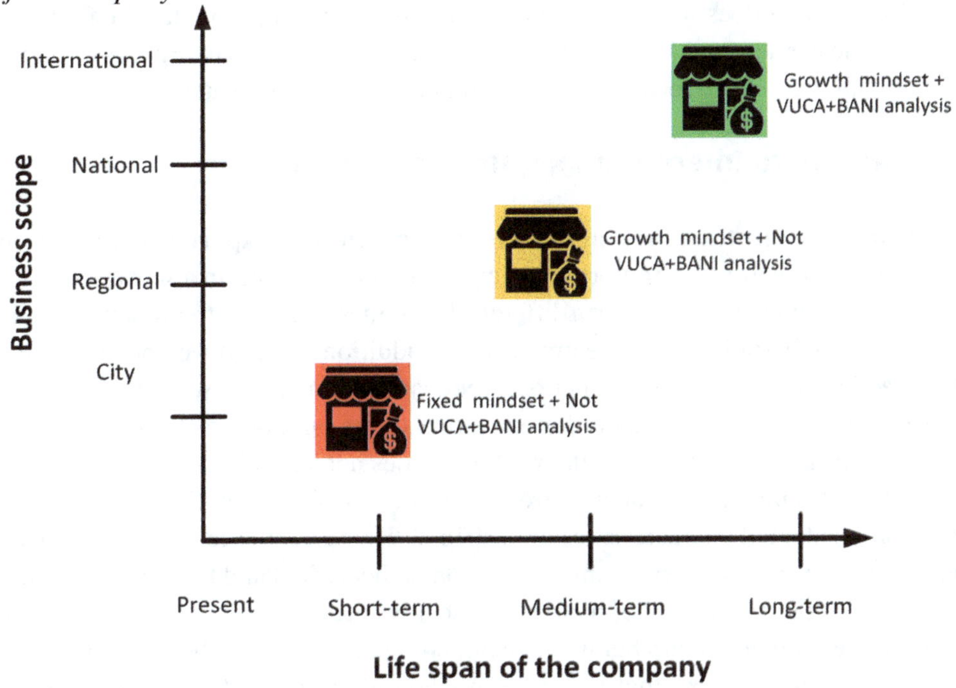

Figure 3 shows the impact of the entrepreneurial mindset and the VUCA-BANI analysis on the life expectancy and physical scope of the companies. It can be seen that when the entrepreneurs have a fixed mindset without analyzing the VUCA-BANI environment, the life expectancy of the companies is reduced (i.e. short term) and the scope is limited (e.g. only in one city). On the other hand, if the entrepreneurs have a growth mindset and carry out the analysis of the VUCA+BANI environment, the life expectancy is likely to be long (i.e. long-term) and the reach is national and international.

5 BARRIERS AND FACILITATORS IN THE UNIVERSITY CONTEXT

In the broad context of promoting international entrepreneurship, it is necessary to identify the barriers and facilitators that could have a negative or positive impact on the promotion of entrepreneurship. In a specific context, such as higher education, it is also important to identify, define, and address all barriers and facilitators to the development of international entrepreneurship. Before analyzing these barriers and facilitators, it is important to make clear that this documentary research provides a broad vision and does not prejudice certain universities in particular. In addition, many of the barriers and facilitators identified apply not only to international entrepreneurship but also to local, regional, and national entrepreneurship.

5.1 Barriers to international entrepreneurship

Reduced institutional and personal entrepreneurship experience. The role of the professor is extremely important in any educational model. In a scenario with a high level of collaboration between different disciplines, such as entrepreneurship, the role of the professor is even more important. In addition to the above, the theoretical and practical aspects of entrepreneurship education are necessary. Considering the above, the ideal professor model for educating future entrepreneurs must have the above characteristics. If a particular professor does not have all the necessary characteristics, it is important that, as a group of professors from a particular university, the aforementioned characteristics are fulfilled. However, the reality is that many people who teach entrepreneurship do so from a theoretical and historical perspective, without the experience of having started a business, i.e., professors who teach aspects of entrepreneurship but who are not entrepreneurs. The above is fully valid in a professional context, that is, a person who only wants to teach topics related to entrepreneurship without actually applying them (Aldana-Rivera et al., 2019; Joensuu-Salo et al., 2021). Thus, in 2022, in the United States of America, 96% of business professors worked only in universities without having any other main business activity, while only 3% of business professors have as their main activity being part of companies in the private sector (mainly in the manufacturing sector) and 1% belong to the public sector (Zippia, 2023).

Inadequate curricular and extracurricular (co-curricular) structure

Firstly, it is important to distinguish between curricular and extracurricular (or co-curricular) activities. Curricular activities allow them to be validated or accredited within the framework of certain courses according to a specific study plan, e.g., attendance at classes, seminars, workshops, laboratory and field placements, among others. On the other hand, extracurricular activities are voluntary and cannot be validated for one or more courses, such as membership in artistic, sports, or academic groups and various societies, among others. However, extra-curricular activities are part of a student's overall education. Once the curricular and extracurricular activities have been defined, it is necessary to contextualize these activities within a curricular and extracurricular structure to promote the entrepreneurial mindset. Sometimes the curricular structure of an educational institution takes into account general aspects that can be accredited and that are framed in the educational objectives. However, if the educational objectives of the educational institution are not related to the entrepreneurial mindset, there will be no curricular activities that can be credited to students for promoting the entrepreneurial mindset. Therefore, it is important first to define the educational objectives that have an impact on entrepreneurship and then to design curricular activities to promote entrepreneurship. Even if an educational institution has curricular activities that promote entrepreneurship, these activities require an internal and external audit process regarding their real impact on the entrepreneurial mindset. On the other hand, Extracurricular activities are more complex to contextualize in the entrepreneurial mindset, and generally, institutions only consider them as part of the overall development of students, without considering the entrepreneurial mindset (Mogul et al., 2020; Rauch & Hulsink, 2015; Pocek et al., 2022; Andalibi, 2019). Despite the above, well-designed extra-curricular activities can have a significant impact on entrepreneurial mindset.

Efforts to generate a workforce (employees), but not entrepreneurs

Educational institutions measure educational success based on several parameters, one of which is the Labor Insertion Index (LII). Specifically, the LII is the percentage of graduates from an institution who have been hired by a company in a given period. For example, the LIN analysis of university students in 2023 in the European Union shows that the Netherlands has the highest labor insertion (95.2%), while Greece is the country with the worst labor insertion (63.5%). In addition to conventional labor insertion, the Highly Specialized Labor Insertion Index (HSLII) is also used (Perez et al., 2023). In this way, an educational institution with a high LII could have a low HSLII. Given the above, a common mistake made by university educational institutions is to focus their efforts only on increasing the labor insertion index, without considering indicators related to entrepreneurship. In fact, educational institutions generally do not have entrepreneurship indicators for their graduates (Handayati et al., 2020; Roca-Hurtuna & Sanz-Ponce, 2023; Fernández-Salinero et al., 2020).

No structured model between research, development, innovation, and entrepreneurs

Research and Development (R&D) is an aspect that universities have to consider in their daily activities. Thus, R&D has evolved into Research, Development, and Innovation (R&DI). In the same sense, the term R&DI has evolved into Research, Development, Innovation, and Entrepreneurship (R&DI+E). In light of the above,

R&D has its challenges and opportunities, which is why sometimes both activities cannot be articulated. R&DI and R&DI+E are no exception. Therefore, the articulation of all R&DI+E activities is very important to reach the final step of research, which is the creation of a company offering a product, service, and experience to a market segment. This is the case of technology-based companies (TBCs). However, few educational institutions have a consolidated R&DI+E model, which would imply that all activities are properly planned with a specific end goal, i.e. the creation of a company. In reality, many universities have a weak structure in terms of R&DI+E and there is no short, medium, or long-term planning. Given the above, entrepreneurial activity is perceived as unrelated to R&DI (Rustiana et al., 2022; Rossoni et al., 2023; Salomaa & Caputo, 2021; Cui & Li, 2022).

Inefficient promotion of international culture

International culture is a fundamental element in the promotion of international entrepreneurship. In particular, if an educational institution does not have a well-designed framework for promoting international culture, it will be very difficult for that university to be a reference for international entrepreneurship. In general, most universities have departments responsible for student life, which may include aspects of international culture. However, even if an educational institution has a framework of international activities that could in some way support international entrepreneurship, this is not enough, nor does it ensure an increase in international entrepreneurship rates. Planning is needed to establish and implement specific activities to promote an international culture that has a direct and indirect impact on international entrepreneurship. For example, a university student who does not participate in an extra-curricular activity involving interaction with international students, professors, and entrepreneurs will be less likely to start an international venture (Ierapetritis, 2019; Futagami, 2021; Zhang & Goodson, 2011).

5.2 Facilitators for international entrepreneurship

Divergence and convergence of ideas based on generational diversity

In the university environment, there may be collaboration between people from different generations, such as Baby Boomers (1946-1964), Generation X (1965-1980), Millennials or Generation Y (1984-1996), and Generation Z or Zoomers (1997-2012). This generational diversity means that the characteristics of each generation also influence how decisions are made and projects are managed in the context of university life. Although there are important differences between the generations that could hinder international entrepreneurship, if they are properly managed by organizational leadership, the characteristics of each individual belonging to a certain generalization could be used to promote the entrepreneurial mindset. In particular, the creative process of divergence and convergence between people belonging to different generations can be a strength in some R&DI+E projects. For example, the divergence of thinking and ways of doing things may be evident within the framework of R&DI+E, but after an adequate management period and based on leadership, the convergence process will lead to unifying thinking and ways of doing things to achieve a final objective (Samaniego et al., 2022; Reynoso-Arcos et al., 2022; Schjoedt et al., 2013; Lowell & Morris, 2019).

Public and private stakeholders

Due to the nature of a university, the relationship with stakeholders from the public and private sectors is very important. For clarification, stakeholders are those individuals or organizations in the public and private sectors who are formally or informally involved with an educational institution and who are in some way positively or negatively affected by the institution's decisions. For example, some stakeholders are part of the councils of certain faculties, so they hold regular meetings to discuss various aspects related to education, innovation, research, networking, and entrepreneurship, among others. Given the above, a stakeholder related to the university environment will play an active role in the decision-making process involving the promotion of entrepreneurship at local, regional, national, and international levels. In this way, active collaboration between universities and stakeholders will make it possible to address aspects of international entrepreneurship from different approaches, and consequently increase the quantity and quality of proposals to strengthen the entrepreneurial mindset of students. Conversely, a university that does not have a network of public and private sector stakeholders will have a version of entrepreneurial reality that reduces the likelihood of success of international ventures (Kusio & Fiore, 2020; Radko et al., 2023; Siegel & Wright, 2015; Ellikkal & Rajamohan, 2023).

Multidisciplinarity, interdisciplinarity, and transdisciplinarity

In the university environment, and considering the variety of disciplines that coexist in the same institution, it is possible to propose an environment of multidisciplinary, interdisciplinary, and transdisciplinary collaboration that directly and indirectly supports international entrepreneurship. In general, the multidisciplinary environment addresses problems or situations from separate disciplinary perspectives, while the interdisciplinary environment makes a mixture of approaches to the object of study, but with clearly identifiable perspectives. On the other hand, transdisciplinary cooperation addresses a problem from a single perspective, where this perspective does not exist in the multidisciplinary and interdisciplinary context, i.e. it is a novel perspective. Given the above, the promotion of international entrepreneurship through the R&DI+E process can be strengthened in the university environment. In this way, the collaboration between engineering sciences, social sciences, and management sciences, among others, can contribute to the generation of new ideas with the potential to create a new product, process, or service within the framework of the creation of a new company at the international level. Finally, although there are many advantages to multidisciplinary, interdisciplinary, and transdisciplinary collaboration, it is also true that there are many challenges and barriers that need to be addressed (Jamira et al., 2021; Butt & Dimitrijević, 2022; Galvão et al., 2021; Villa et al., 2017; Mainzer, 2011).

Academic accreditations at national and international level

Educational accreditation is the result of a systematic and voluntary process of evaluation and monitoring of the fulfillment of the functions of a university, which makes it possible to obtain reliable and objective information on the quality of education. In addition, educational accreditation provides society with assurance about the quality of the human resources trained and the various processes developed in an educational institution. In view of the above, national accreditation allows universities to compare themselves with other universities in the same country, while international accreditation allows them to compare themselves with other universities in other countries. In general, each educational accreditation system, both national and international, has its requirements and elements, such as research, teaching, employability, internationalization, academic development, facilities, social impact and responsibility, online learning, innovation, arts and culture, inclusiveness, environmental impact, entrepreneurship, among others. In this way, national and international accreditation systems that include the impact on entrepreneurship as a direct or indirect assessment parameter can serve as an external incentive for universities to promote and measure entrepreneurship among their students (Sziegat, 2021; Muslim et al., 2023; Aburas et al., 2021; Sababha, 2021).

Having identified some barriers and facilitators to promoting international entrepreneurship in the university context, it is important to clarify that the impact of each barrier or facilitator is not equal. The above implies that some barriers have a greater negative impact and some facilitators have a greater positive impact, so a specific weight (w) must be assigned to each element mentioned. This task is the responsibility of each university after the organizational analysis. Figure 4 shows the relationship between different hypothetical barriers and facilitators with different weights, which causes the probability of entrepreneurship to increase or decrease depending on the number and weight of the barriers and facilitators. Although only 5 barriers and 4 facilitators for international entrepreneurship in the university context were identified, there may well be more barriers and facilitators based on a more detailed analysis of each university.

Figure 4. Barriers and facilitator's entrepreneurship.

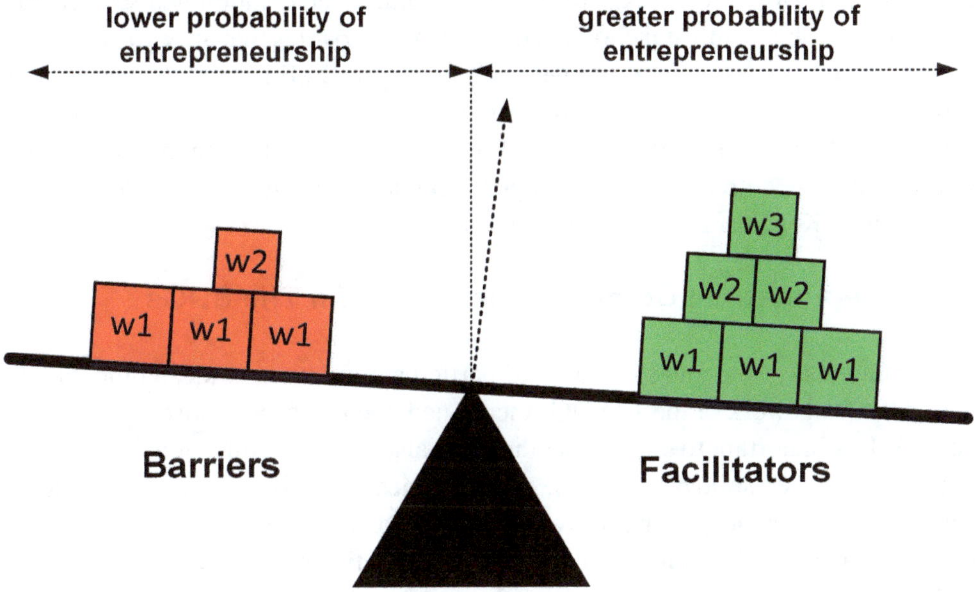

6 INTERDISCIPLINARY STRATEGIES IN THE UNIVERSITY CONTEXT

Previously, the barriers and facilitators to promoting international entrepreneurship in the university context were mentioned. The relationship between the international entrepreneurship mindset and VUCA-BANI frameworks has also been addressed. In this way, many strategies and activities can be used in the university environment, which can be framed in curricular and extra-curricular activities, as well as in formal, non-formal, and informal educational activities. However, the likelihood of success of any strategy to promote international entrepreneurship needs to be assessed in the context of the university's organizational culture. Otherwise, the strategies and activities developed to promote international entrepreneurship will fail (Tallman, et al., 2023).

6.1 Labs, Business Incubators and Business Accelerators

Formal structures for entrepreneurial development need to be created and strengthened. Some examples are laboratories, incubators, and business accelerators. The main difference is that incubators help to bring business ideas to the market and business accelerators provide support and assistance to projects that are already in development. Labs, on the other hand, allow entrepreneurs' business ideas to be experimented with at low risk. This strategy requires the creation and strengthening of relationships with stakeholders to identify companies that are early adopters of new ventures. It also requires a well-structured R&D+E model. Because of the above, the university needs to involve as many disciplines and students as possible from the earliest stages of their studies. It is recommended that the involvement of students in these entrepreneurship support structures be semi-controlled and with well-defined Key Performance Indicators (KPIs).

6.2 Entrepreneurial Competitions Based On The SDGs

For university students to be able to participate in business idea competitions within the framework of the 17 SDGs mentioned, the institution must have internal options. It is important to clarify that there are also external competencies, but it is important to have a solid base of these competencies within the university. Entrepreneurship competencies, taking into account the SDGs, must start from a basic level to a specialized level, taken into account in collaborative work between disciplines. In this way, we can train entrepreneurs with a collaborative mindset between different disciplines, which is very important in the business world.

6.3 Courses That Focus On Experience Rather Than Theory

Universities wishing to improve their international entrepreneurship indicators need to analyze and strengthen the entrepreneurship-related courses included in each academic program. In particular, it is necessary to eliminate, add, and/or modify courses that directly contribute to the entrepreneurial mindset. Furthermore, it is important to propose the time devoted to theory and practice concerning the workload of these courses. Sometimes many courses in academic programs related to business and entrepreneurship focus on theoretical aspects in the curriculum framework, but technical aspects or practices are not considered as part of the curriculum activity. Changes in curricula need to be made taking into account the opinions of public and private stakeholders related to business and entrepreneurship aspects. Furthermore, these courses must be designed and implemented in a multidisciplinary, interdisciplinary, and transdisciplinary working model.

6.4 Updating and Strengthening Reference Professors

As mentioned above, the majority of professors who deliver aspects of business and entrepreneurship in universities do not have experience in the real world of business and entrepreneurship. It is therefore important to update the recruitment policy for new professors involved in the education of new international entrepreneurs. For example, the percentage of professors required to have business training and experience should be set. On the other hand, some professors are hired by the educational institution but do not have business experience. In this particular case, it is important to ensure that these professors start the process of training entrepreneurs based on their technical skills, i.e. that they try to do some kind of entrepreneurship based on the knowledge and technical skills of their discipline. For example, a software development specialist could analyze the possibility of creating an innovative product or service that would lead to the creation of a new company. The above must be coordinated with the R&DI+E processes. If the above has significant complications, the collaboration of professors and researchers in entrepreneurship projects can be analyzed, helping to raise awareness of the entrepreneurial mindset while using their technical skills.

6.5 Recognition of Entrepreneurship and Graduated Requirement

In general, universities grant recognition to students according to different aspects, such as 1) academic regularity, 2) final or partial grades, 3) good conduct, 4) participation in activities that reflect the comprehensive education, e.g. cultural, sports, international, social, bonding, among others. Sometimes, some universities recognize entrepreneurial activities, but in an unstructured or non-formal way, i.e. the reason for recognition can be very simple, e.g. participation in entrepreneurial activities, but not the creation of a small business. Given the above, universities must create mechanisms to recognize formal entrepreneurship, and in this case, depending on the circumstances of each educational institution, consider entrepreneurship as a requirement or opinion for graduating from university.

6.6 Networking and Internships with Other Entrepreneurs

An important aspect of developing an entrepreneurial mindset is the creation of experiences. Therefore, universities need to analyze and implement different activities that allow students to experience the contexts of the business world. One activity that promotes the above is networking. In particular, networking must consider the interaction of students with leading business people to create or expand the network of professional contacts, as well as promote the ability to maintain these professional connections over time. For the above, hard skills are less relevant, while soft skills are very important. If networking events are well-designed and planned, the international entrepreneurial mindsets will be created and reinforced. On the other hand, it is also important for students to undertake internships in companies where the spirit of innovation, creativity, and entrepreneurship are important elements. This will allow students to immerse themselves in an unfamiliar context, while at the same time developing their personalities and acquiring and reinforcing the hard and soft skills needed to create competitive businesses. Nevertheless, it is important to note that most universities already have processes for internships, but they have generally neglected processes and the impact on the entrepreneurial mindset is marginal, focusing rather on increasing the labor insertion index.

Finally, it is important to clarify that it is not only a matter of defining strategies, but also of determining the best time during the academic life for the application of these strategies. Figure 5 illustrates the above proposal and, although it is not intended to be a general application rule, it allows us to visualize that the different strategies for promoting international entrepreneurship must be offered from the initial academic stage to the final academic stage. Thus, some strategies are not present in all academic stages, e.g. strategy 1 is only present in the initial academic stage, strategy 5 is present in the middle and final stages, and strategy 6 is present in all academic stages.

Figure 5. Deployment of strategies according to the academic stage.

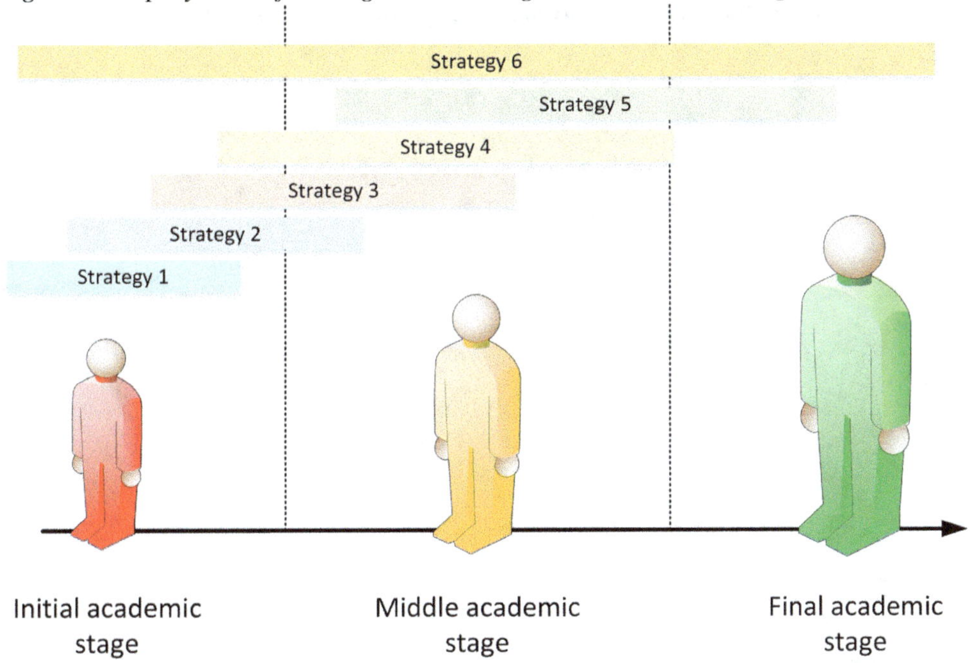

7 CONCLUSIONS

The development of international entrepreneurial mindsets is an important element for society as a whole, i.e. the development of internationally competitive entrepreneurs has a direct and indirect impact on the quality of life of people at local, regional, national, and international levels. Given this relevance, the ways in which universities (but also other institutions at other levels of education) have sought to have a positive impact on international entrepreneurship need to be reconsidered. This is because the positive impact on international entrepreneurship appears to be marginal, and they have focused more on local and regional entrepreneurship, although not with the best results. In light of the above, this research can serve as a starting point for universities to propose a short-, medium-, and long-term roadmap in terms of KPIs that impact the international entrepreneurship intention of their students. In particular, this research has some limitations. The main one is the complexity of addressing the promotion of an international entrepreneurship mindset from an interdisciplinary perspective, which seemed easy in theory, but is very difficult in practice. Furthermore, due to the wide variety of educational models of universities around the world, it is almost impossible to establish specific metrics and strategies to better promote students' international entrepreneurship intentions.

REFERENCES

Aburas, R., Nurunnabi, M., & Atyah, R. (2021). Tensions between local and international accreditation: Insights into interior design learning outcomes. *The International Journal of Design Education, 15*(1), 145–164. DOI: 10.18848/2325-128X/CGP/v15i01/145-164

Al-Qahtani, M., Zguir, M. F., Ari, I., & Koç, M. (2022). Female Entrepreneurship for Sustainable Economy and Development—Challenges, Drivers, and Suggested Policies for Resource-Rich Countries. *Sustainability (Basel), 14*(20), 13412. DOI: 10.3390/su142013412

Aldana-Rivera, E., Tafur-Castillo, J., Gil, I., & Mejía, C. (2019). Práctica pedagógica de emprendimiento en docentes de educación superior en Institución Educativa Universitaria de Barranquia. *Archivos Venezolanos de Farmacología y Terapéutica, 38*(2), 9–18.

Amir, M. T., & Prabawani, B. (2023). Sustainability-oriented innovation through shaping the ecosystem; a case of an e-bus industry in Indonesia. *Cogent Business & Management, 10*(2), 1–20. DOI: 10.1080/23311975.2023.2218681

Andalibi, M. (2019). Early incorporation of entrepreneurship mindset in an engineering curriculum. *International Journal of Higher Education, 8*(4), 98–107. DOI: 10.5430/ijhe.v8n4p98

Anderson, C. C., Denich, M., Warchold, A., Kropp, J. P., & Pradhan, P. (2022). A systems model of SDG target influence on the 2030 Agenda for Sustainable Development. *Sustainability Science, 17*(4), 1459–1472. DOI: 10.1007/s11625-021-01040-8 PMID: 34659581

Angrisani, M., Dell'Anno, D., & Hockaday, T. (2022). From ecosystem to community. Combining entrepreneurship and university engagement in an open innovation perspective. *International Journal of Technology Management, 88*(1), 71–92. DOI: 10.1504/IJTM.2022.121443

Baskoro, G. (2023). From VUCA to BANI: A Challenge of Strategic Environment for Higher Education in Indonesia. Proceedings of the 3rd International Conference on Business and Engineering Management (ICONBEM 2022) In Advances in Economics, Business and Management Research (pp. 229–235). DOI: 10.2991/978-94-6463-216-3_18

Baumol, W. J. (1968). Entrepreneurship in economic theory. *The American Economic Review, 58*, 64–71.

Baumol, W. J. (2018). Entrepreneurship in Economic Theory: In The Microtheory of Innovative Entrepreneurship (pp. 9–22). Princeton University Press. DOI: 10.2307/j.ctt21668j9.7

Bernard, D. T. K. (2015). Microfinance Services: Facilitating Entrepreneurial Success of Poor Women. *Review of Contemporary Business Research*, *4*(2), 57–66. DOI: 10.15640/rcbr.v4n2a5

Bezanilla, M. J., García-Olalla, A., Paños-Castro, J., & Arruti, A. (2020). Developing the entrepreneurial university: Factors of influence. *Sustainability (Basel)*, *12*(3), 842. DOI: 10.3390/su12030842

Bozorgi, J., & Mohammad, J. (2021). The Culture of the University Entrepreneurship Ecosystem, The Drivers of Social Entrepreneurship Development. *Journal of Cultural Management*, *15*(51), 45–57.

Bushuyev, S., Piliuhina, K., & Chetin, E. (2023). Transformation of values of the high technology projects from a VUCA to a BANI environment model. *Innovative Technologies and Scientific Solutions for Industries*, *2*(24), 191–199. DOI: 10.30837/ITSSI.2023.24.191

Butt, A. N., & Dimitrijević, B. (2022). Multidisciplinary and Transdisciplinary Collaboration in Nature-Based Design of Sustainable Architecture and Urbanism. *Sustainability (Basel)*, *14*(16), 10339. DOI: 10.3390/su141610339

Cantillon, B. J., & Higgs, H. (1932). Essai sur la Nature du Commerce en General. *Journal of the Royal Statistical Society*, *95*(1), 131–133. DOI: 10.2307/2341977

Cui, Z., & Li, E. (2022). Does Industry-University-Research Cooperation Matter? An Analysis of Its Coupling Effect on Regional Innovation and Economic Development. *Chinese Geographical Science*, *32*(5), 915–930. DOI: 10.1007/s11769-022-1308-y

De Brito, S., & Leitão, J. (2021). Mapping and defining entrepreneurial ecosystems: A systematic literature review. *Knowledge Management Research and Practice*, *19*(1), 21–42. DOI: 10.1080/14778238.2020.1751571

De Vries, M. (1977). The entrepreneurial personality - a person at the cross-roads. *Journal of Management Studies*, *14*(1), 34–47. DOI: 10.1111/j.1467-6486.1977.tb00616.x

Dhanabhakyam, M. P. M. (2021). Sustainability Strategies for Developing SMEs and Entrepreneurship. In Baporikar, N. (Ed.), *Handbook of Research on Sustaining SMEs and Entrepreneurial Innovation in the Post-COVID-19 Era* (pp. 527–547). IGI Global., DOI: 10.4018/978-1-7998-6632-9.ch025

Dweck, S. C. (2015). Carol Dweck Revisits the "Growth Mindset". *Education Week, 35*(05), 20–24.

Eckhardt, J. T., Ciuchta, M. P., & Carpenter, M. (2018). Open innovation, information, and entrepreneurship within platform ecosystems. *Strategic Entrepreneurship Journal, 12*(3), 369–391. DOI: 10.1002/sej.1298

Ellikkal, A., & Rajamohan, S. (2023). Factors Influencing Entrepreneurial Intentions and the Role of Entrepreneurship Education in Indian Universities: A Stakeholder Perspective. International. *Journal of Professional Business Review*, *8*(7), e02663. DOI: 10.26668/businessreview/2023.v8i7.2663

Fernández-Bedoya, V. H., Meneses-La-Riva, M. E., Suyo-Vega, J. A., & Stephanie Gago-Chávez, J. de J. (2023). Mental health problems of entrepreneurs during the COVID-19 health crisis: Fear, anxiety, and stress. *A systematic review. F1000Research, 12*, 1062. DOI: 10.12688/f1000research.139581.1

Fernández-Salinero De Miguel, C., & García-Álvarez, J. (2020). Graduate's labour insertion through personal contacts. A proposal from the knowledge management. Teoria de La Educacion. *Ediciones Universidad de Salamanca*. DOI: 10.14201/teri.20196

Futagami, T. (2021). On Motivations for Mobility of International Students Studying at Japanese Research-Intensive Universities. *Journal of Comparative & International Higher Education*, *13*(1), 82–102. DOI: 10.32674/jcihe.v13i1.2100

Galvão, C., Faria, C., Viegas, W., Branco, A., & Goulão, L. (2021). Inquiry in higher education for sustainable development: Crossing disciplinary knowledge boundaries. *International Journal of Sustainability in Higher Education*, *22*(1), 291–307. DOI: 10.1108/IJSHE-02-2020-0068

Gifford, E., & McKelvey, M. (2019). Knowledge-intensive entrepreneurship and S3: Conceptualizing strategies for sustainability. *Sustainability (Basel)*, *11*(18), 4824. DOI: 10.3390/su11184824

Glenn, D. (2010). Carol Dweck ' s Mindset. *The Chronicle of Higher Education*, *56*, 4–9.

Grabmeier, S. (2020). *BANI versus VUCA: A New Acronym to Describe the World.* Stephan Grabmeier Blog.

Handayati, P., Wulandari, D., Soetjipto, B. E., Wibowo, A., & Narmaditya, B. S. (2020). Does entrepreneurship education promote vocational students' entrepreneurial mindset? *Heliyon*, *6*(11), e05426. Advance online publication. DOI: 10.1016/j.heliyon.2020.e05426 PMID: 33235932

Hassan, N. T., Alotaibi, S. M., & Hussein, R. (2022). Sustainable Development, Entrepreneurship and Accounting Education: An Exploratory Study for Saudi Universities. *Information Sciences Letters, 11*(6), 2101–2110. DOI: 10.18576/isl/110620

Hierro, B. (2020). *Adiós tiempo del VUCA, bienvenido BANI.* Quint Group.

Hill, S., Ionescu-Somers, A., Coduras, A., Guerrero, M., Menipaz, E., Boutaleb, F., Zbierowski, P., Schøtt, T., Sahasranamam, S., & Shay, J. (2023). *Global Entrepreneurship Monitor 2022/2023 Global Report. Global Entrepreneurship Research Association.* GERA.

Hisrich, R., Michael, P., & Shepherd, D. A. (2005). Definition of entrepreneur today. *McGraw-Hill Irwin, 6*(1), 2.

Howorth, C., Tempest, S., & Coupland, C. (2005). Rethinking entrepreneurship methodology and definitions of the entrepreneur. *Journal of Small Business and Enterprise Development, 12*(1), 24–40. DOI: 10.1108/14626000510579626

Ierapetritis, D. G. (2019). Discussing the role of universities in fostering regional entrepreneurial ecosystems. *Economies (Basel), 7*(4), 119. DOI: 10.3390/economies7040119

Jamira, A., Agustiningsih, N., & Febriani, Y. (2021). THE IMPLEMENTATION OF BUSINESS MODEL CANVAS (BMC) TO IMPROVE STUDENTS' ENTREPRENEURSHIP MINDSET. *Dinasti International Journal of Education Management and Social Science, 2*(3), 395–403. DOI: 10.31933/dijemss.v2i3.751

Joensuu-Salo, S., Peltonen, K., Hämäläinen, M., Oikkonen, E., & Raappana, A. (2021). Entrepreneurial teachers do make a difference – Or do they? *Industry and Higher Education, 35*(4), 536–546. DOI: 10.1177/0950422220983236

Jufriyono, B. T. (2017). Entrepreneurship,Organizational Culture and Emotional Intelligence in Determining Organizational Commitment. *International Journal of Managerial Studies and Research, 5*(6), 29–35. DOI: 10.20431/2349-0349.0506004

Kalamaki, F. R., Mahmoudi, G., & Charati, J. Y. (2021). A Model for Organizational Entrepreneurship with Organizational Culture Approach in Iran's Teaching Hospitals. *Ethiopian Journal of Health Sciences, 31*(2), 419–428. DOI: 10.4314/ejhs.v31i2.25 PMID: 34158794

Kerti - Yasa, N. N., Gde-Sukaatmadja, I. P., Vedanta-Putra, A. A., Dewi-Rahmayanti, P. L. (2022). Entrepreneurship Education Development Strategies to Increase Students' Entrepreneurship Intentions in Bali. *BOHR International Journal of Operations Management Research and Practices, 1(1)*, 45–51. DOI: 10.54646/BIJOMRP.006

Kusio, T., & Fiore, M. (2020). The perception of entrepreneurship culture by internal university stakeholders. *European Business Review, 32*(3), 443–457. DOI: 10.1108/EBR-05-2019-0087

Liu, H., Kulturel-Konak, S., & Konak, A. (2021). Key elements and their roles in entrepreneurship education ecosystem: Comparative review and suggestions for sustainability. *Sustainability (Basel), 13*(19), 10648. DOI: 10.3390/su131910648

Lowell, V. L., & Morris, J. M.Jr. (2019, March 20). Multigenerational classrooms in higher education: Equity and learning with technology. *International Journal of Information and Learning Technology., 36*(2), 78–93. DOI: 10.1108/IJILT-06-2018-0068

Mainzer, K. (2011). Interdisciplinarity and innovation dynamics. On convergence of research, technology, economy, and society. *Poiesis & Praxis : International Journal of Ethics of Science and Technology Assessment, 7*(4), 275–289. DOI: 10.1007/s10202-011-0088-8 PMID: 21874129

Mei, W., & Symaco, L. (2022). University-wide entrepreneurship education in China's higher education institutions: Issues and challenges. *Studies in Higher Education, 47*(1), 177–193. DOI: 10.1080/03075079.2020.1735330

Mogul, A., Laughlin, E., & Lynch, S. (2020). A co-curricular activity to introduce pharmacy students to the concepts of innovation and entrepreneurship. *American Journal of Pharmaceutical Education, 84*(8), 1077–1084. DOI: 10.5688/ajpe7805 PMID: 32934385

Muslim, A. B., Hamied, F. A., Gaffar, M. F., Asuan, M. E., Samsudin, S., Diteeyont, W., Margana, M., Suryani, A. W., Jessie, P. N. G., Solihat, R., Priyantin, T., Cassandra, N., Gunadi, G., & Sitthikorn, S. (2023). Benefits, mechanisms and challenges of international accreditation for teacher education: ASEAN academics' perspectives. *Quality Assurance in Education, 31*(4), 538–555. Advance online publication. DOI: 10.1108/QAE-10-2022-0183

Nambisan, S., Siegel, D., & Kenney, M. (2018). On open innovation, platforms, and entrepreneurship. *Strategic Entrepreneurship Journal, 12*(3), 354–368. DOI: 10.1002/sej.1300

Nguyen, T. T. T., Nguyen, T. T. H., & Pham, T. T. H. (2020). The effect of corporate entrepreneurship, organizational culture on supply chain management and business performance in chemical industry. *Uncertain Supply Chain Management, 8*(1), 67–76. DOI: 10.5267/j.uscm.2019.8.005

Osterwalder, A. (2004). The business model ontology a proposition in a design science approach. Doctoral Dissertation, Université de Lausanne, Faculté Des Hautes Études Commerciales.

Peñalver Martínez, A. (2022). De un entorno VUCA a un entorno BANI para dar sentido a este mundo de transformación constante. *Capital Humano: Revista Para La Integración y Desarrollo de Los Recursos Humanos, 376*, 24.

Pérez, F., Aldás, J., Aragón, R., & Zaera, I. (2023). *ANÁLISIS DE LA INSERCIÓN LABORAL DE LOS UNIVERSITARIOS, Diferencias entre titulaciones*. Fundación BBVA.

Pitaloka, L. K., Melati, I. S., & Setiawan, A. B. (2021). Selection of priority strategies for developing social entrepreneurship for women. *Academy of Entrepreneurship Journal, 27*(4), 1–8.

Pocek, J., Politis, D., & Gabrielsson, J. (2022). Entrepreneurial learning in extra-curricular start-up programs for students. *International Journal of Entrepreneurial Behaviour & Research, 28*(2), 325–345. DOI: 10.1108/IJEBR-04-2020-0206

Radko, N., Belitski, M., & Kalyuzhnova, Y. (2023). Conceptualising the entrepreneurial university: The stakeholder approach. *The Journal of Technology Transfer, 48*(3), 955–1044. DOI: 10.1007/s10961-022-09926-0

Rauch, A., & Hulsink, W. (2015). Putting Entrepreneurship Education Where the Intention to Act Lies: An Investigation into the Impact of Entrepreneurship Education on Entrepreneurial Behavior. *Academy of Management Learning & Education, 14*(2), 187–204. DOI: 10.5465/amle.2012.0293

Reeves, P. M., Zappe, S. E., & Follmer, D. J. (2019). A Comparison of the Types of Problems Encountered by Entrepreneurial Students and Successful Professional Entrepreneurs. *Entrepreneurship Education and Pedagogy, 2*(3), 214–244. DOI: 10.1177/2515127419829396

Reynoso-Arcos, S., Gallardo-Lolandes, Y., Padilla Vento, P., Mori-Holguin, J. Y., & Barraza-Regalado, C. A. (2022). Generational diversity in digital education in teachers of the Administration career of a private university. *RISTI - Revista Iberica de Sistemas e Tecnologias de Informacao*, 2022(E48), 180–195.

Roca-Hurtuna, M., & Sanz-Ponce, R. (2023). The Perception of University Students towards People with Disabilities and Their Labor Insertion. *Education Sciences, 13*(1), 79. Advance online publication. DOI: 10.3390/educsci13010079

Rodríguez, A. (2009). Nuevas perspectivas para entender el emprendimiento empresarial. *Pensamiento & Gestión, 26*, 4–119.

Rossoni, A. L., de Vasconcellos, E. P. G., & de Castilho Rossoni, R. L. (2023). *Barriers and facilitators of university-industry collaboration for research, development and innovation: a systematic review*. Management Review Quarterly., DOI: 10.1007/s11301-023-00349-1

Rustiana, Mohd, O. B., & Mohamad, N. B. (2022). The Triangulation Model Distribution of Entrepreneurship Education, Entrepreneurship Knowledge, and Entrepreneurship Mindset. *Journal of Distribution Science*, *20*(9), 47–59. DOI: 10.15722/jds.20.09.202209.47

Sababha, B. H., Al-Qaralleh, E., & Al-Daher, N. (2021). A New Student Learning Outcome to Strengthen Entrepreneurship and Business Skills and Mindset in Engineering Curricula. In 2021 Innovation and New Trends in Engineering, Technology and Science Education Conference, IETSEC 2021. Institute of Electrical and Electronics Engineers Inc. DOI: 10.1109/IETSEC51476.2021.9440489

Salomaa, M., & Caputo, A. (2021). Business as usual? Assessing the impact of the COVID-19 pandemic to research, development and innovation (RDI) activities of universities of applied sciences. *Tertiary Education and Management*, *27*(4), 351–366. DOI: 10.1007/s11233-021-09079-z PMID: 40477712

Samaniego, J. R. V., Arroyo, K. M. C., & Quispe, A. S. L. (2022). Generational Diversity: Challenges for University Education in the 21st Century. *Revista de Filosofía (Venezuela)*, *39*(102), 664–673. DOI: 10.5281/zenodo.7063329

Schjoedt, L., Monsen, E., Pearson, A., Barnett, T., & Chrisman, J. J. (2013). New Venture and Family Business Teams: Understanding Team Formation, Composition, Behaviors, and Performance. *Entrepreneurship Theory and Practice*, *37*(1), 1–15. DOI: 10.1111/j.1540-6520.2012.00549.x

Setyaningrum, R. P., Norisanti, N., Fahlevi, M., Aljuaid, M., & Grabowska, S. (2023). Women and entrepreneurship for economic growth in Indonesia. *Frontiers in Psychology*, *13*, 1–11. DOI: 10.3389/fpsyg.2022.975709 PMID: 36698571

Sharma, L. (2022). Assessing the "entrepreneurship as emancipation" perspective among women in STEM. *Management Decision*, *60*(6), 1585–1605. DOI: 10.1108/MD-06-2020-0696

Siddegowda, P. A. (2020). A Study on Problems of Women Entrepreneurs at Mysore District, India. *Our Heritage*, *68*(1), 9183–9200.

Siegel, D. S., & Wright, M. (2015). Academic Entrepreneurship: Time for a Rethink? *British Journal of Management*, *26*(4), 582–595. DOI: 10.1111/1467-8551.12116

Sigüenza-Orellana, S. C., Álava-Atiencie, N. G., Pinos-Ramón, L. D., & Peralta-Vallejo, X. K. (2022). University students' perception of the entrepreneurial ecosystem and social entrepreneurial intention. *Retos (Ecuador)*, *12*(24), 248–266. DOI: 10.17163/ret.n24.2022.04

Subramaniam, R., & Shankar, R. K. (2020). Three Mindsets of Entrepreneurial Leaders. *The Journal of Entrepreneurship*, *29*(1), 7–37. DOI: 10.1177/0971355719893498

Suvarna, T., Chithirairajan, B., Thangamayan, S., & Rajarethinam, E. (2019). Economic problems of women entrepreneurs in chennai sub urbans. *International Journal of Innovative Technology and Exploring Engineering, 8(7C2)*, 362–365.

Sziegat, H. (2021). The response of German business schools to international accreditation in global competition. *Quality Assurance in Education*, *29*(2–3), 135–150. DOI: 10.1108/QAE-01-2020-0008

Tallman, S., Shenkar, O., & Wu, J. (2023). "Culture Eats Strategy for Breakfast": Use and Abuse of Culture in International Strategy Research. *Strategic Management Review*, *4*(2), 193–229. DOI: 10.1561/111.00000057

Tsyfra, T., Moholivets, A., & Vershigora, D. (2022). Digital-skills of building economists in the era of VUCA and BANI-WORLD. *Ways to Improve Construction Efficiency*, *1*(49), 192–205. DOI: 10.32347/2707-501x.2022.49(1).192-205

Usup, U., Supriyono, S., Hardika, H., & Redjeki, E. S. (2020). Development of Student Entrepreneurship Skills in LKP Kresna Informatika. *EDUCATIO: Journal of Education*, *5*(1), 84–91. DOI: 10.29138/educatio.v5i1.241

Utama, H. (2021). Strategy for Enhancing Students' Entrepreneurship in Reducing Reduction in Knowledge Management's View. *International Journal of Research and Review*, *8*(5), 292–298. DOI: 10.52403/ijrr.20210537

Villa, C. F. H., Arango, D. A. G., Mesa, E. D. A., García, A. G., Aconcha, R. B., Movilla, J. G. S., & Lopez, A. P. A. (2017). Multidisciplinariedad, interdisciplinariedad y transdisciplinariedad en la formación para la investigación en ingeniería. *Revista Lasallista de Investigación*, *14*(1), 179–197. DOI: 10.22507/rli.v14n1a16

Yu, C. W. (2018). Understanding the ecosystems of Chinese and American entrepreneurship education. *Journal of Entrepreneurship Education*, *21*(2), 1–18.

Zakharov, Y. (2022). Comparative analysis of approaches to world concepts: Spod society, vuca society and bani society. *Society and Economy*, (64), 149–158. DOI: 10.26565/2524-2547-2022-64-13

Zhang, J., & Goodson, P. (2011). Acculturation and psychosocial adjustment of Chinese international students: Examining mediation and moderation effects. *International Journal of Intercultural Relations*, *35*(5), 614–627. DOI: 10.1016/j.ijintrel.2010.11.004

Zimmerman, M. A. (2013). Motivation, Success, and Problems of Entrepreneurs in Venezuela. *Journal of Management Policy and Practice*, *14*(2), 76–90.

Zippia (2023). BUSINESS TEACHER DEMOGRAPHICS AND STATISTICS IN THE US. Zippia, Inc. https://www.zippia.com/business-teacher-jobs/demographics/

Ziyae, B., Sadeghi, H., Shahamat Nejad, M., & Tajpour, M. (2021). A framework of urban entrepreneurship for women breadwinners. *Foresight (Cambridge)*, *23*(5), 597–609. DOI: 10.1108/FS-12-2020-0137

Section 3
Educational Research, Data Analytics, and Technology

Chapter 9
Educational Research and Data-Driven Decision Making for Future-Focused Higher Education Planning

Vipin Tyagi
http://orcid.org/0000-0003-4994-3686
Jaypee University of Engineering and Technology, Guna, India

ABSTRACT

Higher education institutions worldwide are working in an increasingly unstable environment shaped by fluctuating enrollments, constrained funding, evolving faculty expectations and ongoing limits on international mobility. This chapter examines how systematic educational research, together with responsible use of institutional and learning analytics, can inform strategic decisions related to curriculum design, student recruitment and retention, faculty workload planning and resource allocation across diverse higher education contexts. The chapter reviews key sources and there effects of educational data such as enrollment trends, student engagement indicators, learning outcomes and faculty performance metrics. It also addresses challenges related to data quality, interpretation, ethical use and contextual variation across institutions. The chapter concludes that integrating educational research into strategic planning is essential for building sustainable, inclusive and responsive higher education institutions capable of addressing both immediate pressures and long-term goals.

DOI: 10.4018/979-8-2600-2606-9.ch009

1. INTRODUCTION

Higher education is presently undergoing a period of structural strain that many higher education institutions were not designed to withstand. Declining number of enrollments, reduced public funding, increased accountability expectations and increasing diversity within student have collectively created an unprecedented pressure on institutional planning and governance processes. These challenges are not confined to any single region or sector; public and private universities across the globe face similar strategic issues. Institutions must increasingly compete with difficult decisions regarding the allocation of limited resources, the expansion or restructuring of academic programs and the improvement of student retention outcomes while continuing to uphold academic standards and educational quality. Recent research shows that these pressures are further increased by digital transformation, globalization of education markets, and post-pandemic disruptions that have reshaped student expectations and institutional delivery models. Data-informed governance is now considered as an integral component for institutional resilience and strategic agility (Daniel, 2020; Marginson, 2016). The growing reliance on data-driven approaches is further reinforced by advances in big data analytics, artificial intelligence (AI), and machine learning, which enable institutions to derive actionable insights, personalize learning experiences, and improve administrative efficiency (Jain et al., 2026). These technologies are increasingly central to institutional transformation, though they also introduce concerns related to data privacy, algorithmic bias, and governance.

At the center of these issues lies a renewed emphasis on evidence. Decisions that were once guided largely by professional judgment or tradition are now expected to be justified through systematic analysis of data. This shift has increased the role of educational research and data-driven decision making from a supporting function to a core institutional capability. For students and early-career researchers, understanding this shift is no longer optional. It is part of the professional literacy of modern higher education. This shift aligns with broader movements toward evidence-based management, where organizational decisions are systematically informed by the best available data and research evidence rather than intuition alone (Pfeffer & Sutton, 2006).

This chapter examines how educational research methods and data analytics inform planning and decision making in higher education institutions operating under uncertainty. While the discussion takes examples from different institutional contexts, the emphasis is on principles rather than prescriptions. Data do not make decisions on their own. They inform decisions made by people operating within social, cultural and organizational constraints. Recognizing this difference is essential for making decisions.

The chapter proceeds by first relating data-driven decision making in the traditions of educational research. It then discusses key data sources used in institutional planning, methodological considerations and ethical constraints. Later sections examine practical applications in enrollment management, curriculum planning and student success initiatives. The chapter concludes by discussion on limitations and future directions.

2. EDUCATIONAL RESEARCH AS AN INFRASTRUCTURE FOR DECISION MAKING

Educational research provides the conceptual and methodological foundation upon which meaningful data-driven decision making rests. Without this foundation, institutional data risk being reduced to surface-level indicators, attractive dashboards or compliance-oriented reports that offer limited explanatory or predictive value. Numbers alone do not constitute evidence. Evidence emerges only when data is considered within coherent research designs, informed by theory and interpreted in relation to context. Educational research provides this interpretive scaffolding by clarifying what is being measured, why it matters and how findings should be understood within the complex social systems that characterize higher education.

At its core, educational research encourages institutions to move beyond asking what is happening toward asking why it is happening and under what conditions change might occur. This shift is subtle but consequential. For example, a decline in enrollment can be observed through administrative records, but understanding whether that decline shows market shifts, perceptions of program relevance, financial barriers, or institutional climate requires a research-informed approach. Educational research frames such questions in ways that acknowledge both structural forces and human experience.

Historically, educational research has drawn on two broad methodological traditions: quantitative and qualitative inquiry. Quantitative approaches emphasize measurement, statistical inference, modeling and generalizability. These methods are well suited to identifying patterns across large populations, testing hypotheses and estimating relationships between variables. In institutional planning, quantitative analyses often underpin forecasting models, performance indicators and accountability metrics. However, their strength in abstraction can also be a limitation. Quantitative results frequently mask variation within groups and may obscure the mechanisms that generate observed outcomes.

Qualitative approaches address this limitation by focusing on meaning, process and context. Through interviews, observations, document analysis and case studies, qualitative research captures how policies and practices are experienced by students, faculty and staff. These methods are particularly valuable in times of organizational change when formal structures shift faster than institutional cultures. Qualitative findings often surface unintended consequences, informal practices, or sources of resistance that remain invisible in aggregate data.

In modern planning contexts, these paradigms are rarely treated as mutually exclusive. Instead, mixed methods research has gained prominence as a practical and epistemologically coherent approach. By intentionally integrating quantitative and qualitative data, mixed methods designs allow institutions to connect numerical trends with lived experience and institutional narratives. According to Creswell and Plano Clark (2017), mixed methods research is especially useful when addressing complex problems that cannot be fully understood through a single form of evidence. In higher education planning, such problems are the norm rather than the exception. This integrative approach is particularly useful in complex institutional environments where quantitative indicators alone cannot capture the social and organizational dynamics shaping outcomes (Johnson, Onwuegbuzie, & Turner, 2007).

Student retention provides a clear description of this integrative logic. Quantitative models can identify patterns in withdrawal rates across demographic categories, academic programs, or points in the student lifecycle. These models may reveal, for instance, that attrition is highest after the first year or concentrated within particular gateway courses. Yet such findings, while informative, rarely explain why students disengage or how institutional practices contribute to their decisions. Qualitative interviews and focus groups can uncover factors such as financial precarity, limited access to mentoring, perceived irrelevance of coursework, or a lack of belonging within academic communities. When these insights are brought into dialogue with quantitative trends, institutions gain a more complete understanding of both risk and opportunity.

The value of this integration lies not only in explanation but also in action. Interventions informed by mixed evidence are more likely to be appropriately targeted and contextually sensitive. For example, a retention initiative based only on predictive analytics may focus on monitoring student behavior, whereas one informed by qualitative research may prioritize redesigning advising structures or revising curricular pathways. Educational research thus shapes not only what decisions are made but how solutions are conceived.

In this way, educational research functions as institutional infrastructure rather than as a secondary activity. It influences how problems are defined, how evidence is weighed and how success is evaluated over time. Institutions that invest in research capacity develop shared languages for discussing evidence, mechanisms for critical reflection and norms that value inquiry over assumption. Such institutions are better positioned to move beyond reactive decision making driven by short-term pressures. Instead, they cultivate the ability to anticipate challenges, test interventions and learn systematically from outcomes. Recent studies suggest that AI-driven educational systems and data-centric decision models enhance institutional responsiveness by enabling predictive insights and adaptive learning environments (Mekić et al., 2024; Jain et al., 2026). However, the effectiveness of such systems depends on the integration of ethical safeguards and transparency in algorithmic decision-making.

Importantly, treating educational research as infrastructure also implies continuity. Data-driven decision making is not a one-time exercise but an iterative process. Research-informed institutions revisit assumptions, refine models and adapt strategies as conditions change. In periods of uncertainty, this capacity for learning becomes a defining feature of institutional resilience.

Figure 1. Educational research as an institutional infrastructure for data-driven decision making in higher education planning.

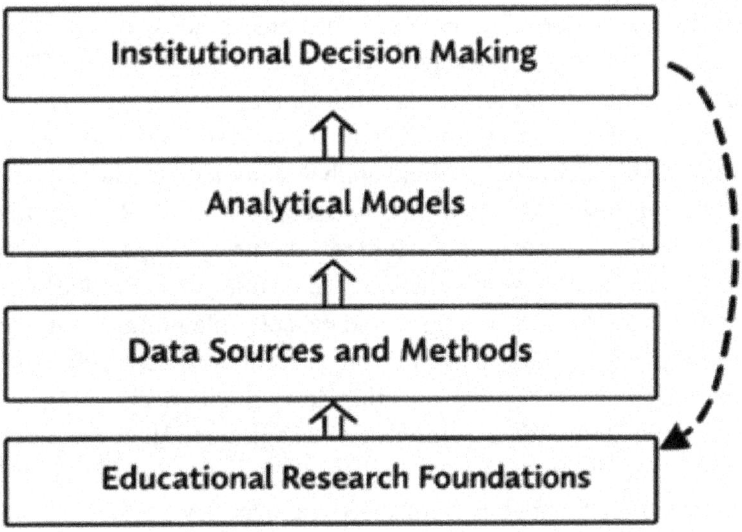

To clarify the role of educational research as a foundational layer, Figure 1 conceptualizes research as an institutional infrastructure that supports data collection, analysis and decision making through iterative feedback loops.

3. SOURCES OF DATA IN HIGHER EDUCATION PLANNING

Data-driven decision making in higher education is only as robust as the data on which it relies. While the phrase institutional data often suggests a single coherent resource, in practice higher education data ecosystems are fragmented, layered and historically dependent. Data are generated by different offices for different purposes, collected at varying levels of granularity and governed by distinct norms of access and interpretation. Understanding the nature of these data sources is therefore a prerequisite for responsible planning and sound analysis.

Broadly speaking, data used in higher education planning can be grouped into administrative data, learning and engagement data, survey-based data, qualitative data and external contextual data. Each category offers distinct insights and carries specific limitations. Educational research provides the tools to assess their validity, reliability and relevance within particular decision contexts.

3.1 Administrative Data and Institutional Records

Administrative data form the backbone of most institutional analytics efforts. These data are generated through routine operations and include student admissions records, enrollment histories, course registrations, grades, credit accumulation, completion outcomes, financial aid records and staffing information. Their primary strength lies in scale and continuity. Administrative datasets typically cover entire populations rather than samples and extend across multiple academic years. This makes them well suited for longitudinal analyses and cohort tracking.

For planning purposes, administrative data support trend analysis and forecasting. Enrollment projections, for example, often rely on historical patterns of application volume, yield rates and progression between academic years. Similarly, completion data inform estimates of time to degree and capacity planning. In engineering and science programs, where progression through sequenced curricula is critical, administrative data can reveal bottlenecks that delay graduation.

However, administrative data were not originally designed for research or planning. They are operational byproducts. As a result, they reflect institutional definitions and constraints that may not align with analytical needs. Variables such as full-time status, retention or academic standing are often defined differently across institutions or even across units within the same institution. Without careful documentation and standardization, comparisons over time or across contexts can be misleading.

Educational research emphasizes the importance of data provenance. Analysts must ask how a variable was generated, under what assumptions and for what purpose. A change in policy or information system can produce apparent trends that reflect administrative shifts rather than substantive change. This issue becomes particularly salient during periods of organizational restructuring or rapid policy reform.

3.2 Learning Management Systems and Engagement Data

The widespread adoption of learning management systems has dramatically expanded the volume and granularity of educational data. These systems generate detailed records of student interaction with course materials, including logins, page views, discussion participation and assignment submissions. Such data are often described as behavioral or trace data because they capture actions rather than self-reports.

Learning analytics research has explored the potential of these data to predict academic performance and identify students at risk of disengagement (Siemens & Baker, 2012). Subsequent studies have further shown the predictive capacity of learning analytics while also emphasizing the need for pedagogical interpretation (Ferguson, 2012).

For planners, engagement data offer a window into instructional practices at scale. Patterns of access and participation can inform decisions about course design, instructional support and digital infrastructure.

Yet the interpretive challenges associated with learning management system data are substantial. Engagement metrics are proxies rather than direct measures of learning. A student who downloads materials may not read them. Another may engage deeply offline. Moreover, patterns of engagement vary by discipline, pedagogy and assessment design. Comparing engagement metrics across courses without contextual knowledge can lead to erroneous conclusions.

Educational research cautions against decontextualized analytics. Engagement data should be interpreted alongside curricular structures, instructional intentions and student characteristics. Mixed methods approaches are particularly valuable here. Quantitative engagement patterns gain meaning when complemented by qualitative insights from instructors and students. The integration of machine learning and statistical modeling techniques further strengthens the analytical value of educational data by uncovering hidden patterns and supporting evidence-based evaluation of learning outcomes (Xu, 2025). These approaches enable more accurate forecasting of educational demand and resource allocation.

3.3 Survey Data and Perceptual Measures

Survey-based data play a central role in higher education planning because they capture dimensions of the educational experience that administrative records cannot. Surveys measure perceptions, attitudes, motivations and self-reported behaviors.

Common survey domains include student satisfaction, sense of belonging, perceived learning gains and engagement with faculty.

National and international surveys such as the National Survey of Student Engagement have been widely adopted as benchmarking tools (Kuh, 2009). These instruments allow institutions to situate their performance within broader sectoral patterns. For planners, survey data can highlight areas of relative strength and concern that warrant further investigation.

Despite their utility, survey data require careful methodological consideration. Response rates vary across groups and low participation can introduce bias. Survey instruments are shaped by theoretical assumptions that may not align perfectly with local contexts. For example, constructs such as engagement or belonging may manifest differently across cultures or institutional types.

Educational research provides guidance on survey design, validation and interpretation. Triangulation is particularly important. Survey findings should be examined alongside administrative and qualitative data to assess consistency and plausibility. When used thoughtfully, survey data enrich planning by foregrounding student and faculty voices. Issues of validity and reliability in surveys have been widely discussed, particularly in relation to cultural sensitivity and construct equivalence across institutional contexts (Porter, 2013).

3.4 Qualitative Data and Narrative Evidence

Qualitative data occupy a distinctive place in data-driven decision making. Unlike administrative or survey data, qualitative evidence is not easily aggregated or summarized numerically. Its value lies in depth rather than breadth.

Interviews, focus groups, open-ended survey responses and document analysis reveal how institutional policies and practices are experienced by individuals. These data illuminate processes, meanings and relationships that shape outcomes. In planning contexts, qualitative data often surface unintended consequences or implementation challenges that quantitative indicators overlook.

For example, an institution may observe declining enrollment in a particular program. Quantitative data can identify when the decline began and which student groups are affected. Qualitative interviews with current and prospective students may reveal perceptions of outdated curricula, limited career pathways or inadequate advising. Such insights are critical for designing effective responses.

Qualitative data also play an important role in organizational learning. Planning decisions frequently involve trade-offs and competing priorities. Narrative evidence can help stakeholders understand the rationale behind decisions and build shared understanding. From an educational research perspective, qualitative data support reflexivity by encouraging institutions to question assumptions and attend to context.

3.5 External and Contextual Data Sources

Higher education institutions do not operate in isolation. External data sources provide essential context for planning and strategic alignment. These data include demographic projections, labor market information, economic indicators and policy data.

Demographic data inform long-term enrollment planning. Changes in secondary school completion rates, population age structures and migration patterns shape the pool of prospective students. In regions experiencing demographic decline, institutions must consider alternative recruitment strategies or program diversification.

Labor market data are particularly salient for professional and technical programs. Employment projections, skill demand analyses and wage data inform curriculum development and program viability. Engineering programs often draw on industry data to justify new specializations or revise learning outcomes.

Policy data shape planning constraints and opportunities. Funding formulas, accreditation requirements and visa regulations influence institutional strategies. Educational research helps planners interpret these data within broader policy frameworks and anticipate potential impacts.

3.6 Integrating Multiple Data Sources

The true power of data-driven decision making emerges when multiple data sources are integrated. No single dataset provides a complete picture. Administrative data describe what happens. Survey data suggest how it is perceived. Qualitative data explain why it unfolds as it does. External data situate institutional patterns within societal trends.

Integration requires both technical infrastructure and conceptual alignment. Data warehouses and analytics platforms facilitate technical integration but do not resolve conceptual differences. Educational research contributes frameworks for aligning data sources around shared questions and evaluative criteria.

For example, a retention initiative may combine administrative progression data, engagement metrics from learning management systems, survey measures of belonging and qualitative feedback from students. Together, these data support a nuanced understanding of retention dynamics and inform targeted interventions.

To make explicit how different forms of data contribute to planning decisions, Table 1 summarizes common data sources used in higher education planning, the types of questions they support and their primary strengths and limitations.

Table 1. Data sources, analytical uses and limitations in higher education planning

Data source	Typical examples	Primary planning questions supported	Key strengths	Key limitations
Administrative data	Enrollment records, grades, credit accumulation, completion data	What is happening over time? Where are bottlenecks or attrition points?	Comprehensive coverage, longitudinal continuity, population-level analysis	Definitions may change, limited insight into student experience, operational bias
Learning management system data	Logins, submissions, discussion activity	How are students engaging with instructional environments?	Fine-grained behavioral traces, near real-time monitoring	Engagement is a proxy for learning, highly context-dependent
Survey-based data	Student satisfaction, sense of belonging, faculty climate surveys	How are experiences and perceptions distributed across groups?	Captures attitudes and self-reported outcomes, supports benchmarking	Response bias, construct validity concerns, cultural variation
Qualitative data	Interviews, focus groups, open-ended responses	Why are patterns occurring? How are policies experienced?	Contextual depth, explanatory power, surfaces unintended effects	Limited generalizability, resource-intensive analysis
External contextual data	Demographic projections, labor market data, policy indicators	How do external conditions shape institutional options?	Strategic foresight, alignment with societal trends	Projections are uncertain, may lag rapid change

The range of data sources that inform institutional planning and their convergence around shared decision questions is shown in Figure 2, which indicates a simplified institutional data ecosystem. In practice, integration is iterative. Initial analyses raise new questions that prompt additional data collection or refinement. Institutions that treat data integration as an ongoing research process rather than a one-time project are better equipped to adapt to change.

Figure 2. Core data sources

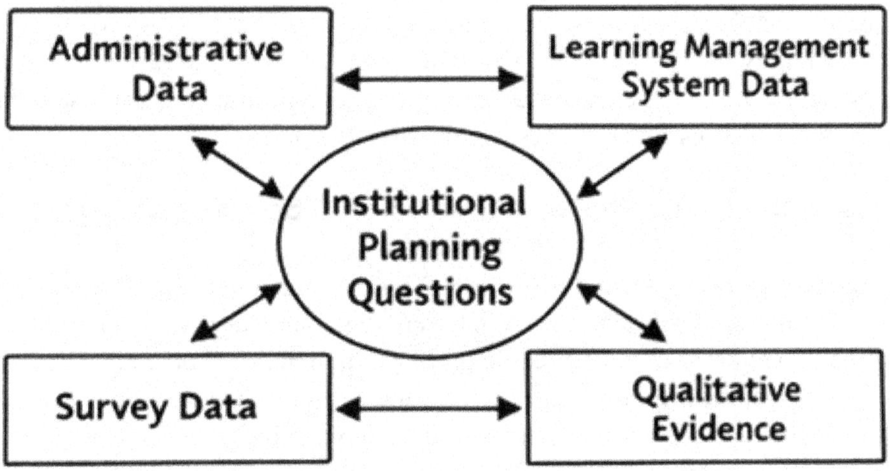

In conclusion, sources of data in higher education planning are diverse in form, purpose and interpretive demands. Educational research equips institutions to navigate this complexity by emphasizing methodological rigor, contextual awareness and ethical responsibility. As subsequent sections will show, the effective use of these data sources depends not only on technical capacity but also on organizational culture and leadership commitment. Data integration in higher education analytics is increasingly considered as a socio-technical process requiring both infrastructure and interpretive alignment (Bichsel, 2012).

4. METHODOLOGICAL CONSIDERATIONS, ANALYTICAL MODELS AND INTERPRETIVE LIMITS

The availability of diverse data sources does not by itself guarantee sound decision making. Data become actionable only through methodological choices that determine how patterns are identified, relationships are inferred and uncertainty is managed. In higher education planning, methodological rigor is not a technical luxury. It is a practical necessity. Decisions informed by weak models or poorly specified analyses can carry long-term consequences for students, faculty and institutional sustainability. The application of analytics in higher education is often seen within the broader domain of academic analytics, which integrates institutional data with predictive modeling to support decision making (Goldstein & Katz, 2005).

Educational research provides a methodological compass for navigating these challenges. It emphasizes that analytical models are representations rather than reflections of reality. Every model encodes assumptions about which variables matter, how they relate to one another and what counts as meaningful change. Understanding these assumptions is essential for responsible interpretation.

4.1 Descriptive Analytics and Institutional Self-Knowledge

Descriptive analytics form the starting point for most planning efforts. These analyses summarize historical data to answer basic questions about institutional performance. Trends in enrollment, retention, graduation rates and course demand are typically examined through counts, percentages and visualizations.

Although often not considered as preliminary, descriptive analyses play a crucial role in institutional self-knowledge. They establish baselines against which change can be assessed and they surface patterns that warrant deeper investigation. For example, a steady decline in enrollment within a specific program may generate questions about curriculum relevance or market alignment.

However, descriptive analytics are inherently backward-looking. They describe what has happened but offer limited guidance about what might happen next or why observed patterns emerged. Educational research cautions against treating descriptive stability as predictive certainty. Historical trends may mask underlying shifts in student behavior or external conditions that only become visible when change accelerates.

4.2 Inferential Statistics and Hypothesis Testing

Inferential statistical methods extend descriptive analysis by allowing institutions to test hypotheses and estimate relationships between variables. Techniques such as regression analysis, analysis of variance and survival analysis are commonly used in institutional research.

For example, regression models may be used to examine the relationship between financial aid levels and student persistence while controlling for academic preparation and demographic characteristics. Survival analysis can model time to degree or time to withdrawal, accounting for censoring and varying exposure periods.

These methods provide a degree of generalizability and statistical confidence that descriptive analytics lack. Yet they also introduce risks of misinterpretation. Statistical significance does not imply practical importance. A small effect size may be statistically detectable in large datasets but irrelevant for planning decisions.

Educational research emphasizes the importance of aligning statistical methods with substantive questions. Analysts must consider whether model assumptions such as linearity or independence are reasonable in educational contexts. When assumptions are violated, results may be unstable or misleading.

4.3 Predictive Analytics and Risk Modeling

Predictive analytics has gained prominence in higher education planning due to advances in computing power and data availability. Predictive models aim to estimate the likelihood of future outcomes such as student attrition, course failure or enrollment yield. Common predictive techniques include logistic regression, decision trees and machine learning algorithms such as random forests. These models are often evaluated based on accuracy metrics such as precision, recall or area under the receiver operating characteristic curve. In practice, predictive models are frequently used to support early intervention systems. Students identified as high risk may be offered additional advising or academic support. From a planning perspective, predictive analytics can inform resource allocation by identifying where interventions are likely to have the greatest impact. Research highlights that AI-driven predictive systems, including recommendation engines and intelligent tutoring systems, significantly enhance personalized learning and institutional decision-making, though their deployment must be accompanied by ethical oversight and bias mitigation strategies (Jain et al., 2026).

However, predictive performance should not be conflated with explanatory power. A model may accurately predict outcomes without providing insight into underlying mechanisms. This distinction matters because interventions based on opaque predictions may fail to address root causes. Moreover, predictive models are sensitive to context. Models trained on historical data assume continuity in institutional practices and student behavior. When conditions change rapidly, such as during shifts to remote instruction or policy reforms, predictive validity can deteriorate. Educational research discuss for continuous model evaluation and recalibration. Concerns regarding bias, fairness and unintended consequences in predictive models have been considered in recent literature on algorithmic decision making (O'Neil, 2016). Figure 3 shows commonly used analytical techniques along a progression from descriptive reporting to causal inference.

Figure 3. Progression of analytical approaches used in higher education planning

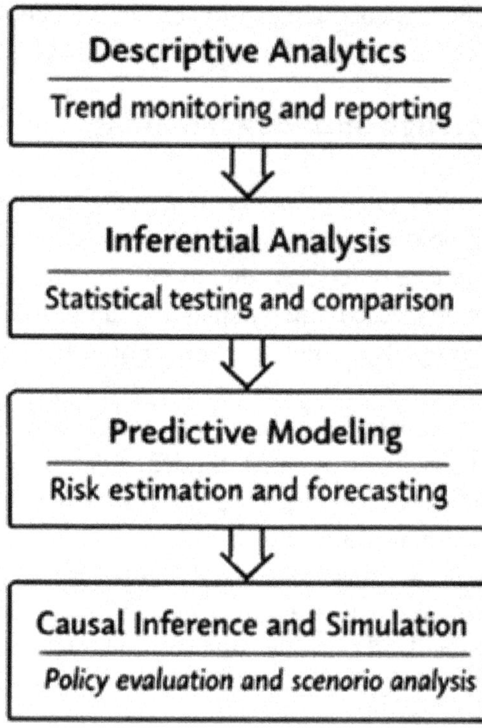

In Table 2, a comparison of common analytical approaches used in higher education planning in terms of their purpose, outputs and typical risks of misinterpretation is provided.

Table 2. Analytical approaches and their roles in higher education planning

Analytical approach	Typical methods	Primary purpose	Appropriate planning use	Common risks
Descriptive analytics	Counts, percentages, trend analysis	Summarize past and current patterns	Baseline assessment, monitoring change	Mistaken as predictive or explanatory
Inferential statistics	Regression, ANOVA, survival analysis	Estimate relationships and test hypotheses	Identifying correlates, informing policy debates	Overemphasis on statistical significance
Predictive analytics	Logistic regression, machine learning models	Estimate likelihood of future outcomes	Early warning systems, resource targeting	Opacity, model drift, equity concerns
Causal inference	Quasi-experimental designs	Estimate program impact	Evaluating interventions, scaling decisions	Strong assumptions, sensitivity to design flaws
Simulation and scenarios	System dynamics, scenario modeling	Explore plausible futures	Strategic planning under uncertainty	Misuse as precise forecasts

4.4 Causal Inference and Program Evaluation

Planning decisions often require answers to fundamental questions. Did a new advising program improve retention? Did curriculum redesign shorten time to degree? Answering such questions is methodologically challenging in educational settings.

Randomized controlled trials remain rare at institutional scale due to ethical, logistical and political constraints. As a result, planners often rely on quasi-experimental designs. Methods such as propensity score matching, regression discontinuity and difference-in-differences analysis attempt to approximate fundamental inference under nonrandom conditions (Shadish et al., 2002).

These approaches require careful design and transparent reporting. Small violations of assumptions can produce biased estimates. Educational research underscores the importance of sensitivity analysis and robustness checks to assess the stability of findings. Fundamental evidence plays a critical role in scaling interventions. Without credible estimates of impact, institutions risk expanding initiatives that are popular but ineffective. Conversely, promising programs may be discontinued prematurely if evaluation designs fail to capture their effects.

4.5 Simulation Models and Scenario Planning

Beyond analysis of existing data, higher education planning increasingly employs simulation and scenario modeling. These models explore how systems might respond to hypothetical changes such as enrollment declines, funding shifts or policy reforms.

Simulation models are particularly useful for examining complex interactions among variables. For example, changes in enrollment affect tuition revenue, which in turn influences staffing levels and course availability. Modeling these interactions helps decision makers anticipate unintended consequences.

Scenario planning acknowledges uncertainty explicitly. Rather than predicting a single future, planners explore multiple plausible futures and assess their implications. Educational research contributes frameworks for identifying critical uncertainties and structuring scenarios in ways that support strategic thinking.

Importantly, simulation models are tools for exploration rather than prediction. Their value lies in clarifying trade-offs and constraints rather than delivering precise forecasts.

4.6 Data Quality, Governance and Interpretive Limits

Methodological sophistication cannot compensate for poor data quality. Missing values, inconsistent coding and changes in data definitions undermine analytical validity. Data governance structures that establish clear ownership, documentation and quality assurance processes are therefore integral to data-driven planning.

Equally important are interpretive limits. No model can fully capture the social complexity of educational institutions. Quantitative analyses abstract away individual narratives and organizational cultures. Educational research reminds planners that models should inform deliberation rather than replace it.

Transparent communication of uncertainty is essential. Confidence intervals, model limitations and alternative interpretations should be communicated clearly to decision makers. This transparency fosters trust and encourages responsible use of evidence.

In summary, methodological and analytical models are central to translating data into decisions. Educational research equips institutions with tools to select appropriate methods, interpret results critically and integrate evidence into planning processes. As discussed in the next sections, the effectiveness of these models depends on how they are embedded within institutional practices and ethical commitments.

5. ETHICAL AND EQUITY CONSIDERATIONS

Ethical considerations in data use are often formed through principles of justice, beneficence and respect for persons, adapted from broader research ethics frameworks (Beauchamp & Childress, 2019). As higher education institutions increasingly rely on data to inform planning and policy, ethical considerations move from the periphery of decision making to its center. Data-driven approaches are often presented as neutral or objective, yet educational research has long demonstrated that data are socially constructed. Choices about what to measure, how to measure it and how results are interpreted are shaped by institutional values, power relations and historical context. Ethical reflection is therefore not an optional add-on to analytics. It is a core component of responsible decision making. Recent literature also underscores that ethical concerns such as data privacy, algorithmic discrimination, and unequal access remain underexplored in AI-driven educational systems, despite their growing adoption (Mena Guacas et al., 2026). Addressing these gaps is essential for ensuring inclusive and equitable data-driven decision-making.

One of the most immediate ethical concerns involves privacy. Higher education institutions collect extensive data about students, faculty and staff. Administrative records, learning management systems and survey instruments together create detailed profiles of individual behavior and performance. While such data can support timely interventions and institutional improvement, they also raise questions about consent, surveillance and autonomy.

From a research perspective, the principle of informed consent is well established. In operational settings, however, consent is often implicit rather than explicit. Students may be unaware of the extent to which their digital interactions are monitored or how those data are used in predictive models. Educational research urges institutions to articulate clear policies regarding data collection and use and to communicate these policies transparently. Ethical practice requires not only legal compliance but also respect for individuals as participants in educational systems rather than mere data sources.

Closely related to privacy is the issue of data security. Breaches of institutional data systems can have serious consequences for individuals and institutional trust. Planning processes that rely on centralized data repositories must therefore incorporate robust governance structures and technical safeguards. Ethical responsibility extends beyond analysis to stewardship.

Equity considerations introduce further complexity. Predictive analytics and performance metrics are often promoted as tools for identifying risk and allocating resources efficiently. Yet when these tools are trained on historical data, they may reflect and reinforce existing inequalities. For example, if students from certain socioeconomic backgrounds have historically experienced lower completion rates, predictive models may label them as high risk. Without careful interpretation, such labels can lead to deficit-oriented interventions or lowered expectations.

Educational research emphasizes the distinction between correlation and causation in equity analysis. Disparities in outcomes rarely arise from individual characteristics alone. They are produced through interactions between institutional practices, structural barriers and social context. Ethical data use requires shifting attention from identifying who is at risk to understanding why risk is unevenly distributed.

The relationship between analytical sophistication and ethical reflection is summarized in Figure 4, which shows how technically advanced methods do not necessarily correspond to responsible decision making.

Figure 4. Relationship between analytical sophistication and ethical reflection in data-driven decision making.

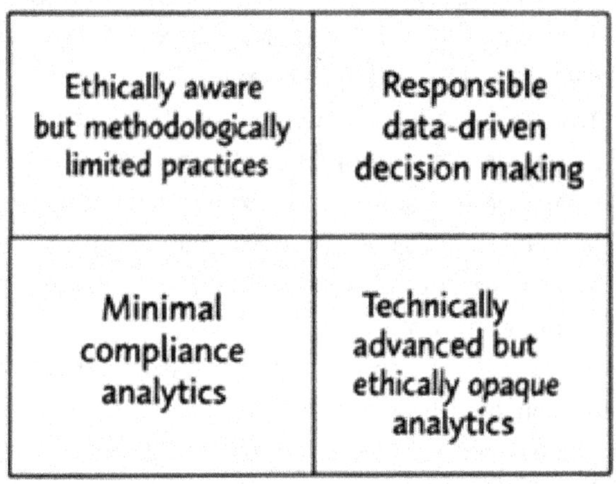

Disaggregation of data by demographic variables is a common equity strategy. When used thoughtfully, disaggregation can reveal patterns that would otherwise remain hidden in aggregate metrics. For instance, overall retention rates may appear stable while masking significant variation across student groups. However, disaggregation also carries risks. Small sample sizes can compromise confidentiality and simplistic interpretations can stigmatize groups rather than illuminate systemic issues.

Transparency is another ethical imperative. Decision makers and stakeholders should be able to understand how data-informed conclusions are reached. Black-box models that deliver predictions without explanation challenge principles of accountability and shared governance. In academic environments, where deliberation and critique are valued, opaque analytics can undermine trust.

Educational research supports the use of interpretable models and participatory approaches to data analysis. Involving faculty, advisors and students in interpreting findings can surface contextual knowledge that improves decision quality. Such participation also distributes ethical responsibility rather than concentrating it within technical units.

The ethical use of data also extends to evaluation and accountability. Metrics are powerful because they shape behavior. When performance indicators are tied to funding or evaluation, they influence priorities and incentives. Overemphasis on easily measurable outcomes can marginalize activities that are central to institutional mission but less quantifiable such as mentoring, community engagement or interdisciplinary collaboration.

From a planning perspective, ethical evaluation requires balance. Quantitative indicators should be complemented by qualitative evidence and professional judgment. Educational research traditions provide models for holistic evaluation that attend to processes and outcomes as well as intended and unintended effects.

Finally, ethical data-driven decision making requires reflexivity. Institutions must continually ask whose interests are served by particular analyses and whose voices are absent. Data can illuminate inequity but they can also obscure it if used uncritically. The ethical challenge is not to abandon analytics but to embed them within value-conscious frameworks.

In this light, equity is not simply an outcome to be measured but a lens through which planning decisions are made. Institutions that approach data-driven decision making as a moral as well as technical endeavor are better positioned to navigate uncertainty with integrity. As the following sections illustrate, ethical awareness shapes how data are applied in concrete domains such as enrollment management, curriculum design and faculty workload planning.

6. APPLICATIONS IN ENROLLMENT MANAGEMENT AND RETENTION

Enrollment management represents one of the most visible and consequential arenas in which data-driven decision making operates within higher education. Enrollment levels directly influence institutional revenue, staffing capacity and program viability. At the same time, enrollment decisions intersect with mission commitments related to access, equity and academic quality. Educational research provides frameworks for navigating these tensions by grounding enrollment strategies in systematic evidence rather than short-term reaction.

Traditionally, enrollment management focused on recruitment and admissions. Contemporary approaches are broader and encompass the entire student lifecycle from initial inquiry through completion. This shift reflects growing recognition that retention and progression are as important as recruitment in sustaining institutional stability. Data-driven enrollment management therefore integrates multiple forms of evidence across time.

6.1 Recruitment Analytics and Admissions Planning

Recruitment planning relies heavily on predictive and descriptive analytics. Institutions analyze application trends, yield rates and demographic patterns to estimate incoming class size and composition. These analyses often incorporate historical data alongside external indicators such as regional demographics or secondary school completion rates.

From a methodological standpoint, yield modeling illustrates both the power and limitations of data-driven approaches. Regression models or machine learning techniques may predict the probability that an admitted student will enroll based on academic preparation, financial aid offers and geographic proximity. Such models can support strategic allocation of scholarships and outreach efforts.

However, educational research cautions against treating predicted yield as an objective truth. Applicant behavior is influenced by perceptions, institutional reputation and economic uncertainty. During periods of volatility, such as global disruptions to mobility, historical models may lose predictive accuracy. Institutions that recognize these limitations use analytics as decision support rather than as deterministic tools.

Equity considerations are especially salient in recruitment analytics. Financial aid optimization models that maximize enrollment revenue may disadvantage students with greater financial need. Research-informed planning requires explicit articulation of values. Institutions must decide whether efficiency or access takes priority and under what conditions trade-offs are acceptable.

6.2 Retention Analysis and Early Warning Systems

Student retention has become a central concern in higher education planning due to its implications for student success and financial sustainability. Data-driven retention strategies often begin with identification of risk factors associated with withdrawal or delayed progression.

To make visible where data-informed interventions can occur along the student lifecycle, Figure 5 presents a simplified representation of student progression pathways with associated data inputs and intervention points. Administrative data reveal patterns in course failure, credit accumulation and academic standing. When analyzed longitudinally, these data can identify critical transition points where students are most vulnerable. First-year persistence and progression through gateway courses frequently emerge as focal areas.

Figure 5. Student progression pathways

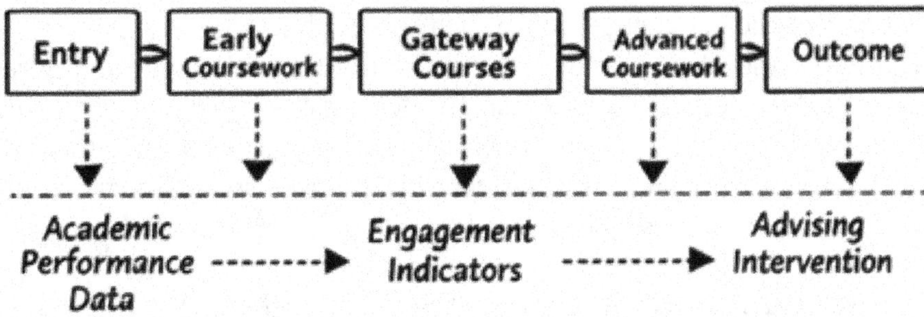

Predictive models are commonly used to flag students at risk of attrition. These models may incorporate academic performance, engagement metrics and demographic variables. Early warning systems built on such models aim to trigger timely interventions such as advising or tutoring. Educational research shows that the effectiveness of early warning systems depends less on predictive accuracy than on institutional response. Alerts that are not acted upon or that result in generic interventions offer limited benefit. Moreover, labeling students as at risk can unintentionally shape expectations and interactions. Ethical practice requires that risk indicators be used to mobilize support rather than to categorize students.

Qualitative research enriches retention analysis by revealing student perspectives. Interviews and focus groups often reveal that decisions to leave are shaped by cumulative experiences rather than isolated events. Financial stress, misalignment between academic expectations and reality and lack of connection to faculty frequently interact. Such insights inform interventions that address structural conditions rather than symptoms alone.

6.3 Program-Level Retention and Curriculum Pathways

Retention dynamics vary across disciplines. In structured programs such as engineering, progression through sequenced curricula plays a critical role. Data analysis may reveal that failure in specific courses correlates strongly with delayed graduation or withdrawal.

Educational research supports the use of pathway analysis to examine how students move through curricula over time. Course sequencing data can identify bottlenecks and unintended barriers. For example, limited availability of required courses may delay progression even for academically successful students. Curriculum reforms informed by such analyses often involve redesigning gateway courses, offering supplemental instruction or adjusting prerequisite structures. Evaluating the impact of these reforms requires longitudinal data and comparison groups. Quasi-experimental designs can help assess whether observed improvements are attributable to curricular changes rather than cohort effects.

Retention should also be understood as an institutional responsibility rather than an individual deficit. Data-driven planning that focuses solely on student characteristics risks overlooking institutional practices that contribute to attrition. Educational research encourages a shift from asking why students leave to asking how institutions can better support persistence.

6.4 Integrating Enrollment and Retention Data

Effective enrollment management integrates recruitment and retention data into a coherent planning framework. Decisions about class size, program capacity and staffing should account for both incoming cohorts and continuing students. For example, aggressive recruitment without corresponding investment in advising and instructional capacity may strain resources and undermine retention. Conversely, improved retention can stabilize enrollment even when recruitment slows. Simulation models can help planners explore these interactions and anticipate resource implications.

Integration also requires cross-unit collaboration. Admissions offices, academic departments and student support services often operate with distinct data systems and priorities. Educational research emphasizes the importance of shared metrics and common interpretive frameworks to align decision making.

6.5 Limitations and Adaptive Planning

Despite advances in analytics, enrollment management remains uncertain. External factors, policy changes and shifting student preferences can disrupt even well-designed models. Data-driven planning should therefore be adaptive rather than rigid. Institutions that approach enrollment management as an ongoing research process are better positioned to respond to change. Continuous monitoring, evaluation of interventions and willingness to revise assumptions are hallmarks of effective practice.

In conclusion, data-driven enrollment management and retention strategies illustrate how educational research translates evidence into action. When grounded in methodological rigor and ethical awareness, these approaches support institutional resilience while advancing student success. The following section extends this discussion to curriculum planning and program evaluation, where similar principles apply within academic structures.

7. CURRICULUM PLANNING AND PROGRAM EVALUATION

Curriculum planning and program evaluation occupy a central position in higher education planning because they sit at the intersection of academic mission, student learning and institutional sustainability. Decisions about what is taught, how learning is structured and which programs are sustained or discontinued carry long-term consequences that extend beyond enrollment cycles. In this domain, data-driven decision making must be particularly attentive to disciplinary norms, educational values and the limits of quantification.

Educational research provides conceptual frameworks for understanding curriculum as both a formal structure and a lived experience. From a planning perspective, curricula are often represented through course catalogs, credit requirements and learning outcomes. From a student perspective, curricula are navigational pathways shaped by sequencing, assessment practices and instructional quality. Data-driven approaches must account for both representations if they are to support meaningful improvement.

7.1 Learning Outcomes and Assessment Data

Outcome-based education has become a dominant paradigm in curriculum planning and evaluation. Institutions are increasingly expected to articulate clear learning outcomes and demonstrate that students achieve them. Assessment data therefore play a prominent role in program review and accreditation processes. The principle of constructive alignment suggests coherence between learning outcomes, teaching activities and assessment practices as a foundation for meaningful curriculum design (Biggs, 1996).

Direct assessment measures include examinations, project evaluations, portfolios and capstone experiences. These measures provide evidence of student learning aligned with disciplinary standards. Indirect measures such as students' self-report or alumni surveys complement direct assessments by capturing perceived learning and longer-term outcomes.

Educational research emphasizes the importance of alignment among learning outcomes, instructional practices and assessment methods. Misalignment can produce misleading data. For example, a program may report strong learning outcomes while relying on assessments that do not reflect stated objectives. Data-driven curriculum planning requires scrutiny of assessment validity as well as results.

Longitudinal analysis of assessment data can reveal trends in learning outcomes across cohorts. Such analyses support evidence-based curriculum revision. However, interpreting these trends requires caution. Changes in student preparation, instructional staffing or assessment design can influence results independently of curriculum quality.

7.2 Curriculum Pathways and Structural Analysis

Beyond learning outcomes, data-driven planning examines how curricula are structured and navigated. Pathway analysis draws on administrative data to trace student movement through courses over time. This approach is particularly relevant in programs with tightly sequenced requirements. In engineering and applied sciences, pathway analysis often reveals that certain courses function as critical junctures. High failure rates or limited availability in these courses can delay progression and increase attrition. Identifying these patterns allows institutions to target instructional support or redesign course sequences. Educational research frames pathway analysis within broader discussions of curricular coherence. A coherent curriculum supports cumulative learning and reduces unnecessary complexity. Data-driven insights into course-taking patterns can expose hidden complexity such as excessive prerequisites or scheduling conflicts that disproportionately affect certain student groups.

Importantly, pathway data must be interpreted alongside qualitative evidence. Faculty insights into course content and pedagogical challenges provide context for observed patterns. Students can offer perspectives on workload, relevance and support. Integrating these perspectives helps avoid reductive conclusions based solely on completion metrics.

7.3 Program Demand and Viability Analysis

Program evaluation also involves assessing demand and viability. Enrollment trends, graduation rates and market data inform decisions about program continuation, expansion or consolidation. These decisions are among the most politically sensitive in higher education planning.

Educational research cautions against equating enrollment size with program value. Some programs serve strategic or mission-driven purposes that are not captured by market metrics alone. For example, programs that support regional workforce needs or interdisciplinary collaboration may justify continued investment despite modest enrollment.

Market data add an external dimension to program evaluation. Employment projections, skill demand analyses and alumni outcomes provide evidence of program relevance. In professional fields, such data often influence curriculum updates and the introduction of new specializations.

However, market data are themselves projections subject to uncertainty. Planning based solely on current demand risks chasing short-term trends at the expense of foundational education. Educational research encourages balance between responsiveness and disciplinary integrity.

7.4 Program Review and Evidence Integration

Formal program review processes provide structured opportunities to integrate diverse forms of evidence. Reviews typically combine quantitative indicators such as enrollment and completion with qualitative self-studies and external evaluations. Data-driven program review benefits from clear evaluative criteria. Ambiguous standards invite selective use of data to support predetermined conclusions. Educational research advocates for transparent frameworks that specify how evidence will be weighed and how decisions will be justified.

Evaluation should also be developmental rather than punitive. When program review is framed as an opportunity for learning and improvement, faculty engagement increases. Data become tools for reflection rather than instruments of control.

Feedback loops are essential. Recommendations emerging from program reviews should be tracked over time to assess implementation and impact. Without such follow-up, data-driven evaluation risks become interrupted rather than transformative.

7.5 Balancing Innovation and Stability

Curriculum planning operates within a tension between innovation and stability. Institutions must adapt to changing knowledge domains and student needs while preserving academic rigor and coherence. Data-driven approaches can support this balance by providing evidence about the effects of change. Pilot programs and incremental reforms offer opportunities for experimentation. Educational research designs such as formative evaluation allow institutions to test innovations and adjust based on evidence. This approach reduces risk while fostering continuous improvement.

At the same time, planners must recognize that not all educational value is immediately measurable. Intellectual development, professional identity formation and ethical reasoning often unfold over extended periods. Data-driven curriculum planning must therefore be complemented by scholarly judgment and disciplinary expertise.

In summary, curriculum planning and program evaluation show both the promise and complexity of data-driven decision making in higher education. Educational research provides the methodological tools and interpretive frameworks needed to use data responsibly in academic contexts. As the next section will show, similar principles apply to organizational planning related to faculty workload and institutional capacity, where data intersect with professional norms and governance structures.

7.6 Faculty Workload and Organizational Planning

While curriculum planning and program evaluation focus primarily on student learning and academic structures, these decisions are inseparable from organizational capacity and faculty workload. Changes in curricula, program portfolios, or instructional modalities directly affect academic labor and institutional resources. For this reason, the discussion now turns from curriculum-focused planning to faculty workload and organizational planning as a connected but analytically distinct domain of data-driven decision making.

Faculty workload and organizational planning represent domains where data-driven decision making intersects most directly with professional identity, governance and institutional culture. Unlike enrollment or curriculum metrics, which often concern aggregated student outcomes, workload data touch individual careers and academic norms. As a result, their use requires particular sensitivity and methodological care. Educational research offers essential guidance for navigating these complexities while supporting institutional sustainability.

Faculty work in higher education is multifaceted. Teaching, research and service responsibilities are distributed unevenly across disciplines, career stages and institutional missions. Planning processes that rely on simplistic workload indicators risk misrepresenting this diversity. Data-driven approaches must therefore begin with clear conceptual models of academic work rather than relying solely on easily quantifiable outputs.

7.7 Sources of Faculty Workload Data

Institutions collect a wide range of data related to faculty activity. Teaching loads are often measured through course counts, student credit hours or contact hours. Research activity is tracked through publications, grants and citations. Service contributions may be documented through committee assignments or administrative roles.

Each of these indicators captures only a portion of academic labor. For example, two courses may carry equivalent credit values while differing substantially in preparation time, assessment complexity or student support demands. Similarly, publication counts do not reflect differences in disciplinary norms or the intellectual labor involved in collaborative research.

Educational research emphasizes the importance of contextualizing workload data within disciplinary and institutional frameworks. Benchmarking across departments or institutions requires careful adjustment for mission, field and resource conditions. Without such adjustment, comparisons may be perceived as inequitable and erode trust.

7.8 Workload Modeling and Capacity Planning

From an organizational planning perspective, workload data support capacity modeling. Institutions use these models to assess whether staffing levels align with enrollment demand and curricular requirements. In periods of enrollment fluctuation, such models inform decisions about hiring freezes, adjunct appointments or program consolidation.

Capacity models often combine enrollment projections with assumptions about average teaching loads. While useful for scenario planning, these models depend heavily on their assumptions. Educational research encourages planners to test multiple scenarios rather than relying on single-point estimates. For example, a model assuming stable teaching loads may underestimate strain during periods of curricular reform or increased student support needs. Incorporating qualitative input from faculty can improve model realism and legitimacy. The balanced integration of data, professional expertise and institutional values in organizational planning is shown in Figure 6.

Figure 6. Integrating data, professional judgment and institutional values in faculty workload and organizational planning.

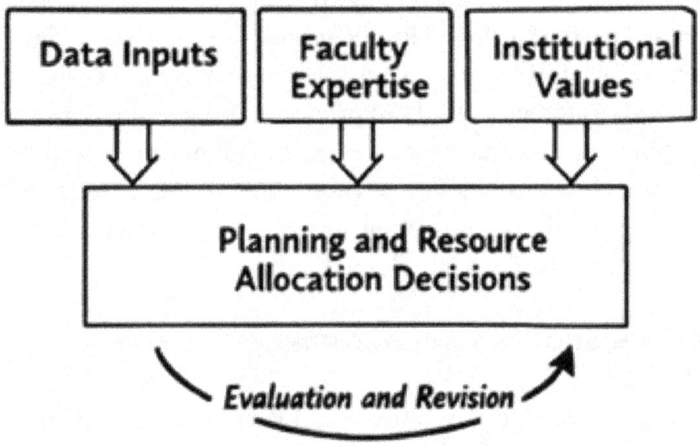

7.9 Evaluation, Accountability and Professional Norms

Data-driven approaches to faculty evaluation have expanded alongside performance-based funding and accountability regimes. Teaching evaluations, publication metrics and grant income increasingly inform promotion, tenure and contract renewal decisions. Educational research has raised concerns about overreliance on narrow metrics. Student evaluations of teaching, while widely used, are influenced by factors unrelated to instructional quality. Citation metrics vary widely across fields and disadvantage interdisciplinary work. Responsible use of workload and performance data requires pluralistic evaluation frameworks. Quantitative indicators should be complemented by peer review and narrative evidence. Such frameworks align more closely with academic values and support holistic assessment.

Importantly, transparency in evaluation criteria is essential. Faculty are more likely to engage constructively with data-driven systems when expectations are clear and processes are perceived as fair. Educational research on organizational trust highlights the role of shared governance in legitimizing data use. Trust in data-driven systems is closely linked to transparency and shared governance, which are central features of academic institutions (Kezar, 2004).

7.10 Organizational Change and Data-Informed Decision Making

Faculty workload planning often occurs within broader organizational change initiatives. Mergers of departments, introduction of new programs or shifts in instructional modality all affect academic labor.

Data-driven planning can support change by clarifying constraints and trade-offs. For instance, modeling the workload implications of introducing a new program can inform decisions about staffing and resource allocation. However, data alone cannot resolve value-based disagreements about priorities. Educational research shows the importance of participatory planning processes. Engaging faculty in interpreting data and exploring options fosters shared understanding and reduces resistance. Minor digressions in planning discussions often surface concerns that are not captured in formal analyses but are critical to implementation.

7.11 Limitations and Human Judgment

Despite advances in analytics, faculty workload planning remains an area where human judgment is indispensable. Academic work involves creativity, mentorship and intellectual risk-taking that resist standardization. Excessively rigid data-driven systems can discourage innovation by rewarding easily measured outputs. Educational research cautions against unintended consequences of metric-driven cultures such as goal displacement or burnout. Effective institutions treat data as a tool for dialogue rather than as a mechanism of control. Workload data can highlight inequities and support resource advocacy when used constructively. They can also exacerbate tension when used punitively.

In conclusion, faculty workload and organizational planning illustrate the need for data-informed rather than data-determined decision making. Educational research provides the conceptual and empirical grounding needed to align analytics with academic values.

7.12 Limitations and Risks of Data-Driven Planning

Despite its promise, data-driven decision making has limitations. Overreliance on metrics can narrow institutional vision. Not everything that matters can be easily measured.

Data lag is another challenge. Planning decisions often must be made before complete data are available. During periods of rapid change, historical data may be misleading.

There is also a risk of technocratic governance where decisions are justified by data without genuine deliberation. Educational research cautions against treating evidence as value-neutral. Values shape which questions are asked and which outcomes are prioritized.

8. FUTURE DIRECTIONS

This chapter has discussed that educational research is not only a technical support function for higher education planning but a foundational infrastructure that shapes how institutions understand themselves, interpret evidence and navigate uncertainty. Across domains ranging from enrollment management to curriculum design and faculty workload planning, data-driven decision making emerges as a complex practice that intertwines methodological rigor, ethical judgment and organizational culture.

Building on the discussions throughout the chapter, future directions in higher education planning will increasingly depend on how institutions extend, rather than restate, research-informed and ethically grounded approaches to data use. The most effective planning decisions draw on multiple forms of evidence rather than privileging a single dataset or analytic technique. Quantitative analyses provide scale and comparability while qualitative research supplies depth and context. External data situate institutional patterns within broader social and economic trends. Educational research offers the tools to align these sources around shared questions and to reconcile apparent contradictions through systematic inquiry. Ethical and equity considerations are inseparable from technical analysis. Decisions informed by data affect access, opportunity and professional life within higher education. Predictive models and performance metrics carry implicit values that must be made explicit and examined critically. Treating equity as a lens rather than an outcome, reframes planning as a moral as well as strategic endeavor. Institutions that embed ethical reflection into their data practices are more likely to sustain trust and legitimacy during periods of change.

Data-driven planning operates within human systems. Faculty workload models, curriculum pathways and retention strategies all intersect with professional identities, disciplinary cultures and governance structures. Educational research underscores that evidence is most effective when used to support dialogue and learning rather than to enforce compliance. Participatory interpretation of data strengthens decision quality and fosters shared ownership of outcomes.

Looking forward, the role of educational research in higher education planning is likely to expand. Advances in analytics and artificial intelligence promise more sophisticated modeling of institutional dynamics. At the same time, these tools raise new questions about transparency, accountability and autonomy. Future research will need to address not only what can be predicted but also what should be predicted and for what purposes. Emerging trends such as explainable AI (XAI), federated learning, blockchain-based credentialing, and immersive technologies like extended reality (XR) are expected to reshape future learning environments and institutional planning processes (Jain et al., 2026)

For advanced undergraduate and graduate students, the implications are clear. Expertise in educational research methods is increasingly central to leadership and planning roles within higher education. Technical skills must be accompanied by theoretical grounding and ethical awareness. The challenge is not to replace judgment with data but to enrich judgment through evidence.

In an era marked by instability and constraint, higher education institutions face difficult choices. Educational research does not eliminate uncertainty but it provides disciplined ways of engaging with it. By treating data-driven decision making as an ongoing research process rather than a set of tools, institutions can navigate shifting conditions with greater coherence, integrity and resilience. The integration of artificial intelligence in higher education analytics further increases both the potential and risks of data-driven planning, particularly in areas of automation, personalization and decision support (Holmes et al., 2019).

9. CONCLUSION

This chapter has emphasized educational research as a vital foundation for informed decision making in contemporary higher education. Across areas such as enrollment planning, curriculum development, student retention and faculty workload, the central message is clear: data are only meaningful when interpreted through rigorous research frameworks and ethical, contextual understanding. Without this grounding, decision making risks becoming reactive or detached from educational values.

The discussion has shown that research enables institutions to move beyond surface-level metrics toward deeper insight. While dashboards and indicators are useful starting points, research-informed approaches support better questions, more careful evaluation and a clearer understanding of long-term consequences. The integration of quantitative and qualitative methods is especially important, as it connects institutional trends with lived experiences and well-being.

Finally, the chapter shows that data-driven planning is shaped by organizational culture, governance and ethical responsibility. As higher education faces continued uncertainty and rapid technological change, the challenge is not simply to adopt new analytical tools but to embed them within research practices that support human judgment, equity and institutional learning. Treated as a core infrastructure, educational research enables planning that remains thoughtful, adaptive and aligned with the mission of higher education.

REFERENCES

Beauchamp, T. L., & Childress, J. F. (2019). *Principles of biomedical ethics* (8th ed.). Oxford University Press.

Bichsel, J. (2012). *Analytics in higher education: Benefits, barriers, progress, and recommendations*. EDUCAUSE Center for Applied Research.

Biggs, J. (1996). Enhancing teaching through constructive alignment. *Higher Education, 32*(3), 347–364. DOI: 10.1007/BF00138871

Creswell, J. W., & Plano Clark, V. L. (2017). *Designing and conducting mixed methods research* (3rd ed.). Sage Publications.

Daniel, J. (2020). Education and the COVID-19 pandemic. *Prospects, 49*(1-2), 91–96. DOI: 10.1007/s11125-020-09464-3 PMID: 32313309

Ferguson, R. (2012). Learning analytics: Drivers, developments and challenges. *International Journal of Technology Enhanced Learning, 4*(5–6), 304–317. DOI: 10.1504/IJTEL.2012.051816

Goldstein, P. J., & Katz, R. N. (2005). *Academic analytics: The uses of management information and technology in higher education*. EDUCAUSE.

Holmes, W., Bialik, M., & Fadel, C. (2019). *Artificial intelligence in education*. Center for Curriculum Redesign.

Jain, R., Upreti, K., Shankar, U., Radhakrishnan, G., Sharma, A., & Malik, K. (2026). *Data-driven education: Leveraging big data, AI, and machine learning for smarter learning environments. Intelligent systems for neurocognition and human-robot-computer interaction*. Academic Press., DOI: 10.1016/B978-0-443-41660-6.00003-X

Johnson, R. B., Onwuegbuzie, A. J., & Turner, L. A. (2007). Toward a definition of mixed methods research. *Journal of Mixed Methods Research, 1*(2), 112–133. DOI: 10.1177/1558689806298224

Kezar, A. (2004). What is more important to effective governance: Relationships, trust, and leadership, or structures and formal processes? [Object Identifier]. *New Directions for Higher Education, 2004*(127), 35–46. DOI: 10.1002/he.154

Kuh, G. D. (2009). The National Survey of Student Engagement: Conceptual and empirical foundations. *New Directions for Institutional Research, 2009*(141), 5–20. DOI: 10.1002/ir.283

Marginson, S. (2016). *The Dream Is Over: The Crisis of Clark Kerr's California Idea of Higher Education*. University of California Press. https://www.jstor.org/stable/10.1525/j.ctt1kc6k1p

Mekić, E., Fetahović, I., Kuk, K., Popović, B., & Čisar, P. (2024). *Data-driven educational decision-making model for curriculum optimization., Ethics in online AI-based systems*. Academic Press., DOI: 10.1016/B978-0-443-18851-0.00002-0

Mena Guacas, A. F., Mellado-Moreno, P.-C., Calderón-Cisneros, J.-T., & Pelicano Piris, N. (2026). Mapping artificial-intelligence-driven innovation in higher education: A bibliometric review. *Social Sciences & Humanities Open*, *13*, 102561. DOI: 10.1016/j.ssaho.2026.102561

O'Neil, C. (2016). *Weapons of math destruction*. Crown Publishing.

Pfeffer, J., & Sutton, R. I. (2006). *Hard facts, dangerous half-truths, and total nonsense: Profiting from evidence-based management*. Harvard Business School Press.

Porter, S. R. (2013). Self-reported learning gains: A theory and test of college student survey response. *Research in Higher Education*, *54*(2), 201–226. DOI: 10.1007/s11162-012-9277-0

Shadish, W. R., Cook, T. D., & Campbell, D. T. (2002). *Experimental and quasi-experimental designs for generalized causal inference*. Houghton Mifflin.

Siemens, G., & Baker, R. S. J. d. (2012). Learning analytics and educational data mining: Towards communication and collaboration. *Proceedings of the 2nd International Conference on Learning Analytics and Knowledge*, 252–254. DOI: 10.1145/2330601.2330661

Tinto, V. (1993). *Leaving college: Rethinking the causes and cures of student attrition* (2nd ed.). University of Chicago Press.

Xu, Y. (2025). Educational evaluation and decision-making based on statistical data. *International Journal of Decision Support System Technology*, *17*(1), 1–24. Advance online publication. DOI: 10.4018/IJDSST.392480

Chapter 10
Conceptual Foundations of AI-Powered Learning Analytics in Education 4.0: A Theoretical Review

Ivan Marcelo Arguello
http://orcid.org/0000-0003-4749-1225
Torrens University, Australia

Justin Pierce
http://orcid.org/0000-0003-3681-2302
Torrens University, Australia

Alex Bolt
Torrens University, Australia

ABSTRACT

This conceptual review synthesizes the theoretical foundations of AI-powered Learning Analytics (LA) in higher education within the framework of Education 4.0. Drawing on an extensive literature base, it examines how major learning theories—behaviorism, cognitivism, constructivism, and connectivism—along with methodological approaches such as Educational Data Mining and LA process models, inform the design and application of AI-driven analytics systems. Adoption theories, including the Technology Acceptance Model, Theory of Planned Behaviour, and Diffusion of Innovations, are analyzed to explain factors shaping institutional uptake. Ethical and sociotechnical issues, such as algorithmic bias, surveillance, and data privacy, are integrated to emphasize responsible implementation. The review

DOI: 10.4018/979-8-2600-2606-9.ch010

argues that these perspectives must converge to frame AI-powered LA as a socio-technical educational practice. The synthesis provides a structured conceptual map to guide theory-informed research, policy, and practice in the evolving landscape of AI in higher education.

1. INTRODUCTION

Education 4.0, defined by the integration of Artificial Intelligence (AI), Internet of Things (IoT), and big data analytics, is reshaping higher education by prioritising personalised, technology-driven learning experiences (Bonfield et al., 2020). In Higher Degree by Research (HDR) programmes, AI-Powered Learning Analytics (AI-LA) analyses data from learning management systems to deliver predictive feedback and support at-risk students (Arguello Villa, 2025; Castro et al., 2024). This technological shift redefines HDR education by addressing challenges such as student isolation and time management, yet its adoption faces resistance from faculty due to ethical concerns and misalignment with traditional supervisory roles (Daou & Hajj, 2023). Without a robust theoretical foundation, AI-LA risks becoming a purely instrumental technology, overlooking critical pedagogical, cognitive, and socio-cultural dimensions that underpin effective learning.

Early milestones in learning analytics laid essential groundwork for the current AI-driven era. Pioneering efforts in the late 2000s and early 2010s focused primarily on descriptive and diagnostic analytics derived from learning management systems, enabling educators to track basic engagement patterns and identify at-risk students through simple dashboards (Siemens & Long, 2011; Gašević et al., 2016). These initial systems emphasised human interpretation of aggregated data rather than automated prediction or personalisation. The transition accelerated with the integration of machine learning techniques around 2015, which introduced predictive capabilities and shifted the focus toward proactive interventions (Romero & Ventura, 2020). However, these pre-AI approaches remained largely limited by manual rule-based models and lacked the adaptive, real-time intelligence that characterises contemporary systems. Education 4.0 builds directly upon this foundation by recombining advanced artificial intelligence with big data and IoT infrastructures, thereby enabling dynamic, context-aware analytics that respond instantaneously to learner behaviours (Castro et al., 2024; Makarenko et al., 2024). This evolution underscores the need for theoretical frameworks that bridge historical developments with emerging socio-technical demands, ensuring that innovations enhance rather than supplant pedagogical values.

This article emerges from a comprehensive literature review conducted as part of a broader exploration of AI-LA's role in Education 4.0, building on the conceptual groundwork laid in a previously published study (Arguello Villa, 2025). It synthesises key theoretical perspectives that inform the design, implementation, and ethical and equity implications permeate the discussion (see Section 2.5) of AI-LA, with a specific focus on HDR contexts in Australian universities. This framework serves as a diagnostic lens, enabling the analysis and adaptation of AI-LA across diverse educational institutions and countries, fostering globally scalable insights (Castro et al., 2024). For instance, it can address global challenges such as unequal access to AI technologies in developing nations, ensuring inclusive educational innovation (Castro et al., 2024). The review draws on established learning theories—behaviourism, cognitivism, constructivism, and socio-cultural frameworks—to understand how AI-LA quantifies observable behaviours, infers cognitive states, and supports collaborative knowledge construction . Connectivism, as articulated by Siemens (2018), provides a lens to explore networked learning in digital ecosystems, while Educational Data Mining (EDM) and Learning Analytics (LA) frameworks guide data processes from collection to predictive analytics (Gašević et al., 2016; Castro et al., 2024).

Adoption models further shape this discourse. The Technology Acceptance Model (TAM) of Davis (1989), the Theory of Planned Behaviour (TPB) of Ajzen (1991), and the Diffusion of Innovations (DOI) theory of Rogers (2010) offer insights into faculty perceptions, highlighting barriers such as perceived complexity and ethical concerns like data privacy (Daou & Hajj, 2023). A hybrid TAM/TPB/DOI framework is proposed to address these challenges, aligning AI-LA with institutional goals.

The article's objectives are threefold: first, to map the theoretical landscape underpinning AI-LA, illustrating how these perspectives interconnect to support personalised learning; second, to evaluate their implications for policy, practice, and future research in HDR programmes; and third, to propose a structured conceptual framework that guides responsible implementation. Two diagrams (Figures 1 and 2) visualise the convergence of pedagogical, adoption, and ethical perspectives, while a third (Figure 3) outlines research priorities. This review, not an empirical study, builds on faculty perception insights from Australian HDR contexts to offer a diagnostic lens for educators, researchers, and policymakers.

The significance of this work lies in its potential to bridge theoretical insights with practical applications, ensuring AI-LA enhances equitable and innovative education. As Education 4.0 evolves, the need for a multi-faceted theoretical approach becomes critical to navigate the opportunities and challenges of AI-driven learning. This article aims to lay the foundation for future scholarship, informing the development of AI-LA tools that are pedagogically sound, ethically robust, and tailored to the unique demands of HDR programmes in Australia and beyond.

2. THEORETICAL LANDSCAPE OF AI IN EDUCATION 4.0

The emergence of Education 4.0, driven by the Fourth Industrial Revolution, calls for pedagogical approaches that are personalized, technology-enabled, and oriented toward future-ready skills (Ramírez-Montoya et al., 2021; Schwab & Davis, 2018). Central to this transformation is the integration of Artificial Intelligence (AI) and Learning Analytics (LA), which form the backbone of data-informed, adaptive learning environments in higher education and beyond (Karmakar & Das, 2024; Kazimova et al., 2025; Makarenko et al., 2024). These technologies reshape educational practices by enabling personalized learning, optimizing resource allocation, and addressing complex challenges in teaching and learning (Kazimova et al., 2025).

The conceptual framework of AI-powered LA in Education 4.0 rests on a convergence of disciplines—learning sciences, data analytics, ethics, and educational technology—and a reconceptualization of core educational values such as equity, agency, and assessment. The current literature provides foundational insight into the socio-technical logics underpinning these systems, emphasizing the need to link technological advancements with robust educational theory (Chatti et al., 2014; Castro et al., 2024).

2.1. Personalization, Adaptation, and Intelligent Feedback

AI-powered Learning Analytics enables personalised learning experiences through intelligent feedback loops and adaptive learning systems. These capabilities are rooted in behavioural and cognitive models that track learner interactions in real time (Arockia et al., 2025; Gonzalez-Sanchez et al., 2011; Slomp et al., 2024). For instance, Intelligent Tutoring Systems (ITS) employ diagnostic models to identify misconceptions and recommend targeted interventions, mimicking human tutoring (Rajput, 2025; Riaz et al., 2019). AI-driven tools in flipped learning models enhance classroom problem-solving by tailoring content to individual needs (Rajput, 2025), while assessment tools adapt to learner performance to provide formative feedback applicable to higher education contexts (Zhang, 2024).

Recent advancements in generative artificial intelligence, particularly large language models (LLMs), have transformed intelligent feedback mechanisms within AI-powered Learning Analytics. These models generate contextually rich, natural-language responses that simulate tutor-like explanations, scaffold critical thinking, and adapt explanations in real time to individual learner needs (Castro et al., 2024). For instance, LLMs can analyse draft research proposals or literature review excerpts submitted by HDR students, offering personalised suggestions on structure, argumentation gaps, or theoretical alignment—tasks that traditionally demand substantial supervisory time. Educators should integrate such capabilities cautiously, ensuring that generative outputs serve as augmentative tools rather than autonomous substitutes for human judgement. This approach aligns with the combinatorial logic of Education 4.0, where legacy pedagogical practices recombine with generative technologies to enhance formative support while preserving learner agency (Makarenko et al., 2024; Arguello Villa, 2025).

We argue that the conceptual challenge lies in defining meaningful adaptation. Balancing pedagogical goals with ethical considerations is essential to ensure personalisation broadens rather than narrows learning pathways (Castro et al., 2024; Romero Alonso et al., 2025) as discussed in Section 2.5.

2.2. Education 4.0 as a Socio-technical System

Education 4.0 is a socio-technical system that redefines the roles of students, educators, and institutions. It integrates AI with technologies like IoT and big data to support distributed, mobile, and lifelong learning (Ciolacu et al., 2018; Zhang & Leong, 2025). Within this paradigm, learners are both autonomous agents and data subjects, as elaborated in Section 2.5. These tensions are evident in academic contexts, particularly in research supervision and curriculum design, where AI reconfigures agency and participation (Webb et al., 2020). Education 4.0 prioritizes real-time data visibility and predictive intervention, necessitating theoretical scrutiny of how knowledge is valued and operationalized (Makarenko et al., 2024).

Educators should view Education 4.0 as the outcome of combinatorial technological evolution, where novel educational configurations arise from the creative recombination of existing tools and practices rather than from gradual accumulation or isolated invention (Arthur, 2009; Pauw, 2021). We draw on seminal works in technological philosophy to illuminate the non-linear, combinatorial dynamics underpinning Education 4.0, thereby extending the socio-technical foundations outlined in prior conceptual work (Arguello Villa, 2025). Also, we argue that this process mirrors broader socio-technical dynamics: technologies do not evolve in isolation but through symbiotic interactions with cultural, economic, and pedagogical contexts, generating emergent systems that redefine roles and interactions across institutions (Richta, 2018).

To illustrate this combinatorial process in practice, consider a hypothetical HDR candidate in a social sciences programme who struggles with time management and conceptual integration during the literature review phase. An AI-powered Learning Analytics system recombines data from the learning management system (submission timestamps, document annotations), supervisor feedback logs, and basic sentiment analysis of draft sections. Rather than replacing supervisory input, the system generates targeted alerts—such as suggesting open-access resources on thematic synthesis or flagging potential methodological inconsistencies—while prompting the supervisor to review a summarised progress dashboard. The supervisor then integrates these insights into a focused mentoring session, adjusting guidance to foster deeper critical thinking. This example demonstrates how Education 4.0 recombines existing tools (LMS data, human expertise, generative suggestions) into an adaptive configuration that addresses isolation and skill gaps without diminishing relational agency. Educators should design such recombinations deliberately, ensuring they amplify rather than automate the supervisory dialogue central to HDR success (Arguello Villa, 2025; Castro et al., 2024).

This combinatorial logic demands a paradigm shift in educational thinking. Rather than refining traditional models incrementally, leaders must embrace radical re-evaluations and creative restructurings that fuse predictive analytics with connectivist networking and ethical governance frameworks (Kuhn, 2012). We contend that these shifts allow institutions to move beyond static pedagogical approaches toward flexible, future-oriented systems that prioritise continuous adaptation in rapidly changing digital landscapes. Educational leaders should therefore cultivate environments where interdisciplinary teams explore emergent synergies, ensuring that technological recombinations enhance rather than constrain learner agency and epistemic diversity (Gašević et al., 2016).

In diverse global higher education contexts, this perspective informs proactive and inclusive planning. Resource-constrained institutions can recombine accessible, open-source analytics tools with localised pedagogical traditions to bridge access inequities and support personalised interventions without requiring extensive infrastructure (Abulibdeh et al., 2024). In contrast, well-resourced universities should lead in advanced integrations, such as multimodal analytics fused with immersive collaborative platforms, to foster cross-border knowledge construction and innovation (Castro et al., 2024). Across both scenarios, leaders must anticipate future recombinations—such as the convergence of real-time predictive models with explainable AI—to design adaptable policies that respond to evolving technological affordances while safeguarding equity and human-centred values (Muñoz, 2024; Himmetoğlu et al., 2020).

We propose that educational leaders adopt combinatorial foresight as a core planning strategy. This involves systematically mapping potential recombinations of existing technologies with pedagogical principles, then iteratively testing their alignment with institutional goals and ethical imperatives (Zhao, 2019). Such an approach transforms Education 4.0 from a reactive response to technological change into a deliberate, co-evolutionary process between pedagogy and innovation. By fostering reflexivity and stakeholder participation in these recombinations, leaders ensure that AI-LA serves as a catalyst for transformative, equitable educational strategies that prepare diverse learners and institutions for an uncertain yet opportunity-rich future (Arguello Villa, 2025; Richta, 2018).

Educational leaders play a pivotal role in steering this combinatorial evolution toward equitable and transformative outcomes. We argue that leaders should actively cultivate institutional cultures that embrace deliberate recombination, guiding faculty and stakeholders in mapping synergies between AI-powered analytics, pedagogical traditions, and ethical safeguards. By prioritising interdisciplinary collaboration and reflexive planning, leaders ensure that emerging configurations amplify learner agency rather than constrain it (Arguello Villa, 2025).

Leaders must champion foresight exercises where teams anticipate future technological recombinations—such as integrating predictive models with connectivist networks—and align them with institutional missions of inclusion and innovation (Castro et al., 2024). This proactive stance enables institutions to navigate digital disruptions responsibly, fostering adaptive strategies that balance efficiency with human-centred values. Ultimately, effective leadership in Education 4.0 transforms potential technological determinism into deliberate co-evolution, where educators and learners co-construct knowledge pathways that are both technologically empowered and pedagogically meaningful (Makarenko et al., 2024; Floridi et al., 2018).

In Higher Degree by Research programmes, where supervision constitutes the core pedagogical relationship, Education 4.0 demands careful reconfiguration rather than disruption of the supervisory role. Supervisors guide candidates through complex, open-ended inquiry, fostering intellectual independence, ethical rigour, and resilience amid uncertainty. AI-powered Learning Analytics augments this process by surfacing patterns in progress, engagement, or conceptual gaps—such as delays in literature synthesis or methodological inconsistencies—thereby enabling more targeted, timely conversations (Arguello Villa, 2025; Castro et al., 2024). Educators should therefore design systems that position supervisors as active interpreters of analytics rather than passive recipients, preserving the relational and dialogic essence of HDR supervision. This human-centred integration ensures that technology supports rather than supplants the nuanced judgement supervisors exercise when navigating disciplinary norms, candidate agency, and long-term intellectual development (Makarenko et al., 2024).

2.3. AI and Learning Analytics: Beyond Prediction

Learning Analytics, initially grounded in Educational Data Mining (EDM), has evolved to include predictive analytics, sentiment analysis, and collaborative learning support to enhance decision-making (Murwaningsih et al., 2024; Siemens & Long, 2011; Romero & Ventura, 2020). AI enhances the scale and sophistication of LA but raises questions about what forms of knowledge are prioritized (Ouyang et al., 2024) as addressed in Section 2.5. LA should focus on understanding learning processes, supporting formative assessment, and facilitating metacognition, aligning with constructivist principles (Gašević et al., 2016). Strategies leveraging AI-integrated analytics can optimize educational performance by providing actionable insights for instructors and institutions (Murwaningsih et al., 2024).

2.4. Connectivism and Networked Learning

Connectivism views learning as the ability to construct and traverse knowledge networks (Siemens, 2005). Siemens (2018) extends this by emphasizing digital networks' role in fostering collaborative learning, aligning with AI-LA's capacity to map and enhance knowledge-sharing communities in higher education. AI-powered LA maps learner interactions and optimizes networks, promoting knowledge discovery and peer interaction (Castro et al., 2024). However, algorithmic curation risks creating echo chambers, limiting epistemic diversity (Chatti et al., 2014). See Section 2.5.

Generative AI further reshapes connectivist networks by functioning as an active node within knowledge ecosystems. Large language models can synthesise information from diverse sources, suggest connections between disparate concepts, and facilitate cross-disciplinary dialogue in virtual research communities (Castro et al., 2024). In HDR contexts, for example, an LLM might bridge isolated supervisory discussions by recommending relevant literature or highlighting synergies between student projects across institutions. However, educators must remain vigilant: algorithmic curation risks reinforcing existing biases or narrowing network diversity if not deliberately diversified through inclusive design. We argue that intentional governance—such as prompt engineering that prioritises epistemic pluralism—enables generative tools to expand rather than constrain connectivist learning pathways (Gašević et al., 2016; Muñoz, 2024).

2.5. Ethical, Equity, and Sociotechnical Considerations in AI-Powered Learning Analytics

We contend that the integration of AI-powered Learning Analytics (AI-LA) into Education 4.0 demands explicit ethical and equity safeguards if it is to support rather than undermine pedagogical values and social justice (Arguello Villa, 2025). Faculty perceptions reveal persistent concerns over data privacy, algorithmic bias, surveillance, and the erosion of learner agency—issues that become particularly acute in Higher Degree by Research (HDR) contexts where supervision relies on nuanced human judgement and trust (Arguello Villa, 2025).

Data privacy emerges as a foundational risk. Continuous monitoring of student interactions generates vast datasets that, without robust safeguards, may expose sensitive information and erode trust between learners and institutions. We argue that privacy-by-design principles must guide system architecture from the outset, limiting data collection to what is strictly necessary and ensuring informed consent mechanisms (Floridi et al., 2018). Such measures align with calls for accountable data governance that respect individual autonomy while enabling meaningful analytics (Abulibdeh et al., 2024).

Algorithmic bias poses an equally pressing threat to equity. Predictive models can perpetuate or amplify existing disparities if trained on unrepresentative data, disadvantaging students from non-dominant cultural or epistemic backgrounds and narrowing rather than broadening educational opportunities (Arguello Villa, 2025; Muñoz, 2024). Educators should therefore mandate regular bias audits, diverse training datasets, and inclusive design processes that incorporate varied perspectives. These steps help ensure AI-LA promotes fairness rather than reinforcing structural inequities in access, representation, and outcomes (Abulibdeh et al., 2024).

Surveillance tensions further complicate personalisation efforts. While real-time analytics enable timely interventions, they risk creating power imbalances that reduce learners to data subjects under constant observation (Bates et al., 2020). In HDR settings, where independent inquiry and agency are central, excessive monitoring may diminish the reflective, self-directed nature of research learning. We advocate for transparent system design—through explainable AI (XAI)—that renders decision-making processes intelligible to users, thereby restoring agency and mitigating perceptions of control (Floridi et al., 2018).

Learners themselves emerge as critical stakeholders whose perspectives merit explicit consideration. In HDR programmes, candidates often value autonomy and self-direction highly; continuous data collection and algorithmic nudging can evoke feelings of surveillance or diminished agency, particularly when predictive interventions appear prescriptive rather than supportive (Arguello Villa, 2025; Bates et al., 2020). Students may perceive themselves reduced to data subjects whose behaviours are optimised for institutional metrics rather than personal growth, potentially eroding trust in supervisory relationships and the broader learning ecosystem. Educators should therefore incorporate learner voices into system design—through participatory mechanisms or transparent communication about data usage—to ensure that nudges enhance rather than undermine intrinsic motivation and epistemic ownership. This student-centred lens complements faculty concerns and strengthens the case for equitable, reflexive implementation across diverse institutional contexts (Abulibdeh et al., 2024; Muñoz, 2024).

Datafication introduces additional risks by reducing multifaceted learning processes to quantifiable metrics, potentially oversimplifying complex phenomena such as motivation, creativity, or cultural context (Knox et al., 2020). This reductionism threatens to privilege certain forms of knowledge while marginalising others, limiting epistemic diversity. Connectivist frameworks, in particular, require deliberate mechanisms to prevent algorithmic curation from fostering echo chambers that homogenise perspectives (Siemens, 2005).

Sociotechnical approaches offer a way forward by treating AI-LA as interdependent with human and institutional systems rather than purely technical artefacts (Bates et al., 2020). We propose stakeholder engagement—faculty, students, and administrators—in co-design and governance to align systems with educational justice and inclusion goals (Al-Mseidin et al., 2023). Institutions should embed ongoing reflexivity, including ethical impact assessments and professional development that builds capacity to interpret analytics critically.

By foregrounding these considerations, educators can harness AI-LA to empower rather than constrain learners. Ethical and equitable deployment thus becomes not an optional add-on but a core requirement for responsible innovation in Education 4.0 (Arguello Villa, 2025; Floridi et al., 2018).

2.6. Adoption and Acceptance: Technology Acceptance Model (TAM), Theory of Planned Behavior (TPB), Diffusion of Innovations (DOI), and Beyond

The adoption of AI-powered LA depends on faculty perceptions and institutional support. The Technology Acceptance Model (TAM) posits that perceived usefulness and ease of use drive technology adoption (Davis, 1989; Bansah & Agyei, 2022). The Theory of Planned Behavior (TPB) highlights attitudes, subjective norms, and perceived behavioral control as predictors of adoption intent (Ajzen, 1991). The Diffusion of Innovations (DOI) theory explains technology spread through factors like relative advantage and trialability (Rogers, 2010). Pedagogical beliefs also influence the adoption of generative AI, as shown in studies using the UTAUT2 model (Cabero-Almenara et al., 2024). These frameworks are critical for understanding barriers and facilitators to AI-LA adoption in higher education (Gupta et al., 2022).

2.7. Intersections and Diagrammatic Model: Synthesizing Theoretical Perspectives

AI-powered LA requires a multi-theoretical approach combining behaviorist, cognitivist, constructivist, connectivist, and ethical frameworks. These theories intersect to inform pedagogy, technology design, and ethical deployment, ensuring AI-LA supports equitable and meaningful learning (Siemens, 2005; Gašević et al., 2016;).

Figure 1. Scopus-based conceptual mapping of AI in Education 4.0

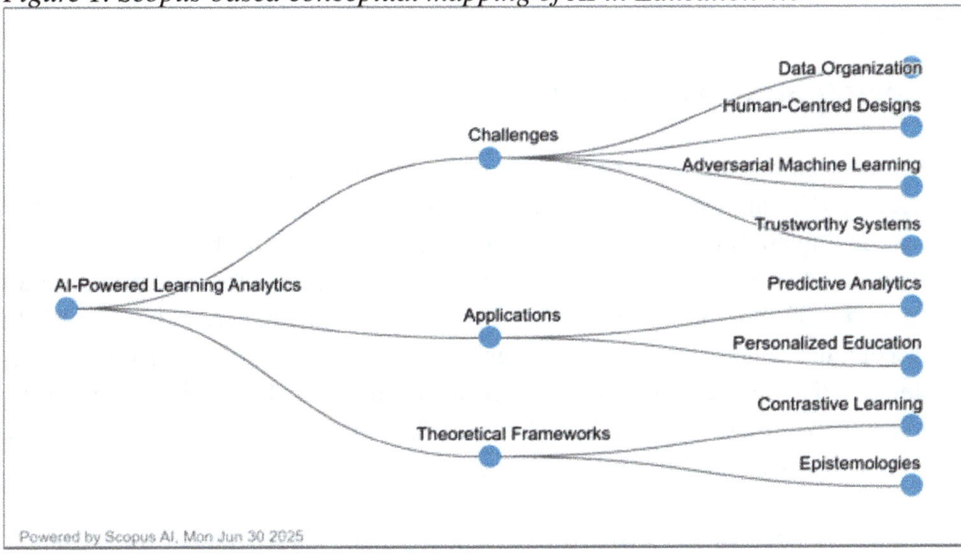

Figure 1. Scopus-based conceptual mapping of AI in Education 4.0 illustrates the convergence of Artificial Intelligence (AI) and Learning Analytics (LA) with foundational learning theories—behaviorism, cognitivism, constructivism, and connectivism—alongside adoption models (Technology Acceptance Model, Theory of Planned Behaviour, Diffusion of Innovations) and ethical frameworks. This diagram, derived from 2018-2025 literature, highlights key themes in Higher Degree by Research (HDR) contexts, including personalization, network learning, and ethical deployment, providing a visual synthesis for educators and policymakers. Examples include AI-driven feedback loops and network mapping in HDR thesis tracking, sourced from Castro et al. (2024).

3. METHODOLOGICAL APPROACH TO THE LITERATURE REVIEW

We adopted a systematic yet interpretive approach to synthesise the theoretical foundations of AI-powered Learning Analytics (AI-LA) within Education 4.0. This conceptual review combines elements of systematic literature review protocols with thematic synthesis to map interconnections among learning theories, adoption models, socio-technical frameworks, and ethical considerations (Thomas & Harden, 2008; Xiao & Watson, 2019). Rather than aiming for exhaustive enumeration, we prioritised depth and conceptual integration to inform future-focused educational planning.

3.1 Search Strategy and Sources

We conducted searches across academic databases including Scopus, Web of Science, ERIC, and Google Scholar, focusing on peer-reviewed articles, books, and proceedings published between 2015 and 2025 to capture the rapid evolution of Education 4.0 and AI-LA. Initial searches used combinations of terms such as "Education 4.0", "AI-powered learning analytics", "learning theories", "technology acceptance", "socio-technical systems", and "ethical AI in education". We supplemented database searches with backward and forward citation tracking from seminal works (e.g., Gašević et al., 2016; Floridi et al., 2018; Siemens, 2005/2018) to identify foundational and emergent perspectives.

3.2 Search Terms and Inclusion/Exclusion Criteria

Inclusion criteria required sources to: (1) address AI-LA or related analytics in higher education contexts; (2) engage explicitly with learning theories, adoption models, or socio-technical/ethical dimensions; (3) offer conceptual or theoretical insights rather than purely empirical data; and (4) be published in English. We excluded purely technical reports, non-peer-reviewed blogs, and studies focused exclusively on primary/secondary education or non-AI analytics tools. After initial screening of 380 titles/abstracts, we retained 142 sources for full-text review, ultimately synthesising 78 core references that directly informed the theoretical landscape.

3.3 Analysis and Synthesis

We employed thematic synthesis to integrate findings (Thomas & Harden, 2008). First, we inductively coded sources for recurring concepts (e.g., personalisation, agency, bias, adoption barriers). Second, we organised codes into higher-order themes: pedagogical foundations, adoption dynamics, socio-technical interdependence, and ethical imperatives. Third, we mapped interconnections across themes to construct a reflexive conceptual framework. Iterative discussions refined these mappings, ensuring alignment with Education 4.0's emphasis on convergence and reconceptualisation of educational values (Arguello Villa, 2025). This interpretive process prioritised theoretical coherence over quantitative aggregation, enabling a diagnostic lens for diverse institutional planning. This review does not present original empirical findings from primary data collection; instead, it offers a theoretically grounded synthesis of existing literature to guide responsible and future-oriented implementation of AI-powered Learning Analytics in diverse higher education contexts.

This methodological approach balances rigour with conceptual flexibility, providing a transparent foundation for the synthesis presented in subsequent sections.

4. FOUNDATIONAL LEARNING THEORIES APPLIED TO AI-POWERED LEARNING ANALYTICS

As Artificial Intelligence and Learning Analytics (AI-LA) become increasingly embedded in Education 4.0, a critical examination of their theoretical underpinnings is essential. This section explores how foundational learning theories—behaviorism, cognitivism, constructivism, sociocultural theory, and connectivism—provide conceptual scaffolding for AI-LA integration into educational design and practice.

4.1 Behaviorism and Data-Driven Monitoring

Behaviorism views learning as a change in observable behavior triggered by external stimuli and reinforced through feedback (Riaz et al., 2019). AI-LA systems track metrics like login frequency and quiz scores to provide immediate feedback, supporting early identification of at-risk students (Slomp et al., 2024). However, overreliance on behavioral metrics risks oversimplifying learning and neglecting motivation or context (Chatti et al., 2014; Gašević et al., 2016).

4.2 Cognitivism and AI-Driven Personalization

Cognitivism emphasizes mental processes like memory and cognitive load. AI-LA systems adapt content based on learner performance, maintaining optimal cognitive load through advanced algorithms like eXtreme Gradient Boosting (Cosar, 2024; Dayal et al., 2023; Gonzalez-Sanchez et al., 2011). These systems enhance personalization by tailoring learning experiences to individual needs in higher education (Imran et al., 2024). Psychological aspects, such as motivation and engagement, further enhance these experiences (Kok et al., 2024). However, they may overlook social and emotional factors, requiring integration with broader perspectives.

4.3 Constructivism and Learner-Centered Design

Constructivism posits that learners actively build knowledge through experience and reflection. AI-LA platforms support this through open-ended exploration and reflection prompts (Arockia et al., 2025; Romero Alonso et al., 2025;). However, algorithmic curation must balance guidance with learner autonomy to avoid limiting exploration (Chatti et al., 2014).

4.4 Sociocultural and Situated Learning

Sociocultural theory emphasizes social and cultural mediation (Vygotsky, cited in Siemens & Long, 2011). AI-LA visualizes peer interactions and supports collaboration, but risks misinterpreting cultural nuances (Al-Mseidin et al., 2023). Systems must incorporate contextual metadata for cultural responsiveness.

4.5 Connectivism and Networked Learning Environments

Connectivism views knowledge as distributed across networks (Siemens, 2005). Siemens (2018) highlights the role of digital platforms in enabling networked learning, supporting AI-LA's capacity to foster interdisciplinary collaboration and knowledge discovery in HDR contexts. AI-LA maps learner networks and recommends connections, fostering interdisciplinary dialogue (Castro et al., 2024). However, there is a risk of algorithmic echo chambers, necessitating mechanisms to promote diverse connections (Siemens, 2005).

Table 1. Comparative Matrix of Foundational Learning Theories and AI-LA Practices summarizes the key principles, applications, and limitations of behaviorism, cognitivism, constructivism, sociocultural theory, and connectivism in the context of AI-powered Learning Analytics, providing a structured overview for HDR educational design.

Table 1. Comparative Matrix of Foundational Learning Theories and AI-LA Practices

Learning Theory	**Key Principles**	**AI-LA Applications**	**Risks and Limitations**
Behaviourism	Observable behaviour, reinforcement	Dashboards, clickstream analysis	Reduces learning to metrics; ignores motivation
Cognitivism	Information processing, cognitive load	Adaptive tutoring, scaffolding	Limited social/emotional awareness
Constructivism	Active knowledge construction	Simulations, reflection prompts	Risk of over-guidance; limits autonomy
Sociocultural Theory	Social mediation, cultural tools	Peer collaboration, discourse visualization	Misinterpretation of cultural cues
Connectivism	Networked knowledge formation	Network analytics, resource recommendation	Risk of echo chambers; algorithmic bias

4.6 Tensions and Theoretical Gaps

Behaviorist and cognitivist approaches excel in data-driven adaptation but often neglect social and cultural dimensions. Constructivist and sociocultural frameworks restore context, while connectivism bridges individual and collective learning. Collaborative learning analytics, supported by AI, can address some of these gaps by fostering peer interaction and knowledge sharing (Ouyang et al., 2024). A hybrid framework is needed to ensure equitable, context-aware AI-LA systems (Siemens, 2005; Gašević et al., 2016).

4.7 Critical Synthesis: Recombination in Education 4.0

While behaviourism informs observable metrics and reinforcement loops in early analytics dashboards, cognitivism underpins diagnostic models that infer mental states from interaction patterns, and constructivism supports collaborative scaffolding through networked feedback. Socio-cultural perspectives emphasise co-construction of knowledge in diverse communities, whereas connectivism positions learning as navigation across digital nodes. We argue that Education 4.0 does not privilege one paradigm over others; instead, it recombines elements from all five traditions into hybrid configurations. For instance, predictive nudges draw behavioural reinforcement while generative explanations scaffold cognitive processes, and network mapping fosters connectivist knowledge flows—all within socio-cultural contexts that demand equity and inclusion (Gašević et al., 2016; Castro et al., 2024).

This recombination transcends additive integration: educators should actively orchestrate synergies to avoid reductionist applications that prioritise quantifiable outcomes over epistemic depth. Over-emphasising behavioural metrics risks narrowing learning to compliance, whereas excessive reliance on connectivist networks without critical scaffolding may fragment knowledge construction. A balanced, reflexive approach—grounded in ethical governance (as discussed in Section 2.5)—enables AI-powered Learning Analytics to support personalised, adaptive, and socially just HDR experiences. Institutions must therefore cultivate interdisciplinary teams that map these recombinations against institutional missions, ensuring that theoretical pluralism translates into equitable practice across diverse global settings (Makarenko et al., 2024; Abulibdeh et al., 2024; Muñoz, 2024).

5. IMPLICATIONS FOR POLICY AND PRACTICE IN AI-DRIVEN EDUCATIONAL LEADERSHIP

The integration of AI-Powered Learning Analytics (AI-LA) into Education 4.0 presents transformative opportunities for Higher Degree by Research (HDR) programmes, yet its success hinges on addressing faculty perceptions and contextual challenges, as highlighted in the literature (Maynard, 2015; Schwab & Davis, 2018). Building on the theoretical foundations (Section 2) and interconnections among learning theories, adoption models, and ethical frameworks (Section 3), this section explores practical implications for educational leadership, policy development, pedagogical transformation, and overcoming implementation barriers. Drawing on seminal works (e.g., Davis, 1989; Ajzen, 1991; Rogers, 2010; Wang, 2021;), it proposes strategies to align AI-LA with institutional goals and ethical standards, particularly in the context of HDR programmes at Adelaide universities, where faculty perceptions shape adoption (Daou & Hajj, 2023)

5.1. Redefining Educational Leadership in the AI Era

Educational leaders must proactively redefine their roles to harness AI-powered Learning Analytics (AI-LA) as a catalyst for transformative change in Education 4.0 (Arguello Villa, 2025). We argue that leadership extends beyond administrative oversight to encompass strategic visioning that integrates data-driven insights with pedagogical values, ensuring technology serves human-centred learning goals rather than dictating them.

Leaders should champion a vision that positions AI-LA as an enabler of personalised, adaptive educational ecosystems. This vision requires them to foster institutional cultures where faculty view analytics not as surveillance tools but as supportive mechanisms that enhance decision-making in supervision and curriculum design (Castro et al., 2024). By prioritising transparency and explainability in AI systems, leaders build trust and encourage adoption, aligning technological affordances with core educational principles such as agency and equity (Floridi et al., 2018).

We contend that effective leadership in this era demands the cultivation of hybrid expertise: leaders must develop sufficient technical literacy to interpret analytics meaningfully while maintaining pedagogical expertise to contextualise insights within disciplinary norms. Institutions benefit when leaders establish cross-functional teams—comprising educators, data specialists, and ethicists—that co-design AI-LA implementations. Such collaborative approaches mitigate risks of technological determinism and ensure systems reflect diverse stakeholder needs (Makarenko et al., 2024).

Globally, educational leaders in diverse higher education contexts face varying challenges in redefining their roles. In resource-constrained settings, leaders should advocate for scalable, low-cost AI-LA solutions that bridge digital divides, promoting inclusive access to personalised support (Abulibdeh et al., 2024). In contrast, leaders in well-resourced institutions must focus on ethical governance frameworks that prevent over-reliance on predictive models and preserve the relational essence of learning (Muñoz, 2024). Across both contexts, leaders play a pivotal role in embedding reflexivity: they should institutionalise regular reviews of AI-LA impacts on equity and learner outcomes, adjusting strategies to respond to evolving technological landscapes.

This redefinition positions educational leaders as stewards of responsible innovation. We propose that they lead by modelling ethical engagement with AI-LA, demonstrating to faculty and students how data-informed practices can amplify human potential without compromising values. Through strategic foresight, professional development programmes, and policy advocacy, leaders pave the way for AI-LA to support equitable, future-oriented education in diverse institutional environments (Arguello Villa, 2025).

5.2. Policy Frameworks for Responsible AI Implementation

Institutions must develop robust policy frameworks that embed responsible AI implementation at the core of their strategic planning in Education 4.0 (Arguello Villa, 2025). We argue that effective policies go beyond compliance checklists to foster proactive governance that balances technological innovation with ethical imperatives and educational equity.

Policymakers should prioritise frameworks grounded in principles of transparency, accountability, and fairness. Such frameworks require institutions to mandate privacy-by-design in AI-LA systems, ensuring data collection remains minimal, purposeful, and consented (Floridi et al., 2018). Leaders should establish clear protocols for data governance that specify who accesses analytics outputs, under what conditions, and with what oversight mechanisms. These measures protect learner autonomy while enabling meaningful use of insights for personalised support (Abulibdeh et al., 2024).

We contend that policies must explicitly address algorithmic bias and epistemic justice. Institutions should require regular independent audits of predictive models to detect and mitigate disparities that could disadvantage underrepresented groups or non-dominant knowledge traditions (Muñoz, 2024). Policymakers should mandate inclusive design processes that incorporate diverse stakeholder input from the earliest stages, thereby preventing the reinforcement of structural inequities in access and outcomes across global higher education contexts.

In diverse institutional settings, policy frameworks should accommodate contextual variations. Resource-limited institutions benefit from scalable, open-source AI-LA guidelines that emphasise low-bandwidth solutions and capacity-building for local implementation (Castro et al., 2024). Well-resourced universities, conversely, should lead in developing advanced governance models, such as explainable AI (XAI) mandates that render decision logic accessible to faculty and students alike. Across all contexts, policies should institutionalise ongoing ethical impact assessments that evaluate AI-LA's influence on agency, collaboration, and knowledge diversity (Makarenko et al., 2024).

We propose that responsible implementation demands multi-level policy alignment: institutional policies should harmonise with national and international standards on AI ethics while allowing flexibility for disciplinary and cultural adaptations. Educational leaders play a central role in translating these frameworks into practice through mandatory training programmes that equip faculty to engage critically with analytics outputs. By embedding reflexivity and stakeholder participation, policies transform AI-LA from a potential source of control into a tool for empowerment and inclusive educational planning (Arguello Villa, 2025; Floridi et al., 2018).

5.3. Transforming Pedagogical Practice with AI-Driven Insights

AI-LA transforms pedagogical practice by enabling personalised learning and data-driven teaching design in HDR programmes. Tan et al. (2025) highlight that intelligent tutoring systems (ITS) provide real-time feedback tailored to individual HDR student needs, enhancing engagement (Mougiakou et al., 2022). Faculty in Adelaide universities see potential in AI-LA for identifying learning difficulties, yet question its relevance for the thesis stage, where independent research dominates (Daou & Hajj, 2023)

Learning analytics informs teaching design by validating pedagogical assumptions. Lockyer and Dawson (2011) argue that AI-LA offers objective insights into student behaviour, enabling timely interventions. However, faculty require technical expertise to leverage these insights, a barrier noted by Nguyen et al. (2020). Professional development programmes, incorporating AI-driven tools, can enhance data interpretation skills while addressing faculty concerns about increased workload .

Maintaining educator autonomy is crucial. AI-LA can reduce administrative burdens, but risks diminishing faculty agency if algorithms dominate decision-making (Bates et al., 2020). Faculty in HDR contexts value human-AI collaboration, preferring tools that complement rather than replace their expertise (Urmeneta & Romero, 2024). Institutions must design AI-LA systems that empower educators, ensuring pedagogical practices remain learner-centred.

5.4. Addressing Implementation Challenges

Implementing AI-LA in HDR programmes faces challenges, including ethical concerns, scalability, and stakeholder trust. Salloum et al. (2024) highlight data privacy and algorithmic bias as key issues, echoing faculty concerns in Adelaide universities (Smith et al., 2024). Ethical guidelines, such as privacy-by-design principles, are essential to ensure transparency and fairness (Chatti et al., 2014). Anagnostopoulou et al. (2024) advocate for user-centred design to build trust in AI-LA systems, addressing faculty scepticism through transparent and inclusive implementation strategies. Faculty also worry about reduced human interaction, necessitating strategies to preserve HDR supervision's relational aspects (Daou & Hajj, 2023)

Scalability is a significant barrier. Khalil and Prinsloo (2025) note that diverse data sources hinder generalisability, particularly in HDR's unique context. Standardised interoperability protocols can facilitate integration, but require institutional investment (Abraham et al., 2019). Faculty perceptions of increased workload due to training demands further complicate adoption .

Building trust is critical. Corbeil and Corbeil (2021) emphasise that transparency and ethical AI use foster faculty confidence. Engaging faculty in AI-LA development, as suggested by Rogers (2010), can address scepticism by demonstrating relative advantage and compatibility with HDR needs. Pilot programmes offering trial trialability and observability can further enhance adoption, aligning AI-LA with Education 4.0's goals.

Figure 2. Priorities for Implementing AI-LA in Educational Leadership

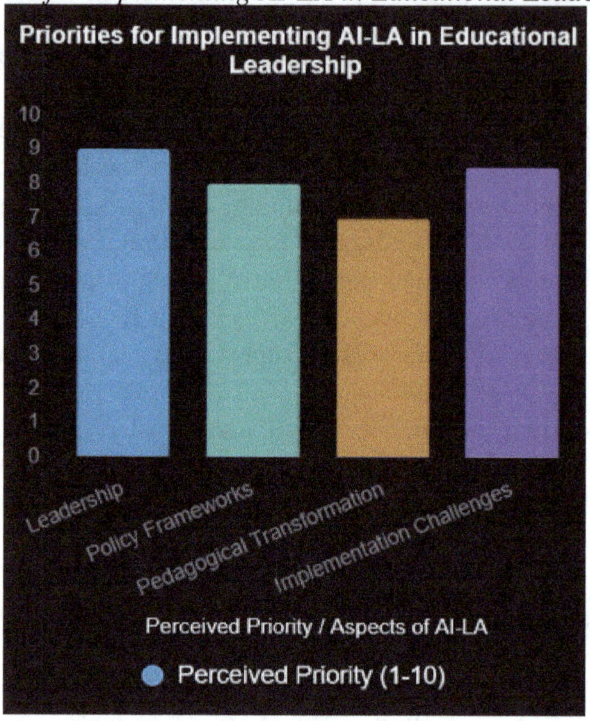

Figure 2. Priorities for Implementing AI-LA in Educational Leadership visualizes the relative importance of redefining leadership roles, establishing robust policy frameworks, transforming pedagogical practices, and addressing implementation challenges. This chart emphasizes their critical interplay in fostering responsible AI-LA adoption in HDR programmes, drawing on faculty perceptions and institutional strategies from Australian universities. For instance, policy audits and training pilots in Adelaide universities address workload concerns .

5.5 Institutional Strategies for AI-LA Adoption

Institutional strategies are pivotal to the successful integration of AI-Powered Learning Analytics (AI-LA) in Higher Degree by Research (HDR) programmes, bridging theoretical insights with practical implementation. These strategies must address faculty adoption barriers, ethical concerns, and scalability challenges, aligning with the frameworks discussed in Sections 2–5. Drawing on Abraham et al. (2019), effective data governance models standardise processes for quality, security, and accountability, ensuring AI-LA systems meet HDR's ethical standards. Policies should mandate regular audits and compliance with Australia's data protection laws

(Australia, 2018), addressing faculty concerns about privacy highlighted by Daou & Hajj (2023).

Professional development is a cornerstone of these strategies. Anagnostopoulou et al. (2024) advocate for tailored training programmes that enhance AI literacy and ethical data use, countering resistance driven by perceived workload increases . Leong and Zhang (2025) suggest incorporating Explainable AI (XAI) training to demystify algorithms, fostering trust among supervisors. Pilot programmes, as recommended by Rogers' (2010) Diffusion of Innovations (DOI), can offer trialability, allowing faculty to test AI-LA tools in controlled HDR settings, such as thesis progress tracking (Mougiakou et al., 2022).

Expanding on data governance, Abraham et al. (2019) recommend real-time monitoring systems to ensure compliance with Australia's privacy laws (Australia, 2018), addressing faculty concerns about data breaches (Daou & Hajj, 2023) Professional development should include workshops on XAI, as Leong and Zhang (2025) suggest, to build technical confidence, with follow-up surveys to measure efficacy . Incentive programmes could offer research grants for AI-LA adoption, aligning with TAM's perceived usefulness (Davis, 1989), and pilot projects in HDR thesis tracking could test scalability (Mougiakou et al., 2022). Ethical leadership requires ethics committees to conduct biannual reviews, mitigating biases as per Floridi et al. (2018), while cultural sensitivity training ensures tools meet diverse needs (Wang, 2025). Collaborative platforms, per Castro et al. (2024), should integrate AI-LA with existing HDR forums, enhancing interdisciplinary dialogue.

Incentive structures further support adoption. Institutions can offer recognition or reduced teaching loads for faculty engaging with AI-LA, aligning with the Technology Acceptance Model (TAM) of Davis (1989), where perceived usefulness drives uptake. Khalil and Prinsloo (2025) note that diverse data sources require interoperable systems, necessitating investment in infrastructure. Collaborative platforms, as suggested by Castro et al. (2024), can integrate AI-LA with existing tools, enhancing collaboration networks in HDR.

Ethical leadership is critical to sustain these efforts. Floridi et al. (2018) emphasize accountability frameworks to mitigate biases, while Muñoz (2024) proposes user-centred design to ensure inclusivity. Institutions should establish ethics committees to oversee AI-LA deployment, addressing surveillance concerns raised by Banerjee et al. (2024). In Australian HDR contexts, where cultural diversity is prevalent, these strategies must accommodate varied student needs, as Wang (2025) advocates for equitable tools.

5.6 Discussion and Future Research Directions

The integration of AI-Powered Learning Analytics (AI-LA) into Education 4.0, as explored in Sections 1–4, represents a pivotal shift in higher education, particularly within Higher Degree by Research (HDR) programmes. Building on the theoretical foundations of the Technology Acceptance Model (TAM), Theory of Planned Behaviour (TPB), and Diffusion of Innovations (DOI) from Section 2, and the practical implications outlined in Section 4, this section synthesises these contributions, evaluates the limitations of the theoretical review, and proposes a research agenda to advance AI-LA in educational contexts. Drawing on seminal works (Davis, 1989; Ajzen, 1991; Rogers, 2010; An et al., 2024; Chan et al., 2025), it addresses the ethical and practical challenges highlighted in Chapter 2 of the thesis, ensuring alignment with the needs of HDR programmes and the broader goals of Education 4.0.

Planning for AI-powered Learning Analytics in diverse higher education institutions requires explicit strategies to safeguard and enhance the supervisory role in HDR programmes. Leaders should prioritise professional development that equips supervisors to interpret analytics critically and integrate insights into supervision meetings without diminishing relational trust. Institutions can foster hybrid models where predictive alerts prompt rather than dictate supervisory decisions, thereby maintaining candidate autonomy while addressing isolation or skill gaps proactively (Arguello Villa, 2025). Such approaches align with future-focused planning by recombining technological affordances with the enduring human elements of mentorship, ensuring equitable support across cultural and disciplinary contexts (Abulibdeh et al., 2024; Muñoz, 2024).

5.6.1 Synthesis of Theoretical Contributions

The theoretical frameworks discussed in Sections 2 and 3—namely TAM, TPB, and DOI—provide a robust foundation for understanding AI-LA adoption in higher education (Davis, 1989; Ajzen, 1991; Rogers, 2010). TAM highlights perceived usefulness (PU) and perceived ease of use (PEOU) as critical drivers of faculty acceptance, suggesting that AI-LA's ability to personalise learning and identify at-risk students enhances its appeal . TPB extends this by incorporating subjective norms and perceived behavioural control, indicating that institutional support and peer influence shape adoption (Daou & Hajj, 2023) DOI complements these by emphasising relative advantage, compatibility, and trialability, which are crucial for integrating AI-LA into the less structured HDR context (Rogers, 2010).

AI-LA applications, such as intelligent tutoring systems (ITS) and predictive modelling, align with Education 4.0's emphasis on data-driven pedagogy (Maynard,

2015; Schwab & Davis, 2018). These tools enable personalised learning experiences and proactive student support, addressing diverse HDR student needs (Mougiakou et al., 2022; Sghir et al., 2022). However, ethical considerations, as noted by Chan et al. (2025), underscore the need for frameworks that ensure transparency and fairness. ElSayary (2025) further advocates for policy frameworks that integrate digital ethics, aligning AI-LA with institutional goals while preserving educator autonomy.

This synthesis reveals that AI-LA's theoretical contributions lie in its potential to bridge technological innovation with pedagogical efficacy, provided ethical and contextual challenges are addressed. The interplay of adoption theories and ethical frameworks (An et al., 2024; Chan et al., 2025) offers a comprehensive lens to guide responsible implementation in HDR programmes, ensuring alignment with Education 4.0's transformative vision.

5.6.2 Limitations of the Theoretical Review

While the theoretical review in Sections 1–4 provides a robust foundation, it faces several limitations, as highlighted in Chapter 2 of the thesis. First, the applicability of AI-LA to HDR programmes remains underexplored due to their unstructured thesis stage, which challenges the utility of generic tools like Learning Management Systems (LMS) tracking (Daou & Hajj, 2023) The review's reliance on general AI-LA applications (e.g., ITS, predictive modelling) may not fully address the nuanced needs of HDR supervision (Bates et al., 2020).

Second, ethical concerns, such as data privacy and algorithmic bias, pose significant limitations. An et al. (2024) note that user concerns about data security and fairness are often inadequately addressed in theoretical models, risking mistrust among faculty and students. Floridi et al. (2018) advocate for an ethical framework grounded in transparency, justice, and non-maleficence to mitigate these risks, ensuring AI-LA systems prioritise fairness and accountability in HDR contexts. Similarly, Wang (2025) highlights that biases in AI algorithms can exacerbate inequities, particularly for marginalised HDR students, limiting the inclusivity of current frameworks.

Third, the theoretical review overlooks the practical burden of AI-LA adoption, such as increased faculty workload due to training demands . While TAM and TPB address perceptions, they do not fully account for operational challenges like system complexity or interoperability, as noted by Bates et al. (2020). These limitations suggest that theoretical models must be contextualised to HDR settings to ensure relevance and efficacy.

5.6.3 Future Research Directions

To address the limitations identified in Section 5.2, future research must prioritise three interconnected areas: developing robust ethical frameworks, enhancing faculty training, and tailoring AI-LA applications to HDR contexts. First, ethical frameworks require urgent attention to ensure responsible AI-LA deployment. Chan et al. (2025) propose a five-step model for responsible AI integration, emphasising transparency, fairness, and accountability. This aligns with Floridi et al.'s (2018) call for principles of justice and non-maleficence, which are critical to mitigate privacy risks and algorithmic bias in HDR settings. Anagnostopoulou et al. (2024) advocate for user-centred ethical guidelines, suggesting that stakeholder engagement can foster trust, particularly where faculty express concerns about data security (Daou & Hajj, 2023). Research could explore Explainable AI (XAI) to enhance transparency, as Chatti et al. (2014) note its potential to demystify algorithmic decisions, ensuring equitable outcomes for diverse HDR students.

Second, faculty training programmes are essential to overcome adoption barriers. Vashishth et al. (2024) highlight the need for professional development to build AI literacy and data interpretation skills, a gap evident in Australian HDR contexts where workload concerns persist (Daou & Hajj, 2023). Anagnostopoulou et al. (2024) recommend comprehensive training and user-centred design to build confidence, suggesting pilot programmes that integrate ethical reasoning with technical proficiency. ElSayary (2025) proposes tailored modules that address faculty autonomy, aligning with the Theory of Planned Behaviour (TPB) of Ajzen (1991), where perceived behavioural control influences acceptance. Future studies could evaluate the efficacy of such training, using the Diffusion of Innovations (DOI) framework of Rogers (2010) to assess trialability and observability in HDR settings.

Third, context-specific AI-LA applications are vital to address HDR's unique demands. Siemens (2018) suggests that connectivism can inform designs fostering collaborative learning networks, enabling HDR students to engage in knowledge-sharing communities. Wang (2025) emphasises equitable tools that accommodate diverse needs, particularly in unstructured research environments. Mougiakou et al. (2022) propose predictive models for thesis progress, while Castro et al. (2024) advocate for network analysis to enhance interdisciplinary dialogue. Research should test these applications, integrating them with adoption models (TAM, TPB, DOI) to ensure alignment with faculty needs and institutional goals. Longitudinal studies could assess their impact on completion rates and student satisfaction, bridging theoretical propositions with empirical evidence.

The prioritization of these research directions necessitates a visual and conceptual framework to guide scholars and practitioners in navigating the complex landscape of AI-Powered Learning Analytics (AI-LA) within Higher Degree by Research

(HDR) programmes. This framework must reflect the current state of development and the perceived relevance of each priority, drawing on the theoretical insights from Sections 2 and 3, as well as the practical challenges outlined in Section 4. For instance, ethical frameworks, while critically underexplored, are deemed essential due to rising concerns over data privacy and algorithmic bias, as evidenced by Chan et al. (2025) and Floridi et al. (2018). Faculty training, though moderately developed through existing professional development initiatives , remains highly relevant to address the skills gap in Australian HDR contexts, where workload and resistance persist (Daou & Hajj, 2023). Context-specific applications, emerging as a response to diverse HDR needs (Wang, 2025), require further theoretical grounding to ensure equitable outcomes, aligning with Siemens' (2018) connectivist principles of networked learning.

To synthesize these priorities, a conceptual mapping is proposed, illustrating their relative development and relevance. This approach avoids premature quantification, instead offering a qualitative lens to stimulate discourse and direct future empirical studies. Such a visualization, rooted in the 2024-2025 literature, underscores the interplay between theoretical propositions and practical implementation, providing a diagnostic tool for educators, policymakers, and researchers. It highlights the urgency of addressing gaps in ethical governance, professional capacity, and contextual adaptability, which are pivotal for the transformative potential of AI-LA in Education 4.0. This expanded context ensures that research efforts are not only reactive but also proactively aligned with the evolving demands of HDR programmes globally.

Building on this conceptual mapping, further exploration of Explainable AI (XAI) could revolutionize transparency, as Chatti et al. (2014) suggest, by making algorithmic decisions accessible to HDR supervisors. Research should test XAI in pilot studies, measuring its impact on trust and adoption rates, particularly among faculty with limited technical skills (ElSayary, 2025). Additionally, longitudinal studies could assess how training programmes influence completion rates, integrating Rogers' (2010) DOI framework to evaluate trialability across diverse HDR cohorts. Wang (2025) proposes equitable AI-LA tools, suggesting studies on adaptive interfaces for non-traditional students, such as those with disabilities, to ensure inclusivity. Collaborative networks, as emphasized by Siemens (2018), require investigation into mitigating echo chambers, potentially through randomized connection algorithms tested in Australian HDR forums (Castro et al., 2024). This holistic approach will align AI-LA with Education 4.0's equity goals.

Figure 3. Priorities for Future AI-LA Research

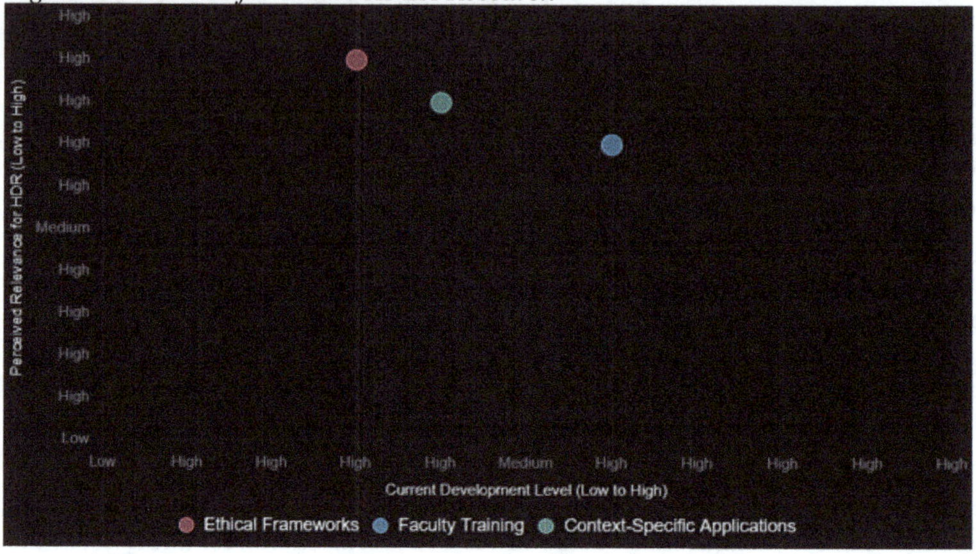

Figure 3. Priorities for Future AI-LA Research visualizes the theoretical relationship between current development levels (low, medium, high) and perceived relevance for HDR (low, medium, high) across ethical frameworks, faculty training, and context-specific applications. Grounded in 2024-2025 literature (e.g., Chan et al., 2025; ; Wang, 2025), this scatter plot serves as a qualitative guide for future research, emphasizing the need to bridge theoretical gaps with practical solutions in Education 4.0, particularly in diverse HDR contexts.

We argue that future scholarship must prioritise longitudinal and comparative investigations to test the convergence of theoretical frameworks in real-world Education 4.0 settings (Arguello Villa, 2025). Researchers should move beyond conceptual mapping to examine how hybrid models—integrating behaviourist monitoring, cognitivist personalisation, constructivist agency, and connectivist networking—evolve over time in diverse higher education institutions.

Scholars should conduct multi-institutional studies that compare AI-LA adoption trajectories across socio-economic and cultural contexts. Such research would illuminate how adoption models (TAM, TPB, DOI) interact with local factors, such as resource availability and institutional maturity, to shape implementation success (Castro et al., 2024). Longitudinal designs would reveal whether initial faculty resistance diminishes as perceived usefulness and behavioural control increase through targeted training and demonstrated value.

We contend that future work must deepen exploration of explainable AI (XAI) as a mechanism to enhance trust and agency. Researchers should investigate how transparent decision-making processes in predictive analytics mitigate surveillance perceptions and empower learners to engage critically with their data profiles (Floridi et al., 2018). This direction holds particular relevance for HDR contexts, where independent inquiry demands systems that augment rather than undermine self-directed learning.

Equity-focused research emerges as a priority. Scholars should develop frameworks to assess and monitor AI-LA's long-term impact on epistemic diversity and access equity in underrepresented groups, including those in developing regions or from non-dominant cultural backgrounds (Abulibdeh et al., 2024; Muñoz, 2024). Comparative analyses would test whether inclusive design practices and bias audits effectively prevent the narrowing of learning pathways and promote broader participation in networked knowledge construction (Makarenko et al., 2024).

We propose that interdisciplinary teams lead future efforts, combining learning sciences, data ethics, and educational policy to co-create adaptive governance models. These models should anticipate emerging technological shifts, such as advancements in real-time multimodal analytics, and prepare institutions for iterative policy refinement. Empirical validation of sociotechnical interdependence would strengthen arguments for stakeholder co-design, ensuring AI-LA remains aligned with pedagogical values across global contexts (Bates et al., 2020).

Future comparative research should examine how combinatorial recombination manifests in distinct global settings. For instance, institutions in sub-Saharan Africa might recombine low-bandwidth, open-source analytics platforms with community-based pedagogical traditions to deliver personalised support despite connectivity constraints (Abulibdeh et al., 2024). Similarly, Latin American universities could integrate predictive models with culturally situated connectivist networks to enhance epistemic inclusion for indigenous and rural learners (Castro et al., 2024). These contextual recombinations would test the adaptability of hybrid theoretical models and inform equitable planning strategies across resource gradients.

Ultimately, this research agenda fosters proactive educational planning. By addressing theoretical gaps through rigorous, context-sensitive inquiry, scholars can guide institutions toward responsible, equitable, and future-oriented integration of AI-powered Learning Analytics, thereby advancing the transformative potential of Education 4.0 (Arguello Villa, 2025; Gašević et al., 2016).

5.7 Practical Case Studies

This section explores practical applications of AI-Powered Learning Analytics (AI-LA) in Higher Degree by Research (HDR) programmes, illustrating how the discussed theories and frameworks translate into real-world settings. Through three case studies, it highlights thesis progress prediction, personalised feedback, and collaboration networks, addressing ethical and adoption challenges.

Case 1: Thesis Progress Prediction with AI-LA

In HDR programmes, tracking thesis progress is challenging due to its unstructured nature. Mougiakou et al. (2022) describe how AI-LA can analyse digital interaction patterns, such as time spent on academic resources and submission frequency, to predict delay risks. For instance, a system might identify that a student with less than 20% activity over six months has a 75% likelihood of not completing on time, enabling early interventions. This aligns with Siemens' (2018) connectivism, emphasising digital networks, and Davis' (1989) Technology Acceptance Model (TAM), where perceived usefulness drives adoption. However, Banerjee et al. (2024) warn of ethical risks, such as privacy invasion, suggesting institutions implement transparency policies to mitigate distrust.

Case 2: Personalised Feedback in HDR Supervision

HDR supervision benefits from AI-LA tools offering personalised feedback. Tan et al. (2025) present a case where an AI system analyses thesis drafts to suggest specific improvements, such as argument clarity or methodological coherence, tailored to each student's level. This reflects constructivist principles, fostering active learning through adaptive feedback . According to Ajzen's (1991) Theory of Planned Behaviour (TPB), acceptance depends on positive attitudes, but supervisors may resist if they perceive a loss of control, a point Muñoz (2024) suggests addressing with ethics-focused teacher training. Integrating these tools requires balancing teacher autonomy with technological support.

Case 3: Collaboration Network Analysis in HDR Forums

Online communities, like research forums, are vital for HDR. Castro et al. (2024) highlight how AI-LA maps student-supervisor interactions, identifying key knowledge nodes and suggesting interdisciplinary connections. For example, analysis might show a 30% productivity boost for an isolated student joining an active group. This case is grounded in connectivism (Siemens, 2018), but raises algorithmic bias concerns, such as "echo chambers" (Banerjee et al., 2024). Rogers' (2010) Diffusion of Innovations (DOI) suggests trialability can boost adoption through pilot testing, while Muñoz (2024) advocates for inclusive system design to avoid disparities.

Reflection on the Cases

These cases demonstrate AI-LA's potential to transform HDR programmes by optimising progress, supervision, and collaboration, but success hinges on overcoming ethical and adoption barriers, including equity considerations (as discussed in Section 2.5). Institutions should adopt hybrid strategies combining technology with human approaches, aligning with established ethical frameworks to ensure inclusive and responsible implementation.

6. CONCLUSION

This theoretical review has elucidated the conceptual foundations of AI-Powered Learning Analytics (AI-LA) in Education 4.0, with a focused lens on Higher Degree by Research (HDR) programmes. Building on the theoretical landscape mapped in Sections 1–5, it underscores the critical role of learning theories—behaviorism, cognitivism, constructivism, and socio-cultural perspectives—in shaping AI-LA's capacity to deliver personalised, data-driven educational experiences. Connectivism, as advanced by Siemens (2018), offers a framework to navigate networked learning in digital ecosystems, while Educational Data Mining (EDM) and Learning Analytics (LA) frameworks provide the technical backbone for data-informed interventions (Gašević et al., 2016). Adoption models, including the Technology Acceptance Model (TAM) of Davis (1989), the Theory of Planned Behaviour (TPB) of Ajzen (1991), and the Diffusion of Innovations (DOI) theory of Rogers (2010), illuminate faculty perceptions and institutional dynamics, proposing a hybrid framework to address resistance (Daou & Hajj, 2023).

The practical implications, explored in Section 4 and the case studies of Section 5.4, highlight AI-LA's transformative potential in HDR. Tools like predictive modelling for thesis progress (Mougiakou et al., 2022) and personalised feedback systems (Tan et al., 2025) enhance student support, while network analysis fosters collaboration (Castro et al., 2024). However, these benefits are contingent on overcoming ethical and adoption challenges. These ethical and equity imperatives, detailed in Section 2.5.

Faculty resistance, driven by workload and mistrust, underscores the importance of training, as advocated by Anagnostopoulou et al. (2024), and institutional strategies to align AI-LA with pedagogical goals.

The review's significance lies in its structured conceptual map, bridging theory and practice to guide future scholarship and policy. Figures 1–3 visualise these interconnections, offering a diagnostic lens for educators and policymakers. Yet, the rapid evolution of AI demands ongoing theoretical refinement, as emerging technologies challenge existing frameworks. Future research, as outlined in Section 5.3, should focus on empirical testing of these propositions, exploring XAI for transparency (Chatti et al., 2014), tailored training modules (ElSayary, 2025), and context-specific tools (Wang, 2025). This iterative approach ensures AI-LA remains pedagogically sound and ethically robust.

The rapid evolution of AI necessitates ongoing adaptation of these frameworks, particularly in HDR's diverse contexts. Empirical studies, as suggested in Section 5.3, should validate XAI's role in enhancing trust, with trials in Australian universities to assess faculty uptake (Chatti et al., 2014). Equity remains a priority, with Wang (2025) urging institutions to monitor AI-LA's impact on underrepresented groups, such as Indigenous HDR students, through targeted interventions. Muñoz (2024) emphasizes data governance policies to ensure inclusivity, while Castro et al. (2024) advocate for scalable network tools to bridge isolation.

In conclusion, this review synthesises a structured conceptual map that integrates pedagogical theories, adoption models, socio-technical dynamics, and ethical imperatives to guide responsible AI-LA integration in Education 4.0. We argue that educational leaders and policymakers should leverage this framework to foster proactive planning: recombining existing technologies with human-centred values, anticipating paradigm shifts, and embedding equity in institutional strategies. By prioritising interdisciplinary reflexivity and contextual adaptability, institutions can transform AI-LA from a potential disruptor into a catalyst for inclusive, future-oriented higher education across diverse global settings. This synthesis not only bridges theoretical insights with practical foresight but also lays a foundation for ongoing scholarship that advances equitable educational innovation in an era of rapid technological convergence (Arguello Villa, 2025; Floridi et al., 2018).

7. REFERENCES

Abraham, R., Schneider, J., & vom Brocke, J. (2019). Data governance: A conceptual framework, structured review, and research agenda. *International Journal of Information Management, 49*, 424–438. Advance online publication. DOI: 10.1016/j.ijinfomgt.2019.07.008

Abulibdeh, A., Zaidan, E., & Abulibdeh, R. (2024). Navigating the confluence of artificial intelligence and education for sustainable development in the era of Industry 4.0: Challenges, opportunities, and ethical dimensions. *Journal of Cleaner Production, 437*, 140527. Advance online publication. DOI: 10.1016/j.jclepro.2023.140527

Ajzen, I. (1991). The theory of planned behavior. *Organizational Behavior and Human Decision Processes, 50*(2), 179–211. DOI: 10.1016/0749-5978(91)90020-T

An, Q., Yang, J., Xu, X., Zhang, H., & Zhang, H. (2024). Decoding AI ethics from users' lens in education. *Heliyon, 10*(20), e39357. Advance online publication. DOI: 10.1016/j.heliyon.2024.e39357 PMID: 39640624

Anagnostopoulou, E., Grammatikos, N. A., Apostolou, D., & Mentzas, G. (2024, September). Trustworthy AI in education: A roadmap for ethical and effective implementation. In *Proceedings of the 13th Hellenic Conference on Artificial Intelligence (SETN 2024)*. ACM. DOI: 10.1145/3688671.3688781

Argüello Villa, I. M. (2025). AI-powered learning analytics in Education 4.0: A study of faculty perceptions in Adelaide Universities [Thesis]. Torrens Figshare. https://torrens.figshare.com/articles/thesis/AI-Powered_Learning_Analytics_in_Education_4_0_A_Study_of_Faculty_Perceptions_in_Adelaide_Universities_/30472238

Arockia, V. J., Vettriselvan, R., Rajesh, D., & Cheelo, C. (2025). Leveraging AI and learning analytics for enhanced distance learning: Transformation in education. In *AI and learning analytics in distance learning*. IGI Global., DOI: 10.4018/979-8-3693-7195-4.ch008

Arthur, W. B. (2009). *The nature of technology: What it is and how it evolves*. Free Press.

Banerjee, A.. (2024). Ethical considerations in AI-driven education: Balancing innovation with responsibility. *Journal of Educational Technology, 50*(3), 123–140.

Bansah, A. K., & Agyei, D. D. (2022). Perceived convenience, usefulness, effectiveness and user acceptance of information technology: Evaluating students' experiences of a learning management system. *Technology, Pedagogy and Education, 31*(4), 431–449. DOI: 10.1080/1475939X.2022.2027267

Bates, T., Cobo, C., Mariño, O., & Wheeler, S. (2020). Can artificial intelligence transform higher education? *International Journal of Educational Technology in Higher Education, 17*(42), 42. Advance online publication. DOI: 10.1186/s41239-020-00218-x

Cabero-Almenara, J., Palacios-Rodríguez, A., Loaiza-Aguirre, M. I., & Andrade-Abarca, P. S. (2024). The impact of pedagogical beliefs on the adoption of generative AI in higher education: Predictive model from UTAUT2. *Frontiers in Artificial Intelligence, 7*, 1497705. Advance online publication. DOI: 10.3389/frai.2024.1497705 PMID: 39484153

Castro, G. P. B., Chiappe, A., Rodríguez, D. F. B., & Sepulveda, F. G. (2024). Harnessing AI for Education 4.0: Drivers of personalized learning. *Electronic Journal of e-Learning, 22*(5), 01–14. Advance online publication. DOI: 10.34190/ejel.22.5.3467

Chan, M. M., Rosales, M., Hernandez-Rizzardini, R., & Amado-Salvatierra, H. R. (2025). Ethical AI in education: A proposed model for responsible integration. In *2025 IEEE Global Engineering Education Conference (EDUCON)*. IEEE. DOI: 10.1109/EDUCON62633.2025.11016451

Chatti, M. A., Dyckhoff, A. L., Schroeder, U., & Thüs, H. (2014). Exploring student interactions: Learning analytics tools for student tracking. In *Lecture Notes in Computer Science* (pp. 50–61). Springer., DOI: 10.1007/978-3-319-20609-7_6

Ciolacu, M., Tehrani, A. F., Binder, L., & Svasta, P. M. (2018). Education 4.0 – Artificial intelligence assisted higher education: Early recognition system with machine learning. In 2018 IEEE 24th International Symposium for Design and Technology in Electronic Packaging (SIITME). IEEE.

Corbeil, M. E., & Corbeil, J. R. (2021). Establishing trust in artificial intelligence in education. In *Trust, organizations and the digital economy* (pp. 49–60). Routledge., DOI: 10.4324/9781003165965-5

Cosar, M. (2024). Utilizing the eXtreme Gradient Boosting Algorithm for artificial intelligence–supported learning analytics application. The Eurasia Proceedings of Science, Technology, Engineering & Mathematics, 28, 277–285. https://dergipark.org.tr/en/download/article-file/4095327

Davis, F. D. (1989). Perceived usefulness, perceived ease of use, and user acceptance of information technology. *Management Information Systems Quarterly, 13*(3), 319–340. DOI: 10.2307/249008

Dayal, G., Verma, P., & Sehgal, S. (2023). A comprehensive review on the integration of artificial intelligence in the field of education. In *Leveraging AI and emotional intelligence in contemporary business organizations*. IGI Global. DOI: 10.4018/979-8-3693-1902-4.ch020

ElSayary, A. (2025). Fostering ethical digital citizenship: A policy framework for integrating digital ethics in education. In *Prompt engineering and generative AI applications for teaching and learning*. IGI Global., DOI: 10.4018/979-8-3693-7332-3.ch016

Floridi, L., Cowls, J., Beltrametti, M., Chatila, R., Chazerand, P., Dignum, V., Luetge, C., Madelin, R., Pagallo, U., Rossi, F., Schafer, B., Valcke, P., & Vayena, E. (2018). AI4People—An ethical framework for a good AI society: Opportunities, risks, principles, and recommendations. *Minds and Machines*, *28*(4), 689–707. DOI: 10.1007/s11023-018-9482-5 PMID: 30930541

Gašević, D., Dawson, S., & Siemens, G. (2016). *Preparing for the digital university: A review of the history and current state of distance, blended, and online learning*. Athabasca University.

Gonzalez-Sanchez, J., Chavez-Echeagaray, M. E., VanLehn, K., & Burleson, W. (2011). From behavioral description to a pattern-based model for intelligent tutoring systems. In *Proceedings of the 2011 ACM Symposium on Applied Computing*. ACM. DOI: 10.1145/2578903.2579164

Gupta, S., Sabitha, A. S., & Choudhary, P. (2022). Factors affecting user acceptance of AI-driven learning analytics in higher education. *Journal of Educational Technology Systems*.

Himmetoğlu, B., Ayduğ, D., & Bayrak, C. (2020). Education 4.0: Defining the teacher, the student, and the school manager aspects of the revolution. *Turkish Online Journal of Distance Education*, *21*(1), 12–28. DOI: 10.17718/tojde.770896

Imran, M., Almusharraf, N., Abdellatif, M. S., & Abbasova, M. Y. (2024). Artificial intelligence in higher education: Enhancing learning systems and transforming educational paradigms. *International Journal of Interactive Mobile Technologies*, *18*(18), 34–48. Advance online publication. DOI: 10.3991/ijim.v18i18.49143

Karmakar, S., & Das, T. (2024). Effect of artificial intelligence on education. In *Optimization and computing using intelligent data-driven approaches for decision-making: Optimization applications*. CRC Press., DOI: 10.1201/9781003536796-8

Kazimova, D., Tazhigulova, G., Shraimanova, G., & Sharzadin, A. (2025). *Transforming university education with AI: A systematic review of technologies, applications, and implications*. International Journal of Engineering Pedagogy., DOI: 10.3991/ijep.v15i1.50773

Knox, J., Williamson, B., & Bayne, S. (2020). Machine behaviourism: Future visions of 'learnification' and 'datafication' across humans and digital technologies. *Learning, Media and Technology*, *45*(1), 31–45. Advance online publication. DOI: 10.1080/17439884.2019.1623251

Kok, C. L., Ho, C. K., Koh, Y. Y., & Teo, T. H. (2024). *Psychological aspects of AI enhanced learning experiences. In 2024 IEEE Region 10 Conference (TENCON)*. IEEE., DOI: 10.1109/TENCON61640.2024.10902839

Kuhn, T. S. (2012). *The structure of scientific revolutions* (4th ed.). University of Chicago Press. DOI: 10.7208/chicago/9780226458144.001.0001

Leong, W. Y., & Zhang, J. B. (2025). *Ethical design of AI for education and learning systems*. ASM Science Journal., DOI: 10.32802/asmscj.2025.1917

Lockyer, L., & Dawson, S. (2011). Learning designs and learning analytics. In *Proceedings of the 2011 LAK Conference*. ACM. DOI: 10.1145/2090116.2090140

Makarenko, O., Borysenko, O., Horokhivska, T., Kozub, V., & Yaremenko, D. (2024). Embracing artificial intelligence in education: Shaping the learning path for future professionals. Multidisciplinary Science Journal, 6, Article e2024ss0720. DOI: 10.31893/multiscience.2024ss0720

Maynard, S. (2015). *The fourth industrial revolution: Opportunities and challenges*. Routledge.

Mougiakou, S., Vinatsella, D., & Sampson, D.. (2022). Optimising teaching using learning analytics. *Frontiers in Education*, *7*, 878279. Advance online publication. DOI: 10.3389/feduc.2022.878279

Murwaningsih, T. Sasmini, Rahardjo, S. S., & Nurhasanah, F. (2024). A well structured strategy development via AI integrated analytics systems to improve performance of education. In 2024 4th International Conference on Advance Computing and Innovative Technologies in Engineering (ICACITE). IEEE. DOI: 10.1109/ICACITE60783.2024.10617260

Nguyen, A., Gardner, L., & Sheridan, D. (2020). A design methodology for learning analytics information systems: Informing learning analytics development with learning design. In *Proceedings of the 53rd Hawaii International Conference on System Sciences*. DOI: 10.24251/HICSS.2020.014

Ouyang, F., & Zhang, L. (2024). AI-driven learning analytics applications and tools in computer-supported collaborative learning: A systematic review. *Educational Research Review*, *44*, 100616. Advance online publication. DOI: 10.1016/j.edurev.2024.100616

Pauw, C. (2021). Combinatorial evolution: A theory of evolution for technology – Fellows' seminar by Brian Arthur. Stellenbosch Institute for Advanced Study. https://stias.ac.za/2019/06/combinatorial-evolution-a-theory-of-evolution-for-technology/

Rajput, R. (2025). Use of artificial intelligence to solve problems in the classroom. In *New technological applications in the flipped learning model*. IGI Global., DOI: 10.4018/979-8-3373-0437-3.ch005

Ramírez-Montoya, M. S.. (2021). Trends for the future of education 4.0. *Education and Information Technologies*. Advance online publication. DOI: 10.1007/s10639-021-10509-4

Riaz, S., Mushtaq, A., & Kaur, M. J. (2019). Intelligent tutoring for informed feedback in interactive learning environments. In *ASET Conference Proceedings*. DOI: 10.1109/ICASET.2019.8714555

Richta, R. (2018). *Civilization at the crossroads: Social and human implications of the Scientific and Technological Revolution*. Routledge.

Rogers, E. M. (2010). *Diffusion of innovations* (5th ed.). Free Press.

Romero, C., & Ventura, S. (2020). Educational data mining and learning analytics: An updated survey. *Wiley Interdisciplinary Reviews. Data Mining and Knowledge Discovery*, *10*(3), e1355. Advance online publication. DOI: 10.1002/widm.1355

Romero Alonso, R., Araya Carvajal, K., & Reyes Acevedo, N. (2025). Role of artificial intelligence in the personalization of distance education: A systematic review. RIED: Revista Iberoamericana de Educación a Distancia.

Salloum, S. A., Salloum, A., & Alfaisal, R. (2024). Objectives and obstacles of artificial intelligence in education. In *Studies in big data*. Springer., DOI: 10.1007/978-3-031-52280-2_38

Schwab, K., & Davis, N. (2018). *Shaping the future of the fourth industrial revolution*. Currency.

Sghir, N., Adadi, A., & Lahmer, M. (2022). Recent advances in predictive learning analytics: A survey of machine learning approaches in education. *Education and Information Technologies*, *28*, 403–426. DOI: 10.1007/s10639-022-11104-0

Siemens, G. (2005). Connectivism: A learning theory for the digital age. *International Journal of Instructional Technology and Distance Learning*, *2*(1), 3–10.

Siemens, G. (2018). Connectivism: A learning theory for the digital age. *International Journal of Instructional Technology and Distance Learning*, *15*(3), 1–8.

Siemens, G., & Long, P. (2011). Penetrating the fog: Analytics in learning and education. *EDUCAUSE Review*, *46*(5), 30–40.

Slomp, E. M., Ropelato, D., Bonatti, C., & Da Silva, M. D. (2024). Adaptive learning in engineering courses: How artificial intelligence can improve academic outcomes. In *EDUNINE Conference Proceedings*. IEEE. DOI: 10.1109/EDUNINE60625.2024.10500580

Smith, J., Brown, T., & Lee, A. (2024). Ethical challenges in AI-driven learning analytics: A review of faculty concerns in higher education. *Journal of Higher Education Policy and Management*, *46*(3), 89–104.

Tan, X., Cheng, G., & Ling, M. H. (2025). Artificial intelligence in teaching and teacher professional development: A systematic review. Computers and Education: Artificial Intelligence. DOI: 10.1016/j.caeai.2024.100355

Thomas, J., & Harden, A. (2008). Methods for the thematic synthesis of qualitative research in systematic reviews. *BMC Medical Research Methodology*, *8*(1), 45. Advance online publication. DOI: 10.1186/1471-2288-8-45 PMID: 18616818

Urmeneta, A., & Romero, C. (2024). Ethical considerations in AI-driven learning analytics. Journal of Educational Technology.

Vashishth, V., & Gautam, P. (2024). Learning analytics in synchronous online education. *E-Mentor*, *86*(4), 54–61. DOI: 10.15219/em86.1482

Wang, V. (2025). Ethics and equity in AI-driven education. In *AI integration into andragogical education*. IGI Global., DOI: 10.4018/979-8-3373-0502-8.ch010

Wang, Y. (2021). Artificial intelligence in educational leadership: A symbiotic role of human-artificial intelligence decision-making. *Journal of Educational Administration*, *59*(3), 256–270. Advance online publication. DOI: 10.1108/JEA-10-2020-0216

Webb, M., Davis, N., & Bell, T. (2020). The development of computer science education globally: A review of current efforts. *Education and Information Technologies*, *25*, 1–32. DOI: 10.1007/s10639-016-9493-x

Xiao, Y., & Watson, M. (2019). Guidance on conducting a systematic literature review. *Journal of Planning Education and Research*, *39*(1), 93–112. DOI: 10.1177/0739456X17723971

Zhang, J. (2024). Application of artificial intelligence tools in educational assessment: Enhancing teaching and learning management in Beijing junior high schools. *Eurasian Journal of Educational Research, 112*, 017. Advance online publication. DOI: 10.14689/ejer.2024.112.017

Zhao, Y. (2019). The future of education: 2030. In *Perspectives on rethinking and reforming education* (pp. 1–24). Springer., DOI: 10.1007/978-981-13-9439-3_1

Chapter 11
Data-Driven Decision Making for Strengthening Educational Policy and Practice

Ashutosh Bhardwaj
http://orcid.org/0009-0008-3311-8335
Poornima University, Jaipur, India

ABSTRACT

Evidence-based strategies have become an essential component of current educational policies and practice creating the chance to enhance learning outcomes, organizational efficiency, and system-wide responsibilities through the use of data-driven decision making. This has been aided by the growing access to digital learning platforms, administrative data, and massive test scores in offering new vistas of reviewing student performance, instructor excellence, and patterns of resource distribution. Educational data, when properly used, can aid in specific interventions, well-informed policymaking, and the steady improvement of all education system levels.This chapter discusses how the use of data-driven methods can enhance educational policy and practice by emphasizing the data source and methodologies of data analysis and system frameworks that can be utilized in supporting decision making that is evidence-based.

DOI: 10.4018/979-8-2600-2606-9.ch011

1. INTRODUCTION

1.1 Evolution of Evidence-Based Educational Governance

The decision making in education has traditionally been based on professional judgment, localized experience and normative policy traditions. Certainly, although these methods have been useful in the development of the system, they were usually not systematic in the process of assessing results on large scale. The increased impetus on accountability and the measurement of performance over the last several decades has changed the way performance in educational systems is evaluated. The governments and institutions are more and more dependent on the quantifiable measures of the student achievement, institutional quality, and policy impact (Simon, 1977).

With the emergence of standardized testing, online platforms of learning and administration information systems, educational data has greatly become more accessible. These advancements have facilitated the longitudinal analysis of student gains, comparative analysis of schools, and determine the effectiveness of programs with a wide range of populations. Consequently, evidence based decision making has been found as one of the key strategies of enhancing transparency and accountability in education systems across the globe.

This development represents a larger trend of evidence-based governance, in which the policy interventions are assessed based on empirical measures instead of referring to ideological or political value consideration. The purpose of this approach in education is to match the resources to quantifiable needs, facilitate the targeted interventions, and constantly revise the instructional recipes, following the results (Kumari et al., 2026).

1.2 Defining Data-Driven Decision Making in Educational Contexts

Data-driven decision making in education -Systematic and coordinated gathering, analysis, and use of information to inform the formulation of policy, instruction, and management in institutions. Contrary to the straightforward which involve reporting systems, the data-informed structures highlight the repetition of feedbacks a process where evidence-based informational structures facilitate planning, implementation, evaluation, and improvement of educational programs. Figure 1 represents the conceptual framework in a graphic representation. The process promotes the promotion of continuous improvement at classroom, school, district, and country level (Lu et al., 2007).

Figure 1. Conceptual Framework of Data-Driven Decision Making for Strengthening Educational Policy and Practice

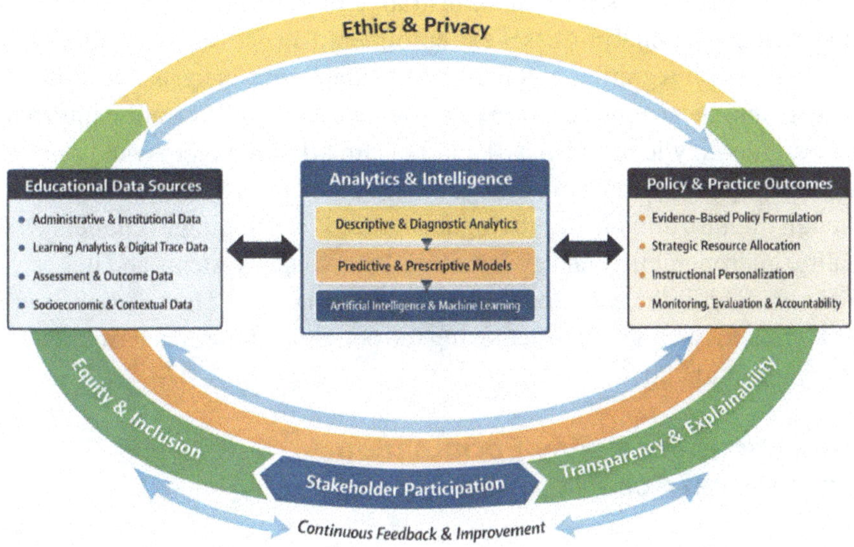

The data on education consists of various aspects including performance levels, behavioral data, school attendance data, economic aspects, and learning patterns. These data sources combined will offer a comprehensive picture of learner experiences and the way the institutions operate. Complex professional techniques enable policy-makers and practitioners to analyze the tendencies, make predictions, as well as analyze the efficiency of particular programs.

Nevertheless, data-based methodologies demand a close contextual understanding. Quantitative hints should be supplied with qualitative insights so that the complex phenomena in education may not be over-simplified. Good decision making will not just solely rely on availability of data but also, on the ability of educators and policymakers in acquiring knowledge of the research findings and converting them into meaningful steps (Chen & Zhang, 2014).

1.3 Role of Digital Transformation in Expanding Educational Data

Digitization of education has greatly increased the information size and fineness. The learning management systems, the adaptive learning platforms and the online tests produce the unending flows of behavioral and performance data. Such online footprints enable teachers to track the learning process in close time, and modify the teaching models (Kumari & Goyal, 2026).

Outside the classroom setting, administrative digitalization has enhanced data coordination in institutional processes e.g. enrolment, finance, staffing and infrastructure planning. This integration will facilitate system wide analysis that contributes to strategic planning and optimization of resources. National education information repositories on policy levels also assist in benchmarking and cross-regional comparisons, which promote reform agendas (Zhang et al., 2015).

Although digitalization is improving analytics, it is bringing in challenges with data quality, interoperability and governance. Dissociated systems and uneven data standards may inhibit the usefulness of analytics programs. The solutions to these structural problems are the key to achieving the potential of the data based education systems (Wang et al., 2016).

1.4 Implications for Policy Formulation and Institutional Accountability

The data driven decision making changes policy development because it allows making more accurate identification of educational gaps, performance gaps. Policymakers are supported to create interventions that are grounded in empirical evidence and not broad self-conceptions thus responding more directly to the policy where a more impartial policy is applicable. This strategy assists in the differentiated funding models, early warning frameworks on the student at-risk, and result-based accountability structures (Sharma et al., 2026).

The structure of institutional accountability depends more and more on the performance indicators that are also associated with student outcomes, the frequency of graduation, and employable skills after the learning process. Evidence-based analysis helps to objectively analyze the performance of institutions and promptly improve it. The overreliance on a single, specific performance measure, though, can have some undesirable side effects of promoting teaching to the test or excluding non-cognitive learning results (Lu et al., 2016).

1.5 Socio-Political Dimensions of Data-Driven Educational Reform

Educational data cannot be neutral as it is based on the social, economic, and political contexts that shape the process of measurement and interpretation. The use of data reforms can serve to reinforce the inequalities of current situations inadvertently in the ease that analytical models do not consider structural disadvantages experienced by marginalized groups. It is therefore the role of policymakers to implement equity-centric models that put performance data into contextualization when it is placed in broader social contexts.

The success of data-driven initiatives is also dependent on the social trust of people. Data-based accountability systems can be seen as a form of punishment; they can seem to be against educational values; in this case, stakeholders can be resistant to such systems. Assessment of confidence in analytical methods involves transparency of communication, democracy of decision-making, and upholding benefits of conformity to moral principles in overseeing data (Bertsimas & Thiele, 2006).

Finally, the reform based on data should be sustainable, which means that technical capacity should be matched with an inclusive system of governance. Data-driven decision making can become a significant tool to reinforce both the educational policy and practice when accompanied by stakeholder participation and ethical consideration (Farooqi et al., 2026).

2. SOURCES AND TYPES OF EDUCATIONAL DATA FOR POLICY AND PRACTICE

2.1 Administrative and Institutional Data Systems

Educational analytics is essentially based on administrative data in the form of enrollment, attendance, test scores, staffing, budget, and infrastructure records. These datasets are normally produced as a normal institutional functionality and they offer crucial information on the capacity of the system and performance. Administrative data allows longitudinal study of trend across policy cycles and academic years due to their continuous collection and in large volume (Lim et al., 2006).

At the institutional level, this data allows monitoring of performance and compliance reporting helping institutions to fit their operations to the requirements of regulators. Even in greater levels of policy decisions, aggregate administrative information has facilitated national benchmarking, identification of regional differences, and resource allocation plans. Such datasets can provide a valid comparison of schools and districts when they are successfully standardized.

Nevertheless, the administrative data tend to represent procedural dimensions of education not pedagogical ones. Unless teaching analytics and contextual variables are complemented, these data might not be able to explain quality of instruction, engagement or even socio-emotional growth of students. Thus, the exclusively administrative measurements can lead to the insufficient completeness of the educational performance (Zadeh, 1965).

2.2 Learning Analytics and Digital Trace Data

With the emergence of digital learning environments, new types of educational data have been added based on interaction of the learner with digital platform. Some of the patterns that are captured by learning management systems include time spent on activities, regularity of operation, paths of content navigation and the number of assessment attempts. Cheating on these digital traces provides highly detailed information on behaviors that could not be easily observed before in learning (Goyal et al., 2026).

Learning analytics will allow the premature identification of academic risk and assist with adaptive interventions in instruction. Teachers are able to detect the tendencies of disengagement, knowledge deficiencies and misunderstandings in almost real-time. Such data may promote the design of curriculum, methods of assessment, and professional development when combined.

However, digital trace information needs to be examined cautiously to prevent any attribute of behavior to learning outcomes. The engagement measures cannot be necessarily directly related to the comprehension, and algorithmic frameworks can reduce sophisticated cognitive tasks to simplicity. There is also the need to incorporate pedagogical knowledge and analytics interpretation in order to make educational progress at the significant level (Bellman & Zadeh, 1970).

2.3 Assessment Data and Outcome Measurement

Assessment data is used to play significant roles in measuring the learning outcomes and effectiveness of the policies. Standardized testing, formative classroom testing and competency-based testing give rise to performance pointers that are utilized to gauge curriculum congruency and student development. These measures can be used to facilitate comparative analysis between institutions and demographic groups.

Many education systems rely on the outcome-based data to inform their accountability systems and their funding allocation systems. Curriculum reforms, teacher training programs and specific support programs are informed by performance trends. Assessment records have the potential to demonstrate more systematic achievement deficiencies when data is longitudinally studied and used to inform systematic intermediary actions (Espinilla et al., 2014).

Nevertheless, assessment-based governance can unintentionally focus instruction, and can reward the use of test-oriented methods in education. Too much focus on quantitative results could undervalue creative, social and critical thinking abilities more difficult to measure. Learning assessment models that incorporate several dimensions of learning are thus what is required during holistic assessment of education (Goyal et al., 2026).

2.4 Socioeconomic and Contextual Data Integration

Socioeconomic factors, family background and community resources all impact significant changes in educational outcomes. Educational analytics get more interpretable power with the addition of contextual information like household income, parental educational level, and geographic accessibility, and health indicators. The multidimensional approach endorses the policy design that is grounded in equity (Zeleny, 1982).

Contextual information can be used to identify structural impediments on learning participation and retention. Policy-makers are able to create specific intervention among the underprivileged population and distribute the resources more efficiently. Geographic information systems also contribute to the spatial analysis of accessibility of services and gaps in infrastructures.

This is as significant as it is; however, socioeconomic data integration poses privacy and ethical issues. Accountable systems of governance should consider safe processes of data management and informed consent. Ethical data use must prioritize the trust of the people and help to cure systemic inequities in evidence-based policies (Yager, 1981).

2.5 Challenges in Data Quality and Interoperability

To achieve effective data-driven decision making, it is necessary to have data accuracy, consistency and compatibility of the systems. The use of disjointed databases and unequal reporting standards in most education systems prevents any significant platform integration. Data silos only allow analysis across sectors and lessen the quality of policy assessments.

There is also an issue with interoperability that makes it hard to track the progress of students across institutions and education levels. Absence of standard identifiers and data-sharing protocols fragment continuity of records making it less effective based on the focus on the learner in policy planning (Dandotiya et al., 2026).

These limitations can be overcome by investing in the modernization of infrastructure, data governance frameworks and professional training. The creation of integrated education data ecosystems can improve the analytical capabilities and can lead to sustainable policy formulation on the basis of valid evidence (Zadeh, 1975).

3. ANALYTICAL METHODS SUPPORTING EDUCATIONAL DECISION MAKING

3.1 Descriptive and Diagnostic Analytics in Education Systems

Descriptive analytics aims at summarizing previous data to determine the performance patterns and trends. Reporting tools and dashboards are used to visualize developments in enrollment, distribution of achievements and attendance. These lessons assist in day-to-day monitoring and benchmarking by an institution.

Diagnostic analytics goes beyond the limits of descriptive analysis in that it analyzes causal relationships of observed outcomes. The correlation between the instructional practices, demographics, and performance outcomes help educators to identify basic causes of the learning difficulties. This method facilitates intervention strategy and program reviews (Herrera & Martínez, 2000).

Though descriptive and diagnostic tools are actively used, their usefulness is determined by the level of data literacy among the educators and administrators. Misinterpretation of trends or the inability of decision makers to identify confounding variables can be made in the absence of proper training and reduce the quality of analytical outputs.

3.2 Predictive Modeling and Early Warning Systems

Predictive analytics involves the use of statistical and machine learning to predict the future based on the former. Predictive models can be implemented in education to abate students who are considered to face a high risk of dropping out, failing, or becoming inactive. The early warning systems facilitate in advance support plans that increase retention and completion rates (Kumari et al., 2026).

Predictive models are also useful in planning the policy by estimating the growth in enrollment, staffing needs and the infrastructure needs. Scenario simulation enables policymakers to evaluate the effectiveness of the alternative intervention early enough thereby improving the strategy (Yager, 1988).

Predictive analytics, however, has ethical implications on the issues of labeling, propagation of biases, and data determinism. However, historically inaccurate algorithm training can contribute to unjust systemic fruitlessness unless it has been well crafted and monitored. Clear model governance and lifelong validation should be ensured to make use of application as equitable.

3.3 Prescriptive Analytics and Decision Optimization

Prescriptive analytics is more than predictive since it proposes the best steps, which is based on the result of the analysis. Optimization models compare different strategies of policy implementation and find the intervention that produces the best outcomes with the available resources. This method embraces evidence based budgeting and priority of the programs (Atanassov, 1986).

Prescriptive systems are used in teaching scenarios as they direct adaptive learning process and individualized instruction. Automated recommendations can assist teachers to customize teaching to the needs of the individual learners without compromising on standards of the curriculum. These instruments assist in the large-scale customization of education.

Irrespective of their potential, prescriptive systems have to be assessed strictly to avoid excessive dependence on automated recommendations. The need to humanize the final decision, consider local factors, and ensure the maintenance of pedagogical principles in the technology-based process of decision making creates the necessity of the human oversight (Kumari et al., 2026).

3.4 Role of Artificial Intelligence and Advanced Analytics

Pattern recognition, natural language processing and real-time accommodating features are artificial intelligence that strengthens educational analytics. AI based systems can assist in identifying latent trends and learning interventions on a personalized basis by looking at large scale datasets. These technologies allow tracing learning paths continuously (Szmidt & Kacprzyk, 2003).

Analysis of qualitative feedbacks, discussion forums and assessment responses can be analyzed using natural language processing. This goes beyond the numerical measures of evaluation, as it involves the perceptions and dynamics of engagement of students. Formative assessment practices are also improved through AI assisted feedback (Wu & Chiclana, 2014).

Nonetheless, there is the issue of algorithmic opaqueness and dependence, which brings about governance challenges. Institutions need to be explainable, fair and accountable in the use of AI. The regulatory framework and ethics are essential in order to ensure that the innovation is balanced with the proper implementation.

3.5 Translating Analytics into Actionable Policy and Practice

The final worth of educational analytics is in its ability to educate significant action. There are joint efforts and processes that must be used to translate data insights to policy decisions through collaboration of educators, administrators, and policy makers. Having stakeholders helps to gain a more understanding of the situation and enhance practical implementation.

Professional development is important because it helps educators to implement findings of classroom practice using analytic methods. Informed teaching needs both technical and pedagogical expertise. The culture of reflective practice and experimentation encourages institutional cultures to embrace the use of data (Sheikh et al., 2026).

The continuous effect will be achieved through incorporation of analytics as part of the continuous improvement cycles as opposed to periodic assessments. Data-driven strategies incorporated into the normal operations of governance provide adaptive education systems that can fulfill the emerging needs of learners (Dong, 2018).

4. DATA-DRIVEN POLICY DESIGN AND IMPLEMENTATION STRATEGIES

4.1 Evidence-Informed Policy Formulation

The process of policy formulation based on data starts with the systematic examination of indicators of educational performance, equity, and variables of the context. Polie based on learning outcomes, institutional capacity and socioeconomic conditions allow the policymakers to set realistic goals that are responsive to the needs of the system. This analytic basis eliminates dependency on ideological presuppositions and makes a case in favor of practical decision making.

The use of dashboards, simulation tools, and scenario modeling to assess alternative strategies of intervention is becoming part and parcel of how the policy is designed. Policymakers may be in a position to evaluate the possible consequences, expenses and risks before them by using these tools. This type of proactive assessment is beneficial in terms of the efficiency of resources, as well as the reduction of the unintended effects of reforms (Xu & Zhao, 2016).

Nevertheless, policymaking based on evidence involves the use of interpretive skills to prevent the overgeneralization of insufficient samples. The precepts and wisdom of the practitioner, as well as qualitative research, will be necessary to put the quantitative findings into perspective. The balanced combination of various sources of evidence guarantees stronger and socially responsible policy formulation (Rodríguez et al., 2014). Evidence-informed policy formulation is reflected through Figure 2 as a data-driven educational policy and practice lifestyle.

Figure 2. Data-Driven Educational Policy and Practice Lifecycle

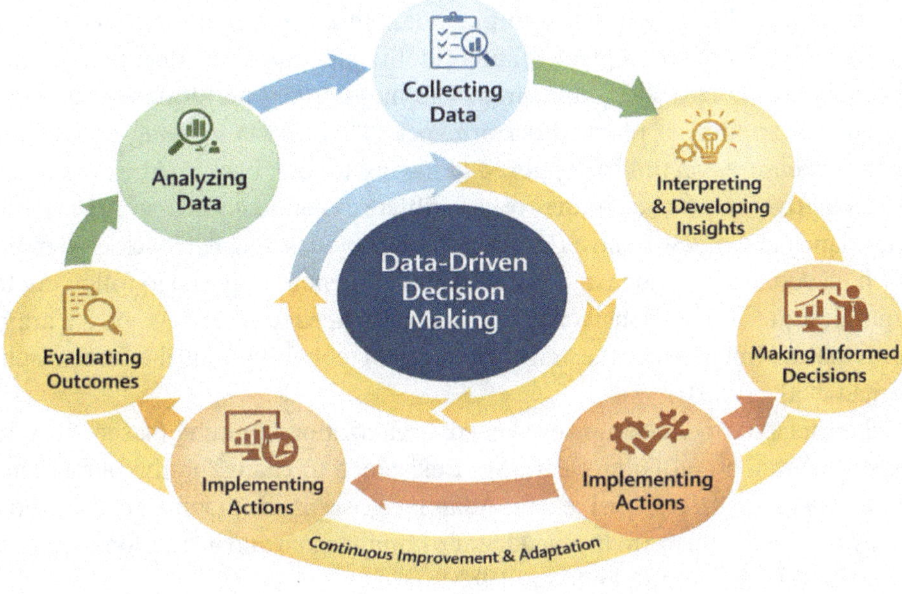

4.2 Strategic Resource Allocation and Budget Optimization

Data analytics is very important in informing equitable and efficient allocation of education resources. Budgeting information, information on teacher deployment and use of infrastructure is made informed by enrollment estimates, teacher deployment data and infrastructure use metrics. Predictive models assist in estimating the future demand in capacity thus lessening reactive funding responses (Torra, 2010).

Performance and demographics indicators are used more frequently to fund vulnerable groups with the help of targeted funding programs. Analytics will allow determining schools in need of further instructional support, technology improvement, or social services. These kinds of targeted investment enhance effectiveness in the policy as well as discourage systemic inequalities.

However, the application of the performance-based funding models can result in unintentional discrimination of the under-resourced institutions. The policy requires special calibration so that data-based allocation systems can generate the support and not competition between schools. The equity sensitive indicators should continue to play key roles in funding structures (Bustince, 2016).

4.3 Implementation Monitoring and Adaptive Governance

After policies have been put into practice, there are monitoring mechanisms that constantly assess the implementation fidelity and outcome effectiveness. Real time dashboards enable the administrators to monitor key performance indicators and identify variation of planned performance. This assists in being able to take corrective measures on time as opposed to having to look back and be post-hoc.

The adaptive governance frameworks facilitate dynamically changing the policy in accordance to the new trends. Feedback loop provides data feedback on iterative data which enhances the idea of constant improvement as opposed to following the original design. This responsiveness is especially needed in fast moving learning systems that are impacted by the transformations of technology and the demographic (Dijkman et al., 1983).

Making adaptive policies, however, needs organizational cultures that are liberated in experimentation and failure learning. Resistance to change in the bureaucracy can defeat data driven responsiveness. Adaptive governance practices can therefore only be preserved with the help of leadership commitment and institutional capacity building (van Laarhoven & Pedrycz, 1983).

This policy entails collaborating with stakeholders to create policies that benefit everyone involved, including employees and customers.

4.4 Policy Co-Creation with Stakeholders

The successful application of the policy requires the interaction with educators, learners, parents, and community organizations. Participatory data-sharing sites enable stakeholders to add the element of context and confirm the analytical interpretation. The joint design enhances the consent and applicability of policy interventions (Palomares et al., 2014).

Transparency in data improves accountability and confidence of people in the process of governance. In case performance indicators and improvement plans are shared, communities will be in a position to interact positively with education authorities. This openness will make people collectively responsible to educational outcomes (Herrera et al., 2009).

However, to engage in it materially, data presentation should be available and digital inclusion tactics should be implemented. Unless participatory governance is democratized through intentional efforts, this may succeed in being confined to technical elites. These inclusive data literacy programs are thus crucial to fair co-creation of the policies.

5. INSTITUTIONAL TRANSFORMATION THROUGH DATA-INFORMED PRACTICE

5.1 Leadership Roles in Data Culture Development

Leadership in education is a critical move to incorporate evidence-based practices in institutions. The evidenced based planning, professional learning, and continuous assessment are the recommendations set by leaders. Their investment affects organizational feelings on adopting analytics and improving instruction.

The strategic leadership is designed to bring the advancement of the goals of the institution and the priorities to use the data. The inclusion of analytics in school improvement strategies can help the leaders to promote the systematic reflection of the educational quality and the student advancement. This congruence is an improvement in the consistency of policy instructions and classroom practice (Zadeh, 1996).

Nonetheless, data cultures led by leadership should not be based on best-down integrity models that deaden teacher agency. These models are collaborative and use a participative style of leadership in order to create more sustainable use of analytics tools with the help of the practitioner expertise. Reflective Practice Trust-based cultures are those that endorse reflective practice instead of punitive accountability.

5.2 Professional Development and Data Literacy Enhancement

Professional development in relation to the analytical interpretation and practical implementation of educational data is important to use it effectively. Teachers need to be placed in a position to translate the performance measures into practical teaching policies. There is increased confidence and competence in evidence-based pedagogy as determined through culture data literacy programs.

Peer learning and solving problems.

Structured data investigatory communities encourage peer learning and community problem solving. When teachers analyze the results of the students in groups, they gain more insight as to what works and what is required in the curriculum. This type of professional collaboration enhances learning in an institution.

However, professional development should be context and workload sensitive. Unnecessary reporting requests can create information apathy and opposition. Incorporating analytics in the current pedagogical processes strengthens the sustainability of the data-driven teaching processes.

5.3 Curriculum Design and Instructional Personalization

Information analytics can shape up curriculum alignment because learning gaps and content sequencing problems are identified. The educators of curriculum design are able to improve instructional aids according to the learning performances and feedback. This helps in evidence based curriculum renewal.

Learner-centered learning plans are highly dependent on the requirements of learners and adjustable learning content. Personalization based on analytics improves the involvement in terms of focusing on the unique learning requirements and speed preferences. This type of customization facilitates the inclusive education models that promote different learning parameters.

The personalization technologies should however have a balance between automation and human pedagogical judgment. High dependency on algorithmic suggestions can be restrictive to the creativity and interpersonal aspects of the education of teachers. Human cultural principles are also fundamental in instructional systems that are data based.

5.4 Evaluation and Continuous Institutional Improvement

Regular evaluation cycles are based on using quantitative and qualitative evidence in regard to institutional effectiveness. Program evaluations are used to determine the effects of instructional interventions, student support services as well as technology integration. Strategic planning and accreditation are supported by evaluation that is based on evidence (Gou et al., 2017).

Comparing performance against other similar institutions can be used to identify best practices and areas of performance improvement. Comparative analytics educates institutional positioning and competition strategy in tertiary markets. Benchmarking of this type is helpful in upholding accountability and quality assurance.

However, assessment systems should not be so metric-focused and compliance oriented that they lose sight of the educational purpose. Balanced scorecard tactical systems that incorporate academic, social and developmental indicators facilitate wholesome institutional measurements and ongoing enhancement.

6. RESPONSIBLE DATA GOVERNANCE AND INCLUSIVE DECISION FRAMEWORKS

6.1 Regulatory Structures and Institutional Accountability

Due to the growing reliance of educational systems on mass data analytics, data practices and governance by a strong regulatory framework are needed to guarantee licit, truthful, and responsible data practices. Regulations stipulate the manner in which student and institutional data is gathered, managed, kept and shared, in the digital platforms. Well-defined legal systems guarantee the rights of individuals and make it possible to use data as an instrument of legitimate educational purposes of monitoring, evaluation, and improvement. In the absence of clearly established governance policies, data-based reforms inevitably face the risk of noncompliance with the law and erosion of the public trust.

The institutional accountability mechanisms create an obligation between the technologies vendors and education ministry, school authorities and vendors involved in data services. The data protection officers and compliance committees, which are formal, make sure presence of operationalization of the policies on the institutional level. Accountability is further ensured through audit system, reporting required and standard documentation procedures, which make it possible to trace how data was accessed and used. The governance practices will make sure that the analytics systems stay true to organizational missions and regulatory pressures.

Nevertheless, the systems of governance should be flexible to changing technologies and pedagogies. Strict regulations can discourage creativity and slow the use of useful analytical tools. Orders that are adaptable to responsible experimentation enable research institutions to investigate evidence-based interventions without losing control. Such policy flexibility and procedural protection provide a long-term sustainability of digital transformation of education.

6.2 Equity-Oriented Data Interpretation and Inclusive Policymaking

Good governance is not restricted to regulation but is also equity-minded understanding of the education information. The analytical models should consider socio-economic differences, linguistic variations, disability, and geographic impediments that determine the outcomes during learning. Neglecting to combine the contextual variables can result in a flawed interpretation of the performance indicators and poor policy reaction to these indicators that ignores the structural disadvantages.

Due to the necessity to address the requirements of the marginalized population, policymaking must be inclusive, which entails disaggregated data analysis.

This analysis can be utilized in the form of specific intervention measures, such as instructional support, community involvement initiatives, and redistribution of resources. The level of equity built in the performance monitoring systems will turn policies to be sensitive to social facts and not to statistic average.

However, equity-based analytics should not stigmatize and deficit-frame the vulnerable groups. Negative labels like low-performing can support negative stereotypes and have an impact on institutional expectations. Identified diversity-driven inclusive governance frameworks hence focus on strengths-driven interpretation and comprehensive accountability to eliminate educational obstacles. This constant scrutiny of analytical assumptions can be effective in the consideration of information that supports empowerment, as opposed to exclusion.

6.3 Transparency, Explainability, and Public Confidence

Openness on the decision-making processes is vital towards building public trust on the system of education based on data. Stakeholders should know the impact of data on the instructional practices, as well as funding allocations and priorities in the policies. Open governance fosters legitimacy and healthy involvement of the educators, parents and community organizations.

Analytical models that are predictive or automated in their mechanisms should be explainable especially when interventions are guided by these methods. When teachers have an opportunity to understand the connection between the indicators and decisions related to the support of learners, there is better trust in technology-assisted governance. Clarity of communication will also minimize the misunderstanding of surveillance and control in online education.

But, not only should there be transparency in the form of technical disclosure but it should be transparency in the form of meaningful public discussion. Intricate analytics is to be converted in easy-to-understand language and graphics. The establishment of data communication literacy by the institutions consolidates the effectiveness of democracy as well as the foundation of evidence-based governance frameworks.

6.4 Institutional Capacity and Sustainable Data Stewardship

Data governance is not a single event but a long-term practice within the organization that needs an institutional ability to handle and manage data in a way that satisfies all the principles of data security and ethics. This involves competent staff, integrated information security, and general cybersecurity, and uniform data-management protocols. Capacity issues promote breaches, abuse and inaccuracy of analyses threatening the credibility of the policies.

Professional development programs increase the technical and interpretive competencies of the administrators and educators. Data security, quality assurance, and responsible analytics training guarantee that institutional practices are of a good governance level. Continuous infrastructure modernization is also a key to sustainable stewardship that is expected to sustain future-proofed data volumes and the complexity of analytics.

However, the lack of capacity consistency among institutions can be a threat of the imbalance of policy application. Schools with poor resourcing can have a problem with complying to the governance requirements, and this poses areas of compliance and blind analysis. The disparities can be addressed through the national coordination and shared services model that offer central technical backup and homogeneous tools.

6.5 Participatory Governance and Collaborative Decision Processes

Comprehensive decision models acknowledge the importance of involvement of stakeholders in determining priorities on the use of data and measuring the consequences of policy. Participatory governance models refer to the inclusion of educators, students, family, and community partners in the process of data interpretation and jointly creating interventions. This type of cooperation contributes to the contextual relevance and the possibility of implementation.

Data query teams encourage collective accountability in institutional change. Once there is joint analysis of the learning outcomes and service delivery indicators by the stakeholders, ownership of the reforms initiatives grows collectively. Participation processes also lead to increased accountability whereby feedback of policy effects and impacts that could be unintended can be obtained.

Nonetheless, beneficial participation presupposes institutional representation of power sharing and transparency. Consultation in form of tokenism and lack of decision-making power can lead to a weakening of governance instead of empowerment. Good participatory mechanisms should incorporate the contribution of stakeholders through official decision-making frameworks and resource distribution procedures.

6.6 Governance Alignment Across Policy Levels

Education systems have multi-level systems of governance indispensable in national ministries, regions and institutional leadership. Coherence in the standards of data, reporting practices, and policy goals can be guaranteed by alignment of these levels. Disjointed governance systems compromise the comparability of data as well as strategic alignment.

The vertical alignment allows the monitoring of policy implementation and evaluation of the outcomes. The collaboration of administrative boundaries is evidenced based by using common indicators and interoperable systems. The successful interventions across jurisdictions can also be scaled up with the aid of coordinated governance.

However, to stay aligned, authority and responsibility has to be negotiated constantly. Decentralized systems should strike a balance between local autonomy and national accountability systems. Good coordination systems enhance adaptive policymaking without interfering with the contextual diversity among educational settings.

7. FUTURE DIRECTIONS AND STRATEGIC PATHWAYS FOR DATA-DRIVEN EDUCATION SYSTEMS

7.1 Artificial Intelligence–Enabled Policy Intelligence

AI-enabled systems of policy intelligence are influencing the future nature of the next stage of data-driven education governance. These systems are the extension of the traditional analytics based on their ability to incorporate machine learning-based algorithms that can handle large-scale multi-dimensional datasets in the academic, behavioural and administrative sectors. Policy intelligence that operates with the help of AI gives decision makers an opportunity to identify complicated patterns that cannot be identified easily by standard statistics and, thus, enhance the level of accuracy in forecasts and the possibility of strategic planning.

AI-based predictive modelling is helping policymakers to forecast enrolment variations, dropout rates and rates, the scarcity of teachers and building requirements more accurately. Scenario modeling would enable officials to model their policy interventions and determine their possible long-term effects before they become policy. This type of anticipatory governance promotes the proactive and not the reactive policy several developments and therefore education systems can respond better to the challenges that arise.

Nonetheless, AI policymaking should be supported by institutional restrictions to make sure policymaking is accountable and interpretable. In the absence of clarifiable models and user-clear validation procedures, the use of automated predictions in policies will destroy confidence in the people. AI needs to be adopted strategically, therefore, governance strategies that do not eliminate human control must be adopted and use computational intelligence.

The extent of understanding within integrative contexts, reconstructing records that mirror the underlying nature of an ER Ecosystem.

7.2 Integrated Cross-Sector Data Ecosystems

Integrated data ecosystems between education systems, healthcare systems, social welfare system, and labor markets will continue to become an important part of future education governance. The ability of cross-sector data integration facilitates comprehensive learning about the paths of learners and life-course outcomes, which has configured coordinated intervention strategy aims which meet various aspects of well-being. These types of ecosystems help in identifying factors of risks other than academic performance.

The connection between education information and system of employment and skills development improves workforce management and economic planning. Researchers are able to assess the level at which the curricula are supporting the changing labor markets. The targeted vocational training and reskilling programs based on the regional economic priorities are also possible through integrated data platforms.

However, cross sector integration brings along technical, legal, and organizational tendencies. Clear information exchange between and among organisations should be aided through the application of data interoperability standards, legal agreements and governance structures. Sustainable integration involves concerted leadership on intergovernmental level among ministries and agencies to defeat institutional silos.

7.3 Global Data Collaboration and Comparative Policy Learning

Global learning assessments and international benchmarking initiatives are important to availability of good prospects of comparative analysis of policy. Worldwide data sets can equip policymakers to explore the effects of various systems of governance on the equity, quality, and innovation of education. Identifying scalable best practices as well as contextualism are helps that comparative analytics provides in identifying reform strategies.

Transnational cooperation brings about more rigor in the methods of research and exchange of knowledge between education systems. Collaborative assessment of pedagogical innovations and governance changes can be helpfully realized in the international proposals of research networks. There is increased reinforcement of evidence-driven policymaking due to the limitations of domestic data with such cooperation.

International comparisons have to be taken with care, though, as a result of cultural, institutional, and socioeconomic disparities. Policy learning needs to be adapted to receive foreign influence instead of recreating it directly. Comparative forms of governance should hence focus on the sensitivity to context and local ability of implementation.

7.4 Personalized Learning Systems and Policy Alignment

Increased developments in learning analytics and adaptive technologies are transforming the expectations of individually tailored delivery of education. The policy frameworks are forcing the adoption of learner-centered theories in which instructional directions are designed through individual performance and engagement patterns. The ability to personalize using data allows education systems to be more responsive and be able to support the needs of a diversified population.

The process of policy coordination with individualized learning programs demands the changes in the evaluation criteria, the education system, and the school training modules. The system of governance needs to be flexible in offering delivery of instruction and be accountable and quality assuring. Individual systems also require continuous monitoring to measure effectiveness and equity influences.

Nonetheless, the schemes of personalization should not support educational stratification with the help of algorithms tracking. There should be policy protection to make sure that adaptive pathways widen chances and does not restrict the movements of the learners. Human control is important as it ensures the maintenance of the holistic development in relation to competencies that can be measured.

7.5 Institutional Resilience and Crisis-Responsive Analytics

Evidence-based governance is essential to making the institutions more resilient to the shocks, including, but not limited to, the outbreak of a new pandemic, economic collapse, and environmental catastrophism. Learning continuity risks and resource deficit during the crisis can be quickly evaluated by using real-time analytics. The mechanisms of early detection are those that provide the opportunity to implement specific support interventions in a timely manner.

Scenario planning systems help the policymakers to prepare contingency plans in the case of emergency response. Simulation models measure the strength of infrastructure, staffing structures and online learning systems during stressful conditions. This preparedness increases continuation of education services in occasions of systemic shock.

Nevertheless, resilience planning needs to be incorporated into long-coming policy pulses instead of reactive crisis planning that is intermittent. Long term preparedness relies on regular stress-testing the governance structures and on the investment of infrastructures. The institutional resilience thus becomes a primary aspect of education governance of the future.

7.6 Building Adaptive Policy Ecosystems

Forthcoming information based educational frameworks have to exist as adaptive policy communities through which they can constantly learn and adapt. Real-world teaching Feedback mechanisms between classroom practice, institutional management and national policy permit real-time optimization of governance policies. Ongoing assessment facilitates progressive change as opposed to inflexible reform processes.

Adaptive ecosystems promote experimentation of innovative teaching patterns, testing and checking plans, and the service delivery systems. Policy sandboxes have been used to test large scale reforms in a controlled manner before enacting the reforms. This kind of experimentation encourages innovation which is evidence-based and reduces systemic risk.

However, the adaptive governance demands cultural changes in the direction of learning-based policy making. The innovation process, teamwork, and reflective practice should be compensated in the form of institutional rewards. Adaptive ecosystems can be used to promote sustainable educational change in social environments that are quickly evolving when they are founded on strong data infrastructure and professional capacity.

CONCLUSION

Evidence-based decision making has evolved to form the core of enhancing educational policy and organizational practice in more complicated and changeable learning settings. With the help of the various data sources and techniques of analysis, education systems will be more able to comprehend the needs of the learners, the performance within the institution and the inequities in the systems. This chapter has also shown how information relates to the development and informed design of policies, how methods of resource allocation, improvement of instruction and constant monitoring of systems can be used to improve effectiveness and accountability in the governance of the education system.

Another important fact mentioned in the analysis is that sustainable data-based transformation involves more than the technological adoption. Good governance systems, organizational ability, data literacy of the professionals, and a consensus-driven decision-making system are needed to make sure that analytics makes a positive contribution to educational growth. Open processes, democratic standards of governance and equity-based practices of interpretation are an important factor in ensuring a high rate of public trust and also it is important to ensure that policy interventions are based on real world instead of abstract measurements. With data and pedagogical capabilities in harmony with community involvement, data can be empowered and not prosecuted.

In the future, the convergence of artificial intelligence, cross-sector data ecosystems, and adaptive systems through governance will increase the role of analytics in the further development of education systems. Nonetheless, innovation and accountability, personalization and equity, and automation and human judgment are the variables that will require balancing in the long term. New models of education keep being developed and in the process, data-oriented decision making will always be a vital source of constructing resilient, inclusive, and future-responsive learning contexts that can address the diversity of learners as well as societal flux.

REFERENCES

Atanassov, K. T. (1986). Intuitionistic fuzzy sets. *Fuzzy Sets and Systems, 20*(1), 87–96. DOI: 10.1016/S0165-0114(86)80034-3

Bellman, R. E., & Zadeh, L. A. (1970). Decision making in a fuzzy environment. *Management Science, 17*(4), B-141–B-164. DOI: 10.1287/mnsc.17.4.B141

Bertsimas, D., & Thiele, A. (2006). Robust and data-driven optimization: Modern decision-making under uncertainty. In *Tutorials in operations research* (pp. 95–122). INFORMS. DOI: 10.1287/educ.1063.0022

Bustince, H., Barrenechea, E., Pagola, M., Fernandez, J., Xu, Z., Bedregal, B., Montero, J., Hagras, H., Herrera, F., & De Baets, B. (2016). A historical account of types of fuzzy sets and their relationships. *IEEE Transactions on Fuzzy Systems, 24*(1), 179–194. DOI: 10.1109/TFUZZ.2015.2451692

Chen, P., & Zhang, C.-Y. (2014). Data-intensive applications, challenges, techniques and technologies: A survey on big data. *Information Sciences, 275*, 314–347. DOI: 10.1016/j.ins.2014.01.015

Dandotiya, M., Goyal, N. K., Yadav, P., Sankhla, K., & Kumari, M. (2026). GENALYTICS: A deep dive into real-time insights via generative AI. In Elbaghazaoui, B. (Eds.), *Generative AI-powered data architectures* (pp. 105–134). IGI Global Scientific Publishing., DOI: 10.4018/979-8-3373-5616-7.ch005

Dijkman, J. G., van Haeringen, H., & de Lange, S. J. (1983). Fuzzy numbers. *Journal of Mathematical Analysis and Applications, 92*(2), 301–341. DOI: 10.1016/0022-247X(83)90253-6

Dong, Y. C., Zha, Q., Zhang, H., Kou, G., Fujita, H., Chiclana, F., & Herrera-Viedma, E. (2018). Consensus reaching in social network group decision making. *Knowledge-Based Systems, 162*, 3–13. DOI: 10.1016/j.knosys.2018.06.036

Espinilla, M., Montero, J., & Rodríguez, J. T. (2014). Computational intelligence in decision making. *International Journal of Computational Intelligence Systems, 7*(Suppl. 1), 1–5. DOI: 10.1080/18756891.2014.853925

Farooqi, A., Das, D., Tripathi, M., Dutta, R., Goyal, N. K., & Sheikh, M. F. (2026). Navigating ethical frontiers in AI-driven geriatric care. In Stolakis, K., & Efthymiou, I. (Eds.), *AI for geriatric care in an aging society* (pp. 243–266). IGI Global Scientific Publishing., DOI: 10.4018/979-8-3373-5462-0.ch009

Gou, X., Liao, H., Xu, Z. S., & Herrera, F. (2017). Double hierarchy hesitant fuzzy linguistic term set and MULTIMOORA method. *Information Fusion*, *38*, 22–34. DOI: 10.1016/j.inffus.2017.02.008

Goyal, N. K., Gulati, K., Avasthi, A., Kapoor, S. K., Keswani, B., & Gupta, S. (2026). Securing the imagination: Security and privacy challenges in generative AI systems. In Elbaghazaoui, B. (Eds.), *Generative AI-powered data architectures* (pp. 239–266). IGI Global Scientific Publishing., DOI: 10.4018/979-8-3373-5616-7.ch010

Goyal, N. K., Kumar, S., Dutta, R., Kothari, V., & Sinha, S. K. (2026). Empowering elderly care through artificial intelligence. In Stolakis, K., & Efthymiou, I. (Eds.), *AI for geriatric care in an aging society* (pp. 1–28). IGI Global Scientific Publishing., DOI: 10.4018/979-8-3373-5462-0.ch001

Herrera, F., Alonso, S., Chiclana, F., & Herrera-Viedma, E. (2009). Computing with words in decision making. *Fuzzy Optimization and Decision Making*, *8*(4), 337–364. DOI: 10.1007/s10700-009-9065-2

Herrera, F., & Martínez, L. (2000). A 2-tuple fuzzy linguistic representation model for computing with words. *IEEE Transactions on Fuzzy Systems*, *8*(6), 746–752. DOI: 10.1109/91.890332

Kumari, M., & Goyal, N. K. (2026). Artificial intelligence in the cryptocurrency ecosystem: Crime mechanisms, detection strategies, and legal perspectives. In Lin, L. (Ed.), *Innovations in cryptocrime and financial fraud* (pp. 245–282). IGI Global Scientific Publishing., DOI: 10.4018/979-8-3373-0675-9.ch007

Kumari, M., Khan, S. T., Gulati, K., Sharma, P., Goyal, N. K., & Sheikh, M. F. (2026). Innovative procedural content generation using generative AI. In Sousa, J., & Tavares, R. (Eds.), *Reshaping the video game landscape with AI and GenAI* (pp. 205–232). IGI Global Scientific Publishing., DOI: 10.4018/979-8-3373-4637-3.ch007

Kumari, M., Kumawat, R., Dutta, R., Khan, S. T., Goyal, N. K., & Sheikh, M. F. (2026). Wireless communication and IoT integration in smart clothing. In Saxena, P. (Eds.), *Next-generation electronic textiles and conductive materials* (pp. 195–232). IGI Global Scientific Publishing., DOI: 10.4018/979-8-3373-4287-0.ch008

Kumari, M., Kumawat, R., Tripathi, M., Suganthi, K., Goyal, N. K., & Sheikh, M. F. (2026). Blockchain for transparency and traceability in supply chains. In Khan, M., Mehmood, T., & Rao, M. (Eds.), *Maximizing operational efficiency at the intersection of supply chain management and marketing* (pp. 35–64). IGI Global Scientific Publishing., DOI: 10.4018/979-8-3373-3109-6.ch002

Lim, A. E., Shanthikumar, J. G., & Shen, Z. M. (2006). Model uncertainty, robust optimization, and learning. In *Tutorials in operations research* (pp. 66–94). INFORMS.

Lu, J., Han, J., Hu, Y., & Zhang, G. (2016). Multilevel decision-making: A survey. *Information Sciences, 346*, 463–487. DOI: 10.1016/j.ins.2016.01.084

Lu, J., Zhang, G., Ruan, D., & Wu, F. (2007). *Multi-objective group decision making: Methods, software and applications with fuzzy set techniques*. World Scientific. DOI: 10.1142/p505

Palomares, I., Martínez, L., & Herrera, F. (2014). A consensus model to detect and manage noncooperative behaviors. *IEEE Transactions on Fuzzy Systems, 22*(3), 516–530. DOI: 10.1109/TFUZZ.2013.2262769

Rodríguez, R. M., Martínez, L., Torra, V., Xu, Z. S., & Herrera, F. (2014). Hesitant fuzzy sets: State of the art and future directions. *International Journal of Intelligent Systems, 29*(6), 495–524. DOI: 10.1002/int.21654

Sharma, P., Kumawat, R., Jain, G., Keswani, G., Goyal, N. K., & Sheikh, M. F. (2026). Machine learning-based intrusion detection systems for healthcare Internet of Things (HIoT). In Shieh, C. (Eds.), *Resilient healthcare Internet of Things systems* (pp. 185–214). IGI Global Scientific Publishing., DOI: 10.4018/979-8-3373-7610-3.ch007

Sheikh, M. F. A., Kapoor, S. K., Goyal, N. K., Tuba, E., & Rao, A. (2026). Enhancing healthcare security with fog computing and blockchain technology. In Nayak, R. (Eds.), *Recent advancements in artificial intelligence* (pp. 1–20). Springer., DOI: 10.1007/978-981-96-7760-3_38

Simon, H. A. (1977). *The new science of management decision*. Prentice-Hall.

Szmidt, E., & Kacprzyk, J. (2003). A consensus-reaching process under intuitionistic fuzzy preference relations. *International Journal of Intelligent Systems, 18*(7), 837–852. DOI: 10.1002/int.10119

Torra, V. (2010). Hesitant fuzzy sets. *International Journal of Intelligent Systems, 25*(6), 529–539. DOI: 10.1002/int.20418

van Laarhoven, P. J. M., & Pedrycz, W. (1983). A fuzzy extension of Saaty's priority theory. *Fuzzy Sets and Systems, 11*(1–3), 229–241. DOI: 10.1016/S0165-0114(83)80082-7

Wang, H., Xu, Z., Fujita, H., & Liu, S. (2016). Towards felicitous decision making: An overview on challenges and trends of big data. *Information Sciences, 367–368*, 747–765. DOI: 10.1016/j.ins.2016.07.007

Wu, J., & Chiclana, F. (2014). A social network analysis trust-consensus based approach to group decision making. *Knowledge-Based Systems*, *59*, 91–107. DOI: 10.1016/j.knosys.2014.01.017

Xu, Z. S., & Zhao, N. (2016). Information fusion for intuitionistic fuzzy decision making. *Information Fusion*, *28*, 10–23. DOI: 10.1016/j.inffus.2015.07.001

Yager, R. R. (1981). A new methodology for ordinal multiobjective decisions based on fuzzy sets. *Decision Sciences*, *12*(4), 589–600. DOI: 10.1111/j.1540-5915.1981.tb00111.x

Yager, R. R. (1988). On ordered weighted averaging aggregation operators in multicriteria decision making. *IEEE Transactions on Systems, Man, and Cybernetics*, *18*(1), 183–190. DOI: 10.1109/21.87068

Zadeh, L. A. (1965). Fuzzy sets. *Information and Control*, *8*(3), 338–353. DOI: 10.1016/S0019-9958(65)90241-X

Zadeh, L. A. (1975). The concept of a linguistic variable and its application to approximate reasoning—I. *Information Sciences*, *8*(3), 199–249. DOI: 10.1016/0020-0255(75)90036-5

Zadeh, L. A. (1996). Fuzzy logic = Computing with words. *IEEE Transactions on Fuzzy Systems*, *4*(2), 103–111. DOI: 10.1109/91.493904

Zeleny, M. (1982). *Multiple criteria decision making*. McGraw-Hill.

Zhang, G., Lu, J., & Gao, Y. (2015). *Multi-level decision making*. Springer-Verlag. DOI: 10.1007/978-3-662-46059-7

Chapter 12
Data-Informed Educational Research and Evidence-Based Decision Making in Modern Education Systems

Shikha Sharma
http://orcid.org/0000-0001-6339-9731
Poornima University, Jaipur, India

ABSTRACT

The growing nature of educational data has altered the manner in which research, policy and practice are being conducted in present education systems. Data-based learning research This approach to learning research focuses on the application of quantitative and qualitative evidence to comprehend the learning processes, assess interventions, and direct learning instruction and institutional decision making. This chapter will look at the premises of data informed and evidence based approaches to education by discussing how various sources of data, the ways data analysis is conducted and how researche designs can be used inform decisions at the classroom, institutional and policy levels. It also explains the purpose of education technologies and learning analytics to produce actionable insights and how to address the ethical, privacy, and equity issues related to the use of data.

DOI: 10.4018/979-8-2600-2606-9.ch012

1. INTRODUCTION

1.1 Emergence of Data-Informed Approaches in Education

The education systems world-wide are in a complete change caused by the growing accessibility of data, and development of analytical technologies. In the traditional approach, educational decision making used to be overly dependent on professional evaluation and experience, and local assessment. Though these are useful methods, they are being supplemented by empirical application of data to guide teaching, institutional practice and policy formulation. This change has seen the emergence of data-informed education; a focus on and importance of the introduction of empirical evidence in educational research and practice.

The advent of mass student data systems, online education systems and standardized assessment systems has dramatically increased the amount and type of educational data. Such advances enable researchers and practitioners to study learning processes on more detailed and wider contexts. The use of data-informed practice can help the stakeholders to gain a better insight into student achievement and teacher performance and system-wide inequities, allowing them to step out of anecdotal data and into stronger findings (Bertrand & Marsh, 2015).

Notably, information-based education does not imply that professional knowledge should be substituted with algorithms and measures. Rather, it is a team-related thing in which data is used as an aid in improving human judgment. Through the integration of empirical and contextual information, it is easy to reach more informed and reflective decisions that answer the needs of a variety of learners (Black & Wiliam, 1998).

1.2 Data-Informed to Data-Driven Decision Making

The concepts of data-driven and data-informed can be used interchangeably, yet they have the different philosophical underpinnings of the way of making decisions in education. Their data-controlled decision making presupposes that decisions are made mostly, or even solely, by the means of quantitative data. Although such a method can facilitate consistency and responsibility, it might fail to recognize contextual aspects of matters like student backgrounds, institutional cultures and pedagogical objectives.

In comparison, data-informed decision-making focuses on the interpretative application of data, in addition to professional experience and qualitative data. The approach acknowledges the fact that educational data is relatively situational and that educational numbers cannot in any meaningful way represent the intricacy of teaching and learning. Evidence based practices promote a closer look on data where teachers may wish to question why things occur the way they do and how interventions can be best suited to fit particular situations (Brown, 2015).

This difference is especially relevant in contemporary education products having the high stakes accountability metrics that can even encourage a limited interpretation of data. An evidence-informed interdisciplinary approach aims to reduce the risks by encouraging the reflective application of evidence, and the culture of inquiry over compliance. This kind of orientation facilitates sustainable enhancement and moral application of educational facts (Datnow & Hubbard, 2015).

1.3 Educational Research and its role in Evidence-Based Practice

Educational research is at the forefront in the translation of the data to the actionable knowledge. Research methods aid in finding relationships between possible causes, assessing interventions, and drawing some insights that can be generalized through a systematic investigation. The use of evidence-based decision making depends on quality research to differentiate between the successful practices and those, which lack support or are limited by the circumstances.

The contemporary educational research tends to embrace mixed-method strategies of integrating both quantitative analysis of data and qualitative research. Big data sets can be used to conduct a statistical modelling and trend analysis, whereas qualitative data allows getting a clearer picture of what learners go through and how institutional organizational processes work. The combination of the two techniques contributes to the validity and applicability of research results (Mandinach & Gummer, 2013).

1.4 Technological Facilitators of Data-Informed Education

The technological innovations in the field of education have contributed greatly to the rapid integration of practices based on data. Learning Management Systems, adaptive learning systems and online assessment tools will generate incessant data concerning student engagement, progress and performance. These technologies deliver feedback in time that may be used to make instructional changes and facilitate personalized learning.

Figure 1. Framework of Data-Informed Educational Research and Evidence-Based Decision Making in Education Systems

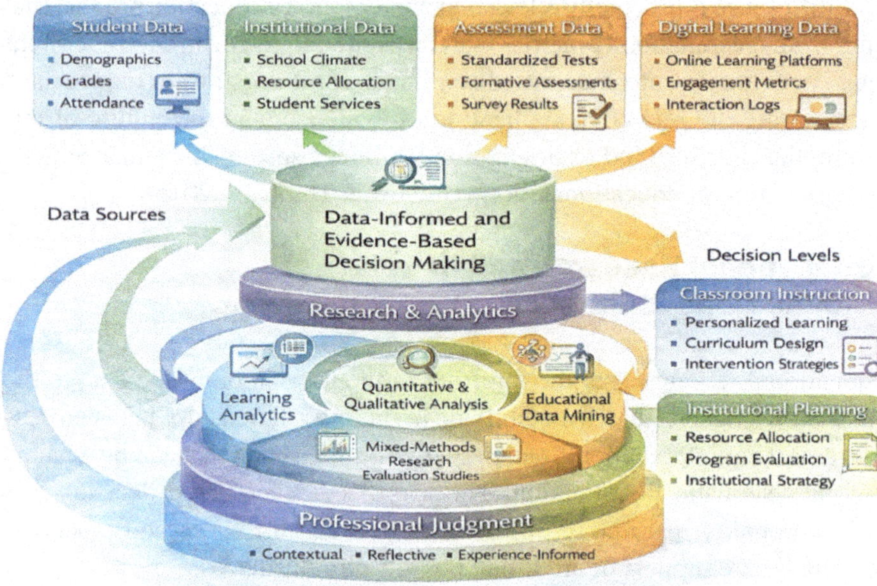

Much educational data mining and learning analytics have become dominant as apply disciplines that use computational methods on education data. These tools allow identifying patterns, predictive modelling, as well as displaying multifaceted data, which is more accessible to teachers and administrators. The analytics used in a responsible manner can facilitate detection of challenges in learning at the initial stage and make informed interventions (Goyal, 2025).

Nonetheless, the introduction of technology into data-informed education also brings to the fore key aspects associated with data quality, interpretation, and equity. Technological tools are to be developed and applied in the manner that facilitates meaningful decision making as opposed to superficial ones. This highlights why data-informed educational research should have solid methodological grounds and ethical principles.

1.5 Scope and Objectives of the Chapter

The chapter will focus on offering an in-depth analysis of the data-driven educational research and evidence-based decision making in the contemporary education systems. It investigates theory, practice and methods to apply data usage in informing educational practice and policy. Placing the use of data in the context of larger educational aims, the chapter makes it evident that the gap between evidence and such values as equity, inclusion, and learner-centeredness should be narrow.

The chapter covers various levels of decision making which are classroom instructions, institutional management and system level policy development. It also highlights the mutuality of data, research, and human judgment and appears to promote the idea of a balanced approach, which does not undermine professional autonomy by using evidence.

Finally, this chapter aims at providing researchers, educators and policymakers with a better grasp of how data-based methods can be used to improve the quality and accountability of education. As it provides a clear background in this introductory part, the chapter preconditions the further discussions of data sources, methods, technologies, ethical issues, and the further perspectives of evidence-based education.

2. CONCEPTUAL FOUNDATIONS OF EVIDENCE-BASED DECISION MAKING IN EDUCATION

2.1 Understanding Evidence-Based Decision Making in Educational Contexts

Evidence-based decision making in education can be defined as the application of the integration of the most optimal version of research evidence with professional skills and situational knowledge to make educational decisions. Compared to either intuition-driven application or tradition-driven application, evidence-based decision-making focuses on the intentional application of empirical evidence to enhance teaching, learning and institutional performance. This strategy acknowledges the fact that learning issues are multifaceted and need to be judged by knowledge and plausible evidence (Schildkamp & Poortman, 2015).

In the learning environment, the evidence can be in several forms, such as research, evaluation data, observations in classrooms, and the input of stakeholders. Evidence-based decision making is grounded on the conceptual level on the belief that the practices in education ought to be constantly tested and improved upon results as opposed to speculation. Such a view gives rise to a culture of asking questions whereby teachers are keen to find other ways of evidence to support instructional and organizational decisions.

Notably, evidence-based decision making does not lay down standardized solutions. The educational settings are very diverse (population of students, resources and cultural demands of students). Consequently, evidence should be perceived considerably with references to local circumstances and priorities. This interpretive aspect is what allows evidence-based practice to be meaningful and not necessarily be a strict application of generalized results (Earl & Katz, 2006).

2.2 Educational Evidence types and Hierarchies

There is a continuum of educational evidence of rigor and relevance. At one extreme are major scale experimental and quasi-experimental studies that seek to determine causal relationships between interventions and outcomes. Such studies are regarded as quality evidence in general due to the rigor of the methodology. On the other end are qualitative insights, practitioner thoughts, and contextual information, who have depth and insight into the how and why of the unfolding of educational processes.

Whereas hierarchies of evidence are popular in other areas like medicine, education is in need of a less hierarchical perspective of evidence. Randomized controlled trials can provide good causal statements, which are not necessarily true, but which do not necessarily reproduce the complexity of a real-world classroom. Unlike the quantitative studies, qualitative ones, case-studies, and design-based research offer helpful insights that are to be used in addition to the quantitative ones (Farley-Ripple et al., 2018).

An educative system with a data-informed approach appreciates different types of evidence and emphasizes the triangulation. Incorporating a variety of different sources of data allows educators and researchers to establish a more detailed picture of education phenomena. The broadness of this inclusive perspective of evidence contributes to more sensitive and contextual decision making.

2.3 Professional Judgment and Contextual Knowledge Role

Evidence-based decision making heavily depends on the professional judgment as an intervening factor between research and practice. Experience, pedagogical skills, and knowledge of needs of the learners do not immediately capture information on data only. This is a human aspect, which is necessary to understand evidence and transform it to fit certain instructional/institutional situations.

The contextual knowledge has an impact on the perception and application of evidence. The priorities of decision making are influenced by the demographics of the students, institutional mission, availability of resources and as well as community values. Evidence-based methods, which fail to take into account such contextual factors, stand a chance of proving ineffective or even counterproductive. The understanding of the interaction between the evidence and context will make the decisions informed and justified (Marsh et al., 2006).

The combination of professional judgment and empirical evidence is the main philosophy of data-informed education. This strategy encourages evidence and experience to be synthesized rather than merely favoring data whereas preference is given to the human intellect. This form of integration promotes reflective practice and scaling aids adamant improvement in the education systems.

2.4 Decision-Making Systems in Education Systems

Conceptual frameworks give guided methods towards integrating evidence in the educational decision making. These models often consist of the identification of problems, gathering of evidence, analysis, interpreting and assessing results. Systematic processes can help educators and administrators be less biased and increase the consistency of decisions.

The decision-making structures in the institutional environment aid in strategic planning, curriculum design and resource allocation. Evidence-based frameworks will provide the leaders with an opportunity to evaluate the effectiveness of programs and initiatives, areas of improvement, and make justification decisions to stakeholders. When making decisions, having them based on the documented evidence improves transparency and accountability (Datnow et al., 2013).

Evidence-based frameworks inspire reforms and large-scale interventions at the policy level. The policymakers use the research syntheses, longitudinal data, and evaluation studies to measure the outcome of the policy. Nevertheless, evidence translation into policy has to be done with keen attention to issues of political, economic and social concerns, which highlights the difficulty of evidence-based governance in education.

2.5 Limitations and Critical perspectives

Although decision making through evidence-based is very advantageous, it is not without flaws. One is that there is a risk it will overvalue measurable outputs to the detriment of things of importance but less measurability like creativity, social development and well-being. Certain conceptualizations of evidence may gender Canadians towards learning prohibitively.

The other problem is the quality and interpretation of data. Poor contextualized, incomplete, and biased data may result in ill-informed decisions. Multidisciplinary practices need a high level of data literacy among the staff and administration to use the information carefully. The evidence-based decision making promise will not be absolutely achieved without proper training (Goyal et al., 2025).

Critical views also focus on the idea that evidence is never neutral which is influenced by methodological arguments and values on which it is based. Given these constraints, people must be more considerate and approach evidence with more critical thinking and action. The evidence-based decision making has a lot to offer to the education systems but must be approached with critical but constructive attitude so that the advantages of evidence-based decision making may be exploited to the benefit of the remedies.

3. DATA SOURCES AND ANALYTICS IN MODERN EDUCATION SYSTEMS

3.1 Types of Educational Data in Contemporary Systems

The present-day education system produces a mass of evidence that can be used to conduct research and make decisions on several levels. Most educational datasets include student level data which is in the form of academic performance, attendance records, and behavioral indicators. Such data can give information about the pace of learning, interaction dynamics, and aspects of learning that a person might need more attention to. Superimposed student records can expose trends which could be used to design instruction and interventions.

In addition to the student data, institutional data is important in the operations of education systems. This contains data on teacher performance, implementation of curriculum, resource distribution as well as administrative procedures. With such data, institutions can measure the effectiveness of a program and its efficiency of operation. On the system level, policy information, demographic data, and high scale evaluation outcomes facilitate comparative examination and strategic design between a region or sector of education (Wayman et al., 2012).

The digitalization of education has increased the number of data sources to incorporate the digital traces that are created in the process of learning using learning management systems, online tests, and educational applications. These data record interactions that are real-time between the learning environment and the learner and provide detailed insights as to the learning behaviours. Nonetheless, such a wide range and quantity of these data sources are also faced with challenges of integration, quality and interpretation.

3.2 Learning Analytics and Educational Data Mining

Learning analytics and educational data mining are very close related fields which utilise analytical techniques to educational data with the aim of enhancing learning and decision making. Learning analytics aims at gauging, gathering, and assessing information regarding the learners and their setting to assist in Oncizing the learning and learning settings. It can also focus on practical implications that can be used to modify the instruction and support systems to students (Hargreaves & Braun, 2013).

By comparison, educational data mining is more interested in the development and application of high-level techniques to extract trends on large collections of educational data. Clustering, classification, and predictive modeling techniques are applied in the identification of relationships among variables and forecasting of the future. These techniques help the researcher to reveal the concealed patterns in data that they may not readily detect by the conventional methods of analysis.

Figure 2. Key Blocks and Workflow of Data-Informed Decision Making in Modern Education Systems

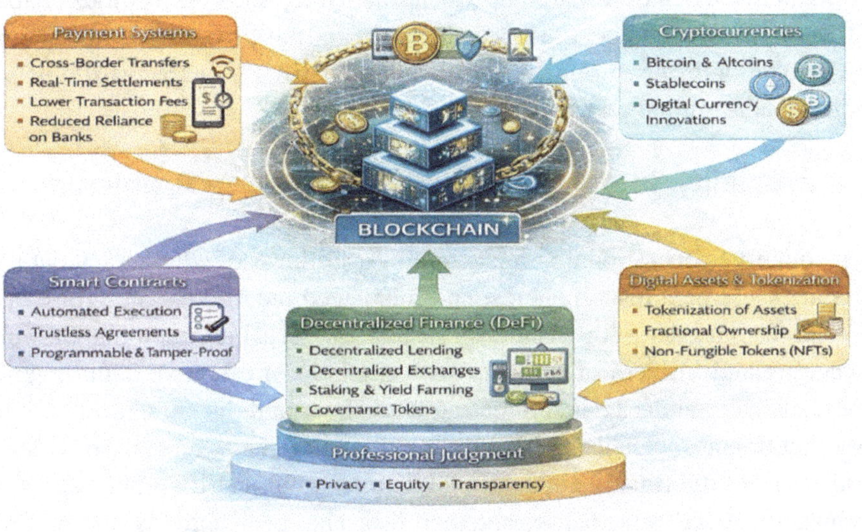

Both disciplines have a role in deterministic education, by converting raw information into valuable output. Nevertheless, they can be effective only when used and interpreted in a way. The results of the analysis have to be placed in pedagogical and institutional context so that the insights could translate into effective steps instead of naive conclusions.

3.3 Analysis and Qualitative and Quantitative methods

The importance of quantitative analytics within data-informed educational research is significant, as it allows measuring, comparing, and making a statistically informed conclusion. The tools that are usually utilized to assess educational interventions and establish factors that are related to student success are descriptive statistics, regression analysis, and experimental designs. The approaches facilitate evidence-based decision making because they offer empirical evidence on instructional and policy decisions.

Qualitative analytics are in the category of supplements that can be used to understand educational processes and experiences on a deeper level that is not addressed by quantitative methods. Sources of data like interviews, classroom observations and open-ended survey responses can contain views that cannot be brought out with numerical data. Through qualitative analysis, it will be possible to determine why some patterns can be noticed and how the stakeholders scale education initiatives (Lai & Schildkamp, 2013).

The need to combine both quantitative and qualitative analytics enhances the validity and relevance of research in education. Mixed-method methods enable the investigator to bring together the research results and answer multifaceted questions, which involve both measurement and meaning. This is a characteristic of strong data-driven educational research.

3.4 Data Quality, Integration and Interpretation Problems

Data quality is operational in the extent of usefulness of educational data. Lack of data, measurement discrepancies, and misplaced records are the problems that may lower the integrity of the results of the analysis. It is important that they ensure the accuracy and fullness of the data with the help of effective data governance policies, such as standard data collection workflows and the validation policies.

Another important challenge to the contemporary education system is data integration. Most of the time the educational data are held on different systems under the management of diverse parties and therefore it has been hard to establish a single perspective of the learners and institutions. Platform integration also needs both technical and organization interoperability and standards (Van Geel et al., 2016).

Perhaps the most important issue of educational analytics is interpretation. Latent data are not eloquently articulated and can be misunderstood with ease, unless they are put in perspective. Teachers and decision makers need to acquire data literacy skills to critically appraise outputs of analytical techniques and to make incorrect conclusions. Accountable interpretation guarantees that decisions that are made using data are relevant and precise (Goyal et al., 2025).

3.5 Research and Decision-Making Implications

The existence of various sources of data and highly refined analytics vastly affects not only the practice but also research in the sphere of education as well.

Researchers can investigate more deeply complicated questions, pertaining to learning processes and equity and performance of the system. Research that is informed by data contributes to the continuous improvement of the data through the provision of consistent assessments of the education interventions.

To practitioners and administrators, analytics give the means of making decisions timely and on target. Students at risk can be identified through the early warning system and evaluation of the program is used to direct resource allocation and strategic planning. Analytics can promote efficiency and responsibility in education systems when it is in line with institutional objectives.

Nevertheless, a growing dependency on data and analytics also requires a close attention to the ethics and equity concerns. Making judgments due to incomplete or biased information may support the existing differences. At the time when educational systems keep adopting the method of data-driven practices, analytical sophistication must still be balanced with human judgment. This ratio will make sure data are an instrument to improve the quality of education and not the goal (Schildkamp et al., 2014).

4. RESEARCH METHODOLOGIES FOR DATA-INFORMED EDUCATIONAL STUDIES

4.1 Quantitative Research Designs in Educational Research

Quantitative research designs are one of the building blocks of data-driven educational research since they offer methodical approaches to the measurement of educational phenomena, and hypothesis testing. These techniques are based on numerical data and statistical methods of studying the relationship between variables, testing interventions, and trends across populations. Familiar quantitative designs are an experimental, quasi-experimental and correlational studies which provide varying degrees of control and inference.

Randomized controlled trials, especially experimental designs are considered as a strong tool of coming up with causal relationships in the field of education. Researchers can isolate the effects of the interventions by randomly assigning the participants to treatment and control group. Working practical and ethical restrictions frequently restrict the viability of full method experimental structures in educational institutions causing scientists to embrace the quasi-experimental techniques that estimate experimental conditions with observational data (Rickinson et al., 2017).

Quantitative large-scale studies are also instrumental in the analysis at the system level. Ways through which researchers can study educational outcomes across time and across contexts are by using national assessment, longitudinal data and administrative records. Although these studies provide general information, the results should be used with caution because statistical significance is not necessarily educational significance.

4.2 Qualitative Methodologies and Interpretive Inquiry

Qualitative methods of research are used to complement the quantitative techniques in that they deal with meaning, context and lived experiences in the learning environments. These methodologies are mostly useful in the study of rich social processes, including classroom dynamics, institutional environments, and perception of the learners. Qualitative research involves interview, focus groups, ethnography, and case studies to provide rich and contextual information that helps in understanding the results better than numerical measures.

Interpretive inquiry focuses on the views of participants, as well as acknowledging the fact that educational realities are socially constructed. This method enables the researcher to examine the relationship between policies and practices and their experiences by students, teachers, and administrators. The nature of qualitative findings offers an insight into the implementation process, implementation barriers, and facilitators, which may not be visible in the case of quantitative data (Weick, 1995).

Qualitative approaches are highly important in data-informed educational studies when explaining patterns detected using analytics. Indicatively, qualitative analysis may provide insight into the factors behind the success of certain interventions in this or that setting. Such an explanatory power increases the usefulness and usability of research results (Datnow & Park, 2018).

4.3 Mixed-Methods and Design-Based Research Methods

Mixed-methods research involves the integration of both the quantitative and qualitative research in one study or research programme. According to this method, complicated educational questions tend to involve several types of evidence. Mixed-methods studies comprise a more detailed view on educational phenomena because they take numerical data in combination with insights articulated by narrative.

Design-based research is a particular mixed-methods method that is especially suitable in an education that is informed by data. It entails repetitive design, implementation, evaluation, and improvement of education interventions in the real world. At the same time, researchers work hand in hand with practitioners in order to formulate solutions that are theoretically based and practically oriented (Goyal et al., 2025).

The mentioned methodologies ensure continuous improvement by producing functional knowledge as opposed to conclusions. Design based research is much related to the principles of evidence-based decision making, in the sense that they focus on flexibility, relevancy on the context, and the continuous assessment. These strategies will narrow the divide between research and practice in the contemporary education systems.

4.4 Ethical in Educational Research methodology

Ethical issues are essential in research based on data in education especially as education research may use extensive and sensitive data. In any research, the researchers have to guarantee informed consent, data security and in addition to this, confidentiality. Institutional review boards are an important aspect of ethical oversight that safeguards the rights and well-being of the participants.

The surveillance, privacy, and ownership of data represent other ethical issues that come up with the utilization of digital data. It is possible that the learners lack awareness of how their data are gathered and utilized, which brings up the attributes of transparency and agency. Scholars should find ways of engaging in ethical data practices treated in such a way so as not to infringe upon the autonomy of the participants as required by the law or the institution (Poortman & Schildkamp, 2016).

Another very important possible ethical aspect is equity. The methodologies used in the research should not be structured in a way that perpetuates the levels of inequalities or even isolate vulnerable groups of people. Data-driven methods can be used to promote equity and social justice in education, and this goal can be achieved through including research practices and considerate approach to the findings.

4.5 Data-Informed Studies Methodological Rigor and Validity

The methodological rigor of educational research is critical to guarantee the data-informed research. Rigor entails meticulous design of the study, use of proper method of data collection, and clear method of analysis. The aspects of validity and reliability are of central concern, as they define the degree in which results are relevant to educational realities.

Rigor in quantitative studies is enhanced by the provision of statistical controls, duplication and sensitivity analysis. The strategies used to attain qualitative rigor include triangulation, member checking and thick description. Mixed-methods research will have to be concerned with rigor in both methodological traditions, with the findings being coherent and integrated (Mandinach et al., 2008).

Finally, methodological rigor elevates the credibility of evidence to be used in decision making. Evidence-based practices are more likely to be embraced by policymakers, educators, and other stakeholders whenever the methods used in research are clear and strong. By basing data-driven education on solid methodology, scientists will be able to play a role in the sustainable and effective change both within the education systems.

5. EVIDENCE-BASED POLICY AND INSTITUTIONAL DECISION MAKING IN EDUCATION

5.1 Evidence Use in Educational Policy Formulation

Evidence based policy making in education entails the achievement of systematic applications of research and data analysis in designing and reforming policies. Empirical evidence becomes more popular with policymakers in order to evaluate the level of educational program efficiency, resources distribution, and intervention development, which will result in better learning outcomes. This transformation indicates an increasing expectation of accountability, transparency and change of public education systems to be demonstrated (Earl, 2015).

The data-informed education policies can be applied to systemic problems like the achievement gap, shortage of teachers, or irrelevancy of the curriculum. The big tests, longitudinal tests, and program tests offer information regarding the influence of policies to me on various groups of students in the long run. Evidence-based policymaking enables governments and educational leaders to minimize reliance on ideological suppositions or in the short-term political concerns.

Nevertheless, research evidence cannot be easily translated into policy. The process of policymaking exists in rather complicated political and social environments, where conflicting priorities and stakeholder interests follow decision making. Evidence should thus be discussed and reported efficiently to inform the policy discussions and be contextually aware.

5.2 Decision making and Strategic Planning at an institutional level

The evidence-based decision making at the institutional level assists in strategic planning, improvement of organization and managements. Data are used in schools, colleges and universities in order to assess the effectiveness of programs, track the student advancement as well as development areas. There is rising interest among institutional leaders to consider data as a strategic asset that makes long-term and operational decisions.

Evidential strategic use makes institutions to be aligned in terms of goal(s) and feedback. Curriculum planning, staffing and support are informed by enrollment statistics, graduation rates and comments made by students. With qualitative knowledge of educators and learners, these data lead to more responses and adaptable institutions (Vanlommel et al., 2017).

Continuous feedback loops are also useful in institutional decision making. Data-driven institutions involve continuous monitoring and evaluation as opposed to using periodical assessment. Such practice promotes prompt adjustments, creation of a continuous improvement culture, which is consistent with evidence-based values.

5.3 Accountability, Evaluation and Performance Measurement

One of the key factors of evidence-based decision making in education systems is accountability. Performance measurement frameworks rely on data in measuring the performance of institutions, programs, policies. These frameworks usually incorporate standardized pointers like test scores and rates of completion and enlistment results.

Although, accountability mechanisms are able to enhance transparency and change, they create issues concerning the narrowing of educational priorities. Christos and Giovoo (2001) enumerate that overemphasis can lead teachers to teach towards the test or overlook the overall education objectives like social development and critical thinking. This is because even in the evidentiary accountability systems, there has to be a balance in measurement and holistic perspective on educational quality (Goyal, 2025).

Assessment is very important in the maintenance of evidence-based decisions producing significant results. Strict assessment tools can be used to determine whether the policies and institutional programs fulfil their intended objectives and unintended outcomes. Results of evaluation are used to make decisions in future refining the process and causing learning within an institution and system (Schildkamp et al., 2016).

5.4 Knowledge Mobilization and Stakeholder Engagement

Evidence based decision making entails proper interactions with the stakeholders, such as educators, students, parents and the community members. Stakeholder views also help in contextual knowledge to complement interpretation of data and the fact that decisions made are more relevant. Inclusive participation creates an understanding of the common ownership of evidence-based moves and encourages a successful implementation.

Knowledge mobilization, which is explained by communication and application of research evidence to practice, is practiced. It is also important that complex research findings should be translated into easy-to-use formats so that they can be utilized by educators and administrators. The link between research and action can be achieved through clear communication strategies which keep evidence contextual as opposed to abstract.

The knowledge mobilization of researchers and practitioners is enhanced by collaborative partnerships. When the stakeholders are present in the research process, the results will be more substantiated to meet the real needs and limitations. These types of partnerships increase the effects of research with data in administering education policy and practice (Weiss, 1998).

5.5 Compromises and Tensions in the Evidence-Based Decision Making

Evidence-based decision making in education has several challenges despite its leverage potentiality. A significant conflict is one of policy and research cycles. The intensive research can take long periods of data gathering and analysis, and policymakers can need fast solutions to urgent matters.

The other issue is the selective application or misuse of evidence. Evidence can also be employed strategically to rationalize decisions that have been made in advance than to lead to an open investigation. This means that disclosing information on the source of data, the methodologies and restrictions of that data are needed to ensure integrity in the use of evidence (Eynon, 2013).

The evidence-based practices adoption is also impacted by capacity constraints. The institutions and those making the policies might not have the information or the necessary resources to collate, analyze and interpret data to their advantage. These issues can be met by investing in data literacy, infrastructures and collaborative cultures where evidence-based conversation is appreciated.

6. EDUCATIONAL TECHNOLOGIES AND LEARNING ANALYTICS IN DATA-INFORMED EDUCATION

6.1 Role of Educational Technologies in Data Generation

Data-informed educational research and decision making are based heavily on the use of educational technologies, which help to produce data in large-scale. Online educational platforms, learning management system, virtual classroom, adaptive learning, and assessment platforms constantly gather information about learners conduct, interest and achievement. Such technologies have given educators and researchers the opportunity to access more than ever before in real-time and longitudinal data relating to education.

Application of technology in teaching and learning has changed the traditional learning processes. Where a previous classroom interaction was weakly ephemeral and therefore hard to replicate, it is now captured in digital remains, and its learning activity can be subsequently analyzed in a systematic way. Such a change allows tracking student progress more accurately and provides the ability to provide feedback and intervention in time. Consequently, educational technologies are being used as data infrastructures that support research and evidence-based practice, in addition to being used as instructional systems (Katz & Dack, 2014).

Nevertheless, data collection through technology should be collected or implemented in a well-thought manner. When using technologies, they should be in line with the pedagogical goals and research objectives in order to make sure that gathered data have a meaning. Ineffectively designed systems may lead to the production of vast amounts of data that cannot be used extensively in education, and this makes deliberate inclusion of technology in data-informed education a commonly sought solution.

6.2 Learning Analytics for Instructional Improvement

Learning analytics is the study of educational data to clarify and enhance learning processes and outcomes. Learning analytics can be used to inform learning by analyzing patterns of student engagement, performance, and progression and using this information to inform learning decisions. Teachers can apply such insights to offer extra support to students and adjust the teaching methods.

Personalized learning with the help of analytics-provided feedback mechanisms would help to adjust the teaching process to individual needs of the learner. Data are represented through dashboards and visualization to create easily understandable formats, which allow educators to process information in a light manner. In the hands of skilled professionals, learning analytics enable teachers to not only respond flexibly to changes in their process but also make all necessary decisions ahead of time, making the teaching process more responsive (Kippers et al., 2018).

Although these are the positive aspects of learning analytics, it has to be used carefully. Excessive use of predictive models can simplify the learning processes and may label students according to the risk categorizations. The application of analytics should be used ethically, and the application should be transparent, interpreted contextually, and evaluated continuously to check the impact on learners.

6.3 Analytics to be used at the Institutional and System level

Learning analytics is beneficial to institutional and system-wide decision making beyond the classroom. Aggregated data is utilised by educational leaders to determine the effectiveness of programs and the allocation of resources and performance of institutions. Analytics is a tool that helps in evidence-based strategic planning as it will give insights into enrollment trends, the retention rate, and also the learning outcomes (Van der Kleij et al., 2015).

On the system level, analytics can be used in policy assessment and reform, based on which patterns in schools or regions are identified. Comparative studies raise the awareness of differences and endorse the specific interventions to advance equity and access. These applications reflect the role of analytics in the systemic improvement through the connection of the data and decision making on several levels.

Nonetheless, institutional and system level analytics demand effective data governance frameworks. The interoperability, accuracy of data, and their security is crucial to rely on the analysis. In the absence of good governance, analytics efforts are likely to yield false conclusions that could lead to lack of confidence in the use of data in decision making (Goyal et al., 2025).

6.4 Technological Use Ethical, Privacy, and Equity

Educational technologies and analytics create major ethical and privacy concerns. Student information usually consists of sensitive data concerning academic achievement, conduct and individual traits. To ensure that this information is safely kept, regulations of the law and ethical guidelines that place the rights and autonomy of learners come first must be followed.

One principle of ethics of data-informed education is transparency. Students and teachers are supposed to know which data are used, with which purposes, and what are the data gathered. The presence of informed consent and communication leads to ethically appropriate use of educational technologies (Hamilton et al., 2009).

Equity is also a factor that needs to be considered. The technology-enhanced analytics can serve to solidify the existing inequalities without even intending to do so in case the data is more biased or depicts uneven allocation of resources. The equitable design and implementation can be ensured when a critical analysis of the sources of data, models of analysis and decision making is conducted. Ethical models assist in making sure that technology can reinforce non-discriminatory and fair educational achievements.

6.5 Future Projections and New Trends

Other new technologies like artificial intelligence and smarter analytics will most probably continue to influence data-based education. Learner-centered systems that change dynamically to meet the needs of learners are promising in improving the concept of personalization and engagement. Natural language processing and multimodal analytics enable the extension of the scope of data to be analyzed and more information about a learning experience is provided.

The integration of technology and the human judgment is also a prerequisite in the future developments. Instead of emerging tools being used to substitute educators, more and more they can aid in decision making providing interpretable insights. Such anthropocentric methodology is in line with the ideas of data-informed education that respects professional knowledge and empirical findings.

Since education systems are undergoing transformation ongoing endeavors must be made in capacity building, ethical governance, and interdisciplinary collaboration to maintain data-informed practices. It is possible to use the educational technologies in a responsible manner and improve how the stakeholders make evidence-based decisions without unjustly damaging the human values that support education. Such a prospective view preconditions the final part of the chapter, which finalizes the main findings and gives recommendations regarding the research, policy, and practice (Zala-Mezö et al., 2018).

CONCLUSION

This increased focus on both data-guided educational research studies, and evidence-based decision making is symptomatic of a larger change in how contemporary education system conceptualizes and enhances learning. As has been shown in this chapter, this systematization of data and research evidence empowers educators, institutional leaders and policymakers to make better, more accountable and transparent decisions. Combining both empirical investigations grounded in the educational practice with the consideration of the complexity of a situation, data-driven methods can offer a solid basis in improving the effectiveness of instruction, the performance of an institution, and the effectiveness of the entire system.

Simultaneously, the chapter brings out the point that the process of evidence based decision making in education is not a purely technical process. The appropriate use of data relies on quality research methods, professionalism and ethical policies. The educational technologies and learning analytics provide potent tools to create insights, and their effect depends on the way evidence is interpreted and implemented in the real-life scenario. Concerns about data quality, privacy, equity, and stakeholder involvement serve as the reminder of the importance of reflective and responsible data practices that do not overlook the importance of values and diversity of the educational communities.

In the future, the data-informed education systems will be sustainably organized through maintaining a balance between analytical innovation and human-centered values. To imprint evidence in purposeful action, investment in areas related to developing and sustaining data literacy, choosing, and performing methods supported by shared culture is a necessity. With the further development of the educational environment, evidence-based decision making might be considered as a lifelong learning and adaptation process instead of a predetermined set of solutions. Combining data, research, and professional experience, the contemporary educational systems will be able not only to promote continuous improvement but also to make the educational decisions oriented to the more general social objectives and the comprehensive development of learners.

REFERENCES

Bertrand, M., & Marsh, J. A. (2015). Teachers' sensemaking of data and implications for equity. *American Educational Research Journal, 52*(5), 861–893. DOI: 10.3102/0002831215599251

Black, P., & Wiliam, D. (1998). Assessment and classroom learning. *Assessment in Education: Principles, Policy & Practice, 5*(1), 7–63. DOI: 10.1080/0969595980050102

Brown, C. (Ed.). (2015). *Leading the use of research and evidence in schools*. Institute of Education Press.

Datnow, A., & Hubbard, L. (2015). Teachers' use of assessment data to inform instruction. *Teachers College Record, 117*(4), 1–26. DOI: 10.1177/016146811511700408

Datnow, A., & Park, V. (2018). Equity and data use in schools. *Journal of Educational Change, 19*(2), 131–152. DOI: 10.1007/s10833-018-9323-6

Datnow, A., Park, V., & Kennedy-Lewis, B. (2013). Affordances and constraints in teacher collaboration for data use. *Journal of Educational Administration, 51*(3), 341–362. DOI: 10.1108/09578231311311500

Earl, L. (2015). Reflections on leading research and evidence use in schools. In *Leading the Use of Research and Evidence in Schools* (pp. 146–152).

Earl, L. M., & Katz, S. (2006). *Leading schools in a data-rich world*. Corwin Press.

Eynon, R. (2013). The rise of big data: What does it mean for education? *Learning, Media and Technology, 38*(3), 237–240. DOI: 10.1080/17439884.2013.771783

Farley-Ripple, E., May, H., Karpyn, A., Tilley, K., & McDonough, K. (2018). Rethinking connections between research and practice in education. *Educational Researcher, 47*(4), 235–245. DOI: 10.3102/0013189X18761042

Goyal, N. K. (2025). Security and privacy in IoT, fog, and blockchain networks. In *Energy-Efficient Deep Learning Approaches in IoT, Fog, and Green Blockchain Revolution* (pp. 371–398). IGI Global. https://doi.org/DOI: 10.4018/979-8-3373-0300-0.ch015

Goyal, N. K. (2025). Weaponizing misinformation and cyberattacks on supply chains. In *Mass Media and Impact of Fake News on Supply Chains* (pp. 177–210). IGI Global., DOI: 10.4018/979-8-3373-2175-2.ch007

Goyal, N. K., Dandotiya, M., Kumari, M., Kaloria, S., & Anushya, A. (2025). AI-powered haptic devices for patient rehabilitation. In *Integrating AI With Haptic Systems for Smarter Healthcare Solutions* (pp. 143–170). IGI Global., DOI: 10.4018/979-8-3373-2307-7.ch007

Goyal, N. K., Dandotiya, M., Kumari, M., Sheikh, M. F., & Sharma, S. (2025). Emerging job roles in the tourism sector leveraging artificial intelligence. In *Empowering Sustainable Performance and Competitive Advantage in Tourism* (pp. 89–126). IGI Global., DOI: 10.4018/979-8-3373-4546-8.ch004

Goyal, N. K., Dandotiya, M., Qurashi, J. A., Kumari, M., & Sharma, S. (2025). AI-driven predictive analytics for disease management. In *Utilizing AI of Medical Things for Healthcare Security and Sustainability* (pp. 231–276). IGI Global., DOI: 10.4018/979-8-3373-0690-2.ch008

Goyal, N. K., Kumari, M., Kushwah, V., Dandotiya, M., & Vijay, A. (2025). Evaluating blockchain security: Trade-offs in consensus mechanisms. *IET Conference Proceedings,* 2024(38), 80–88. https://doi.org/DOI: 10.1049/icp.2025.0775

Hamilton, L. S., Stecher, B. M., & Yuan, K. (2009). *Standards-based reform in the United States*. RAND Corporation.

Hargreaves, A., & Braun, H. (2013). *Data-driven improvement and accountability*. National Education Policy Center.

Katz, S., & Dack, L. A. (2014). Towards a culture of inquiry for data use in schools. *Studies in Educational Evaluation, 42*, 35–40. DOI: 10.1016/j.stueduc.2013.10.006

Kippers, W. B., Poortman, C. L., Schildkamp, K., & Visscher, A. J. (2018). Data literacy challenges for educators. *Studies in Educational Evaluation, 56*, 21–31. DOI: 10.1016/j.stueduc.2017.11.001

Lai, M. K., & Schildkamp, K. (2013). Data-based decision making: An overview. In *Data-Based Decision Making in Education* (pp. 9–21). Springer. DOI: 10.1007/978-94-007-4816-3_2

Mandinach, E., Honey, M., Light, D., & Brunner, C. (2008). A conceptual framework for data-driven decision-making. In *Data-Driven School Improvement* (pp. 13–31). Teachers College Press.

Mandinach, E. B., & Gummer, E. S. (2013). A systemic view of implementing data literacy in educator preparation. *Educational Researcher, 42*(1), 30–37. DOI: 10.3102/0013189X12459803

Marsh, J. A., Pane, J. F., & Hamilton, L. S. (2006). *Making sense of data-driven decision making in education*. RAND Corporation.

Poortman, C. L., & Schildkamp, K. (2016). Solving student achievement-focused problems with data use interventions. *Teaching and Teacher Education, 60*, 425–433. DOI: 10.1016/j.tate.2016.06.010

Rickinson, M., de Bruin, K., Walsh, L., & Hall, M. (2017). What can evidence-use in practice learn from evidence-use in policy? *Educational Research, 59*(2), 173–189. DOI: 10.1080/00131881.2017.1304306

Schildkamp, K., Karbautzki, L., & Vanhoof, J. (2014). Exploring data use practices around Europe. *Studies in Educational Evaluation, 42*, 15–24. DOI: 10.1016/j.stueduc.2013.10.007

Schildkamp, K., & Poortman, C. L. (2015). Factors influencing the functioning of data teams. *Teachers College Record, 117*(4), 1–42. DOI: 10.1177/016146811511700403

Schildkamp, K., Poortman, C. L., & Handelzalts, A. (2016). Data teams for school improvement. *School Effectiveness and School Improvement, 27*(2), 228–254. DOI: 10.1080/09243453.2015.1056192

Van der Kleij, F. M., Vermeulen, J. A., Schildkamp, K., & Eggen, T. J. H. M. (2015). Integrating data-based decision making and formative assessment. *Assessment in Education: Principles, Policy & Practice, 22*, 324–343. DOI: 10.1080/0969594X.2014.999024

Van Geel, M., Keuning, T., Visscher, A. J., & Fox, J. P. (2016). Effects of a school-wide data-based decision-making intervention. *American Educational Research Journal, 53*(2), 360–394. DOI: 10.3102/0002831216637346

Vanlommel, K., Van Gasse, R., Vanhoof, J., & Van Petegem, P. (2017). Teachers' decision-making: Data-based or intuition driven? *International Journal of Educational Research, 83*, 75–83. DOI: 10.1016/j.ijer.2017.02.013

Wayman, J. C., Jimerson, J. B., & Cho, V. (2012). Organizational considerations in establishing the data-informed district. *School Effectiveness and School Improvement, 23*(2), 159–178. DOI: 10.1080/09243453.2011.652124

Weick, K. E. (1995). Sensemaking in organizations. *Sage (Atlanta, Ga.).*

Weiss, C. H. (1998). Have we learned anything new about the use of evaluation? *The American Journal of Evaluation, 19*(1), 21–33. DOI: 10.1177/109821409801900103

Zala-Mezö, E., Strauss, N. C., Müller, D., Häbig, J., Kuster, R., Herzig, P., & Unterweger, G. (2018). Use of research results to improve student participation. *ICSEI Conference Proceedings*.

Compilation of References

Abraham, R., Schneider, J., & vom Brocke, J. (2019). Data governance: A conceptual framework, structured review, and research agenda. *International Journal of Information Management, 49*, 424–438. Advance online publication. DOI: 10.1016/j.ijinfomgt.2019.07.008

Abulibdeh, A., Zaidan, E., & Abulibdeh, R. (2024). Navigating the confluence of artificial intelligence and education for sustainable development in the era of Industry 4.0: Challenges, opportunities, and ethical dimensions. *Journal of Cleaner Production, 437*, 140527. Advance online publication. DOI: 10.1016/j.jclepro.2023.140527

Aburas, R., Nurunnabi, M., & Atyah, R. (2021). Tensions between local and international accreditation: Insights into interior design learning outcomes. *The International Journal of Design Education, 15*(1), 145–164. DOI: 10.18848/2325-128X/CGP/v15i01/145-164

Accreditation Board for Engineering and Technology (ABET). (2025). Criteria for Accrediting Engineering Programs, 2025-2026. Available online: https://www.abet.org/accreditation/accreditation-criteria/criteria-for-accrediting-engineering-programs-2025-2026/ (Accessed March 2025)

Adagale, A. S. (2015). Curriculum development in higher education. *International Journal of Applied Research, 1*(11), 602–605. https://www.allresearchjournal.com/archives/2015/vol1issue11/PartI/1-11-80.pdf

Ajzen, I. (1991). The theory of planned behavior. *Organizational Behavior and Human Decision Processes, 50*(2), 179–211. DOI: 10.1016/0749-5978(91)90020-T

Alam, A., & Mohanty, A. (2024). Integrated constructive robotics in education (ICRE) model: A paradigmatic framework for transformative learning in educational ecosystem. *Cogent Education, 11*(1), 2324487. DOI: 10.1080/2331186X.2024.2324487

Aldana-Rivera, E., Tafur-Castillo, J., Gil, I., & Mejía, C. (2019). Práctica pedagógica de emprendimiento en docentes de educación superior en Institución Educativa Universitaria de Barranquia. *Archivos Venezolanos de Farmacología y Terapéutica, 38*(2), 9–18.

Almasyhari, A. K., Rachmadani, W. S., Sari, Y. P., & Basrowi, . (2025). Strategic decision-making: Linking corporate choices, social responsibility, and environmental accounting in waste management. *Social Sciences & Humanities Open, 11*, 101404. DOI: 10.1016/j.ssaho.2025.101404

Al-Qahtani, M., Zguir, M. F., Ari, I., & Koç, M. (2022). Female Entrepreneurship for Sustainable Economy and Development—Challenges, Drivers, and Suggested Policies for Resource-Rich Countries. *Sustainability (Basel), 14*(20), 13412. DOI: 10.3390/su142013412

Alzahrani, B., Bahitham, H., & Elshennawy, A. (2021). Exploring the applicability of Quality 4.0 in higher education institutions. *Proceedings of the 2021 IEMS Conference*, 27, 1-8. DOI: 10.62704/10057/24719

Amir, M. T., & Prabawani, B. (2023). Sustainability-oriented innovation through shaping the ecosystem; a case of an e-bus industry in Indonesia. *Cogent Business & Management, 10*(2), 1–20. DOI: 10.1080/23311975.2023.2218681

Anagnostopoulou, E., Grammatikos, N. A., Apostolou, D., & Mentzas, G. (2024, September). Trustworthy AI in education: A roadmap for ethical and effective implementation. In *Proceedings of the 13th Hellenic Conference on Artificial Intelligence (SETN 2024)*. ACM. DOI: 10.1145/3688671.3688781

Anand, A., & Singh, P. (2025). Interdisciplinary studies: Issues, perspectives, and challenges from National Education Program 2020. In *Integrating personalized learning methods into STEAM education* (pp. 233–260). IGI Global. DOI: 10.4018/979-8-3693-7718-5.ch011

Andalibi, M. (2019). Early incorporation of entrepreneurship mindset in an engineering curriculum. *International Journal of Higher Education, 8*(4), 98–107. DOI: 10.5430/ijhe.v8n4p98

Anderson, C. C., Denich, M., Warchold, A., Kropp, J. P., & Pradhan, P. (2022). A systems model of SDG target influence on the 2030 Agenda for Sustainable Development. *Sustainability Science, 17*(4), 1459–1472. DOI: 10.1007/s11625-021-01040-8 PMID: 34659581

Angrisani, M., Dell'Anno, D., & Hockaday, T. (2022). From ecosystem to community. Combining entrepreneurship and university engagement in an open innovation perspective. *International Journal of Technology Management, 88*(1), 71–92. DOI: 10.1504/IJTM.2022.121443

An, Q., Yang, J., Xu, X., Zhang, H., & Zhang, H. (2024). Decoding AI ethics from users' lens in education. *Heliyon, 10*(20), e39357. Advance online publication. DOI: 10.1016/j.heliyon.2024.e39357 PMID: 39640624

An, Y., & Mindrila, D. (2020). Strategies and tools used for learner-centered instruction. *International Journal of Technology in Education and Science, 4*(2), 133–143. https://ijtes.net/index.php/ijtes/article/view/1595. DOI: 10.46328/ijtes.v4i2.74

Aoki, T. T. (1993). Legitimating lived curriculum: Toward a curricular landscape of multiplicity. *Journal of Curriculum and Supervision, 8*(3), 255–268.

Argüello Villa, I. M. (2025). AI-powered learning analytics in Education 4.0: A study of faculty perceptions in Adelaide Universities [Thesis]. Torrens Figshare. https://torrens.figshare.com/articles/thesis/AI-Powered_Learning_Analytics_in_Education_4_0_A_Study_of_Faculty_Perceptions_in_Adelaide_Universities_/30472238

Armstrong, C. (2021). Key methods used in qualitative document analysis. *OSF Preprints*, 1-9. DOI: 10.2139/ssrn.3996213

Arockia, V. J., Vettriselvan, R., Rajesh, D., & Cheelo, C. (2025). Leveraging AI and learning analytics for enhanced distance learning: Transformation in education. In *AI and learning analytics in distance learning*. IGI Global., DOI: 10.4018/979-8-3693-7195-4.ch008

Arora, V. (2025). Shifting employment paradigms: Role of the gig economy in transforming traditional jobs. *Indian Journal of Accounting, 57*(1), 38–50. DOI: 10.63637/ija.v57i1.38-50

Arthur, W. B. (2009). *The nature of technology: What it is and how it evolves*. Free Press.

Atanassov, K. T. (1986). Intuitionistic fuzzy sets. *Fuzzy Sets and Systems, 20*(1), 87–96. DOI: 10.1016/S0165-0114(86)80034-3

Ayoub, M. T., Malik, A. H., Tariq, M. J., Ali, S., Abbas, N., & Ftima, M. (2024). 21st Century Skills 4 C's in Higher Education English Language Classroom: Teachers' Perspectives. [JALT]. *Journal of Applied Linguistics and TESOL, 7*(4), 872–883.

Bandura, A. (1977). *Social learning theory*. Prentice Hall.

Banerjee, A.. (2024). Ethical considerations in AI-driven education: Balancing innovation with responsibility. *Journal of Educational Technology, 50*(3), 123–140.

Bansah, A. K., & Agyei, D. D. (2022). Perceived convenience, usefulness, effectiveness and user acceptance of information technology: Evaluating students' experiences of a learning management system. *Technology, Pedagogy and Education, 31*(4), 431–449. DOI: 10.1080/1475939X.2022.2027267

Baskoro, G. (2023). From VUCA to BANI: A Challenge of Strategic Environment for Higher Education in Indonesia. Proceedings of the 3rd International Conference on Business and Engineering Management (ICONBEM 2022) In Advances in Economics, Business and Management Research (pp. 229–235). DOI: 10.2991/978-94-6463-216-3_18

Bates, T., Cobo, C., Mariño, O., & Wheeler, S. (2020). Can artificial intelligence transform higher education? *International Journal of Educational Technology in Higher Education, 17*(42), 42. Advance online publication. DOI: 10.1186/s41239-020-00218-x

Baumber, J. (2023). Developing Ideas-Informed Young Citizens. In *The Ideas-Informed Society* (pp. 265–284). Emerald Publishing Limited. DOI: 10.1108/978-1-83753-010-620231021

Baumol, W. J. (2018). Entrepreneurship in Economic Theory: In The Microtheory of Innovative Entrepreneurship (pp. 9–22). Princeton University Press. DOI: 10.2307/j.ctt21668j9.7

Baumol, W. J. (1968). Entrepreneurship in economic theory. *The American Economic Review, 58*, 64–71.

Beagon, U., & Bowe, B. (2023). Understanding professional skills in engineering education: A phenomenographic study of faculty conceptions. *Journal of Engineering Education, 112*(4), 1109–1144. DOI: 10.1002/jee.20556

Beauchamp, T. L., & Childress, J. F. (2019). *Principles of biomedical ethics* (8th ed.). Oxford University Press.

Becker, G. S. (1993). *The economic way of looking at life* [Nobel Prize lecture]. University of Chicago.

Bellman, R. E., & Zadeh, L. A. (1970). Decision making in a fuzzy environment. *Management Science, 17*(4), B-141–B-164. DOI: 10.1287/mnsc.17.4.B141

Bernard, D. T. K. (2015). Microfinance Services: Facilitating Entrepreneurial Success of Poor Women. *Review of Contemporary Business Research, 4*(2), 57–66. DOI: 10.15640/rcbr.v4n2a5

Bertrand, M., & Marsh, J. A. (2015). Teachers' sensemaking of data and implications for equity. *American Educational Research Journal, 52*(5), 861–893. DOI: 10.3102/0002831215599251

Bertsimas, D., & Thiele, A. (2006). Robust and data-driven optimization: Modern decision-making under uncertainty. In *Tutorials in operations research* (pp. 95–122). INFORMS. DOI: 10.1287/educ.1063.0022

Bezanilla, M. J., García-Olalla, A., Paños-Castro, J., & Arruti, A. (2020). Developing the entrepreneurial university: Factors of influence. *Sustainability (Basel), 12*(3), 842. DOI: 10.3390/su12030842

Bhargava, P. (2022, October 20). The increasing importance of micro-credentials on your international college applications. The Economic Times. https://economictimes.indiatimes.com/nri/study/the-increasing-importance-of-micro-credentials-on-your-international-college-applications/articleshow/94989354.cms

Bhuttah, T. M., Xusheng, Q., Abid, M. N., & Sharma, S. (2024). Enhancing student critical thinking and learning outcomes through innovative pedagogical approaches in higher education: The mediating role of inclusive leadership. *Scientific Reports, 14*(1), 24362. https://www.nature.com/articles/s41598-024-75379-0. DOI: 10.1038/s41598-024-75379-0 PMID: 39420057

Bichsel, J. (2012). *Analytics in higher education: Benefits, barriers, progress, and recommendations*. EDUCAUSE Center for Applied Research.

Biesta, G. (2015). *The beautiful risk of education*. Routledge. DOI: 10.4324/9781315635866

Biggs, J. (1996). Enhancing teaching through constructive alignment. *Higher Education, 32*(3), 347–364. DOI: 10.1007/BF00138871

Billett, S. (2011). Integrating experiences in workplace and university settings: A conceptual perspective. In *Developing learning professionals: Integrating experiences in university and practice settings* (pp. 21–40). Springer. DOI: 10.1007/978-90-481-3937-8_2

Black, P., & Wiliam, D. (1998). Assessment and classroom learning. *Assessment in Education: Principles, Policy & Practice, 5*(1), 7–63. DOI: 10.1080/0969595980050102

Blumberg, P. (2009). *Developing learner-centered teaching: A practical guide for faculty*. Jossey-Bass.

Bond, M., Bedenlier, S., Marín, V. I., & Händel, M. (2021). Emergency remote teaching in higher education: Mapping the first global online semester. *International Journal of Educational Technology in Higher Education, 18*(1), 50. DOI: 10.1186/s41239-021-00282-x PMID: 34778537

Bond, M., Khosravi, H., De Laat, M., Bergdahl, N., & Gašević, D. (2023). A meta-analysis of student engagement in online learning. *Educational Psychology Review, 35*(2), 1–29.

Borkar, P. (2023). NEP 2020: New structural changes in curriculum and pedagogy in education. https://www.iitms.co.in/blog/new-structural-changes-in-curriculum-and-pedagogy-in-education.html

Borsatto, J. M. L. S., Marcolin, C. B., Abdalla, E. C., & Amaral, F. D. (2024). Aligning community outreach initiatives with SDGs in a higher education institution with artificial intelligence. *Cleaner and Responsible Consumption, 12*, 100160. Advance online publication. DOI: 10.1016/j.clrc.2023.100160

Bozorgi, J., & Mohammad, J. (2021). The Culture of the University Entrepreneurship Ecosystem, The Drivers of Social Entrepreneurship Development. *Journal of Cultural Management, 15*(51), 45–57.

Braun, V., & Clarke, V. (2012). Thematic analysis. In H. Cooper, P. M. Camic, D. L. Long, A. T. Panter, D. Rindskopf, & K. J. Sher (Eds.), *APA Handbook of Research Methods in psychology, Vol. 2: Research Designs: Quantitative, Qualitative, Neuropsychological, and Biological* (pp. 57–71). American Psychological Association. DOI: 10.1037/13620-004

Bridgstock, R. (2009). The graduate attributes we've overlooked: Enhancing graduate employability through career management skills. *Higher Education Research & Development, 28*(1), 31–44. DOI: 10.1080/07294360802444347

Brinkmann, S. (2015). Learner-centred education reforms in India: The missing piece of teachers' beliefs. *Policy Futures in Education, 13*(3), 342–359. https://journals.sagepub.com/doi/10.1177/1478210315569038. DOI: 10.1177/1478210315569038

Broo, D. G., Kaynak, O., & Sait, S. M. (2022). Rethinking engineering education at the age of industry 5.0. *Journal of Industrial Information Integration, 25*, 100311. DOI: 10.1016/j.jii.2021.100311

Brown, C. (Ed.). (2015). *Leading the use of research and evidence in schools*. Institute of Education Press.

Brown, C., Luzmore, R., & Groß Ophoff, J. (2023). Facilitating the ideas-informed society: A systematic review. *Emerald Open Research, 1*(1). Advance online publication. DOI: 10.1108/EOR-01-2023-0008

Bushuyev, S., Piliuhina, K., & Chetin, E. (2023). Transformation of values of the high technology projects from a VUCA to a BANI environment model. *Innovative Technologies and Scientific Solutions for Industries, 2*(24), 191–199. DOI: 10.30837/ITSSI.2023.24.191

Bustince, H., Barrenechea, E., Pagola, M., Fernandez, J., Xu, Z., Bedregal, B., Montero, J., Hagras, H., Herrera, F., & De Baets, B. (2016). A historical account of types of fuzzy sets and their relationships. *IEEE Transactions on Fuzzy Systems, 24*(1), 179–194. DOI: 10.1109/TFUZZ.2015.2451692

Butler, C., & Zander, L. (2008). The business of teaching and learning through multicultural teams. *Journal of Teaching in International Business, 19*(2), 192–218. DOI: 10.1080/08975930802118903

Butt, A. N., & Dimitrijević, B. (2022). Multidisciplinary and Transdisciplinary Collaboration in Nature-Based Design of Sustainable Architecture and Urbanism. *Sustainability (Basel), 14*(16), 10339. DOI: 10.3390/su141610339

Cabero-Almenara, J., Palacios-Rodríguez, A., Loaiza-Aguirre, M. I., & Andrade-Abarca, P. S. (2024). The impact of pedagogical beliefs on the adoption of generative AI in higher education: Predictive model from UTAUT2. *Frontiers in Artificial Intelligence, 7*, 1497705. Advance online publication. DOI: 10.3389/frai.2024.1497705 PMID: 39484153

Cantillon, B. J., & Higgs, H. (1932). Essai sur la Nature du Commerce en General. *Journal of the Royal Statistical Society, 95*(1), 131–133. DOI: 10.2307/2341977

Cardno, C. (2018). Policy document analysis: A practical educational leadership tool and a qualitative research method. *Educational Administration: Theory and Practice, 24*(4), 623–640. DOI: 10.14527/kuey.2018.016

Caruana, S. (2011). Accreditation of soft skills in higher education using ICT. *Soft Skill Accreditation*, available at https://www.academia.edu/1561384/Accreditation_of_Soft_Skills_in_Higher_Education_using_ICT (Accessed May 2024)

CASEL. (2023). *What is the CASEL framework?* Collaborative for Academic, Social, and Emotional Learning. https://casel.org

Castro, G. P. B., Chiappe, A., Rodríguez, D. F. B., & Sepulveda, F. G. (2024). Harnessing AI for Education 4.0: Drivers of personalized learning. *Electronic Journal of e-Learning, 22*(5), 01–14. Advance online publication. DOI: 10.34190/ejel.22.5.3467

Chan, C. K. Y., & Hu, W. (2023). Students' voices on generative AI: Perceptions, benefits, and challenges in higher education. *International Journal of Educational Technology in Higher Education*, *4*(1), 100129. DOI: 10.1186/s41239-023-00411-8

Chandel, T. A. (2024). Artificial intelligence in the workplace: The future of learning and developments. In *Gaming, wellness, and technology in the bold global workforce* (pp. 203–234). IGI Global., DOI: 10.4018/979-8-3373-5322-7.ch007

Chandel, T. A. (2024). Emerging technology: Present and future generation leadership. In *Impact of new technology on next-generation leadership* (pp. 1–28). IGI Global., DOI: 10.4018/979-8-3693-1946-8.ch001

Chandel, T. A. (2025). E-collaboration technologies with generative AI tools. In *Humans and generative AI tools for collaborative* (pp. 369–402). IGI Global., DOI: 10.4018/979-8-3693-8332-2.ch016

Chan, M. M., Rosales, M., Hernandez-Rizzardini, R., & Amado-Salvatierra, H. R. (2025). Ethical AI in education: A proposed model for responsible integration. In *2025 IEEE Global Engineering Education Conference (EDUCON)*. IEEE. DOI: 10.1109/EDUCON62633.2025.11016451

Chatti, M. A., Dyckhoff, A. L., Schroeder, U., & Thüs, H. (2014). Exploring student interactions: Learning analytics tools for student tracking. In *Lecture Notes in Computer Science* (pp. 50–61). Springer., DOI: 10.1007/978-3-319-20609-7_6

Chen, P., & Zhang, C.-Y. (2014). Data-intensive applications, challenges, techniques and technologies: A survey on big data. *Information Sciences*, *275*, 314–347. DOI: 10.1016/j.ins.2014.01.015

Chen, Q., Yin, H., & Feng, J. (2023). Construction of course content integrating ideas of engineering education accreditation for higher education in China: An example of geochemistry course. *Sustainability (Basel)*, *15*(17), 12709. DOI: 10.3390/su151712709

Chesters, J. (2020). Preparing for successful transitions between education and employment in the twenty-first century. *Journal of Applied Youth Studies*, *3*(2), 133–151. DOI: 10.1007/s43151-020-00002-8

Ciolacu, M., Tehrani, A. F., Binder, L., & Svasta, P. M. (2018). Education 4.0 – Artificial intelligence assisted higher education: Early recognition system with machine learning. In 2018 IEEE 24th International Symposium for Design and Technology in Electronic Packaging (SIITME). IEEE.

Cipriano, C., Tominey, S. L., & Rivera, M. C. (2023). Supporting social and emotional learning in higher education: A review of emerging evidence. *Educational Psychologist*, *58*(1), 1–18.

Clandinin, D. J. (2013). *Engaging in narrative inquiry*. Routledge.

Coach Space. (2024). The role of the right education in helping leaders succeed. https://thecoachspace.com/blog/role-of-education-in-helping-leaders-succeed/

Corbeil, M. E., & Corbeil, J. R. (2021). Establishing trust in artificial intelligence in education. In *Trust, organizations and the digital economy* (pp. 49–60). Routledge., DOI: 10.4324/9781003165965-5

Cosar, M. (2024). Utilizing the eXtreme Gradient Boosting Algorithm for artificial intelligence–supported learning analytics application. The Eurasia Proceedings of Science, Technology, Engineering & Mathematics, 28, 277–285. https://dergipark.org.tr/en/download/article-file/4095327

Crawford, J., Butler-Henderson, K., Rudolph, J., Malkawi, B., Glowatz, M., Burton, R., Magni, P., & Lam, S. (2020). COVID-19: 20 countries' higher education intra-period digital pedagogy responses. *Journal of Applied Learning & Teaching*, *3*(1), 1–20.

Creswell, J. W., & Plano Clark, V. L. (2017). *Designing and conducting mixed methods research* (3rd ed.). Sage Publications.

Csikszentmihalyi, M. (1990). *Flow: The psychology of optimal experience*. Harper & Row.

Cui, Z., & Li, E. (2022). Does Industry-University-Research Cooperation Matter? An Analysis of Its Coupling Effect on Regional Innovation and Economic Development. *Chinese Geographical Science*, *32*(5), 915–930. DOI: 10.1007/s11769-022-1308-y

Dagtekin, M., & Erkalkan, H. (2025). Artificial intelligence literacy and student engagement in higher education: Implications for responsible AI use in learning environments. *Computers and Education: Artificial Intelligence*, *6*, 100223.

Dandotiya, M., Goyal, N. K., Yadav, P., Sankhla, K., & Kumari, M. (2026). GENALYTICS: A deep dive into real-time insights via generative AI. In Elbaghazaoui, B. (Eds.), *Generative AI-powered data architectures* (pp. 105–134). IGI Global Scientific Publishing., DOI: 10.4018/979-8-3373-5616-7.ch005

Daniel, J. (2020). Education and the COVID-19 pandemic. *Prospects*, *49*(1-2), 91–96. DOI: 10.1007/s11125-020-09464-3 PMID: 32313309

Dart, S., Trad, S., & Blackmore, K. (2021). Navigating the path from technical engineering to engineering education research: A conceptual model of the transition process. *European Journal of Engineering Education, 46*(6), 1076–1091. DOI: 10.1080/03043797.2021.1992609

Das, D. K. (2025). *Problem-based learning for engineering education: Developing the engineers of the future*. Routledge., DOI: 10.1201/9781003529743

Datnow, A., & Hubbard, L. (2015). Teachers' use of assessment data to inform instruction. *Teachers College Record, 117*(4), 1–26. DOI: 10.1177/016146811511700408

Datnow, A., & Park, V. (2018). Equity and data use in schools. *Journal of Educational Change, 19*(2), 131–152. DOI: 10.1007/s10833-018-9323-6

Datnow, A., Park, V., & Kennedy-Lewis, B. (2013). Affordances and constraints in teacher collaboration for data use. *Journal of Educational Administration, 51*(3), 341–362. DOI: 10.1108/09578231311311500

Davis, F. D. (1989). Perceived usefulness, perceived ease of use, and user acceptance of information technology. *Management Information Systems Quarterly, 13*(3), 319–340. DOI: 10.2307/249008

Dayal, G., Verma, P., & Sehgal, S. (2023). A comprehensive review on the integration of artificial intelligence in the field of education. In *Leveraging AI and emotional intelligence in contemporary business organizations*. IGI Global. DOI: 10.4018/979-8-3693-1902-4.ch020

De Brito, S., & Leitão, J. (2021). Mapping and defining entrepreneurial ecosystems: A systematic literature review. *Knowledge Management Research and Practice, 19*(1), 21–42. DOI: 10.1080/14778238.2020.1751571

De Bruijn-Smolders, M., & Prinsen, F. R. (2024). Effective student engagement with blended learning: A systematic review. *Heliyon, 10*(23), e39439. https://linkinghub.elsevier.com/retrieve/pii/S2405844024154709. DOI: 10.1016/j.heliyon.2024.e39439 PMID: 39687123

De Vries, M. (1977). The entrepreneurial personality - a person at the cross-roads. *Journal of Management Studies, 14*(1), 34–47. DOI: 10.1111/j.1467-6486.1977.tb00616.x

Deci, E. L., & Ryan, R. M. (1985). Intrinsic motivation and self-determination in human behavior. Springer. https://link.springer.com/book/10.1007/978-1-4899-2271-7

Dewar, J. (2017). Call for tertiary sector to gear toward University 4.0. https://www.ceda.com.au/news-and-resources/news/education/call-for-tertiary-sector-to-gear-toward-university. (Accessed October 2024)

Dewey, J. (1938). *Experience and education*. Macmillan.

Dhanabhakyam, M. P. M. (2021). Sustainability Strategies for Developing SMEs and Entrepreneurship. In Baporikar, N. (Ed.), *Handbook of Research on Sustaining SMEs and Entrepreneurial Innovation in the Post-COVID-19 Era* (pp. 527–547). IGI Global., DOI: 10.4018/978-1-7998-6632-9.ch025

Dijkman, J. G., van Haeringen, H., & de Lange, S. J. (1983). Fuzzy numbers. *Journal of Mathematical Analysis and Applications*, *92*(2), 301–341. DOI: 10.1016/0022-247X(83)90253-6

Dong, Y. C., Zha, Q., Zhang, H., Kou, G., Fujita, H., Chiclana, F., & Herrera-Viedma, E. (2018). Consensus reaching in social network group decision making. *Knowledge-Based Systems*, *162*, 3–13. DOI: 10.1016/j.knosys.2018.06.036

Doyle, E. (2011). Career development needs of low socio-economic status university students. *Australian Journal of Career Development*, *20*(3), 56–65. DOI: 10.1177/103841621102000309

Drishti, I. A. S. (2026). National credit framework. https://www.drishtiias.com/daily-updates/daily-news-analysis/national-credit-framework-1

Duncan, T., & Buskirk-Cohen, A. A. (2011). Exploring learner-centered assessment: A cross-disciplinary approach. *International Journal on Teaching and Learning in Higher Education*, *23*(2), 246–259. https://eric.ed.gov/?id=EJ946150

Durlak, J. A., Weissberg, R. P., Dymnicki, A. B., Taylor, R. D., & Schellinger, K. B. (2011). The impact of enhancing students' social and emotional learning: A meta-analysis of school-based universal interventions. *Child Development*, *82*(1), 405–432. DOI: 10.1111/j.1467-8624.2010.01564.x PMID: 21291449

Dweck, C. S. (2006). *Mindset: The new psychology of success*. Random House.

Dweck, S. C. (2015). Carol Dweck Revisits the "Growth Mindset". *Education Week*, *35*(05), 20–24.

Earl, L. (2015). Reflections on leading research and evidence use in schools. In *Leading the Use of Research and Evidence in Schools* (pp. 146–152).

Earl, L. M., & Katz, S. (2006). *Leading schools in a data-rich world*. Corwin Press.

Eckhardt, J. T., Ciuchta, M. P., & Carpenter, M. (2018). Open innovation, information, and entrepreneurship within platform ecosystems. *Strategic Entrepreneurship Journal, 12*(3), 369–391. DOI: 10.1002/sej.1298

Edu, N. (2025). The influence of international rankings on higher education reforms and institutional strategies. *International Journal of Innovative Social Sciences & Humanities Research, 13*(1), 273–280. DOI: 10.1201/9781351182003-6

edutiip. (2026). Types of regulatory bodies of higher education in India. https://english.edutiips.com/regulatory-bodies-of-higher-education/

Ellikkal, A., & Rajamohan, S. (2023). Factors Influencing Entrepreneurial Intentions and the Role of Entrepreneurship Education in Indian Universities: A Stakeholder Perspective. International. *Journal of Professional Business Review, 8*(7), e02663. DOI: 10.26668/businessreview/2023.v8i7.2663

ElSayary, A. (2025). Fostering ethical digital citizenship: A policy framework for integrating digital ethics in education. In *Prompt engineering and generative AI applications for teaching and learning*. IGI Global., DOI: 10.4018/979-8-3693-7332-3.ch016

Engineers Australia. (2019). *Stage 1 Competency Standard for Engineering Associates*. Available at: https://www.engineersaustralia.org.au/sites/default/files/2025-05/stage-1-competency-standard-engineering-associate-may-25.pdf (Accessed January 2025)

Engineers Australia. (2019). *Stage 1 Competency Standard for Engineering Technologists*. Available at: https://www.engineersaustralia.org.au/sites/default/files/2025-05/stage-1-competency-standard-engineering-technologist-may-25.pdf (Accessed January 2025)

Engineers Australia. (2019). *Stage 1 Competency Standard for Professional Engineer*. Available at: https://www.engineersaustralia.org.au/sites/default/files/2022-07/stage-1-competency-standard-professional-engineer.pdf (Accessed January 2025)

Engineers Ireland. (2021). *Accreditation Criteria* (January 2021). Available at: https://www.engineersireland.ie/LinkClick.aspx?fileticket=Mz3SCCk_uRg=&portalid=0&resourceView=1&utm (Accessed November 2023)

Espinilla, M., Montero, J., & Rodríguez, J. T. (2014). Computational intelligence in decision making. *International Journal of Computational Intelligence Systems, 7*(Suppl. 1), 1–5. DOI: 10.1080/18756891.2014.853925

European Commission. (2020). *A new skills agenda for Europe*. Publications Office of the European Union.

European Network for Accreditation of Engineering Education (EUR-ACE). (2021). *EUR-ACE® Framework Standards and Guidelines* (November 2021). Available at: https://www.enaee.eu/wp-content/uploads/2023/11/EAFSG-approved-4-Nov-2021.pdf (Accessed June 2024)

Evelyn, L. (2023). Curriculum development models. https://www.evelynlearning.com/blog/curriculum-development-models

Exceed, C. (2025). Types, principles & process of curriculum development. https://exeedcollege.com/blog/principles-and-process-of-curriculum-development/

Eynon, R. (2013). The rise of big data: What does it mean for education, technology, and learning? *Learning, Media and Technology*, *38*(3), 237–240. DOI: 10.1080/17439884.2013.771783

Farley-Ripple, E., May, H., Karpyn, A., Tilley, K., & McDonough, K. (2018). Rethinking connections between research and practice in education. *Educational Researcher*, *47*(4), 235–245. DOI: 10.3102/0013189X18761042

Farooqi, A., Das, D., Tripathi, M., Dutta, R., Goyal, N. K., & Sheikh, M. F. (2026). Navigating ethical frontiers in AI-driven geriatric care. In Stolakis, K., & Efthymiou, I. (Eds.), *AI for geriatric care in an aging society* (pp. 243–266). IGI Global Scientific Publishing., DOI: 10.4018/979-8-3373-5462-0.ch009

Felten, P., & Lambert, L. M. (2020). *Relationship-rich education: How human connections drive success in college*. Johns Hopkins University Press. DOI: 10.1353/book.78561

Ferguson, R. (2012). Learning analytics: Drivers, developments and challenges. *International Journal of Technology Enhanced Learning*, *4*(5–6), 304–317. DOI: 10.1504/IJTEL.2012.051816

Fernández-Bedoya, V. H., Meneses-La-Riva, M. E., Suyo-Vega, J. A., & Stephanie Gago-Chávez, J. de J. (2023). Mental health problems of entrepreneurs during the COVID-19 health crisis: Fear, anxiety, and stress. *A systematic review. F1000Research, 12*, 1062. DOI: 10.12688/f1000research.139581.1

Fernández-Salinero De Miguel, C., & García-Álvarez, J. (2020). Graduate's labour insertion through personal contacts. A proposal from the knowledge management. Teoria de La Educacion. *Ediciones Universidad de Salamanca*. DOI: 10.14201/teri.20196

Ferns, S., Campbell, M., & Zegwaard, K. E. (2014). *Work integrated learning. Higher Education Research and Development Society of Australia*. HERDSA Inc.

Floridi, L., Cowls, J., Beltrametti, M., Chatila, R., Chazerand, P., Dignum, V., Luetge, C., Madelin, R., Pagallo, U., Rossi, F., Schafer, B., Valcke, P., & Vayena, E. (2018). AI4People—An ethical framework for a good AI society: Opportunities, risks, principles, and recommendations. *Minds and Machines*, *28*(4), 689–707. DOI: 10.1007/s11023-018-9482-5 PMID: 30930541

Forum, I. A. S. (2024, February 5). Micro-credentials and higher education in India. https://forumias.com/blog/micro-credentials-and-higher-education-in-india/

Fredricks, J. A., Blumenfeld, P. C., & Paris, A. H. (2004). School Engagement: Potential of the Concept, State of the Evidence. *Review of Educational Research*, *74*(1), 59–109. https://journals.sagepub.com/doi/10.3102/00346543074001059. DOI: 10.3102/00346543074001059

Fullan, M. (2016). *The new meaning of educational change* (5th ed.). Teachers College Press.

Futagami, T. (2021). On Motivations for Mobility of International Students Studying at Japanese Research-Intensive Universities. *Journal of Comparative & International Higher Education*, *13*(1), 82–102. DOI: 10.32674/jcihe.v13i1.2100

Gaftandzhieva, S., Hussain, S., Hilcenko, S., Doneva, R., & Boykova, K. (2023). Data-driven decision making in higher education institutions: State-of-play. *International Journal of Advanced Computer Science and Applications*, *14*(6). Advance online publication. DOI: 10.14569/IJACSA.2023.0140642

Galvão, C., Faria, C., Viegas, W., Branco, A., & Goulão, L. (2021). Inquiry in higher education for sustainable development: Crossing disciplinary knowledge boundaries. *International Journal of Sustainability in Higher Education*, *22*(1), 291–307. DOI: 10.1108/IJSHE-02-2020-0068

Gamage, K. A. A., Ekanayake, S. Y., & Dehideniya, S. C. P. (2022). Embedding sustainability in learning and teaching: Lessons Learned and Moving Forward—Approaches in STEM Higher Education Programmes. *Education Sciences*, *12*(3), 225. DOI: 10.3390/educsci12030225

Gašević, D., Dawson, S., & Siemens, G. (2016). *Preparing for the digital university: A review of the history and current state of distance, blended, and online learning*. Athabasca University.

Gazi, A. I. (2025). AI Meets Academia: How Machine Learning is Transforming Higher Education in China. *Journal of Educational Studies*, *3*(3), 1–13. DOI: 10.1108/EMJB-03-2024-0055

Gazi, M. A. I., Mim, A. T., Masud, A. A., Rahman, M. K. H., Amin, M. B., Senathirajah, A. R. B. S., & Oláh, J. (2025). Paving the way of entrepreneurship for university students: The role of innovativeness, technological adaptability, and self-management. *Cogent Education, 12*(1), 2455230. Advance online publication. DOI: 10.1080/2331186X.2025.2455230

Gelso, C. J., & Lent, R. W. (2000). Scientific training and professional practice in counseling psychology. In S. D. Brown & R. W. Lent (Eds.), *Handbook of counseling psychology* (3rd ed., pp. 117–132). Wiley.

Gifford, E., & McKelvey, M. (2019). Knowledge-intensive entrepreneurship and S3: Conceptualizing strategies for sustainability. *Sustainability (Basel), 11*(18), 4824. DOI: 10.3390/su11184824

Glass, C. R., Kociolek, E., Wongtrirat, R., Lynch, R., & Cong, S. (2021). Uneven experiences: The impact of student-faculty interactions on international students' sense of belonging. *Journal of International Students, 11*(2), 1–20.

Glenn, D. (2010). Carol Dweck ' s Mindset. *The Chronicle of Higher Education, 56*, 4–9.

Godsk, M., & Møller, K. L. (2024). Engaging students in higher education with educational technology. *Education and Information Technologies, 30*(3), 2941–2976. https://link.springer.com/article/10.1007/s10639-024-12901-x. DOI: 10.1007/s10639-024-12901-x

Goel, A. K., & Polepeddi, L. (2016). *Jill Watson: A virtual teaching assistant for online education.* Georgia Institute of Technology Research Brief.

Goldstein, P. J., & Katz, R. N. (2005). *Academic analytics: The uses of management information and technology in higher education.* EDUCAUSE.

Gonzalez-Sanchez, J., Chavez-Echeagaray, M. E., VanLehn, K., & Burleson, W. (2011). From behavioral description to a pattern-based model for intelligent tutoring systems. In *Proceedings of the 2011 ACM Symposium on Applied Computing.* ACM. DOI: 10.1145/2578903.2579164

Goodwin, J. R. (2024). What's the difference? A comparison of student-centered teaching methods. *Education Sciences, 14*(7), 736. https://www.mdpi.com/2227-7102/14/7/736. DOI: 10.3390/educsci14070736

Gou, X., Liao, H., Xu, Z. S., & Herrera, F. (2017). Double hierarchy hesitant fuzzy linguistic term set and MULTIMOORA method. *Information Fusion, 38*, 22–34. DOI: 10.1016/j.inffus.2017.02.008

Goyal, N. K. (2025). Security and privacy in IoT, fog, and blockchain networks. In *Energy-Efficient Deep Learning Approaches in IoT, Fog, and Green Blockchain Revolution* (pp. 371–398). IGI Global. https://doi.org/DOI: 10.4018/979-8-3373-0300-0.ch015

Goyal, N. K. (2025). Weaponizing misinformation and cyberattacks on supply chains. In *Mass Media and Impact of Fake News on Supply Chains* (pp. 177–210). IGI Global., DOI: 10.4018/979-8-3373-2175-2.ch007

Goyal, N. K., Dandotiya, M., Kumari, M., Kaloria, S., & Anushya, A. (2025). AI-powered haptic devices for patient rehabilitation. In *Integrating AI With Haptic Systems for Smarter Healthcare Solutions* (pp. 143–170). IGI Global., DOI: 10.4018/979-8-3373-2307-7.ch007

Goyal, N. K., Dandotiya, M., Kumari, M., Sheikh, M. F., & Sharma, S. (2025). Emerging job roles in the tourism sector leveraging artificial intelligence. In *Empowering Sustainable Performance and Competitive Advantage in Tourism* (pp. 89–126). IGI Global., DOI: 10.4018/979-8-3373-4546-8.ch004

Goyal, N. K., Dandotiya, M., Qurashi, J. A., Kumari, M., & Sharma, S. (2025). AI-driven predictive analytics for disease management. In *Utilizing AI of Medical Things for Healthcare Security and Sustainability* (pp. 231–276). IGI Global., DOI: 10.4018/979-8-3373-0690-2.ch008

Goyal, N. K., Kumari, M., Kushwah, V., Dandotiya, M., & Vijay, A. (2025). Evaluating blockchain security: Trade-offs in consensus mechanisms. *IET Conference Proceedings,* 2024(38), 80–88. https://doi.org/DOI: 10.1049/icp.2025.0775

Grabmeier, S. (2020). *BANI versus VUCA: A New Acronym to Describe the World.* Stephan Grabmeier Blog.

Gupta, S., Sabitha, A. S., & Choudhary, P. (2022). Factors affecting user acceptance of AI-driven learning analytics in higher education. *Journal of Educational Technology Systems.*

Hamilton, L. S., Stecher, B. M., & Yuan, K. (2009). *Standards-based reform in the United States.* RAND Corporation.

Handayati, P., Wulandari, D., Soetjipto, B. E., Wibowo, A., & Narmaditya, B. S. (2020). Does entrepreneurship education promote vocational students' entrepreneurial mindset? *Heliyon, 6*(11), e05426. Advance online publication. DOI: 10.1016/j.heliyon.2020.e05426 PMID: 33235932

Hargreaves, A., & Braun, H. (2013). *Data-driven improvement and accountability.* National Education Policy Center.

Harrell, P. E., & Wendt, J. L. (2016). A learner-centered approach to technology integration. In Keengwe, J., & Onchwari, G. (Eds.), *Handbook of research on learner-centered pedagogy in teacher education and professional development* (pp. 1–22). IGI Global., https://www.igi-global.com/gateway/chapter/163484

Hassan, N. T., Alotaibi, S. M., & Hussein, R. (2022). Sustainable Development, Entrepreneurship and Accounting Education: An Exploratory Study for Saudi Universities. *Information Sciences Letters*, *11*(6), 2101–2110. DOI: 10.18576/isl/110620

Hazrat, M. A., Hassan, N. M. S., Chowdhury, A. A., Rasul, M. G., & Taylor, B. A. (2023). Developing a skilled workforce for future industry demand: The potential of digital twin-based teaching and learning practices in engineering education. *Sustainability (Basel)*, *15*(23), 16433. DOI: 10.3390/su152316433

Healey, M., Flint, A., & Harrington, K. (2021). *Students as partners guide: Student engagement through partnership*. Advance HE.

Healey, M., & Jenkins, A. (2009). *Developing undergraduate research and inquiry*. Higher Education Academy.

Herrera, F., Alonso, S., Chiclana, F., & Herrera-Viedma, E. (2009). Computing with words in decision making. *Fuzzy Optimization and Decision Making*, *8*(4), 337–364. DOI: 10.1007/s10700-009-9065-2

Herrera, F., & Martínez, L. (2000). A 2-tuple fuzzy linguistic representation model for computing with words. *IEEE Transactions on Fuzzy Systems*, *8*(6), 746–752. DOI: 10.1109/91.890332

He, X. (2025). Practical Research on Classroom Teaching Reform Based on AI-Assisted Instructional Design. *IJLAI Transactions on Science and Engineering*, *3*(4), 13–20. DOI: 10.12677/ae.2025.155750

Hierro, B. (2020). *Adiós tiempo del VUCA, bienvenido BANI*. Quint Group.

Higher Education Digest. (2024). Revolutionizing higher education: The role of technology in enhancing student engagement and learning outcomes. https://www.highereducationdigest.com/revolutionizing-higher-education-the-role-of-technology-in-enhancing-student-engagement-and-learning-outcomes/

Hill, S., Ionescu-Somers, A., Coduras, A., Guerrero, M., Menipaz, E., Boutaleb, F., Zbierowski, P., Schøtt, T., Sahasranamam, S., & Shay, J. (2023). *Global Entrepreneurship Monitor 2022/2023 Global Report. Global Entrepreneurship Research Association*. GERA.

Himmetoğlu, B., Ayduğ, D., & Bayrak, C. (2020). Education 4.0: Defining the teacher, the student, and the school manager aspects of the revolution. *Turkish Online Journal of Distance Education, 21*(1), 12–28. DOI: 10.17718/tojde.770896

Hisrich, R., Michael, P., & Shepherd, D. A. (2005). Definition of entrepreneur today. *McGraw-Hill Irwin, 6*(1), 2.

Hodgkinson-Williams, C., & Trotter, H. (2018). A social justice framework for understanding open educational resources and practices in the global south. *Journal of Learning for Development, 5*(3), 204–224. DOI: 10.56059/jl4d.v5i3.312

Holmes, P., & Corbett, J. (Eds.). (2022). *Critical Intercultural Pedagogy for Difficult Times: Conflict, Crisis, and Creativity* (1st ed.). Routledge. DOI: 10.4324/9781003150756

Holmes, W., Bialik, M., & Fadel, C. (2019). *Artificial intelligence in education.* Center for Curriculum Redesign.

Holmes, W., Bialik, M., & Fadel, C. (2022). *Artificial intelligence in education: Promises and implications for teaching and learning*. Center for Curriculum Redesign.

Holstein, K., Wortman Vaughan, J., Daumé, H.III, Dudik, M., & Wallach, H. (2019). Improving fairness in machine learning systems: What do industry practitioners need? *Proceedings of the 2019 CHI Conference on Human Factors in Computing Systems*, 1–16. DOI: 10.1145/3290605.3300830

Hopping, D. (2025). Digitalisation in sustainable higher education campuses. Sustainability Magazine. https://sustainabilitymag.com/articles/digitalisation-in-sustainable-higher-education-campuses

Howorth, C., Tempest, S., & Coupland, C. (2005). Rethinking entrepreneurship methodology and definitions of the entrepreneur. *Journal of Small Business and Enterprise Development, 12*(1), 24–40. DOI: 10.1108/14626000510579626

Huck, C. (2025). How does curriculum development in higher education work? American College of Education. https://ace.edu/blog/how-does-curriculum-development-in-higher-education-work/

Idhalama, O. U., & Makori, E. O. (2024). Artificial intelligence, deep learning, machine learning, robotics and digital transformation: Applications, implications and future. *Ukrainian Journal of Educational Studies and Information Technology, 12*(3), 1–21. DOI: 10.32919/uesit.2024.03.01

Idris, M. D., Feng, X., & Dyo, V. (2024). Revolutionizing higher education: Unleashing the potential of large language models for strategic transformation. *IEEE Access : Practical Innovations, Open Solutions*, *12*, 67738–67757. DOI: 10.1109/ACCESS.2024.3400164

Ierapetritis, D. G. (2019). Discussing the role of universities in fostering regional entrepreneurial ecosystems. *Economies (Basel)*, *7*(4), 119. DOI: 10.3390/economies7040119

Ifenthaler, D., & Yau, J. Y. K. (2020). Utilising learning analytics to support study success in higher education: A systematic review. *Educational Technology Research and Development*, *68*(4), 1961–1990. DOI: 10.1007/s11423-020-09788-z

IFIM Institute. (2026). How quality education shapes future leaders. https://ifim.edu.in/how-quality-education-shapes-future-leaders/

Ilawagbon, O. (2025). The role of regulatory bodies in sustaining educational development in Nigeria: An assessment of the National Universities Commission. *International Journal of Research and Innovation in Social Science*, *9*(4), 2664–2681. DOI: 10.47772/IJRISS.2025.90400198

Immordino-Yang, M. H., & Darling-Hammond, L. (2021). *The brain basis for integrated social, emotional, and academic development*. Aspen Institute.

Imran, M., Almusharraf, N., Abdellatif, M. S., & Abbasova, M. Y. (2024). Artificial intelligence in higher education: Enhancing learning systems and transforming educational paradigms. *International Journal of Interactive Mobile Technologies*, *18*(18), 34–48. Advance online publication. DOI: 10.3991/ijim.v18i18.49143

International Labour Organization. (2020). *Global employment trends for youth 2020*. ILO.

Jackson, D. (2015). Employability skill development in work-integrated learning: Barriers and best practice. *Studies in Higher Education*, *40*(2), 350–372. DOI: 10.1080/03075079.2013.842221

Jackson, D., & Li, I. (2022). Transition to work, mismatch and underemployment among graduates: An Australian longitudinal study. *International Journal of Manpower*, *43*(7), 1516–1539. DOI: 10.1108/IJM-03-2021-0195

Jacob, M. (2025). Micro-credentials in Indian higher education institutions. https://ipsrsolutions.com/academix/micro-credentials-in-indian-higher-education-institutions/

Jain, R., Upreti, K., Shankar, U., Radhakrishnan, G., Sharma, A., & Malik, K. (2026). *Data-driven education: Leveraging big data, AI, and machine learning for smarter learning environments. Intelligent systems for neurocognition and human-robot-computer interaction*. Academic Press., DOI: 10.1016/B978-0-443-41660-6.00003-X

Jamira, A., Agustiningsih, N., & Febriani, Y. (2021). THE IMPLEMENTATION OF BUSINESS MODEL CANVAS (BMC) TO IMPROVE STUDENTS' ENTREPRENEURSHIP MINDSET. *Dinasti International Journal of Education Management and Social Science*, *2*(3), 395–403. DOI: 10.31933/dijemss.v2i3.751

Jamison, C. S. E., Fuher, J., Wang, A., & Huang-Saad, A. (2022). Experiential learning implementation in undergraduate engineering education: A systematic search and review. *European Journal of Engineering Education*, *47*(6), 1356–1379. DOI: 10.1080/03043797.2022.2031895

Joensuu-Salo, S., Peltonen, K., Hämäläinen, M., Oikkonen, E., & Raappana, A. (2021). Entrepreneurial teachers do make a difference – Or do they? *Industry and Higher Education*, *35*(4), 536–546. DOI: 10.1177/0950422220983236

Johnson, R. B., Onwuegbuzie, A. J., & Turner, L. A. (2007). Toward a definition of mixed methods research. *Journal of Mixed Methods Research*, *1*(2), 112–133. DOI: 10.1177/1558689806298224

Judijanto, L., Jata, W., & Istiarsyah, I. (2025). Evolution of curriculum design approaches in education studies. *The Eastasouth Journal of Learning and Educations*, *3*(3), 294–308. DOI: 10.58812/esle.v3i03.801

Jufriyono, B. T. (2017). Entrepreneurship,Organizational Culture and Emotional Intelligence in Determining Organizational Commitment. *International Journal of Managerial Studies and Research*, *5*(6), 29–35. DOI: 10.20431/2349-0349.0506004

Jugessur, Y. S. M. F. (2023). Kerr's model of curriculum design and curriculum development in education. *International Journal of Humanities and Social Science Invention*, *12*(4), 105–107. DOI: 10.35629/7722-1204105107

Kahu, E. R., & Nelson, K. (2022). Student engagement in the educational interface: Understanding the mechanisms of student success. *Higher Education Research & Development*, *41*(5), 1467–1480.

Kalamaki, F. R., Mahmoudi, G., & Charati, J. Y. (2021). A Model for Organizational Entrepreneurship with Organizational Culture Approach in Iran's Teaching Hospitals. *Ethiopian Journal of Health Sciences*, *31*(2), 419–428. DOI: 10.4314/ejhs.v31i2.25 PMID: 34158794

Karmakar, S., & Das, T. (2024). Effect of artificial intelligence on education. In *Optimization and computing using intelligent data-driven approaches for decision-making: Optimization applications*. CRC Press., DOI: 10.1201/9781003536796-8

Katz, S., & Dack, L. A. (2014). Towards a culture of inquiry for data use in schools. *Studies in Educational Evaluation, 42*, 35–40. DOI: 10.1016/j.stueduc.2013.10.006

Kazimova, D., Tazhigulova, G., Shraimanova, G., & Sharzadin, A. (2025). *Transforming university education with AI: A systematic review of technologies, applications, and implications*. International Journal of Engineering Pedagogy., DOI: 10.3991/ijep.v15i1.50773

Kelly, A. V. (2009). *The curriculum: Theory and practice* (6th ed.). SAGE Publications Ltd.

Kern, M. L., Waters, L., Adler, A., & White, M. (2022). A multidimensional approach to measuring well-being in education. *Educational Psychology Review, 34*(1), 1–25. PMID: 34226808

Kerti - Yasa, N. N., Gde-Sukaatmadja, I. P., Vedanta-Putra, A. A., Dewi-Rahmayanti, P. L. (2022). Entrepreneurship Education Development Strategies to Increase Students' Entrepreneurship Intentions in Bali. *BOHR International Journal of Operations Management Research and Practices, 1(1)*, 45–51. DOI: 10.54646/BIJOMRP.006

Kezar, A. (2004). What is more important to effective governance: Relationships, trust, and leadership, or structures and formal processes? [Object Identifier]. *New Directions for Higher Education, 2004*(127), 35–46. DOI: 10.1002/he.154

Kezar, A., & Eckel, P. D. (2002). The effect of institutional culture on change strategies in higher education. *The Journal of Higher Education, 73*(4), 435–460. DOI: 10.1080/00221546.2002.11777159

Kippers, W. B., Poortman, C. L., Schildkamp, K., & Visscher, A. J. (2018). Data literacy challenges for educators. *Studies in Educational Evaluation, 56*, 21–31. DOI: 10.1016/j.stueduc.2017.11.001

Kjellgren, B., & Richter, T. (2021). Education for a sustainable future: Strategies for holistic global competence development at engineering institutions. *Sustainability (Basel), 13*(20), 11184. DOI: 10.3390/su132011184

Knight, P. T., & Yorke, M. (2003). *Assessment, learning and employability*. Open University Press.

Knox, J., Williamson, B., & Bayne, S. (2020). Machine behaviourism: Future visions of 'learnification' and 'datafication' across humans and digital technologies. *Learning, Media and Technology*, *45*(1), 31–45. Advance online publication. DOI: 10.1080/17439884.2019.1623251

Kohl, K., & Hopkins, C. (2021). Aligning higher education's promise of well-being with sustainability as a purpose of education. In van't Land et al. (Eds.), *The Promise of Higher Education: Essays in Honour of 70 Years of IAU* (pp. 355-361). Springer Publishing. DOI: 10.1007/978-3-030-67245-4_53

Kok, C. L., Ho, C. K., Koh, Y. Y., & Teo, T. H. (2024). *Psychological aspects of AI enhanced learning experiences. In 2024 IEEE Region 10 Conference (TENCON).* IEEE., DOI: 10.1109/TENCON61640.2024.10902839

Kolb, D. A. (1984). *Experiential learning: Experience as the source of learning and development*. Prentice-Hall.

Kolmos, A., Egelund Holgaard, J., Worm Routhe, H., Winther, M., & Bertel, L. (2024). Interdisciplinary project types in engineering education. *European Journal of Engineering Education*, *49*(2), 257–282. DOI: 10.1080/03043797.2023.2267476

Koseda, E., Cohen, I. K., Cooper, J., & McIntosh, B. (2025). Embedding employability into curriculum design: The impact of education 4.0. *Policy Futures in Education*, *23*(3), 676–688. DOI: 10.1177/14782103241282121

Küçükuncular, A. (2026). Dehumanising education: AI and the capitalist capture of teaching. *AI and Ethics*, *6*(1), 123. DOI: 10.1007/s43681-026-01006-5

Kuffuor, O., Aggrawal, S., Jaiswal, A., Smith, R. J., & Morris, P. V. (2024). Transformative pathways: Implementing intercultural competence development in higher education using Kotter's change model. *Education Sciences*, *14*(7), 686. DOI: 10.3390/educsci14070686

Kuh, G. D. (2009). The national survey of student engagement: Conceptual and empirical foundations. *New Directions for Institutional Research*, *141*(141), 5–20. https://onlinelibrary.wiley.com/doi/10.1002/ir.283. DOI: 10.1002/ir.283

Kuhn, T. S. (2012). *The structure of scientific revolutions* (4th ed.). University of Chicago Press. DOI: 10.7208/chicago/9780226458144.001.0001

Kumar, M. J. (2024, February 4). Micro-credentials, the next chapter in higher education. The Hindu. https://www.thehindu.com/opinion/op-ed/micro-credentials-the-next-chapter-in-higher-

Kumari, M., & Goyal, N. K. (2026). Artificial intelligence in the cryptocurrency ecosystem: Crime mechanisms, detection strategies, and legal perspectives. In Lin, L. (Ed.), *Innovations in cryptocrime and financial fraud* (pp. 245–282). IGI Global Scientific Publishing., DOI: 10.4018/979-8-3373-0675-9.ch007

Kumari, M., Khan, S. T., Gulati, K., Sharma, P., Goyal, N. K., & Sheikh, M. F. (2026). Innovative procedural content generation using generative AI. In Sousa, J., & Tavares, R. (Eds.), *Reshaping the video game landscape with AI and GenAI* (pp. 205–232). IGI Global Scientific Publishing., DOI: 10.4018/979-8-3373-4637-3.ch007

Kumari, M., Kumawat, R., Dutta, R., Khan, S. T., Goyal, N. K., & Sheikh, M. F. (2026). Wireless communication and IoT integration in smart clothing. In Saxena, P. (Eds.), *Next-generation electronic textiles and conductive materials* (pp. 195–232). IGI Global Scientific Publishing., DOI: 10.4018/979-8-3373-4287-0.ch008

Kumari, M., Kumawat, R., Tripathi, M., Suganthi, K., Goyal, N. K., & Sheikh, M. F. (2026). Blockchain for transparency and traceability in supply chains. In Khan, M., Mehmood, T., & Rao, M. (Eds.), *Maximizing operational efficiency at the intersection of supply chain management and marketing* (pp. 35–64). IGI Global Scientific Publishing., DOI: 10.4018/979-8-3373-3109-6.ch002

Kumaro, M., & Barliana, M. S. (2022, March). Integration of 4 Cs skills into learning by using the Project Based Learning (PBL) model to face the challenges of the 21st century. In *4th International Conference on Innovation in Engineering and Vocational Education* (ICIEVE 2021) (pp. 88–93). Atlantis Press.

Kumar, S. (2025). Education 4.0: Transforming learning for the Fourth Industrial Revolution. *Higher Education for the Future, 12*(2), 144–162. DOI: 10.1177/23476311251326140

Kusio, T., & Fiore, M. (2020). The perception of entrepreneurship culture by internal university stakeholders. *European Business Review, 32*(3), 443–457. DOI: 10.1108/EBR-05-2019-0087

Lai, M. K. (2025). *AI-personalised learning in higher education: A study on learning outcomes and motivation among university students.* International Journal of Research and Innovation in Social Science., DOI: 10.47772/IJRISS.2025.905000473

Lai, M. K., & Schildkamp, K. (2013). Data-based decision making: An overview. In *Data-Based Decision Making in Education* (pp. 9–21). Springer. DOI: 10.1007/978-94-007-4816-3_2

Lantada, A. D. (2022). Engineering education 5.0: Strategies for a successful transformative project-based learning. *Insights into Global Engineering Education after the Birth of Industry 5*, 19. DOI: DOI: 10.5772/intechopen.102844

Leal Filho, W., Wall, T., Rayman-Bacchus, L., Mifsud, M., Pritchard, D., & Lovren, V. (2023). Impacts of climate change education on student awareness and emotional engagement. *International Journal of Sustainability in Higher Education, 24*(2), 295–310.

Leong, W. Y., & Zhang, J. B. (2025). *Ethical design of AI for education and learning systems*. ASM Science Journal., DOI: 10.32802/asmscj.2025.1917

Levin-Goldberg, J. (2012). Teaching Generation TechX with the 4 Cs: Using technology to integrate 21st century skills. *Journal of Institutional Research, 1*, 59–66. Available at: https://files.eric.ed.gov/fulltext/EJ1127608.pdf

Liu, C., Wang, G. C., & Wang, H. F. (2025). The application of artificial intelligence in engineering education: A systematic review. *IEEE Access : Practical Innovations, Open Solutions, 13*, 17895–17910. DOI: 10.1109/ACCESS.2025.3532595

Liu, C., & Zhou, D. (2025). AI Integration in Higher Education: A Software Engineering Perspective on Readiness, Anxiety, and Innovation. *International Journal of Software Engineering and Knowledge Engineering*. Advance online publication. DOI: 10.1142/S0218194025501116

Liu, H., Kulturel-Konak, S., & Konak, A. (2021). Key elements and their roles in entrepreneurship education ecosystem: Comparative review and suggestions for sustainability. *Sustainability (Basel), 13*(19), 10648. DOI: 10.3390/su131910648

Lockyer, L., & Dawson, S. (2011). Learning designs and learning analytics. In *Proceedings of the 2011 LAK Conference*. ACM. DOI: 10.1145/2090116.2090140

López, M. B. (2025). Evolving pedagogy in digital signal processing education: AI-assisted review and analysis. *IEEE Access : Practical Innovations, Open Solutions, 13*, 45559–45567. DOI: 10.1109/ACCESS.2025.3549477

Lowell, V. L., & Morris, J. M.Jr. (2019, March 20). Multigenerational classrooms in higher education: Equity and learning with technology. *International Journal of Information and Learning Technology., 36*(2), 78–93. DOI: 10.1108/IJILT-06-2018-0068

Luckin, R., Holmes, W., Griffiths, M., & Forcier, L. B. (2016). *Intelligence unleashed: An argument for AI in education*. Pearson Education.

Lu, J., Han, J., Hu, Y., & Zhang, G. (2016). Multilevel decision-making: A survey. *Information Sciences*, *346*, 463–487. DOI: 10.1016/j.ins.2016.01.084

Lu, J., Zhang, G., Ruan, D., & Wu, F. (2007). *Multi-objective group decision making: Methods, software and applications with fuzzy set techniques*. World Scientific. DOI: 10.1142/p505

Lyall, A. (2025). Theoretical foundation of curriculum. https://itcollege.ac.in/itdc/assets/images/econtant/Dr-A.Lyl_.pdf

Mahajan, H. (2024). The power of data-driven decision making in higher education. https://www.academiaerp.com/blog/the-power-of-data-driven-decision-making-in-higher-education/

Mainzer, K. (2011). Interdisciplinarity and innovation dynamics. On convergence of research, technology, economy, and society. *Poiesis & Praxis : International Journal of Ethics of Science and Technology Assessment*, *7*(4), 275–289. DOI: 10.1007/s10202-011-0088-8 PMID: 21874129

Makarenko, O., Borysenko, O., Horokhivska, T., Kozub, V., & Yaremenko, D. (2024). Embracing artificial intelligence in education: Shaping the learning path for future professionals. Multidisciplinary Science Journal, 6, Article e2024ss0720. DOI: 10.31893/multiscience.2024ss0720

Mandinach, E. B., & Gummer, E. S. (2013). A systemic view of implementing data literacy in educator preparation. *Educational Researcher*, *42*(1), 30–37. DOI: 10.3102/0013189X12459803

Mandinach, E., Honey, M., Light, D., & Brunner, C. (2008). A conceptual framework for data-driven decision-making. In *Data-Driven School Improvement* (pp. 13–31). Teachers College Press.

Marginson, S. (2016). *The Dream Is Over: The Crisis of Clark Kerr's California Idea of Higher Education*. University of California Press. https://www.jstor.org/stable/10.1525/j.ctt1kc6k1p

Marginson, S. (2016). *Higher education and the common good*. Melbourne University Publishing.

Marginson, S. (2022). Global student mobility and inequality in higher education. *Higher Education*, *84*(1), 1–18. DOI: 10.1007/s10734-004-7649-x PMID: 34584277

Marsh, J. A., Pane, J. F., & Hamilton, L. S. (2006). *Making sense of data-driven decision making in education*. RAND Corporation.

Mayberry, M. (2023, February). You don't need to be "the boss" to be a leader. Harvard Business Review. https://hbr.org/2023/02/you-dont-need-to-be-the-boss-to-be-a-leader

Maynard, S. (2015). *The fourth industrial revolution: Opportunities and challenges*. Routledge.

McCowan, T. (2016). Universities and the post-2015 development agenda: An analytical framework. *Higher Education*, *72*(4), 505–523. DOI: 10.1007/s10734-016-0035-7

McKeown, R., & Hopkins, C. (2017). Quality education and education for sustainable development. In Michelsen, G., & Wells, P. (Eds.), *A Decade of Progress on Education for Sustainable Development: Reflections from the UNESCO Chairs Programme* (pp. 28–38). UNESCO.

Mcmillin, J., & Dyball, R. (2009). Developing a whole-of-university approach to educating for sustainability: Linking curriculum, research and sustainable campus operations. *Journal of Education for Sustainable Development*, *3*(1), 55–64. DOI: 10.1177/097340820900300113

Mei, W., & Symaco, L. (2022). University-wide entrepreneurship education in China's higher education institutions: Issues and challenges. *Studies in Higher Education*, *47*(1), 177–193. DOI: 10.1080/03075079.2020.1735330

Mekić, E., Fetahović, I., Kuk, K., Popović, B., & Čisar, P. (2024). *Data-driven educational decision-making model for curriculum optimization., Ethics in online AI-based systems*. Academic Press., DOI: 10.1016/B978-0-443-18851-0.00002-0

Mena Guacas, A. F., Mellado-Moreno, P.-C., Calderón-Cisneros, J.-T., & Pelicano Piris, N. (2026). Mapping artificial-intelligence-driven innovation in higher education: A bibliometric review. *Social Sciences & Humanities Open*, *13*, 102561. DOI: 10.1016/j.ssaho.2026.102561

Michelsen, G., & Burandt, S. (2017). Sustainable development as a guideline for higher education: An innovative concept for teaching and learning. In G. Michelsen and P. Wells, *A Decade of Progress on Education for Sustainable Development: Reflections from the UNESCO Chairs Programme* (pp. 38-48). UNESCO.

Ministry of Human Resource Development, Government of India. (2020). National education policy 2020. https://www.education.gov.in/sites/upload_files/mhrd/files/NEP_Final_English_0.pdf

Miranda, J., Navarrete, C., Noguez, J., Molina-Espinosa, J. M., Ramírez-Montoya, M. S., Navarro-Tuch, S. A., Bustamante-Bello, M.-R., Rosas-Fernández, J.-B., & Molina, A. (2021). The core components of education 4.0 in higher education: Three case studies in engineering education. *Computers & Electrical Engineering*, *93*, 107278. DOI: 10.1016/j.compeleceng.2021.107278

Mogul, A., Laughlin, E., & Lynch, S. (2020). A co-curricular activity to introduce pharmacy students to the concepts of innovation and entrepreneurship. *American Journal of Pharmaceutical Education*, *84*(8), 1077–1084. DOI: 10.5688/ajpe7805 PMID: 32934385

Monteiro, S., Santos, S., Teixeira, J. N., Torres, L., & Palhares, J. (2025). Determinants of higher education graduates' employability: A scoping review. *Education + Training*, *67*(1), 56–74. DOI: 10.1108/ET-04-2024-0190

Moon, J. A. (2013). *Reflection in learning and professional development: Theory and practice*. Routledge. DOI: 10.4324/9780203822296

Mougiakou, S., Vinatsella, D., & Sampson, D.. (2022). Optimising teaching using learning analytics. *Frontiers in Education*, *7*, 878279. Advance online publication. DOI: 10.3389/feduc.2022.878279

Murphy, L. (2025). The productivity dilemma: Examining the truth behind automation's impact on employment. *The International Journal of Organizational Analysis*, *33*(3), 622–644. DOI: 10.1108/IJOA-04-2024-4430

Murwaningsih, T. Sasmini, Rahardjo, S. S., & Nurhasanah, F. (2024). A well structured strategy development via AI integrated analytics systems to improve performance of education. In 2024 4th International Conference on Advance Computing and Innovative Technologies in Engineering (ICACITE). IEEE. DOI: 10.1109/ICACITE60783.2024.10617260

Muslim, A. B., Hamied, F. A., Gaffar, M. F., Asuan, M. E., Samsudin, S., Diteeyont, W., Margana, M., Suryani, A. W., Jessie, P. N. G., Solihat, R., Priyantin, T., Cassandra, N., Gunadi, G., & Sitthikorn, S. (2023). Benefits, mechanisms and challenges of international accreditation for teacher education: ASEAN academics' perspectives. *Quality Assurance in Education*, *31*(4), 538–555. Advance online publication. DOI: 10.1108/QAE-10-2022-0183

Naixin, Z., Wai Yie, L., Tong, Z., & Changqing, W. (2024). Artificial intelligence in engineering education: A review of pedagogical innovations. *INTI Journal*, *2024*(46), 1–10. DOI: 10.61453/INTIj.202446

Nambisan, S., Siegel, D., & Kenney, M. (2018). On open innovation, platforms, and entrepreneurship. *Strategic Entrepreneurship Journal*, *12*(3), 354–368. DOI: 10.1002/sej.1300

Narong, D. K., & Hallinger, P. (2024). Traversing the evolution of research on engineering education for sustainability: A bibliometric review (1991–2022). *Sustainability (Basel)*, *16*(2), 641. DOI: 10.3390/su16020641

Neendoor, S. (2026). 5 popular curriculum development models you should know. https://www.hurix.com/blogs/popular-curriculum-development-models-you-should-know/

Ngoc, T. N., Tran, Q. N., Tang, A., Nguyen, B., Nguyen, T., & Pham, T. (2023). AI-assisted learning for electronic engineering courses in higher education. *arXiv preprint arXiv:2311.01048. DOI: https://doi.org/*DOI: 10.3102/2198146

Nguyen, A., Gardner, L., & Sheridan, D. (2020). A design methodology for learning analytics information systems: Informing learning analytics development with learning design. In *Proceedings of the 53rd Hawaii International Conference on System Sciences*. DOI: 10.24251/HICSS.2020.014

Nguyen, T. T. T., Nguyen, T. T. H., & Pham, T. T. H. (2020). The effect of corporate entrepreneurship, organizational culture on supply chain management and business performance in chemical industry. *Uncertain Supply Chain Management*, *8*(1), 67–76. DOI: 10.5267/j.uscm.2019.8.005

Nondumiso Shabangu., & Madondo, N. E. (2024). Addressing graduate unemployment: Aligning higher education curricula with labour market demands. In Proceedings of the Focus Conference (TFC 2024). Atlantis Press. https://doi.org/ DOI: 10.2991/978-94-6463-630-7_5

Novawan, A., Ismailia, T., Zuhro, C., Utami, L. D., Pratama, M. R., Karimah, K., & Haq, R. N. (2024). Design thinking approach to powerful material development in educational contexts: From theory to practice. [IJOSSH]. *International Journal of Studies in Social Sciences and Humanities*, *1*(2), 125–145. DOI: 10.25047/ijossh.v1i2.5571

Nunnally, J. C. (1978). *Psychometric theory* (2nd ed.). McGraw-Hill.

Nussbaum, M. C. (2010). *Not for profit: Why democracy needs the humanities.* Princeton University Press.

O'Dea, R., & Stern, N. (2023). Reimagining the civic role of universities in the twenty-first century. *Higher Education Quarterly*, *77*(2), 243–259.

O'Neil, C. (2016). *Weapons of math destruction.* Crown Publishing.

OECD. (2019). *OECD future of education and skills 2030: Conceptual learning framework.* OECD Publishing.

OECD. (2021). *OECD skills outlook 2021: Learning for life.* OECD Publishing.

OECD. (2022). *Education at a glance 2022: OECD indicators.* OECD Publishing.

OECD. (2023). *OECD digital education outlook 2023: Towards an effective digital education ecosystem.* OECD Publishing.

Osterwalder, A. (2004). The business model ontology a proposition in a design science approach. Doctoral Dissertation, Université de Lausanne, Faculté Des Hautes Études Commerciales.

Ouyang, F., & Zhang, L. (2024). AI-driven learning analytics applications and tools in computer-supported collaborative learning: A systematic review. *Educational Research Review, 44*, 100616. Advance online publication. DOI: 10.1016/j.edurev.2024.100616

Pacher, C., Woschank, M., Zunk, B. M., & Gruber, E. (2024). Engineering education 5.0: A systematic literature review on competence-based education in the industrial engineering and management discipline. *Production & Manufacturing Research, 12*(1), 2337224. DOI: 10.1080/21693277.2024.2337224

Palomares, I., Martínez, L., & Herrera, F. (2014). A consensus model to detect and manage noncooperative behaviors. *IEEE Transactions on Fuzzy Systems, 22*(3), 516–530. DOI: 10.1109/TFUZZ.2013.2262769

Pane, J. F., Steiner, E. D., Baird, M. D., & Hamilton, L. S. (2015). *Continued progress: Promising evidence on personalized learning.* RAND Corporation. DOI: 10.7249/RR1365

Parker, J. (2025). Bloom's taxonomy. Center for Teaching Excellence, University of Florida. https://teach.ufl.edu/resource-libraryold/blooms-taxonomy/

Park, S. K., & Bishara, N. D. (2023). Climate change and a just transition to the future of work. *American Business Law Journal, 60*(4), 701–748. DOI: 10.1111/ablj.12235

Partnership for 21st Century Learning (P21). (2019). Framework for 21st century learning definitions. Available at: https://static.battelleforkids.org/documents/p21/p21_framework_definitionsbfk.pdf. (Accessed April, 2025).

Passow, H. J., & Passow, C. H. (2017). What competencies should undergraduate engineering programs emphasize? A systematic review. *Journal of Engineering Education, 106*(3), 475–526. DOI: 10.1002/jee.20171

Pauw, C. (2021). Combinatorial evolution: A theory of evolution for technology – Fellows' seminar by Brian Arthur. Stellenbosch Institute for Advanced Study. https://stias.ac.za/2019/06/combinatorial-evolution-a-theory-of-evolution-for-technology/

Peñalver Martínez, A. (2022). De un entorno VUCA a un entorno BANI para dar sentido a este mundo de transformación constante. *Capital Humano: Revista Para La Integración y Desarrollo de Los Recursos Humanos, 376*, 24.

Peng, L. M., & Mun, B. W. K. (2025). Understanding gig work in paving towards gig economy sustainability: Insights from platform-based companies. *Malaysian Journal of Qualitative Research, 11*(1).

Pérez, F., Aldás, J., Aragón, R., & Zaera, I. (2023). *ANÁLISIS DE LA INSERCIÓN LABORAL DE LOS UNIVERSITARIOS, Diferencias entre titulaciones*. Fundación BBVA.

Pérez-Juárez, M., Serrano-López, A. E., & García-Martínez, I. (2024). Digital well-being and university students: The role of screen time, stress, and academic engagement. *Computers & Education, 203*, 104828.

Pfeffer, J., & Sutton, R. I. (2006). *Hard facts, dangerous half-truths, and total nonsense: Profiting from evidence-based management*. Harvard Business School Press.

Pham, T., Nguyen, T. B., Ha, S., & Ngoc, N. T. N. (2023). Digital transformation in engineering education: Exploring the potential of AI-assisted learning. *Australasian Journal of Educational Technology, 39*(5), 1–19. DOI: 10.14742/ajet.8825

Piaget, J. (1950). *The psychology of intelligence*. Routledge.

Pitaloka, L. K., Melati, I. S., & Setiawan, A. B. (2021). Selection of priority strategies for developing social entrepreneurship for women. *Academy of Entrepreneurship Journal, 27*(4), 1–8.

Pocek, J., Politis, D., & Gabrielsson, J. (2022). Entrepreneurial learning in extra-curricular start-up programs for students. *International Journal of Entrepreneurial Behaviour & Research, 28*(2), 325–345. DOI: 10.1108/IJEBR-04-2020-0206

Poortman, C. L., & Schildkamp, K. (2016). Solving student achievement-focused problems with data use interventions. *Teaching and Teacher Education, 60*, 425–433. DOI: 10.1016/j.tate.2016.06.010

Porter, S. R. (2013). Self-reported learning gains: A theory and test of college student survey response. *Research in Higher Education, 54*(2), 201–226. DOI: 10.1007/s11162-012-9277-0

Press Information Bureau, Government of India. (2026). AI in education: Building India's talent pipeline for global leadership.

Pressbooks. (2026). Curriculum design, development and models: Planning for student learning. https://oer.pressbooks.pub/curriculumessentials/chapter/curriculum-design-development-and-models-planning-for-student-learning-there-is-always-a-need-for-newly-formulated-curriculum-models-that-address-contemporary-circumstance-an/

Prezi. (2015). Approaches to curriculum design. https://prezi.com/rka1dtoahbpr/approaches-to-curriculum-designing/

Qadir, J., Yau, K. L. A., Imran, M. A., & Al-Fuqaha, A. (2020, October). Engineering education, moving into 2020s: Essential competencies for effective 21st century electrical and computer engineers. In *2020 IEEE Frontiers in Education Conference (FIE)* (pp. 1-9). IEEE.

Radko, N., Belitski, M., & Kalyuzhnova, Y. (2023). Conceptualising the entrepreneurial university: The stakeholder approach. *The Journal of Technology Transfer, 48*(3), 955–1044. DOI: 10.1007/s10961-022-09926-0

Rajest, S. S., & Suresh, P. (2018). The "Four Cs" education for 21st century's learners. *Research Guru Online Journal of Multidisciplinary Subjects, XII*, 888–900.

Rajput, R. (2025). Use of artificial intelligence to solve problems in the classroom. In *New technological applications in the flipped learning model*. IGI Global., DOI: 10.4018/979-8-3373-0437-3.ch005

Ramírez-Montoya, M. S.. (2021). Trends for the future of education 4.0. *Education and Information Technologies*. Advance online publication. DOI: 10.1007/s10639-021-10509-4

Rath, K. C., Senapati, A. K., Dalla, V. K., Kumar, A., Sahu, S., & Das, R. P. (2023). Growing role of AI towards digital transformation in higher education systems. In *Advancements in Artificial Intelligence, Blockchain Technology, and IoT in Higher Education* (pp. 3–26). Apple Academic Press., DOI: 10.1201/9781003300458-2

Rauch, A., & Hulsink, W. (2015). Putting Entrepreneurship Education Where the Intention to Act Lies: An Investigation into the Impact of Entrepreneurship Education on Entrepreneurial Behavior. *Academy of Management Learning & Education, 14*(2), 187–204. DOI: 10.5465/amle.2012.0293

Reeves, P. M., Zappe, S. E., & Follmer, D. J. (2019). A Comparison of the Types of Problems Encountered by Entrepreneurial Students and Successful Professional Entrepreneurs. *Entrepreneurship Education and Pedagogy, 2*(3), 214–244. DOI: 10.1177/2515127419829396

Reid-Griffin, A., Croson, J., Fisher, S., & Lopez, N. (2023). Collaborative partnership: Helping adolescents to develop a STEM mindset. *PDS Partners: Bridging Research to Practice, 18*(1), 43–53. DOI: 10.1108/PDSP-01-2023-0002

Reynoso-Arcos, S., Gallardo-Lolandes, Y., Padilla Vento, P., Mori-Holguin, J. Y., & Barraza-Regalado, C. A. (2022). Generational diversity in digital education in teachers of the Administration career of a private university. *RISTI - Revista Iberica de Sistemas e Tecnologias de Informacao*, 2022(E48), 180–195.

Riaz, S., Mushtaq, A., & Kaur, M. J. (2019). Intelligent tutoring for informed feedback in interactive learning environments. In *ASET Conference Proceedings*. DOI: 10.1109/ICASET.2019.8714555

Richta, R. (2018). *Civilization at the crossroads: Social and human implications of the Scientific and Technological Revolution*. Routledge.

Rickinson, M., de Bruin, K., Walsh, L., & Hall, M. (2017). What can evidence-use in practice learn from evidence-use in policy? *Educational Research, 59*(2), 173–189. DOI: 10.1080/00131881.2017.1304306

Riessman, C. K. (2008). Narrative methods for the human sciences. *Sage (Atlanta, Ga.)*.

Roberts, P., & Green, B. (2013). Researching rural places. *Qualitative Research Journal, 13*(1), 2–12. DOI: 10.1108/14439881311314496

Roca-Hurtuna, M., & Sanz-Ponce, R. (2023). The Perception of University Students towards People with Disabilities and Their Labor Insertion. *Education Sciences, 13*(1), 79. Advance online publication. DOI: 10.3390/educsci13010079

Rodríguez, A. (2009). Nuevas perspectivas para entender el emprendimiento empresarial. *Pensamiento & Gestión, 26*, 4–119.

Rodríguez, R. M., Martínez, L., Torra, V., Xu, Z. S., & Herrera, F. (2014). Hesitant fuzzy sets: State of the art and future directions. *International Journal of Intelligent Systems, 29*(6), 495–524. DOI: 10.1002/int.21654

Rogers, E. M. (2010). *Diffusion of innovations* (5th ed.). Free Press.

Romero Alonso, R., Araya Carvajal, K., & Reyes Acevedo, N. (2025). Role of artificial intelligence in the personalization of distance education: A systematic review. RIED: Revista Iberoamericana de Educación a Distancia.

Romero, C., & Ventura, S. (2020). Educational data mining and learning analytics: An updated survey. *Wiley Interdisciplinary Reviews. Data Mining and Knowledge Discovery*, *10*(3), e1355. Advance online publication. DOI: 10.1002/widm.1355

Rossoni, A. L., de Vasconcellos, E. P. G., & de Castilho Rossoni, R. L. (2023). *Barriers and facilitators of university-industry collaboration for research, development and innovation: a systematic review*. Management Review Quarterly., DOI: 10.1007/s11301-023-00349-1

Rouvrais, S., & Gaultier Le Bris, S. (2018). Breadth experiential courses to flexibly meet new programme outcomes for engineers. In *Engineering Education for a Smart Society: World Engineering Education Forum & Global Engineering Deans Council* (pp. 326-342). Springer International Publishing. DOI: 10.1007/978-3-319-60937-9_25

Rustiana, Mohd, O. B., & Mohamad, N. B. (2022). The Triangulation Model Distribution of Entrepreneurship Education, Entrepreneurship Knowledge, and Entrepreneurship Mindset. *Journal of Distribution Science*, *20*(9), 47–59. DOI: 10.15722/jds.20.09.202209.47

Ryff, C. D. (1989). Happiness is everything, or is it? Explorations on the meaning of psychological well-being. *Journal of Personality and Social Psychology*, *57*(6), 1069–1081. DOI: 10.1037/0022-3514.57.6.1069

Ryff, C. D. (2014). Psychological well-being revisited: Advances in the science and practice of eudaimonia. *Psychotherapy and Psychosomatics*, *83*(1), 10–28. DOI: 10.1159/000353263 PMID: 24281296

Sababha, B. H., Al-Qaralleh, E., & Al-Daher, N. (2021). A New Student Learning Outcome to Strengthen Entrepreneurship and Business Skills and Mindset in Engineering Curricula. In 2021 Innovation and New Trends in Engineering, Technology and Science Education Conference, IETSEC 2021. Institute of Electrical and Electronics Engineers Inc. DOI: 10.1109/IETSEC51476.2021.9440489

Salloum, S. A., Salloum, A., & Alfaisal, R. (2024). Objectives and obstacles of artificial intelligence in education. In *Studies in big data*. Springer., DOI: 10.1007/978-3-031-52280-2_38

Salomaa, M., & Caputo, A. (2021). Business as usual? Assessing the impact of the COVID-19 pandemic to research, development and innovation (RDI) activities of universities of applied sciences. *Tertiary Education and Management, 27*(4), 351–366. DOI: 10.1007/s11233-021-09079-z PMID: 40477712

Samaniego, J. R. V., Arroyo, K. M. C., & Quispe, A. S. L. (2022). Generational Diversity: Challenges for University Education in the 21st Century. *Revista de Filosofia (Venezuela), 39*(102), 664–673. DOI: 10.5281/zenodo.7063329

Sanyal, S., & Kumar, S. (2025). The digital transformation of work: How will automation alter future workplaces? In *Advancements in intelligent process automation* (pp. 1–22). IGI Global.

Schildkamp, K., Karbautzki, L., & Vanhoof, J. (2014). Exploring data use practices around Europe. *Studies in Educational Evaluation, 42*, 15–24. DOI: 10.1016/j.stueduc.2013.10.007

Schildkamp, K., & Poortman, C. L. (2015). Factors influencing the functioning of data teams. *Teachers College Record, 117*(4), 1–42. DOI: 10.1177/016146811511700403

Schildkamp, K., Poortman, C. L., & Handelzalts, A. (2016). Data teams for school improvement. *School Effectiveness and School Improvement, 27*(2), 228–254. DOI: 10.1080/09243453.2015.1056192

Schjoedt, L., Monsen, E., Pearson, A., Barnett, T., & Chrisman, J. J. (2013). New Venture and Family Business Teams: Understanding Team Formation, Composition, Behaviors, and Performance. *Entrepreneurship Theory and Practice, 37*(1), 1–15. DOI: 10.1111/j.1540-6520.2012.00549.x

Schwab, K., & Davis, N. (2018). *Shaping the future of the fourth industrial revolution*. Currency.

Seely, B. E. (2005). Patterns in the history of engineering education reform: A brief essay. In *Educating the engineer of 2020: Adapting engineering education to the new century* (pp. 114–130). National Academic Press.

Seligman, M. E. P. (2011). *Flourish: A visionary new understanding of happiness and well-being*. Free Press.

Seligman, M. E. P. (2018). PERMA and the building blocks of well-being. *The Journal of Positive Psychology, 13*(4), 333–335. DOI: 10.1080/17439760.2018.1437466

Selwyn, N. (2019). *Should robots replace teachers? AI and the future of education*. Polity Press.

Setyaningrum, R. P., Norisanti, N., Fahlevi, M., Aljuaid, M., & Grabowska, S. (2023). Women and entrepreneurship for economic growth in Indonesia. *Frontiers in Psychology*, *13*, 1–11. DOI: 10.3389/fpsyg.2022.975709 PMID: 36698571

Sghir, N., Adadi, A., & Lahmer, M. (2022). Recent advances in predictive learning analytics: A survey of machine learning approaches in education. *Education and Information Technologies*, *28*, 403–426. DOI: 10.1007/s10639-022-11104-0

Shadish, W. R., Cook, T. D., & Campbell, D. T. (2002). *Experimental and quasi-experimental designs for generalized causal inference*. Houghton Mifflin.

Shah, P. J. (2015). Regulatory structure of higher education in India (Working paper). International Growth Centre. https://www.theigc.org/sites/default/files/2015/11/Shah-2015-Working-paper.pdf

Sharma, L. (2022). Assessing the "entrepreneurship as emancipation" perspective among women in STEM. *Management Decision*, *60*(6), 1585–1605. DOI: 10.1108/MD-06-2020-0696

Sharma, P., Kumawat, R., Jain, G., Keswani, G., Goyal, N. K., & Sheikh, M. F. (2026). Machine learning-based intrusion detection systems for healthcare Internet of Things (HIoT). In Shieh, C. (Eds.), *Resilient healthcare Internet of Things systems* (pp. 185–214). IGI Global Scientific Publishing., DOI: 10.4018/979-8-3373-7610-3.ch007

Sheikh, M. F. A., Kapoor, S. K., Goyal, N. K., Tuba, E., & Rao, A. (2026). Enhancing healthcare security with fog computing and blockchain technology. In Nayak, R. (Eds.), *Recent advancements in artificial intelligence* (pp. 1–20). Springer., DOI: 10.1007/978-981-96-7760-3_38

Shermis, M. D., & Burstein, J. (Eds.). (2013). *Handbook of automated essay evaluation: Current applications and new directions*. Routledge. DOI: 10.4324/9780203122761

Short, E. (2025). Curriculum design, development and models: Planning for student learning. In Curriculum essentials. Pressbooks. https://oer.pressbooks.pub/curriculumessentials/chapter/curriculum-designdevelopment-and-models-planning-for-student-learning-there-is-always-a-need-for-newlyformulated-curriculum-models-that-address-contemporary-circumstance-an/

Shree Adhitya Education. (2026). Shaping the future: How Ministry of Education powers higher education in India. https://touchcampus.in/blog/shaping-the-future-how-the-ministry-of-education-powers-higher-education-in-india

Shuman, L. J., Besterfield-Sacre, M., & McGourty, J. (2005). The ABET "professional skills"—Can they be taught? Can they be assessed? *Journal of Engineering Education, 94*(1), 41–55. DOI: 10.1002/j.2168-9830.2005.tb00828.x

Siddegowda, P. A. (2020). A Study on Problems of Women Entrepreneurs at Mysore District, India. *Our Heritage, 68*(1), 9183–9200.

Siegel, D. S., & Wright, M. (2015). Academic Entrepreneurship: Time for a Rethink? *British Journal of Management, 26*(4), 582–595. DOI: 10.1111/1467-8551.12116

Siemens, G. (2005). Connectivism: A learning theory for the digital age. *International Journal of Instructional Technology and Distance Learning, 2*(1), 3–10.

Siemens, G., & Baker, R. S. J. d. (2012). Learning analytics and educational data mining: Towards communication and collaboration. *Proceedings of the 2nd International Conference on Learning Analytics and Knowledge*, 252–254. DOI: 10.1145/2330601.2330661

Siemens, G., & Long, P. (2011). Penetrating the fog: Analytics in learning and education. *EDUCAUSE Review, 46*(5), 30–40.

Sigahi, T. F., & Sznelwar, L. I. (2022). Exploring applications of complexity theory in engineering education research: A systematic literature review. *Journal of Engineering Education, 111*(1), 232–260. DOI: 10.1002/jee.20438

Sigüenza-Orellana, S. C., Álava-Atiencie, N. G., Pinos-Ramón, L. D., & Peralta-Vallejo, X. K. (2022). University students' perception of the entrepreneurial ecosystem and social entrepreneurial intention. *Retos (Ecuador), 12*(24), 248–266. DOI: 10.17163/ret.n24.2022.04

Simon, H. A. (1977). *The new science of management decision*. Prentice-Hall.

Singh, S. (2024, February 14). Micro credentials: An innovation in Indian higher education institutes.

Skvarenina, T. (2008, June). Incorporating and Assessing ABET "Soft Skills" in the Technical Curriculum. In *2008 Annual Conference & Exposition* (pp. 13-727). DOI: 10.18260/1-2--4089

Slade, S., & Prinsloo, P. (2013). Learning analytics: Ethical issues and dilemmas. *The American Behavioral Scientist, 57*(10), 1510–1529. DOI: 10.1177/0002764213479366

Slomp, E. M., Ropelato, D., Bonatti, C., & Da Silva, M. D. (2024). Adaptive learning in engineering courses: How artificial intelligence can improve academic outcomes. In *EDUNINE Conference Proceedings*. IEEE. DOI: 10.1109/EDUNINE60625.2024.10500580

Smith, J., Brown, T., & Lee, A. (2024). Ethical challenges in AI-driven learning analytics: A review of faculty concerns in higher education. *Journal of Higher Education Policy and Management*, *46*(3), 89–104.

Southworth, J., Migliaccio, K., Glover, J., Glover, J. N., Reed, D., McCarty, C., Brendemuhl, J., & Thomas, A. (2023). Developing a model for AI across the curriculum: Transforming the higher education landscape via innovation in AI literacy. *Computers and Education: Artificial Intelligence*, *4*, 100127. DOI: 10.1016/j.caeai.2023.100127

Subramaniam, R., & Shankar, R. K. (2020). Three Mindsets of Entrepreneurial Leaders. *The Journal of Entrepreneurship*, *29*(1), 7–37. DOI: 10.1177/0971355719893498

Succi, C., & Canovi, M. (2019). Soft skills to enhance graduate employability: Comparing students and employers' perceptions. *Studies in Higher Education*, *45*(9), 1834–1847. DOI: 10.1080/03075079.2019.1585420

Suvarna, T., Chithirairajan, B., Thangamayan, S., & Rajarethinam, E. (2019). Economic problems of women entrepreneurs in chennai sub urbans. *International Journal of Innovative Technology and Exploring Engineering, 8(7C2)*, 362–365.

Sziegat, H. (2021). The response of German business schools to international accreditation in global competition. *Quality Assurance in Education*, *29*(2–3), 135–150. DOI: 10.1108/QAE-01-2020-0008

Szmidt, E., & Kacprzyk, J. (2003). A consensus-reaching process under intuitionistic fuzzy preference relations. *International Journal of Intelligent Systems*, *18*(7), 837–852. DOI: 10.1002/int.10119

Tallman, S., Shenkar, O., & Wu, J. (2023). "Culture Eats Strategy for Breakfast": Use and Abuse of Culture in International Strategy Research. *Strategic Management Review*, *4*(2), 193–229. DOI: 10.1561/111.00000057

Tan, X., Cheng, G., & Ling, M. H. (2025). Artificial intelligence in teaching and teacher professional development: A systematic review. Computers and Education: Artificial Intelligence. DOI: 10.1016/j.caeai.2024.100355

Taylor, R. D., Oberle, E., Durlak, J. A., & Weissberg, R. P. (2017). Promoting positive youth development through school-based social and emotional learning interventions: A meta-analysis. *Child Development*, *88*(4), 1156–1171. DOI: 10.1111/cdev.12864 PMID: 28685826

Team Creatrix. (2026). Bloom's taxonomy: The dean's guide to curriculum design. https://www.creatrixcampus.com/blog/blooms-taxonomy-in-higher-education

Thomas, J., & Harden, A. (2008). Methods for the thematic synthesis of qualitative research in systematic reviews. *BMC Medical Research Methodology*, *8*(1), 45. Advance online publication. DOI: 10.1186/1471-2288-8-45 PMID: 18616818

Thomas, L. (2012). *Building student engagement and belonging in higher education*. Higher Education Academy.

Thornhill-Miller, B., Camarda, A., Mercier, M., Burkhardt, J. M., Morisseau, T., Bourgeois-Bougrine, S., Vinchon, F., El Hayek, S., Augereau-Landais, M., Mourey, F., Feybesse, C., Sundquist, D., & Lubart, T. (2023). Creativity, critical thinking, communication, and collaboration: Assessment, certification, and promotion of 21st century skills for the future of work and education. *Journal of Intelligence*, *11*(3), 54. Advance online publication. DOI: 10.3390/jintelligence11030054 PMID: 36976147

Tilak, J. B. G. (2015). How inclusive is higher education in India? *Social Change*, *45*(2), 185–223. DOI: 10.1177/0049085715574178

Tinto, V. (1993). *Leaving college: Rethinking the causes and cures of student attrition* (2nd ed.). University of Chicago Press.

Tomlinson, M. (2017). Forms of graduate capital and their relationship to graduate employability. *Education + Training*, *59*(4), 338–352. DOI: 10.1108/ET-05-2016-0090

Torra, V. (2010). Hesitant fuzzy sets. *International Journal of Intelligent Systems*, *25*(6), 529–539. DOI: 10.1002/int.20418

Trevisan, L. V., Eustachio, J. H. P. P., Dias, B. G., Filho, W. L., & Pedrozo, E. Á. (2024). Digital transformation towards sustainability in higher education: State-of-the-art and future research insights. *Environmental Science and Pollution Research International*, *26*, 2789–2810.

Trigwell, K., Prosser, M., & Ginns, P. (2005). Phenomenographic pedagogy and a revised approaches to teaching inventory. *Higher Education Research & Development*, *24*(4), 349–360. https://www.tandfonline.com/doi/abs/10.1080/07294360500284730. DOI: 10.1080/07294360500284730

Tsyfra, T., Moholivets, A., & Vershigora, D. (2022). Digital-skills of building economists in the era of VUCA and BANI-WORLD. *Ways to Improve Construction Efficiency*, *1*(49), 192–205. DOI: 10.32347/2707-501x.2022.49(1).192-205

Ülker, N., & Otrar, M. (2025). University 4.0 essentials: Influence of industry 4.0 on higher education. *Industry and Higher Education*, *39*(5), 528–538. DOI: 10.1177/09504222241295625

UNESCO. (2020). *Education for sustainable development. A roadmap*, UNESCO, Paris. Available at: https://unesdoc.unesco.org/ark:/48223/pf0000374802 (Accessed March 2024)

UNESCO. (2020). *Education for sustainable development: A roadmap*. UNESCO.

UNESCO. (2021). *Reimagining our futures together: A new social contract for education*. UNESCO.

UNESCO. (2023). *Higher education in a time of global disruption: Policy perspectives*. UNESCO.

UNESCO. 2017. Education for sustainable development goals: Learning objectives. Available at: https://unesdoc.unesco.org/ark:/48223/pf0000247444 (Accessed December 2023)

Urmeneta, A., & Romero, C. (2024). Ethical considerations in AI-driven learning analytics. Journal of Educational Technology.

Uslu, N. (2025). Digital well-being and self-regulation in higher education learning environments. *Education and Information Technologies*, *30*(1), 1–18.

Usup, U., Supriyono, S., Hardika, H., & Redjeki, E. S. (2020). Development of Student Entrepreneurship Skills in LKP Kresna Informatika. *EDUCATIO: Journal of Education*, *5*(1), 84–91. DOI: 10.29138/educatio.v5i1.241

Utama, H. (2021). Strategy for Enhancing Students' Entrepreneurship in Reducing Reduction in Knowledge Management's View. *International Journal of Research and Review*, *8*(5), 292–298. DOI: 10.52403/ijrr.20210537

Van der Kleij, F. M., Vermeulen, J. A., Schildkamp, K., & Eggen, T. J. H. M. (2015). Integrating data-based decision making and formative assessment. *Assessment in Education: Principles, Policy & Practice*, *22*, 324–343. DOI: 10.1080/0969594X.2014.999024

Van Dijk, J. (2020). *The digital divide*. Polity Press.

Van Geel, M., Keuning, T., Visscher, A. J., & Fox, J. P. (2016). Effects of a school-wide data-based decision-making intervention. *American Educational Research Journal*, *53*(2), 360–394. DOI: 10.3102/0002831216637346

van Laarhoven, P. J. M., & Pedrycz, W. (1983). A fuzzy extension of Saaty's priority theory. *Fuzzy Sets and Systems*, *11*(1–3), 229–241. DOI: 10.1016/S0165-0114(83)80082-7

VanLehn, K. (2011). The relative effectiveness of human tutoring, intelligent tutoring systems, and other tutoring systems. *Educational Psychologist*, *46*(4), 197–221. DOI: 10.1080/00461520.2011.611369

Vanlommel, K., Van Gasse, R., Vanhoof, J., & Van Petegem, P. (2017). Teachers' decision-making: Data-based or intuition driven? *International Journal of Educational Research*, *83*, 75–83. DOI: 10.1016/j.ijer.2017.02.013

Vashishth, V., & Gautam, P. (2024). Learning analytics in synchronous online education. *E-Mentor*, *86*(4), 54–61. DOI: 10.15219/em86.1482

Vehrer, A., & Pálfalusi, N. (2025). Artificial intelligence in higher education: Opportunities and risks for academic integrity and student learning. *Higher Education Policy*, *38*(2), 1–20.

Villa, C. F. H., Arango, D. A. G., Mesa, E. D. A., García, A. G., Aconcha, R. B., Movilla, J. G. S., & Lopez, A. P. A. (2017). Multidisciplinariedad, interdisciplinariedad y transdisciplinariedad en la formación para la investigación en ingeniería. *Revista Lasallista de Investigación*, *14*(1), 179–197. DOI: 10.22507/rli.v14n1a16

Vithanage, V., & Nakashima, N. (2025) The Role Played by the Student-Centred Approach in the Acquisition and Development of 4 Cs of 21st Century Skills Through a Project-Based STEM Curriculum ISSN: 2186-5892 – The Asian Conference on Education 2024: Official Conference Proceedings (pp. 595-610) DOI: 10.22492/issn.2186-5892.2025.53

Vyas, K. (2024). Data-driven decision-making in higher education. https://www.sogolytics.com/blog/data-driven-decisions-higher-education/

Wang, H., Xu, Z., Fujita, H., & Liu, S. (2016). Towards felicitous decision making: An overview on challenges and trends of big data. *Information Sciences*, *367–368*, 747–765. DOI: 10.1016/j.ins.2016.07.007

Wang, V. (2025). Ethics and equity in AI-driven education. In *AI integration into andragogical education*. IGI Global., DOI: 10.4018/979-8-3373-0502-8.ch010

Wang, Y. (2021). Artificial intelligence in educational leadership: A symbiotic role of human-artificial intelligence decision-making. *Journal of Educational Administration*, *59*(3), 256–270. Advance online publication. DOI: 10.1108/JEA-10-2020-0216

Wan, Y. (2025). A study on the impact of AI-assisted project-based learning design on innovation ability. *Frontiers in Interdisciplinary Educational Methodology*, *2*(3), 210–223. DOI: 10.1109/ICEIB53692.2021.9686424

Wayman, J. C., Jimerson, J. B., & Cho, V. (2012). Organizational considerations in establishing the data-informed district. *School Effectiveness and School Improvement*, *23*(2), 159–178. DOI: 10.1080/09243453.2011.652124

Webb, M., Davis, N., & Bell, T. (2020). The development of computer science education globally: A review of current efforts. *Education and Information Technologies*, *25*, 1–32. DOI: 10.1007/s10639-016-9493-x

Weick, K. E. (1995). Sensemaking in organizations. *Sage (Atlanta, Ga.)*.

Weimer, M. (2002). *Learner-centered teaching: Five key changes to practice*. Jossey-Bass.

Weiss, C. H. (1998). Have we learned anything new about the use of evaluation? *The American Journal of Evaluation*, *19*(1), 21–33. DOI: 10.1177/109821409801900103

White, C., & Hastings, D. (2018). An International Study of Faculty Perceptions on Communication Development in Engineering Education. In Auer, M., & Kim, K. S. (Eds.), *Engineering Education for a Smart Society. GEDC WEEF 2016 2016. Advances in Intelligent Systems and Computing* (Vol. 627). Springer. DOI: 10.1007/978-3-319-60937-9_21

Williamson, B. (2017). Big data in education: The digital future of learning, policy and practice. *Sage (Atlanta, Ga.)*. Advance online publication. DOI: 10.4135/9781529714920

Williamson, B., Bayne, S., & Shay, S. (2020). The datafication of teaching in higher education: Critical issues and perspectives. *Teaching in Higher Education*, *25*(4), 351–365. DOI: 10.1080/13562517.2020.1748811

World Economic Forum. (2020). The future of jobs report. World Economic Forum.

Wu, J., & Chiclana, F. (2014). A social network analysis trust-consensus based approach to group decision making. *Knowledge-Based Systems*, *59*, 91–107. DOI: 10.1016/j.knosys.2014.01.017

Xiao, Y., & Watson, M. (2019). Guidance on conducting a systematic literature review. *Journal of Planning Education and Research*, *39*(1), 93–112. DOI: 10.1177/0739456X17723971

Xu, L. (2024). Innovative interdisciplinary models in engineering education: Transforming practices across global universities. *Engineering Education Review*, *2*(3), 129–144. DOI: 10.54844/eer.2024.0846

Xu, X., Lu, Y., Vogel-Heuser, B., & Wang, L. (2021). Industry 4.0 and industry 5.0-Inception, conception and perception. *Journal of Manufacturing Systems*, *61*, 530–535. DOI: 10.1016/j.jmsy.2021.10.006

Xu, Y. (2025). Educational evaluation and decision-making based on statistical data. *International Journal of Decision Support System Technology*, *17*(1), 1–24. Advance online publication. DOI: 10.4018/IJDSST.392480

Xu, Z. S., & Zhao, N. (2016). Information fusion for intuitionistic fuzzy decision making. *Information Fusion*, *28*, 10–23. DOI: 10.1016/j.inffus.2015.07.001

Yager, R. R. (1981). A new methodology for ordinal multiobjective decisions based on fuzzy sets. *Decision Sciences*, *12*(4), 589–600. DOI: 10.1111/j.1540-5915.1981.tb00111.x

Yager, R. R. (1988). On ordered weighted averaging aggregation operators in multicriteria decision making. *IEEE Transactions on Systems, Man, and Cybernetics*, *18*(1), 183–190. DOI: 10.1109/21.87068

Yorke, M. (2006). *Employability in higher education: What it is – what it is not.* Higher Education Academy.

Yorke, M., & Knight, P. T. (2006). Curricula for economic and social gain. *Higher Education*, *51*(4), 565–588. DOI: 10.1007/s10734-004-1704-5

Yoshida, H. (2025). Regulatory bodies in higher education. https://www.scribd.com/document/846820711/Regulatory-bodies-in-education

Yu, C. W. (2018). Understanding the ecosystems of Chinese and American entrepreneurship education. *Journal of Entrepreneurship Education*, *21*(2), 1–18.

Zadeh, L. A. (1965). Fuzzy sets. *Information and Control*, *8*(3), 338–353. DOI: 10.1016/S0019-9958(65)90241-X

Zadeh, L. A. (1975). The concept of a linguistic variable and its application to approximate reasoning—I. *Information Sciences*, *8*(3), 199–249. DOI: 10.1016/0020-0255(75)90036-5

Zadeh, L. A. (1996). Fuzzy logic = Computing with words. *IEEE Transactions on Fuzzy Systems*, *4*(2), 103–111. DOI: 10.1109/91.493904

Zakharov, Y. (2022). Comparative analysis of approaches to world concepts: Spod society, vuca society and bani society. *Society and Economy*, (64), 149–158. DOI: 10.26565/2524-2547-2022-64-13

Zala-Mezö, E., Strauss, N. C., Müller, D., Häbig, J., Kuster, R., Herzig, P., & Unterweger, G. (2018). Use of research results to improve student participation. *ICSEI Conference Proceedings*.

Zawacki-Richter, O., Marín, V. I., & Bond, M. (2022). Systematic review of research on artificial intelligence applications in higher education. *International Journal of Educational Technology in Higher Education, 19*(1), 1–23. PMID: 35013716

Zeleny, M. (1982). *Multiple criteria decision making*. McGraw-Hill.

Zhai, X., & Du, X. (2022). Digital resilience and well-being in higher education during COVID-19. *Computers & Education, 179*, 104410.

Zhang, G., Lu, J., & Gao, Y. (2015). *Multi-level decision making*. Springer-Verlag. DOI: 10.1007/978-3-662-46059-7

Zhang, J. (2024). Application of artificial intelligence tools in educational assessment: Enhancing teaching and learning management in Beijing junior high schools. *Eurasian Journal of Educational Research, 112*, 017. Advance online publication. DOI: 10.14689/ejer.2024.112.017

Zhang, J., & Goodson, P. (2011). Acculturation and psychosocial adjustment of Chinese international students: Examining mediation and moderation effects. *International Journal of Intercultural Relations, 35*(5), 614–627. DOI: 10.1016/j.ijintrel.2010.11.004

Zhang, Y., Zhang, M., Wu, L., & Li, J. (2025). Digital transition framework for higher education in AI-assisted engineering teaching: Challenge, strategy, and initiatives in China. *Science & Education, 34*(2), 933–954. DOI: 10.1007/s11191-024-00575-3

Zhao, Y. (2019). The future of education: 2030. In *Perspectives on rethinking and reforming education* (pp. 1–24). Springer., DOI: 10.1007/978-981-13-9439-3_1

Zimmerman, M. A. (2013). Motivation, Success, and Problems of Entrepreneurs in Venezuela. *Journal of Management Policy and Practice, 14*(2), 76–90.

Zippia (2023). BUSINESS TEACHER DEMOGRAPHICS AND STATISTICS IN THE US. Zippia, Inc. https://www.zippia.com/business-teacher-jobs/demographics/

Ziyae, B., Sadeghi, H., Shahamat Nejad, M., & Tajpour, M. (2021). A framework of urban entrepreneurship for women breadwinners. *Foresight (Cambridge), 23*(5), 597–609. DOI: 10.1108/FS-12-2020-0137

About the Contributors

Caroline M. Crawford, Ed.D., is a Professor of Instructional Design and Technology at the University of Houston-Clear Lake in Houston, Texas, United States of America. She earned her doctoral degree from the University of Houston in Houston, Texas, United States of America, in 1998, with specialization areas in Instructional Technology and Curriculum Theory, and began her tenure at the University of Houston-Clear Lake (UHCL) the same year. At this point in Dr. Crawford's professional career, her main areas of interest focus upon student success, engagement, and belonging, within learning environments. Further, Dr. Crawford's areas of expertise extend into communities of learning and the appropriate and successful integration of technologies into the learning environment; the learning environment may be envisioned as face-to-face, blended and online (virtual or text-driven) environments, as well as microlearning and micro-assist deliverables.

***

Ashutosh Bhardwaj is a contributing author and currently is an Assistant Professor at Poornima University in Jaipur, Rajasthan, India.

Tarana Afrin Chandel is an Associate Professor in Integral University, had M. Tech degree from UPTU & B. Tech degree from Magadha University, Bihar in the year 2009 and 2002 and Ph.D. from Integral University. She is Principal Investigator of the project "Performance Analysis of 1MW Grid Connected Solar Photovoltaic System using Image Analysis. She is honored as Indo Asian – Best Researcher Award 2022 in Renewable Energy & VLSI on 28.02.2022, International Teaching Excellence Award 2021 on 18.12.2021, Incredible Academician of INDIA-21 by Record Owner, 25.09.2021, Excellence in Research 30.06.2021, Recognition of Academic Excellence & Recognition of Research Excellence (Ph.D) on 16.01.2021, Excellence in Reviewing in recognition of an outstanding contribution on 21.09.2020, Best Research Award 2020 NESIN 2020, on 18.11.2020, Pride of India on 12.09.2018, Excellent Teaching award in Higher Education for on 8.03.2018, Best Faculty award in Rural Institution on 25.11.2017, Best Paper Award: 19th - 20th Feb 2016, "Rashtriya Gaurav Award" on 24.05.2010.Life member of Solar Energy Society of India, The Institution of Engineers (India), President and Life member of Robotic Society

J. Vijaya Barathy, M.Sc, MCA, M.Phil, (Ph.D)., is serving as an Assistant Professor in the Department of Computer Applications at Perunthalaivar Kamarajar Arts College, Pondicherry. And also pursuing Ph.D(Computer Science) in Annamalai University. She has nearly 10 years of experience in Teaching, Research and innovations. Her research interests include Networking, Machine Learning and IoT. Her profound interest in research has made her publish various papers and articles in the international journals. She has participated in several National and International conferences and presented papers. She keeps updating herself with the latest knowledge in her discipline and likes to interact with the students on contemporary topics.

Preet Kanwal is an Associate Professor at the Mittal School of Business, Lovely Professional University, with over 22 years of academic and research experience in Human Resource Management. A Post-Doctoral Fellow from the University of Quebec in Montreal, she holds a PhD in HRM from I.K. Gujral Punjab Technical University. Her research interests include quality of work life, labour laws, industrial relations, organisational behaviour, and workforce well-being. She has published widely in Scopus-indexed and UGC-listed journals, authored books and numerous book chapters, and presented at several national and international conferences. She has taught internationally for Victoria University (Online), Australia, and Sunway University (Online), Malaysia. She recently completed an ICSSR-funded project as Co-Principal Investigator on empowering women artisans for Vision Viksit Bharat@ 2047 and is currently a Co-Investigator on an ongoing ICSSR-funded project on enhancing Social-Emotional Learning (SEL) in government schools across Punjab.

M. C. Savithri is an Assistant Professor in the Department of Computer Science and Engineering at JKKMCT college, Tamil Nadu, India. My research interests include Artificial Intelligence and Network Security.

Priyal Malhotra is an educator with experience in higher education across India and Singapore. Currently pursuing a Ph.D. in Educational Psychology from CHRIST (Deemed to be University), her research interests include adolescent development, well-being, educational innovation, and curriculum development. She is actively involved in initiatives that promote student well-being, reflective practice, and emotional resilience within educational settings.

Sialia Karina Mellink-Méndez, Master in Education with a specialty in Organizational Development and Bachelor in Graphic Design, both from the CETYS University. Coordinator of the Bachelor's Degree in Graphic Design and the Bachelor's Degree in Graphic Design and Creative Innovation at CETYS University, Ensenada campus. Recognition for Educational Excellence 2023 in the Category of Developing Researcher and Educational Excellence 2022 in the Category of Full-Time Professor of Administration and Business at CETYS University. With teaching certifications in experiential learning, development of information skills, corporate social responsibility and communication issues.

P. Nagaraj is currently serving as an Associate Professor in the Department of Computer Science and Engineering at SRM Institute of Science and Technology, Tiruchirappalli. He holds a Ph.D. in Computer Science and Engineering and brings over 16 years of rich experience in teaching, research, academic leadership, and scholarly mentorship. Dr. Nagaraj's research expertise spans Data Science and Analytics, Artificial and Computational Intelligence, Machine Learning, Recommendation Systems, and Intelligent Healthcare Systems. His primary research focus lies in the application of data analytics, deep learning, optimization techniques, and explainable AI to healthcare problems, including diabetes management, medical image analysis, disease prediction, and decision-support systems, along with intelligent engineering applications. He has an outstanding research record with over 200 publications in SCI- and Scopus-indexed international journals, conferences, and edited volumes, and has authored several international book chapters published by leading global publishers. He actively contributes to the research ecosystem as a Guest Editor for Frontiers in Artificial Intelligence and serves as a reviewer for multiple high-impact international journals, ensuring rigorous peer-review and research quality. In his academic career, Dr. Nagaraj has guided more than 100 undergraduate projects and 20 postgraduate projects, and is currently supervising ten Ph.D. scholars in the domains of AI, Data Science and Analytics, and Image Processing. He is also a sought-after Resource Person and has delivered expert lectures in seminars, Faculty Development Programs (FDPs), workshops, and conferences across India. Dr. Nagaraj has played a significant leadership role in professional bodies. He previously served as the Faculty Sponsor of the KARE ACM Student Chapter (Chapter ID: 170084), under whose guidance the chapter received the Outstanding Recruitment Program Award (2023) and Honorable Mention in Outstanding Chapter Award (2024) from ACM India. In recognition of his sustained research impact, Dr. Nagaraj has been listed among the World's Top

2% Scientists by Stanford University for three consecutive years (2023, 2024, and 2025) based on Scopus-indexed citation metrics. As of now, he has accrued 2,862 citations, with an h-index of 33 and an i10-index of 67, reflecting his strong and consistent contributions to the global research community.

Sathish P is a faculty member at CHRIST (Deemed to be University), Bannerghatta Road Campus, Bengaluru, since 2021. He holds a Ph.D. from VIT University, Vellore, with specialization in Finance and Accounting. He earned a B.Com. from SRM University, Chennai, securing the Gold Medal and First Rank, and an MBA from Anna University, where he was the class topper and secured the 39th University Rank. His research interests include institutional investment, green finance, sustainability, capital markets, and macroeconomic determinants. He has published in reputed Scopus-indexed, Web of Science, ABDC-listed, and EBSCO-indexed journals, and has contributed book chapters with Elsevier, Emerald, Springer, and IGI Global. He has served as a resource person, guest speaker, and session chair at various academic events. His awards include the VIT Research Award (2017), Best Researcher Award (2020), Early Career Researcher with Impact Award (2024), and Young Researcher Award (2025).

S. Gokulraj is currently serving as an Associate Professor in the Department of Cyber security at Dr.N.G.P.Institute of Technology, Coimbatore, and Tamil Nadu. He holds a Ph.D. in Computer Science and Engineering from Anna University, Chennai. He has completed his Bachelor of Engineering Degree in CSE from Paavai Engineering College, Anna University, Chennai; he did his Master of Engineering in Computer Science and Engineering from Paavai Engineering, College, Anna University, Chennai. He received his doctor of philosophy in Computer Science and Engineering from Anna University, Chennai with Cloud Computing and Optimization as his research realm. He has guided more than 100 Post and Undergraduate students. He has published as many as 20 papers in reputed International Journals, International and National Conferences. He also has published 5 patents in Indian patent journal and 1 Copyrights.

Sneha Saha is an accomplished Associate Professor and Head Department of Psychology, CHRIST (Deemed to be University), Delhi-NCR. She has over a decade of experience in teaching and research. Her doctoral work focused on the effectiveness of positive youth development interventions.

Shikha Sharma is a contributing author and currently is an Associate Professor at Poornima University in Jaipur, Rajasthan, India.

Anjali Sharma is currently serving as an Associate Professor at the Mittal School of Business, Lovely Professional University, Phagwara, Punjab—an esteemed institution accredited by ACBSP, USA, and ranked 31st among Indian universities in the NIRF 2025 rankings. She has conducted over five faculty development workshops and has been invited to deliver guest lectures at reputed institutions including Amity International Business School, Amity University, and Akal Business School, Akal University. Demonstrating a strong commitment to continuous professional development, she has successfully completed more than 20 certified training and development programs. Her academic contributions include the design of university-level syllabi and the creation of e-content, including recorded online lectures, supporting the advancement of digital pedagogy within the institution. As a dedicated researcher, she has presented papers at various national and international conferences and authored five Scopus-indexed journal articles, six book chapters, and two conference proceedings. She has also edited four academic books with national publishers and has mentored seven capstone research projects, reflecting her commitment to fostering scholarly inquiry and applied learning.

K. Muthamil Sudar received his B.Tech. degree in computer science and engineering from Kalasalingam University, Srivilliputhur, India, in 2014, the M.E. degree in computer science and engineering from RVS College of Engineering and Technology, Coimbatore, India, in 2016, and the Ph.D. degree in computer science and engineering from Kalasalingam Academy of Research and Education, Srivilliputhur, India, in 2021. He is currently working as an Assistant Professor in the Department of Computer Science and Engineering, Mepco Schlenk Engineering College, Sivakasi, Tamil Nadu, India. His research interests include network security, software-defined networking, and machine learning techniques. He has published more than 55 research articles in reputed international journals and leading conferences.

Vipin Tyagi is a distinguished academician, researcher and author, currently serving as Dean (Academics and Research) at Jaypee University of Engineering and Technology in Guna, Madhya Pradesh. With a rich background in Computer Science, his expertise spans across Image Processing, Cyber Forensics and Speech Recognition. Prof. Tyagi has a prolific publication record, contributing significantly to his fields of interest. His scholarly work includes numerous journal articles, conference papers, and books. Some of his notable publications are in the areas of image forgery detection, image denoising and content-based image retrieval. He has authored and edited several books and papers in the field of Computer Science, such as "Digital Image Forgery Detection: Techniques, Challenges and Applications", "Predictive Computing and Information Security" and "Content-Based Image

Retrieval: Ideas, Influences, and Current Trends" published by Springer Singapore. His book "Understanding Digital Image Processing" using MATLAB, published by Taylor and Francis is highlighted by Mathworks at: https://in.mathworks.com/academia/books/understanding-digital-image-processing-tyagi.html His scholarly work has earned him a respectable h-index and numerous citations in the academic community.

Nilüfer Ülker is an Associate Professor of educational sciences and Director of School of Foreign Languages at Istanbul Technical University (ITU). She completed her PhD in Educational Administration and Supervision at Marmara University, Türkiye. She was a post-doctoral research scholar at Montana State University, USA between 2015-2016 and a visiting professor at the College of Education, University of Illinois Urbana Champaign, USA between 2023-2025, aside from her academic and administrative duties at ITU. She also served as an international accreditation reviewer between 2011-2025. Her research mainly focuses on administration, internationalization, quality and accreditation of higher education, administration of foreign language education and innovative practices in higher education teaching, learning and administration. She has articles published in international peer-reviewed journals, a book, book chapters and projects on various aspects of higher education and foreign language education. She has participated as a presenter and moderator in several national and international conferences with a focus on education. She is an associate editor of the Higher Education Section of the journal Frontiers in Education, an International Editorial Advisory Board Member of the journal Research in Post-Compulsory Education and serves as a reviewer for some other journals with a focus on education.

Diana Esther Woolfolk-Ruiz, 20 years of experience in the field of Higher Education. Focused mainly in the areas of leadership, work teams, strategic management, entrepreneurship, gender. Emphasis on collaborative work, continuous improvement, internationalization, global vision.

Index

Symbols

A

B

C

D

E

F

G

H

I

L

N

O

P

Q

R

S

T

V

W

www.ingramcontent.com/pod-product-compliance
Lightning Source LLC
LaVergne TN
LVHW062323300926
849161LV00007B/1545
* 9 7 9 8 2 6 0 0 2 6 0 6 9 *